WRAPPING AUTHORITY

Women Islamic Leaders in a Sufi Movement in Dakar, Senegal

Since around 2000, a growing number of women in Dakar, Senegal, have come to act openly as spiritual leaders for both men and women. As urban youth turn to the Fayḍa Tijāniyya Sufi Islamic movement in search of direction and community, these women provide guidance in practising Islam and cultivating mystical knowledge of God. While women Islamic leaders may appear radical in a context where women have rarely exercised religious authority, they have provoked surprisingly little controversy. *Wrapping Authority* tells these women's stories and explores how they have developed ways of leading that feel natural to themselves and those around them.

Addressing the dominant perceptions of Islam as a conservative practice, with stringent regulations for women in particular, Joseph Hill reveals how the female leaders integrate values typically associated with pious Muslim women into their leadership. These women present spiritual guidance as a form of nurturing motherhood; they turn acts of devotional cooking into a basis of religious authority and prestige; they connect shyness, concealing clothing, and other forms of feminine "self-wrapping" to exemplary piety, hidden knowledge, and charismatic mystique. Yet like Sufi mystical discourse, their self-presentations are profoundly ambiguous, insisting simultaneously on gender distinctions and on the transcendence of gender through mystical unity with God.

(Anthropological Horizons)

JOSEPH HILL is an associate professor in the Department of Anthropology at the University of Alberta.

ANTHROPOLOGICAL HORIZONS

Editor: Michael Lambek, University of Toronto

This series, begun in 1991, focuses on theoretically informed ethnographic works addressing issues of mind and body, knowledge and power, equality and inequality, the individual and the collective. Interdisciplinary in its perspective, the series makes a unique contribution in several other academic disciplines: women's studies, history, philosophy, psychology, political science, and sociology.

For a list of the books published in this series see page 319.

JOSEPH HILL

Wrapping Authority

Women Islamic Leaders in a Sufi Movement in Dakar, Senegal

UNIVERSITY OF TORONTO PRESS
Toronto Buffalo London

Toronto Buffalo London
utorontopress.com
Printed in Canada

ISBN 978-1-4875-0307-9 (cloth) ISBN 978-1-4875-2244-5 (paper)

♾ Printed on acid-free, 100% post-consumer recycled paper with vegetable-based inks.

(Anthropological Horizons)

Library and Archives Canada Cataloguing in Publication

Hill, Joseph, 1974–, author
Wrapping authority : women Islamic leaders in a Sufi movement in Dakar, Senegal / Joseph Hill.

(Anthropological horizons)
Includes bibliographical references and index.
ISBN 978-1-4875-0307-9 (hardcover)

1. Muslim women – Senegal – Dakar. 2. Islamic leadership – Senegal – Dakar. 3. Sufism – Senegal – Dakar. I. Title. II. Series: Anthropological horizons

HQ1170.H55 2018 305.48′697 C2018-900946-2

University of Toronto Press acknowledges the financial assistance to its publishing program of the Canada Council for the Arts and the Ontario Arts Council, an agency of the Government of Ontario.

Canada Council for the Arts Conseil des Arts du Canada

ONTARIO ARTS COUNCIL
CONSEIL DES ARTS DE L'ONTARIO
an Ontario government agency
un organisme du gouvernement de l'Ontario

Funded by the Government of Canada Financé par le gouvernement du Canada Canada

Contents

Figures and Tables

Figures

Tables

Preface

If someone had predicted when I began researching the Fayḍa Tijāniyya Sufi (mystical Islamic) movement in Senegal in 2001 that my first monograph on this movement would focus on its female spiritual leaders, or *muqaddamas*, I would have been incredulous. Not only had I never considered studying women Islamic leaders in Senegal, but I was largely unaware of their existence. The extensive body of literature on the political influence of Senegalese Islamic groups since the early colonial period had only turned up a single female Senegalese Islamic leader, an apparent anomaly whose father had died leaving no sons (Coulon 1988; Coulon and Reveyrand 1990; Creevey 1996). Hence my surprise when, soon after I arrived in the Fayḍa movement's spiritual capital of Medina Baay in 2001, my research assistant (El Hadj Ibrahima "Baay" Thiam) drew up a list of nearby Islamic leaders to visit and included one woman. Over the following three years, I interviewed that woman and then several others. However, although I was probably the first scholar to mention multiple cases of women Islamic leaders in Senegal (Hill 2007), I only later began to think seriously about these women's rarity in the global Islamic context and about the questions concerning gender and religious authority that they raised.

As I began researching the question in earnest, starting in 2009, for what I imagined would be a single short article, I realized that the phenomenon of women's religious leadership in the Fayḍa was far more widespread than I had imagined. I also came across oral and written accounts showing that women had been appointed as spiritual guides in the Tijānī Sufi order for well over a century, even if their appointments were little known and the few who came to act as spiritual guides usually led fellow women. I also realized that the form of women's leadership I was witnessing – women openly leading gender-mixed groups of disciples – had been almost non-existent before 2000.

The newness of most of these women's appointments suggested that the phenomenon of women's religious leadership was growing and transforming before my eyes, especially in urban areas like Dakar. The extent of women's often hidden yet decisive leadership roles repeatedly surprised me, as did their ingenious ways of reimagining Islamic leadership as harmonious with their conventional roles as mothers, wives, and pious Muslims. I gradually perceived a need to expand my short article into a book.

After four more months of research in 2014, my book expanded into two companion volumes. The current volume is the first to be completed, although the second book, tentatively entitled *Women Who Are Men*, is in some ways logically and chronologically prior. *Women Who Are Men*, whose title comes from Sufi discourses of gender transcendence discussed below, focuses on the historical and doctrinal origins of women's often hidden authority in the Fayḍa Tijāniyya. Combining interviews with analysis of Arabic texts, it discusses women directly appointed and taught by Fayḍa founder Shaykh Ibrāhīm Niasse, including his elder daughters and other notable women. It continues with examples of more recent women leaders in and around Medina Baay. The current volume, in contrast, is a collection of essays primarily on spiritual guides I call the "new *muqaddama*s" who have emerged in Dakar since 2000. This book also discusses several female *sikkarkat*s, or Sufi chanters, who also exercise religious authority in new ways. While both books are intended to stand on their own, they complement each other in providing an account of the roots, the current manifestations, and the complexities of women's spiritual leadership in the Fayḍa.

One obvious irony and indeed contradiction of this project is that both I and the various assistants I have worked with over the years are men. In 2004 in Medina Baay, I worked with a group of more than a dozen local collaborators that initially included two women – a schoolteacher and a high-school student – both of whom soon dropped out because they were not confident about approaching people for interviews. In Medina Baay's semi-rural environment and in the surrounding Saalum villages, most women I met were highly reserved in speaking to gatherings or in claiming the authority to tell their own stories. This reticence was linked to feminine piety and respect for their husbands and male elders. Although this region of Senegal does not enforce the level of gender segregation I observed in Mauritania, I still tended to be led into male-dominated circles and to men perceived as legitimate spokesmen. I had to make conscious efforts to interact with women.

Even after I shifted much of my research to Dakar starting in late 2004, I continued to collaborate primarily with the young men I had worked with since 2004 in Medina Baay, most of whom had come to Dakar to study or work. Although I might have found more women there who were willing and able to assist with my research, my short trips left me with little time to recruit and train new collaborators. Although a weakness of this study, this contradiction is an artefact of the very dynamics of pious feminine self-wrapping I describe in this book.

Certainly my own and my local collaborators' gender shaped and limited the results in subtle and not-so-subtle ways, although it never barred our access to women leaders. Many of these women had more male than female disciples, and young men often filled their living rooms. The limited gender segregation I usually encountered in the Fayḍa community in Senegal meant that I had no problem in sitting and talking with these women, usually in the presence of male and female disciples and relatives. I visited most of the women discussed in this book multiple times over many years, developing friendships with them and their families. Nonetheless, I had little opportunity for the intimacy that a female researcher living in the same household might develop.

Consequently, this book focuses more on women's narratives and public performances of authority than on subtle everyday interactions and household dynamics. Female anthropologists who have participated extensively in women's social spaces inside and outside their homes have more richly captured the texture of Muslim women's everyday lives, whether in Senegal (Buggenhagen 2012a; Augis 2014), in other West African countries (Alidou 2005; S.J. Rasmussen 2006; Masquelier 2009), or elsewhere (Fernea 1965; Abu-Lughod 1993). Still, even if my account is admittedly partial, as someone with a unique perspective on the Senegalese Fayḍa community I felt an urgent responsibility to bring to light this heretofore little-studied phenomenon. I hope this incomplete account depicts these women's lives, struggles, and visions in a way that they might find truthful.

Perhaps more than most ethnographers, I am indebted not only to a countless number of interlocutors but to many local collaborators who actively shaped the direction of research. The local collaborators who have most actively contributed to my research on women leaders are Cheikh Baye Thiam, El Hadj Abdoulaye ("Aas") Bitèye, Abdoulaye

("Baay Laay") Niang, Alioune Seck, and Nazirou Thiam. Other local collaborators who have contributed to my long-term research project on the Fayḍa Tijāniyya in Senegal include Ady Fall (d. 2012), Baye Seck, Amadou Ndiaye, Ahmed "Ndaara" Seck, Baye Samb, Seydina Babacar "Ḥaraka" Thiam (d. 2015), El Hadj Thiam, and Younoussa Thiam. Throughout this book, I speak of interviewees speaking to "us," since nearly all interviews were conversations between me, these local collaborators, and our interviewees.

Of course, this book would also not have been possible without the active and enthusiastic participation of the women leaders who are its subjects. All gladly talked to me, in most cases multiple times, and insisted that I attribute their life stories and views to them by name. My policy is to identify interlocutors by their real name when speaking of their public roles, personae as religious leaders, and life narratives, while anonymizing aspects of their family or personal life that are not public knowledge. Usually with my collaborators, I have interviewed at least twenty-three *muqaddama*s in Senegal, ten of them in Dakar. I interviewed all in Wolof, except for one Mauritanian *muqaddama* I interviewed in Arabic. Several of these *muqaddama*s are daughters of Shaykh Ibrāhīm Niasse: Shaykha Maryam, Sayyida Ruqayya ("Yata Baay"), Sayyida Nafīsatu ("Nafi Baay"), Sayyida Ndèye Khady, and Sayyida Ndèye Aïda. In the Dakar area, I also interviewed *Sayyida*s Moussoukoro Mbaye, Aïda Thiam, Diarra Ndiaye, Seynabou Mbathie, Awa Cissé, Mame Diarra Bousso Dramé, Khady Fall, Ndèye Maguète Niang, and Diénaba Seck. In Kaolack, in addition to Shaykh Ibrāhīm's daughters who live there, I interviewed *Sayyida*s Diénaba Guèye, Ndèye Ndiaye, and Néné Thiam. In Mbour I interviewed Ami Sall, and in Nioro I interviewed Habibatou Mbaye, Khady Thiongane, and Mati ("Caama") Thiam (who lives in Sokone). I am indebted to each of them.

My research as a whole would have been impossible without the support of Medina Baay's leaders. When I began my research in 2001, Imam Shaykh Hassan Cissé (d. 2008) and the *khalīfa* Ahmed "Daam" Niasse (d. 2010) were Medina Baay's principal authorities. I benefited greatly from their hospitality and generosity. The current leaders, the Medina Baay's Imam Shaykh Tijānī Cissé and the *khalīfa* Shaykh Tijānī Niasse, have also generously provided books, interviews, and their blessing for my research activities. Shaykh Māḥī Niasse, Shaykh Makkī Niasse, Shaykh Māḥī Cissé, and other descendants of Shaykh Ibrāhīm Niasse and Shaykh ʿAlī Cissé also patiently answered my questions and supported this research, as did dozens of other leaders. Their support was indispensable in undertaking this project.

Ever since Professor Ousmane Kane graciously introduced me to his student from Medina Baay, El Hadj Ibrahim ("Baay") Thiam, in 2001, members of the extended family of his father, Barham Thiam "Casamance," have provided the backbone of my social life and research in Senegal. They effectively adopted me, gave me a new name (Abdoulaye Thiam), and made sure I had a place to stay and people to work with wherever I went. Fatou Thiam ("Joolaa"), Moustapha Thiam, Rokhy Thiam, Souleymane Thiam, the late Mbaye Dièye Bitèye, and the late Diaye Bitèye and their families always cared for me and have given me a socially rich and personally fulfilling life in Senegal. While I was in Mauritania, Al-Ḥājj wuld Mishrī and his disciples also took care of my every need and contributed significantly to this research project while I studied Arabic in the village of Maatamoulana. More generally, I have benefited from the hospitality and help of hundreds of Fayḍa Tijāniyya community members in Medina Baay, Dakar, and dozens of villages and towns in Senegal, Mauritania, and beyond. Although this book focuses on Dakar, it grows out of research in dozens of towns and villages among people too numerous to name here.

Drafts, segments, and ideas from this book over the past several years have benefited from comments from many people, including Adeline Masquelier, Ousseina Alidou, Britta Frede, Ousmane Kane, Thomas Gibson, Emil Homerin, Anthea Butler, Rüdiger Seesemann, Andrew Conroe, Lucia Cantero, Omolade Adunbi, Mark Westmoreland, John Schaefer, Amy Austin Holmes, Agnes Czajka, Marwa Ali Sabbah, Sarah Michelle Leonard, Claralyn Hill, and many others. My classmates at Yale, Richard Payne, Molly Margaretten, Seth Curley, Gavin Whitelaw, Allison Alexy, and the late Jennifer Jackson, have all pushed me and encouraged me in important ways. This book builds on dissertation research advised by Kamari M. Clarke and read by Joseph Errington, Eric Worby, and Leonardo Villalón. In my initial foray into Senegal fieldwork in 1998, I benefited from the wise mentorship of Michael Phillips, G. Wesley Johnson, Donald Marshall, and David Crandall.

Stages of research, writing, and relevant language study were generously funded by a Fulbright-Hays Doctoral Dissertation Research Abroad grant, a Social Science Research Council International Dissertation Research Fellowship grant, a United States Foreign Language and Area Studies grant, the Yale University Program in Agrarian Studies, the Yale University Graduate School, the University of Rochester's

Frederick Douglass Institute for African and African-American Studies, the American University in Cairo, and the University of Alberta.

Several passages in this book are adapted from material that has appeared elsewhere. Several brief passages originate in my dissertation at Yale University, *"Divine Knowledge and Islamic Authority: Religious Specialization among Disciples of Baay Ñas"* (Hill 2007). Several chapters incorporate and expand on material previously published in the article "'All Women Are Guides': Sufi Leadership and Womanhood among Taalibe Baay in Senegal" (Hill 2010) in the *Journal of Religion in Africa*, published by Brill. Parts of chapter 5 originated in the chapter "Entrepreneurial Discipleship: Cooking Up Women's Sufi Leadership in Dakar" (Hill 2016a) in the volume *Cultural Entrepreneurship in Africa*, published by Routledge. These adapted passages are published with the permission of the original publishers.

I am grateful to the hundreds of Taalibe Baay women and men who so generously shared their stories with me and my collaborators. I hope that this book will not only contribute to the academic literatures on gender, Islam, and West Africa but will also respect these disciples' wish to convey to the world their religious mission and that of Shaykh Ibrāhīm Niasse.

My parents, Ned and Claralyn Hill, have gone above and beyond in supporting my research, visiting me, and truly becoming part of my life in Senegal, Mauritania, and Egypt. Their love and encouragement has kept me going all these years.

Finally, I express my gratitude to the Sufi woman who has, in her own way, acted as my own spiritual guide, Marwa Fikry. She has inspired and accompanied me in every aspect of life, including the process of researching for and writing this book. I dedicate this book to her and to Zidan, who does not yet know that he is one result of this book project.

Transliteration Note

This book extensively uses transliterated terms and translated utterances from three primary languages: Wolof, Arabic, and French. In this multilingual context, even speakers themselves may not be entirely sure to which language a term or name belongs. Transliteration in this context requires a sometimes arbitrary compromise between intelligibility, phonemic accuracy, and adherence to conventions. Most of the non-English terms and quotations in this book are from Wolof and Arabic. All interviews discussed here were conducted in Wolof. Unless noted, all Islam-related terms and quoted textual passages are from Arabic. Wherever the language is not obvious from the context or where I am introducing terms for the first time, I specify the language (Ar., Wol., Fr.). I identify Arabic and French terms embedded in Wolof interviews as such. It is usually easy to differentiate Wolof from Arabic terms because of contrasting phonological systems and transliteration conventions. For example, Wolof words may contain the letters "à," "c," "e/é/ë," "g," "ñ," "o/ó," "x," and doubled vowels, while Arabic words may contain "ā," "ī," "ū," "ay," "aw," "kh," "gh," "sh," "ʿ," and "ʾ."

In transliterating Arabic terms and phrases that maintain the same meaning across contexts, I follow the conventions of the *International Journal of Middle Eastern Studies (IJMES),* preserving diacritics. For example, I write *tarbiya, ṭarīqa,* and *fanāʾ*. However, I transliterate some Arabic loanwords that have been localized in Wolof-speaking contexts using Wolof conventions. For example, *daayira* (Wolof: religious association) comes from Arabic *dāʾira* (circle), while *sikkar* (Sufi chant or a Sufi chant gathering) comes from the Arabic *dhikr* (mentioning, remembrance). Of course, the line between Wolof and Arabic religious terms is fluid, and the decision is often arbitrary, as terms inevitably change in pronunciation and meaning from context to context.

More contentious is the question of how to transliterate names, which in Senegalese government documents follow French conventions yet usually combine Arabic and Wolof elements. Although public schooling and state documents have habituated most Senegalese to writing their names according to French conventions, in rural communities and Islamic contexts many people are more used to writing their name using Arabic or *ʿajamī* script (Arabic characters adapted to write non-Arabic languages). A single speaker may pronounce and write his or her own name in various ways depending on the linguistic context. The French conventions followed in government documents and Western academic works fail to preserve Wolof and Arabic phonemic distinctions.

In some writings I have consistently used Wolof spellings to reflect actual pronunciation of names and other terms (for example, Hill 2007, 2011), as have some scholars of Senegal before me (for example, Heath 1990), while elsewhere I have accommodated readers more familiar with French spellings (Hill 2010). In this book, I compromise between using French, Arabic, and Wolof conventions for people's names. I transcribe nicknames and titles of Wolof origin (Pàppa, Sëriñ, Soxna, Baay, Yaay) using Wolof orthography; I write Arabic titles and Islamic leaders' given names using Arabic conventions (Muḥammad, Al-Ḥājj, Shaykh, Sayyida, Sīdī); and I otherwise render official Wolof given and family names using French conventions as they would most likely appear on an identity card. Consequently, I may write a person's full name, including a title, nickname, and family name, combining all three conventions (for example, Shaykh Ibrāhīm "Baay" Niasse or Shaykha Maryam "Yaay-bóoy" Niasse).

The resulting pastiche will certainly not satisfy everyone, but I believe it balances the need to reflect the heteroglossic nature of Senegalese Muslims' identities with the need to keep names recognizable to research participants and readers familiar with Senegal.

Wolof Transliteration

Aside from proper names of people and places, I transliterate Wolof terms according to the transliteration system advanced by the Centre de linguistique appliquée de Dakar (CLAD). However, as mentioned above, I spell the official names of people and places according to French conventions most often used in official documents.

The CLAD system designates long vowels and strong consonants using doubled letters. Most consonants are pronounced approximately as in English, including *"j,"* which is usually represented as *di[e]* in French-style transliterations. The following consonants are pronounced differently. The letter *"c"* (*thi[e]* in French conventions) is pronounced approximately as *ch* in the English "charm." *"Ñ"* is similar to the same letter in Spanish (pronounced as *n*ʸ, written as *gn[e]* in French conventions). The letter *"ŋ"* is pronounced like "ng" in the English "running." *"X"* and *"q"* are both pronounced as in the International Phonetic Alphabet (IPA): *"x"* is a voiceless velar fricative similar to German *ach-laut*, and *"q"* is a more percussive voiceless uvular plosive similar to the Arabic *qāf*. (French conventions represent both as *"kh."*) *"G"* (*g[u]* in French conventions) is always hard as in "gone." All vowels can be lengthened through doubling except *"ë"* and *"à"*, which are length-neutral. The unaccented *"e"* is pronounced as the "e" in "set" in North American English, while the accented *"é"* sounds somewhat like the "a" in "take." The vowel *"ë"* sounds similar to the "u" in "put" in American English or the "e" in the French word *le*. The accented *"à"* is open and is not distinguished by length.

Although I do not use these conventions in writing legally recognized names of people and places, I use the CLAD transliteration system for all other Wolof terms, including Wolof personal nicknames (Baay, Maam) and the names of historical regions (Saalum, Jolof) that no longer function as administrative units. I do so in order to convey the precise pronunciation and meaning of these terms even if the literature sometimes represents them according to French conventions.

Arabic Transliteration

For the most part, I transliterate Arabic terms and names using American Library Association-Library of Congress (ALA-LC) conventions, preserving diacritics for long vowels and emphatic consonants. Accordingly, I always write the definite article as *al-* even when it is assimilated into a sun letter. The final *tāʾ marbūṭa* is simplified as *-a* except where part of a possessive *(iḍāfa)* construction, where it is represented as *-at*. Long vowels are represented with a diacritical mark *(ā, ī, ū)*. The masculine *nisba* ending is simplified as *ī* while the feminine *nisba* is represented as *-iyya*.[1] *Hamza* (ʾ, glottal stop) is preserved in the middle or end position but omitted in the initial position. *Hamzat waṣl* (elided initial vowel) is rendered as an apostrophe. The guttural consonant *'ayn* is represented with the character " ' " and is never omitted.

For simplicity's sake, I generally pluralize Arabic and Wolof nouns by appending the letter "s" in default type rather than using the more complex Arabic plurals (thus *muqaddama*s rather than *muqaddamāt*). The exception is commonly used plural terms referring to collectivities (for example, *'ulamā'* [scholars] rather than *'ālim*s).

The table below shows how some of the proper names and titles encountered in this book might be transliterated in French, Wolof, and Arabic:

Table TN.1. Equivalent transliterations in French, Wolof, and Arabic.

French	Wolof	Arabic	French	Wolof	Arabic
Abdoulaye	*Abdulaay*	*'Abdallāh*	*Malick*	*Maalik*	*Mālik*
Astou Diankha	*Astu Jànqa*		Mbathie	*Mbaj*	
Cheikh	*Shéex, séex*	*Shaykh*	*Mbitéyène*	*Mbittéyeen*	
Cissé	*Siise*	*Sīsī*	*Ndèye*	*Ndey*	
Diarra	*Jaara*		Ndiaye	*Njaay*	
Dieupeul	*Jëppël*		Niasse	*Ñas*	*Inyās, Nyās*
Diop	*Jóob*		Niassène	*Ñaseen*	
El Hadj	*Allaaji*	*Al-Ḥājj*	*Zeyda*	*Zeydaa*	*Sayyida*
Ibrahima	*Ibrayima*	*Ibrāhīm*	*Sokhna*	*Soxna*	
Kaolack	*Kawlax*	*Kawlakh*	*Thiam*	*Caam*	
Khady	*Xadi*	*Khadīja*	*Rokhy*	*Roqi*	
Kossi	*Kóosi*		Thioub	*Cubb*	

Glossary

Wolof Terms

awukat (from Wol. *awu*: to echo, repeat + *-kat*). A supporting chanter who sings the response the chant leaders call in a religious chant meeting.

baay. Father. Alone, Shaykh Ibrāhīm's nickname; also used as a title for some elder leaders.

barke (from Ar. *baraka*: blessing). Divine blessing. By extension, material wealth. Often described as being transmitted through people and objects. Sometimes contrasted to *tuyaaba* (Ar.: *thawāb*).

daara (from Ar. *dār al-Qur'ān*: house of the Qur'ān). Qur'ānic school, usually run inside a house. The principal teacher is called a *sëriñ daara*.

daayira (from Ar. *dā'irah*: circle). A circle or association of disciples. It may be made up of co-disciples sharing a neighbourhood, workplace, school, or *muqaddam*.

daraja (from Ar. *daraja*: degree or rank). Social prestige, status, or rank.

gàmmu. See *mawlid* (Ar.).

géwal. Griot, or member of an endogamous caste of praise singers, musicians, oral historians, and public speakers.

ibaadu. See *Jamā'at 'Ibād al-Raḥmān* (Ar.).

jébbalu. To submit to a religious leader. The term is used among various Senegalese Islamic groups, but the submission ritual is most institutionalized among Murids.

jinne (from Ar. *jinnī*). A category of intelligent beings, along with humans and angels, mentioned in the Qurʾān. Although a *jinne* can be good or bad, human interactions with *jinne*s are usually negative, so the term is often glossed as "devil" or "demon."

Jolof. A historical kingdom in northwest Senegal; now the geographical area corresponding to that kingdom. Its inhabitants are called *Jolof-Jolof*.

kaala. Any scarf or turban worn around the head or shoulders by a man or woman.

kersa. Shame, dignified restraint. Sometimes translated as *sangfroid*, nobility, honour, docility.

kurus (Ar. *subḥa, tasbīḥ, misbaḥa*). Rosary, prayer beads.

mbaxana. Hat or cap. Usually, a man's rimless cap covering the top part of the head, often embroidered.

mbóot. A secret or an important matter. (Also, a cockroach.)

mëlfa. See *malaḥfa*.

Ñaseen (Fr. *Niassène)*. A member of the Niasse (*Ñas*) family; of or pertaining to the Ñas family. Often used by outsiders to designate all those affiliated with a Ñaseen leader, although Taalibe Baay rarely use the term in this way.

piri (from Wol. *firi*: to interpret). Interpretation; also *piri Alxuraan*, the act or event of interpreting the Qurʾān, *tafsīr*.

rab. Bush spirit. Often treated synonymously with *jinne*, although some insist that they are two distinct kinds of being or even that *rab* are an un-Islamic African superstition.

Saalum. A former *Séeréer*-ruled kingdom in west-central Senegal; the corresponding geographical area today.

Saalum-Saalum. Of, from, or pertaining to *Saalum*.

sëriñ (Fr. *marabout)*. Any person who works in a religious function – for example, as a producer of esoteric cures, Sufi *shaykh*, or teacher of the Qurʾān or other Islamic texts. *Sëriñ bi*: "sir," a respectful title.

sikkar (from Ar. *dhikr*: mention, remembrance, invocation). See *dhikr*. Also, the activity of repeating *dhikr*; a meeting organized to chant *dhikr* communally.

sikkarkat (from Ar. *dhikr*: mention, remembrance [of God's name] + *-kat*, an agentive suffix [one who]). Someone who chants the *dhikr* (*sikkar*) and other sacred chants at religious meetings.

soxna. A noble or holy woman; wife. *Soxna si*: Ma'am. Similar to Ar. *sayyida*.

taalibe (from Ar. *ṭālib* or *ṭālib al-ʿilm*: seeker of knowledge, student). A Qurʾānic student; a disciple of a *shaykh*.

Taalibe Baay (lit. "disciple of Baay"). A follower of Shaykh Ibrāhīm Niasse and adherent of the Fayḍa Tijāniyya.

tuyaaba (Ar. *thawāb*). Divine reward for an individual's good deeds. Cf *barke*.

xam-xam (from Wol. *xam*: to know). Knowledge; in Islam, the Islamic disciplines studied after studying the Qurʾān. Often a gloss of Arabic *ʿilm* (textual knowledge) or *ʿulūm* (studies, disciplines).

yaay. Mother. A title or form of address for senior women and female leaders.

yëngu (lit. "moving oneself"). A genre of practice that accompanies *sikkar (dhikr)* chant with percussion and frenetic dancing. Originating in eastern Saalum (east of Kaolack) in the 1980s, this controversial practice has gained popularity among some Taalibe Baay youth.

Arabic Terms

ʿālim (pl. *ʿulamāʾ*). A learned person or religious scholar (active participle of *ʿalima*, "to know" [a fact]).

ʿārif (lit. "one who knows"). In Sufism, *ʿārif bi-'Llāh* ("knower of God") possesses deep experiential knowledge of God and sacred matters. The verb *ʿarafa* implies experiential knowledge *(maʿrifa)*, whereas the verb *ʿalima* implies factual knowledge *(ʿilm)*. Cf *ʿālim*.

baraka. Blessing from God.

bāṭin. Inside. The esoteric, hidden nature of things. (Ant.: *ẓāhir*.)

dhikr (lit. "mentioning [God]"). Any phrase repeated to remind one of or invoke God, including the ninety-nine names of God and various prayer formulas. A *dhikr* that is transmitted from shaykh to disciple, usually to be recited at set times, is called a *wird* (litany). Wolofized as *sikkar*.

Fanāʾ. Extinction, obliteration. In Sufism, a state in which one ceases to be aware of oneself and is only aware of God.

Fatḥ. Opening. In Sufism, the attainment of an experience of God, in which the self dissolves in the experience of God through *fanāʾ*.

Fātiḥa (lit. "beginning" or "opening"). The first chapter *(sūra)* in the Qurʾān. (Not to be confused with the *Ṣalāt al-Fātiḥ*.)

Fayḍa (also *Fayḍ*). Flood, emanation. Fayḍa Tijāniyya: Flood of the Tijānī Order; the movement and community started by Shaykh Ibrāhīm Niasse in 1929. The name comes from a prediction of Shaykh Aḥmad at-Tijānī that someone would flood the earth with the Tijānī Order.

fiqh. Islamic jurisprudence. The branch of Islamic study that interprets God's law *(sharīʿa)*, drawing primarily on Qurʾān and *ḥadīth*. It governs worship and daily practice *(ʿibādāt)* and interpersonal relations *(muʿāmalāt)*.

ḥadīth. An account of the sayings or deeds of Muḥammad. Alongside the Qurʾān, *ḥadīths* form the basis of the prescriptions of Islamic jurisprudence *(fiqh)*.

ḥaḍra (lit. "presence" or "place of presence," glossed in Wol. as "*péey*"). In Sufism, any of the levels of presences through which God manifests himself to the gnostic. *Ḥaḍrat al-jumʿa*: The Friday afternoon Tijānī litany, ideally chanted in unison, consisting primarily of repeating *Lā ilāha illā Allāh* ("There is no god but Allāh"). *Ḥaḍrat al-Shaykh Ibrāhīm*: The community of Shaykh Ibrāhīm's presence, i.e., the Fayḍa community.

***ḥājj* (fem. *ḥājja*)**. Someone who has made the pilgrimage *(ḥajj)* to Mecca.

ḥāl. State. In Sufism, a state of spiritual growth on the way to a higher *maqām* (station). Colloquially, it refers to altered states of consciousness and ecstatic manifestations, often experienced during religious activities.

ḥaqīqa. Reality. In Sufism, the reality of the divine presence and unity underlying all things. It is often contrasted to *sharīʿa*, the law, representing order and differentiation.

ijāza. Diploma, certificate, authorization. In Sufism, the authorization (usually written) to represent a *ṭarīqa* and to induct new members. In the Tijāniyya, there are two kinds, *muqayyada* (limited) and *muṭlaqa* or *iṭlāq* (absolute).

imām (from *amāma*: in front of). One who leads prayer, especially by appointment in a mosque; figuratively, a leader (in a community, branch of knowledge).

Jamāʿat ʿIbād al-Raḥmān. Association of Servants of the Merciful. The best-known Sunnī reformist organization in Senegal, with roots in Salafism. Its adherents and other reformists are colloquially known in Wolof as *ibaadu*.

khalīfa. Successor (of the Prophet, another religious figure, or a patriarch); leader of the religious community or a family, usually the senior surviving male; a religious community's official representative in a region.

khalwa. Independent seclusion; a personal spiritual retreat.

Lā ilāha illā 'Llāh. "There is no god but Allāh." Part of the two-part Islamic declaration of faith *(shahādah)*. Among Taalibe Baay, one of the most commonly repeated *dhikr*s, pronounced hundreds of times per day during the Tijānī *wird*s, during meetings, and during *tarbiya*.

malaḥfa. A long piece of fabric, often multicoloured, used as a loose wrap to cover all but a woman's face and hands. Worn by most Mauritanian women and by a growing number of pious Senegalese women.

maʿrifa. Experiential or intuitive knowledge (in contrast to *ʿilm*); in Sufism, direct knowledge of God *(maʿrifa ilāhiya)*.

mawlid. Birth; celebration of a birth, especially of the Prophet Muḥammad or a major saint such as Shaykh Ibrāhīm Niasse. *Mawlid an-nabī* (birth of the Prophet) or *al-mawlid an-nabawī* (the Prophetic birth): celebration of Muḥammad's birth, held on the twelfth night of the Islamic month of Rabīʿ al-awwal. Minor *mawlid*s are held throughout the year. (Wol. *gàmmu*.)

***muqaddam* (fem. *muqaddama*)**. Someone holding an *ijāza*, or authorization to represent and induct into a Sufi order. In the Fayḍa, a *muqaddam* often acts as a *shaykh murabbī* or provider of spiritual education, and *muqaddam*s today oversee religious associations (Wol. *daayira*s).

***qaṣīda* (pl. *qaṣāʾid*)**. An Arabic poem, usually following one of several classical metres, each line ending with the same letter. In Sufism, usually a panegyric poem in Arabic about the Prophet Muḥammad or another religious figure.

Ṣalāt al-Fātiḥ. "Prayer of the Opener." A prayer for the Prophet Muḥammad that is part of the standard Tijānī *wird*s, believed by Tijānīs to have powerful effects.

sayyida. A noble or holy woman. Used as a title for women religious figures. Cf Wol. *soxna*.

sayr. Progress; procession; pursuance. In the Fayḍa, one's continued spiritual development under a *shaykh* after *tarbiya* through conversation and performing further litanies.

sharī'a. The law of God, revealed in the Qur'ān and *Sunna* (Prophetic example) and interpreted through *fiqh*. In Sufism, it is often contrasted to *ḥaqīqa* (truth). Among Taalibe Baay, it usually suggests Islamic prescriptions, not a state-enforced legal code.

***sirr* (pl. *asrār*)**. Secret. By extension, esoteric power and authority transmitted along with sacred phrases. (Wol. *mbóot*.)

sūra. A chapter in the Qur'ān.

tafsīr (from *fassara*: to interpret, explain). Interpretation (e.g., of a text). As a discipline, it refers to Qur'ānic interpretation. (Wol. *piri*.)

tarbiya. Education or upbringing; in Sufism, the process of spiritual training at the hands of a *shaykh murabbī*. Shaykh Ibrāhīm Niasse formulated a particular process involving the transmission of *wirds*.

***ṭarīqa* (pl. *ṭuruq*)**. Way or path. In Sufism, a spiritual lineage and set of practices originating in a founding shaykh. Often glossed as "Sufi order," or misleadingly as "brotherhood."

thawāb. Divine reward for good deeds.

Tijāniyya. The Tijānī Sufi order, founded by North African Shaykh Aḥmad al-Tijānī (1735–1815). The Fayḍa is the largest branch of the Tijāniyya worldwide.

***'ulamā'* (sing. *'ālim*)**. (Islamic) scholars.

waẓīfa. Occupation, duty. In the Tijāniyya, a litany pronounced once daily, ideally in the evening as a group.

***wird* (pl. *awrād*)**. Any litany consisting of repeated sacred phrases *(dhikr)*, transmitted from shaykh to disciple, to be recited at regular times. Entrance into the Tijānī order is marked by "receiving" the Tijānī *wird* from a *muqaddam*. The Tijānī *wird* actually includes three litanies: the *wird lāzim* ("obligatory *wird*"), recited individually and silently morning and afternoon; the *waẓīfa*, most commonly recited after sunset, as a group if possible; and *ḥaḍrat al-jum'a* or *dhikr al-jum'a*, recited on Friday afternoon, also as a group if possible. Sometimes used interchangeably with the broader term *dhikr*.

ẓāhir. Apparent, manifest. The visible or exoteric side of reality. (Ant.: *bāṭin*.)

zāwiya. A religious centre established by a shaykh or a community of disciples, often including one or more central houses, a mosque (either in its own structure or in a house), one or more religious schools, and potentially the tomb of the founder.

ziyāra. Visit. In Sufism, it often refers to a more or less ritualized visit to a religious personality in which a gift *(hadiyya)* may be given to the leader. Blessing *(baraka)* is often said to result from such visits.

French Terms

conférence. Conference. In this context, a large religious meeting organized around a keynote speech by an invited Islamic scholar on a chosen theme.

marabout (from Ar. *murābiṭ)*. In the Sahara, an Islamic teacher; historically, an adherent of the Islamic reform movement "*al-Murābiṭūn*" (Almoravids). Anyone (usually a Muslim) practising a religious occupation. In Senegal, usually a gloss for "*sëriñ*." While common colloquially and in scholarship, the term does not delineate a clear analytical category.

WRAPPING AUTHORITY

Women Islamic Leaders in a Sufi Movement in Dakar, Senegal

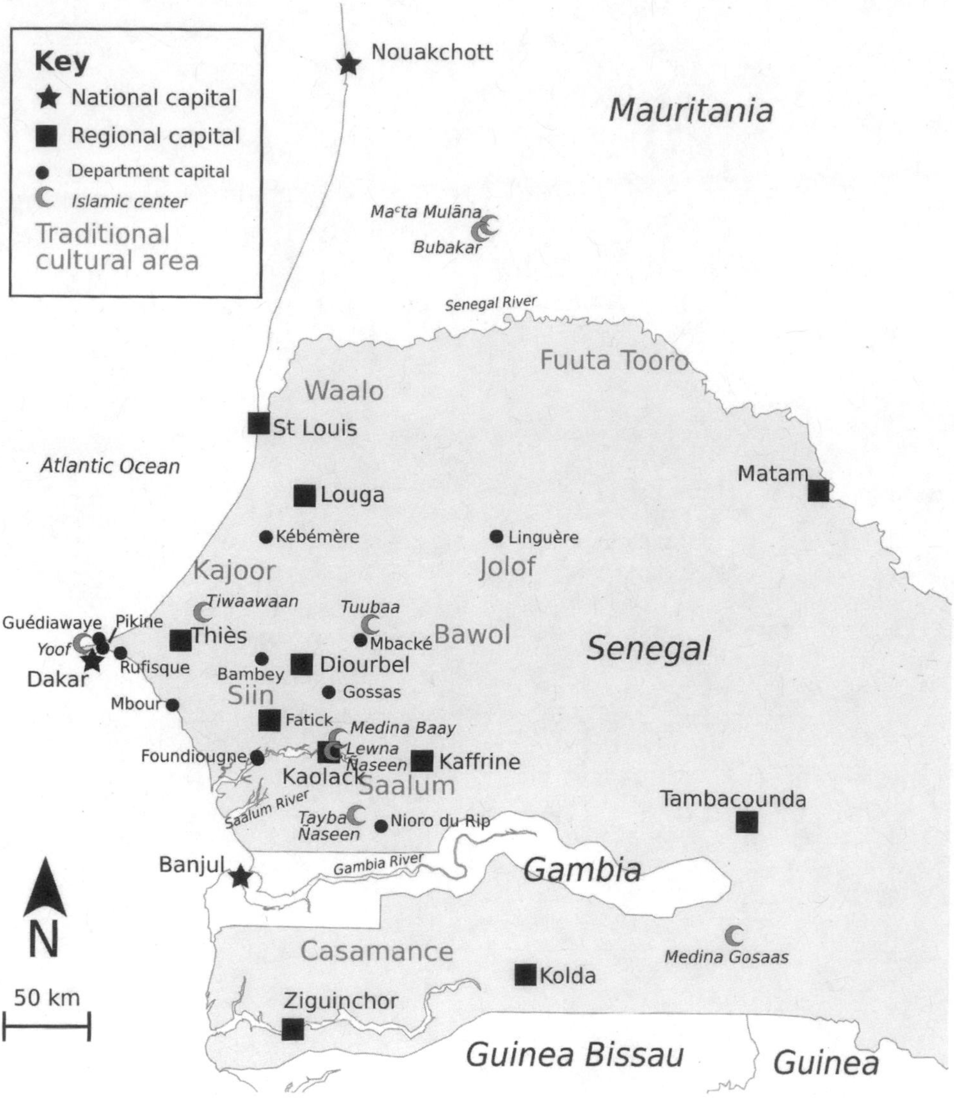

Figure I.1 Map of western Senegal and southwestern Mauritania.

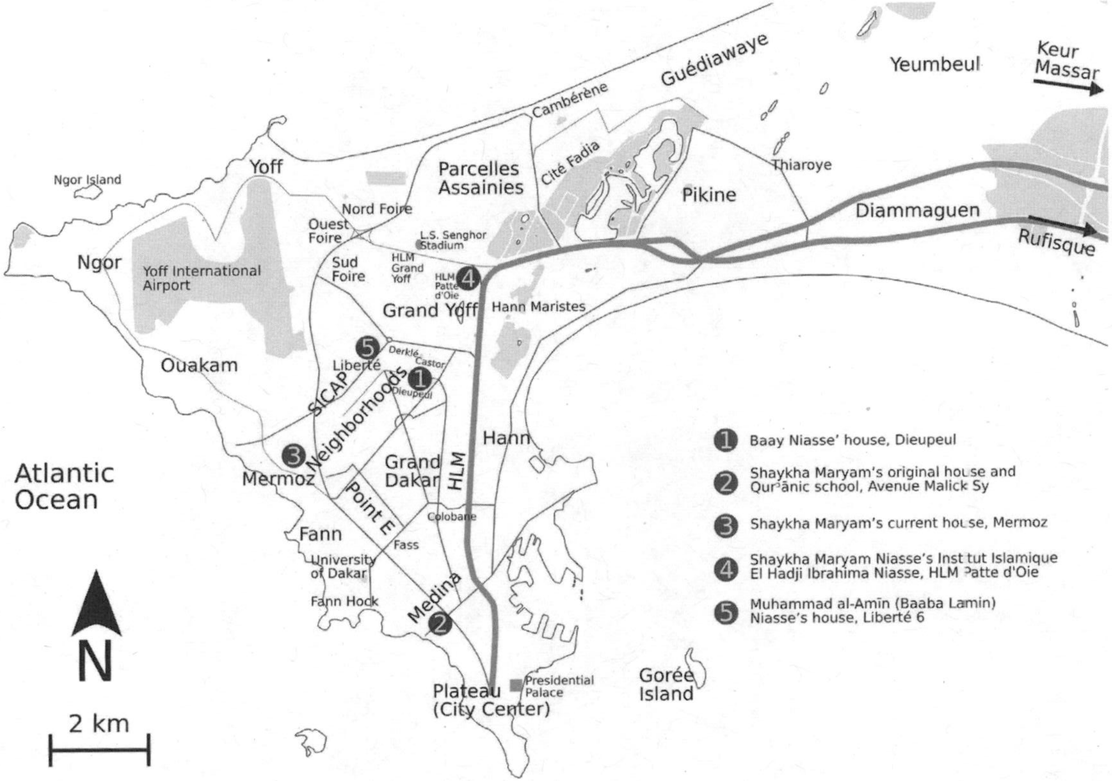

Figure I.2 Map of Greater Dakar, the Cap Vert Peninsula.

Introduction

New Spaces of Religious Authority

Sayyida[1] Diarra Ndiaye was likely the first woman to initiate disciples into the Fayḍa Tijāniyya Islamic movement in Dakar through guiding them through the process of *tarbiya* (Ar.), or spiritual training, the Fayḍa movement's distinctive initiation practice. During *tarbiya,* an authorized spiritual guide (Ar. *muqaddam*) instructs a disciple to meditate on a series of litanies, usually over a period of two weeks to a month, until attaining experiential knowledge of God. Sayyida Diarra's house in Mermoz, a middle-class neighbourhood in west-central Dakar, overlooks a busy highway leading to Dakar's northern suburbs. A small restaurant she built in front sells sandwiches and cold drinks. By the time I met her in 2004, though, she had delegated the running of the restaurant to others, in order to devote more time to giving *tarbiya* and further spiritual guidance (Ar. *sayr*) to the disciples who filled her house daily.

Sayyida Diarra was in her mid-fifties when I first visited her, along with her husband and mother. As we sat and talked in their living room, disciples emerged from a bedroom leading a woman in her late teens who was feverishly sobbing and repeating *"Lā ilāha illā Allāh"* (Ar. "There is no divinity but Allāh") and seating her on a sofa. This initiate had just reached the final stage of *tarbiya,* the ecstatic state of *fanā*ʾ (Ar.), the obliteration of the self in which one is conscious of nothing but the all-encompassing reality of God. As is standard during each stage of *tarbiya,* Sayyida Diarra asked her a series of questions to assess her spiritual state. Asked who she was, the young woman interrupted her sobbing repetitions to answer, "I am God" (*man maay Yàlla*). Sayyida Diarra explained to me that she would soon "bring down" (Wol. *wàcce*) the young woman from this state, allowing her to continue to deepen her experience of divine reality (Ar. *ḥaqīqa*) while having the presence of mind to observe God's dictates (Ar. *sharīʿa*) such as fasting and prayer. More than anything else, Fayḍa adherents describe themselves as drawn to the Fayḍa by this promise of directly "knowing God." They credit this unique knowledge to the Fayḍa's founder, Shaykh Ibrāhīm Niasse (1900–1975), known to his disciples as "Baay" – "Father" in Wolof, Senegal's lingua franca. Members of Senegal's Fayḍa community call themselves "Taalibe Baay" – "disciples of Baay."

A close companion of Baay appointed Sayyida Diarra as a *muqaddama* – or a female spiritual guide – in 1980 while she was visiting the Fayḍa's spiritual capital, Medina Baay. Yet instead of immediately announcing her appointment, she only began giving *tarbiya* several years later when prospective disciples approached her and asked her for *tarbiya* (see chapter 1). Before her appointment, during the late 1970s, Sayyida Diarra and her neighbour Astou Diop had already been pioneers in organizing the Fayḍa community in Mermoz. When Diarra and her husband moved into the new house in the 1970s, it had no upper level, and where the highway is now a brushy expanse at Dakar's edge. Starting around 1975, after Diarra underwent *tarbiya* around 1975 and Astou followed, the two would sit on woven mats in the space in front of the house to chant group litanies and "*sikkar*" (Wol., from Ar. *dhikr Allāh),* or remembrance of God. Sometimes Diarra's Taalibe Baay husband would join them, and they soon caught the attention of fellow Taalibe Baay and other passersby. The group grew, and Sayyida Diarra's house eventually became the headquarters of the first highly organized Taalibe Baay *daayira* (Wol. circle of disciples) in Dakar, *Naḥnu Anṣār Allāh* (Ar. "We are God's champions"), often shortened to "Naḥnu."

As central as she and other women had been in forming and running this *daayira,* when its members formalized its structure, men filled the most visible leadership positions. Women mostly held positions in the *daayira*'s Women's Commission, whose main task was to prepare massive communal meals for large gatherings. Only in 2001, as the Fayḍa was transforming into a mass urban youth movement, did Sayyida Diarra form a new *daayira* of which she was officially the leading spiritual guide. Her *daayira* comprised mostly young women and men to whom she had personally given *tarbiya,* primarily nearby high school and university students. She remained active in "Naḥnu," most of whose members were older than herself, serving as president of its Women's Commission for many years.

The Fayḍa Tijāniyya is one of many communities in Senegal growing out of the tradition of Sufism, or "the esoteric or inward (*bāṭin*) aspect of Islam" (Burckhardt 2008, 3), which seeks to understand and realize not just the literal prescriptions of the Qur'ān but also its hidden spiritual qualities. Sufism includes many branches throughout the Muslim world and spans the Sunni/Shī'a divide. Most organized Sufi communities revolve around an aspirant's relationship with a spiritual master who transmits spiritual knowledge and blessing said to trace back to the Prophet Muḥammad (Burckhardt 2008, 7). Since much of Senegal was Islamized by Sufi leaders, for most Senegalese, Islam is essentially Sufi, even if Islamic reform groups have challenged this relationship. Senegal's 2013 census estimates a 96 per cent Muslim population (République du Sénégal 2013, 300).[2] In that census's religion survey, over 90 per cent of Muslim respondents identified with one of four Islamic communities rooted in Sufism: the Tijānīs (58% of Muslims), Murids (26%), Qādirīs (6%), and Laayeen (0.5%) (République du Sénégal 2015). Members of each of these groups may in turn associate with a particular leader (Ar. *shaykh*, Wol. *sëriñ*, Fr. *marabout)* and participate in various ways and to various degrees. The Fayḍa is generally considered the second-largest branch of the Tijāniyya within Senegal, although it has become the dominant branch worldwide.

Any visitor to Senegal immediately sees ubiquitous signs of deep devotion to Islamic leaders. Leaders' photographs and painted images adorn nearly every shop, house, and commercial automobile. At night, loudspeakers in many neighbourhoods amplify melismatic group recitations of poetry written by the saintly founders of Senegal's Sufi lineages. One of the first things one is likely to learn upon meeting any Senegalese person is which Islamic leader they consider their spiritual guide. Because Islamic leaders in Senegal have such a large and devoted following, they have come to exert considerable influence on Senegal's formally secular state institutions. Many have large investments in agriculture and transportation, provide economic opportunities to disciples, and make claims on politicians and state institutions in exchange for political support (Coulon 1981; Villalón 1995; Robinson 2000). However, judging by popular media, ubiquitous iconography, and conversations with many Senegalese, one might easily assume that female Senegalese Islamic leaders do not exist.

Sayyida Diarra was the third *muqaddama* I had become aware of and interviewed by 2004.[3] Although in 2001 I had also met Shaykh Ibrāhīm's daughter Shaykha Maryam, who is perhaps Senegal's best-known

Qur'ānic educator, neither I nor many others were aware at the time that she was a *muqaddama*.[4] Though I was familiar with the voluminous literature on charismatic male Islamic leaders in Senegal, I was surprised to learn of these female Islamic leaders. At first, I wondered if they were a marginal phenomenon that central male leaders would dismiss. Indeed, some male elders I spoke with outside Dakar found the idea of women acting as *muqaddama*s preposterous and assured me that Shaykh Ibrāhīm would never have approved of such a deviation. Yet it turned out that Shaykh Ibrāhīm himself appointed many *muqaddama*s, and nearly all *muqaddama*s I met had close relationships with Shaykh Ibrāhīm's sons and other major leaders. They were among the leading recruiters and organizers in their area. Sayyida Diarra herself served in several leadership positions in the Women's Commission of the Dakar Anṣār al-Dīn ("Champions of the Faith") Federation that regroups all Dakar Taalibe Baay *daayira*s, acting as its president from 2004 to 2013. Sayyida Moussoukoro Mbaye has the title of "Mother" – in this case, the official spiritual adviser – of the large *daayira* grouping of more than a thousand Taalibe Baay students in Dakar's higher education institutions.

Perhaps more remarkable to me than the apparent novelty of having women spiritual guides openly lead mixed-gender disciple communities was the absence of debate surrounding this significant change. These women did not speak of waging a "gender jihad" (Deeb 2006; Wadud 2006) for equal participation in the religious community. They did not call for critical "*ijtihād*" (Ar.), or reexamination of Islamic texts, which some scholars have advocated to challenge patriarchal biases in traditional interpretations (Wadud 1992; Abou El Fadl 2001; Barlas 2002; Safi 2003; in the Senegalese context see Mbow 2001; Sow 2003). Instead, they declared that Islam and the Fayḍa had "liberated" women from the beginning. They acted as if nothing were more natural than women's newly salient Islamic leadership.

During another visit to Sayyida Diarra Ndiaye in 2009, I told her I intended to write about the little-known phenomenon of *muqaddama*s. She downplayed the importance of this title, saying that she and many other women had been calling people to God through teaching and example since long before her appointment. "'*Muqaddam*' is just a word," she said, "but all women are *muqaddam*s, because all women are educators."[5] This statement naturalizes women's new leadership roles, declaring that on a deeper (*bāṭin*) level, motherhood and religious authority are two names for the same thing (see chapter 4). The statement also revalues the work she and other women quietly perform for the religious community, placing women's informal authority on an equal footing with the authority of formally recognized *muqaddams*.

At first, I wondered if I had discovered some long-standing phenomenon that scholars had somehow missed because of their preoccupation with politically powerful male – and usually Murid – Islamic elites. This suspicion was partially correct, since Tijānī women had been quietly appointed as *muqaddama*s since the nineteenth century (al-Idrīsī 2010), and Shaykh Ibrāhīm appointed many women throughout his lifetime. Yet few of these earlier women ended up acting openly as spiritual guides or making their appointments known. Even where they were known, their own communities had often erased them from history. Most of the handful of Tijānī *muqaddama*s who had previously acted as spiritual guides lived outside Senegal, led women in gender-segregated spaces, and acted invisibly and on behalf of a male leader (see, for example, Hutson 1999, 2001; al-Idrīsī 2010). Between 2004 and 2010, several elders told us of four women in the village of Darou Mbitéyène near Kaolack during the Fayḍa's early years (likely the 1930s) appointed directly by Shaykh Ibrāhīm as *muqaddama*s. These women, the elders told me, were "leaders of women," who organized women's cooking for religious events and gave *tarbiya* to women. Yet when I visited the village in late 2010, some of these same elders denied that the women were *muqaddama*s. I wondered if they had second-guessed the propriety of publicly unveiling pious Muslim women. Such reticence partially explains the widespread unawareness of women leaders.

Yet it became clear that I was witnessing a new phenomenon that was developing before my eyes. Each time I have returned to Senegal since beginning my research on the Fayḍa in 2001, I have heard of *muqaddama*s appointed since my previous visit. Although several, including the three mentioned above, were appointed during the 1990s or earlier, all had formed their own *daayira* only since 2000. Far from being marginal, most were appointed by Shaykh Ibrāhīm's sons or close companions, and nearly all were overseeing a quickly growing mixed-gender *daayira* or group of *daayira*s. Most were in Dakar or Kaolack, although several lived in smaller towns throughout Senegal. Unlike most previously known *muqaddama*s – although like the first three I interviewed – none of what I call the "new *muqaddama*s" inherited their saintly status from male kin or had extensive Islamic textual education. Unlike nearly all female Islamic leaders reported in the literature, these women act openly as spiritual guides to men and women and oversee gender-mixed *daayiras*. During the same period, women have also come to act as chant leaders (Wol. *sikkarkats*) in large meetings, another role previously limited to men (see chapter 6).

Rather than inheriting their position, these women had simply earned a reputation as exceptionally devoted disciples possessing mystical knowledge and an ability to lead. They ranged from destitute to wealthy; from unschooled to, in one case (Khadi Fall), a university professor and former government minister with five university diplomas; from members of established Taalibe Baay families to women who had only discovered the Fayḍa after marrying and raising several children. Those in the Dakar area were located everywhere from the colonial "native quarter" of Medina near the city centre to the middle-class SICAP neighbourhoods like Mermoz to the teeming northern suburbs of Parcelles Assainies, Guédiawaye, Pikine, and Yeumbeul.

The changes I have observed among Taalibe Baay coincide with a worldwide rise in women's Islamic leadership due to various global changes (Bano and Kalmbach 2012; Kalmbach 2012). Yet Taalibe Baay *muqaddamas* seem to be unique even compared to other women Islamic leaders. Nearly all the women Islamic leaders and teachers discussed in the academic literature lead and teach women in more or less segregated spaces – like, for example, the Qubaysiyyāt originating in Syria (Islam 2012; Omar 2013). Those who specialize more in Islamic healing and divination as opposed to spiritual leadership are more likely to have a mixed-gender clientele (Flueckiger 2006; Gemmeke 2008). In South Asia, the wives or daughters of male Islamic leaders may exercise de facto spiritual authority and power over men, although not they but their husbands or fathers are acknowledged as disciples' *shaykh* (Flueckiger 2006; Pemberton 2006). Flueckiger showed that, even if such a woman may be reputed as more spiritually powerful than her husband, when her husband dies, she loses her religious role, which is perceived to derive from his authority. The few women who have led mixed congregations in prayer (something not accepted by Taalibe Baay) have been among small groups of self-consciously "progressive" Muslims, often operating in the Western world, South Africa, or Malaysia (Hammer 2010). Taalibe Baay *muqaddamas* are still among a small handful of women Islamic leaders who openly exercise authority over both male and female disciples (see Neubauer 2009 for another exceptional case in Turkey).

This book centres on a simple question: How have these Taalibe Baay women come to occupy positions of religious leadership and authority that have been previously limited to men without openly contesting existing patriarchal norms and authority structures? In answering this question, I highlight a number of factors that have often separated women from Islamic authority, as well as factors that have recently facilitated the changes I have observed. As discussed in chapter 1, global material, ideological, and infrastructural changes have made women objects of hegemonic discourses. Global neoliberal economic conditions have drawn women into more visible roles in the economy, politics, and other spheres, habituating many people to seeing women successfully engaging in such activities. Rapid youth urbanization and a global "resurgence of religion" (Antoun and Heglund 1987; Sahliyeh 1990; Kepel 1994; Westerlund 1996) have yielded an intensely competitive religious scene in which, in the Senegalese context, the Fayḍa has emerged since around 2000 as an immensely popular youth movement. The influx of young women and men seeking *tarbiya* and continued guidance has created a demand for leadership that women and men not from religious specialist backgrounds have gladly filled.

Yet these conditions alone do not account for how seemingly unchanging religious spaces, discourses, and practices adapt to allow unprecedented levels of participation by women. Much of this book focuses on how new performances of religious authority become accepted as "felicitous" (Austin 1962), or socially recognized as legitimate and effective through adhering to established conventions. How does something new gain recognition as harmonious with an apparently timeless tradition? I devote special attention to women leaders' accounts of themselves, through which they situate their religious authority in terms of prevalent discourses and practices in their context. I also examine religious meetings as "cultural performances" (Singer 1955; V. Turner 1987) in which authority is displayed, reflected upon, and reconfigured, sometimes even becoming "social dramas" (V. Turner 1957) in which the boundaries of community are destabilized (see chapter 6). Religious meetings and life stories are not just "stories people tell themselves about themselves" (Geertz 1973, 448) but are innovative meta-performances during which new realities can be ratified.

Through such performances, I show, women Sufi leaders "wrap" themselves – not just their bodies but also their actions and social presence – so as to reconcile their new performances of authority with norms of feminine piety. "Wrapping," a concept developed throughout this book and especially in chapter 3, encompasses the more familiar "veiling" but goes beyond it in at least two important ways. First, whereas "veiling" tends to imply a negative act of concealing, "wrapping" highlights positive acts such as identifying, protecting, proclaiming, embellishing, and so on. Second, as a semiotic process that applies to a broad range of situations, "wrapping" moves beyond the cliché of "the veiled Muslim woman." For example, a woman's display of self-wrapping can iconically connect her to restrained nobility and hidden spiritual knowledge.

In contrast to liberal feminists and even early Sufi women (Nūrbakhsh 1983; M. Smith 1984; Silvers 2010, 2015), the women discussed here do not refuse or distance themselves from conventionally feminine roles and attributes. Instead, they repackage prevalent norms as sources of latent power and as a basis of religious authority. They connect the pious feminine virtues – wifely devotion, humility, and an inward-looking "wrapped" orientation – to saintly self-effacement before God and the veiled nature of mystical truths and spiritual power (chapters 3 and 6). They reimagine spiritual guidance as a form of nurturing motherhood (chapter 4). They consecrate acts of cooking as acts of devotion and leadership (chapter 5). In so doing, they naturalize the connection between womanhood and religious authority, even suggesting that women are more effective as spiritual guides than men because, as Sayyida Diarra said, they are natural mothers and hence educators and guides. However, paradoxically, *muqaddamas* simultaneously use mystical discourses to describe themselves as spiritual "men" and even as transcending gender distinction altogether.

I approach women's accounts of Islam and their own lives as both expressions of their experiences of transcendent realities and as narrative performances of authority. Rather than explicitly engaging in critical *ijtihād*, these women establish new practices largely through what I have called elsewhere "performative apologetics" (Hill 2016b; 2016c). That is, they defend potentially controversial practices less through argumentation than through seeking to demonstrate an excess of piety and knowledge such that an audience can reconcile these practices with their "line" (Goffman 1969) as proper Muslim and Taalibe Baay women.

Before continuing with an introduction to the Fayḍa's history and specificities, I will provide a brief note on this book's terminology and emphasis. Readers familiar with the long literature on Islamic leadership in West Africa may recognize the *muqaddamas* discussed here as examples of the spiritually powerful and socially influential Islamic leaders often called "marabouts." Scholars have described several other Senegalese women as marabouts – for example, the Murid leader

Sokhna Magat Diop (Coulon and Reveyrand 1990, discussed below) and several women in Dakar who use Qur'ānic verses in healing and divination (Gemmeke 2008, 2009). However, while the term is colloquially used throughout West Africa, I do not use "marabout" or its Wolof equivalent, "*sëriñ*," as analytical categories. "Marabout/*sëriñ*" can refer to a Qur'ānic schoolteacher (*sëriñ daara*), an esoteric specialist (*sëriñ taariyaax*) who may or may not use Qur'ānic verses, a major or minor Sufi leader (Ar. *shaykh*, *muqaddam*), or any other Islamic scholar or authority. I have sometimes heard the term used to describe travelling medicine men who were not known to be Muslims. "Maraboutism" today is usually a synonym of "charlatanism" (Gemmeke 2008). Such pejorative overtones resonate with colonial depictions of "maraboutic" African Islam as a debased and syncretistic form of Islam, less authentic yet less threatening than Arab Islam (Seesemann 2011, 12–13). While academic literature tends to identify Middle Eastern Islamic specialists by their specific role – imam, Sufi shaykh, mufti, judge (Ar. *qāḍī*), scholar (Ar. *'ālim*) – West African Islamic specialists are often lumped together as "marabouts." In addition, the term carries gender implications. "*Sëriñ bi*" ("the marabout") is also a form of respectful address for men similar to "Sir," implying a masculine identity. The feminine equivalent is "*soxna si*." Both terms can either refer to a holy person or serve to address a stranger respectfully. Thus, although male esoteric healers and diviners are often called marabout/*sëriñ*, I have seldom heard the term applied to the many women who engage in similar practices.

Most importantly, the women authorities discussed in this book rarely self-apply the term. They most often use the term that formally designates their rank in the Tijānī order – "*muqaddam*" (feminine: "*muqaddama*"), literally "one who is sent forth," in this case to represent the founder of a spiritual lineage. As Wolof lacks grammatical gender, Wolof speakers tend to use the masculine term for men and women, only explicitly gendering when needed ("*muqaddam bu jigéen*" – "female *muqaddam*"). For simplicity's sake, I use the Arabic masculine and feminine forms.

This shift in terminology reflects my shift in approach away from the long-standing academic focus on West African Sufi leaders as "big men" and on disciples as their "clients." Instead, I focus more on Sufism as a spiritual pursuit, one rooted in long traditions and one in which participants describe regular spiritual practice and experience as their primary concern. Much of the academic literature on Sufi Islam in Senegal and its diaspora has focused on the Murid order. Although Murids make up only a quarter of Senegal's population while Tijānīs make up more than half (République du Sénégal 2015), Murids are disproportionately visible in Senegalese politics, economy, and popular culture. Since colonial times, with their profound influence over Senegal's electoral politics and economy and a spiritual capital that acts as a state within a state, Murid leaders have readily lent themselves to political-economic studies approaching "marabouts" as "big men" (Cruise O'Brien 1971; Copans 1980; Coulon 1981). More recently, Murids' highly visible global trade diaspora has attracted further attention to their economic organization (Evers Rosander 1991; Bava 2000, 2003; M. Diouf 2000; Buggenhagen 2004, 2009a, 2012b; Riccio 2004; Salzbrunn 2004, to name but a few). Only a few scholars have seriously thematized Sufi spirituality and Islamic teachings in the Murid context, especially when examining Murid founder Shakyh Aḥmadu Bamba's religious teachings (Babou 2007) or Murid expressive culture (Roberts and Roberts 2000, 2002; Ross 2006; Glover 2007).

Taalibe Baay leaders also participate in exchanges of political favours, social influence, prayer, and religious offerings from disciples (*àddiya*). Yet I shift attention to the neglected question of Sufism as tradition of spiritual practice and knowledge, both because of my own interest in understanding disciples' experiences and my Taalibe Baay interlocutors' overwhelmingly spiritual preoccupations. Because of several differences between Taalibe Baay and Murids – for example, the Fayḍa's more recent popularity; its more diffuse organization; its lack of a large, politically independent geographical core (Hill 2007, ch. 4) – Taalibe Baay have never formed a high-stakes political-economic juggernaut as Murids have. The Fayḍa has not developed an organized trade diaspora, despite being perhaps the largest Sufi movement globally. This is not to say that Taalibe Baay leaders and disciples are less "political" or "worldly" than other Senegalese Muslims. Yet what brings the Fayḍa's diverse discipleship together is a shared interest in cultivating knowledge of God. Consequently, this book relegates the state and marketplace more to the background than most previous studies of Senegalese Islam. Before returning to this book's conceptual themes, I will briefly introduce the Fayḍa Sufi movement and its relationship to women.

The Fayḍa and Women

Shaykh Ibrāhīm Niasse (1900–1975) was one of the younger sons of Al-Ḥājj ʿAbdallāh Niasse (d. 1922), the preeminent Islamic leader and representative of the Tijānī Sufi order in the Siin-Saalum area to the south-east of Dakar. At the annual *gàmmu* (Wol.; Ar. *mawlid),* the celebration of the Prophet Muḥammad's birth, at his father's *zāwiya* (Ar. Islamic centre) of Léona Niassène in 1929, the young Ibrāhīm announced that he was the bringer of the long-awaited "flood" of divine knowledge – the Fayḍa – foretold by the Sufi order's founder Shaykh Aḥmad al-Tijānī well over a century before. Anyone who wanted to know God, he said, must approach him. Ibrāhīm's announcement led to a schism between those who accepted his claim and those who saw such a lofty claim as insubordinate. As tensions rose, Shaykh Ibrāhīm and his close followers founded a new *zāwiya* in 1932 that came to be called Medina Baay. Today, both Léona Niassène and Medina Baay are neighbourhoods in the regional capital, Kaolack, about 180 kilometres southeast of Dakar (see figures I.1 and I.2).

As we have seen, what most clearly distinguished the Fayḍa from its contemporary Senegalese Sufi communities was the practice of *tarbiya,* which promised any seeker to reach "knowledge of God" (Wol. *xam Yàlla,* Ar. *ma'rifa bi-Llāh*) in a short span. The use of meditative litanies (Ar. *dhikr,* pl. *adhkār* or *wird,* pl. *awrād*) to cultivate spirituality, potentially leading to the dissolution of the self (Ar. *fanā' al-nafs*) through an experience of existential unity (Ar. *waḥdat al-wujūd*), is a widespread Sufi practice. Yet such spiritual pursuits have often been reserved for an inner circle who dedicate years to ascetic meditation, while rank-and-file followers depend on this spiritual elite for prayers and divine blessing (Ar. *baraka*). When Shaykh Ibrāhīm announced the "flood" (Ar. *fayḍ*) of divine knowledge and power, he promised to transform every disciple into a charismatic figure directly connected with God. I will revisit the *tarbiya* process and its implications later in this introduction.

The promise of knowing God through *tarbiya* attracted large numbers of followers in Shaykh Ibrāhīm's native western Saalum, and many villages quickly became entirely Taalibe Baay. Yet the interior of French-ruled Senegal was already under the de facto influence of several major Sufi Islamic leaders, limiting the Fayḍa's domestic spread beyond this small area. Still, within a few years of the Fayḍa's beginning, several junior members of the major scholarly lineages of Mauritania's Idaw'ali tribe, whose leaders had introduced the Tijānī Sufi order to West Africa, joined the Fayḍa. Their adherence legitimized it among the clerical elite and provided a base of disciples in Mauritania and beyond (Seesemann 2004, 2011). In 1937, while on pilgrimage to Mecca and Medina, Shaykh Ibrāhīm met the emir (ruler) of Kano, Northern Nigeria. The emir became his disciple, along with many Tijānī leaders of Northern Nigeria and eventually millions of disciples (Paden 1973; Hiskett 1980; Gray 1998). Consequently, almost from its beginning, the Fayḍa had a far larger following outside than inside Senegal. Only during the late 1990s and especially the 2000s did the Fayḍa become a major popular movement in Senegal (see chapter 1).

Women have played important yet usually overlooked roles in the Fayḍa since its inception.[6] Shaykh Ibrāhīm's initial circle of disciples, and possibly Shaykh Ibrāhīm himself, seem initially to have assumed that the mystical knowledge popularized by the Fayḍa was only destined for men. According to some accounts, during the first days of the Fayḍa, Shaykh Ibrāhīm's close follower Shaykh Ibra Fall (not to be confused with the Murid figure of the same name) approached Shaykh Ibrāhīm and told him that the disciples' female kin had been wondering whether they could have this new knowledge of God. Shaykh Ibrāhīm authorized Shaykh Ibra to give *tarbiya* to women, including Shaykh Ibrāhīm's mother and wives. Shaykh Ibra's son Al-Ḥājj ʿAbdallāh Fall told me that Shaykh Ibra gave *tarbiya* to nine women, then refused the tenth. He reasoned that Shaykh Ibrāhīm himself had only given *tarbiya* to five men and, since Islamic law gives two women's testimony the weight of one man's testimony, to initiate a tenth would be to rival his leader. This account suggests that twice as many women as men sought to join the Fayḍa during its early days. Most of these women were wives or mothers of Shaykh Ibrāhīm and his male disciples, so their greater number may stem partly from the polygyny prevalent in the area. After the Fayḍa's initial moment, there was no restriction on which *muqaddam* could initiate women, and it seems that Shaykh Ibrāhīm's *muqaddam*s initiated at least as many women as men wherever they were working. Considering Shaykh Ibra Fall's initial connection with women, it is no surprise that he or his deputies had appointed several of the women leaders I interviewed.

Many women were pillars of the emerging Fayḍa community in their villages, organizing *sikkar* meetings and cooking large quantities of food for work days in fields whose harvest was to be given to Shaykh Ibrāhīm. Shaykh Ibrāhīm appointed women throughout his life, although it seems that few of them ever acted as spiritual guides. The few who are aware of these women's appointments are often wary of mentioning them. As mentioned above, oral accounts actively erase the roles of leaders of women that Shaykh Ibrāhīm reportedly appointed as *muqaddama*s. Shaykh Ibrāhīm also appointed several of his senior daughters as *muqaddamas*, and younger daughters have been appointed since his death in 1975.

Shaykh Ibrāhīm also insisted on his daughters' Islamic education, having them memorize the Qur'ān and other Islamic texts alongside their brothers. Yet his daughters only studied in Medina Baay under their family's protection, while their brothers continued their studies at Arab universities abroad, especially Al-Azhar in Cairo. Most of Shaykh Ibrāhīm's daughters ended their formal studies on marrying, often during their teens. Most married Shaykh Ibrāhīm's *muqaddams* outside Kaolack, many of them throughout West Africa. Several of Shaykh Ibrāhīm's daughters went on to found Qur'ānic schools and Islamic institutes and some oversee large *daayiras*. The best-known of these in Senegal are Sayyida Ruqayya (b. 1930) and Shaykha Maryam (b. 1932), while the daughter with perhaps the largest following overall is Umm al-Khayri, who has lived in Niger since marrying Shaykh Ibrāhīm's main representative there. Many interviewees cited these women's example as evidence that women can do anything men can do and of Shaykh Ibrāhīm's pioneering support for girls' education.

Women, Marginality, and Islamic Authority

Up until the 1980s, research on Islam in West Africa, especially in Senegal, focused overwhelmingly on the political influence of charismatic male Islamic leaders who had become major power brokers during the colonial period (Trimingham 1959; Behrman 1970; Cruise O'Brien 1971; Copans 1980; Coulon 1981). Occasional references to women were limited to abstract discussions of family and kinship (e.g., Monteil 1980). Many scholars of Senegalese Sufi communities, apparently generalizing a widespread Murid position, claim that these communities uniformly bar women from submitting directly to a shaykh and praying in mosques (e.g., Cruise O'Brien 1971, 85–6; Creevey 1991, 1996; Evers Rosander 1997; Mbow 1997; Bop 2005). Research on women in African Muslim communities has often focused on women's marginal relationship to formal Islamic knowledge, authority, and practice (Frede and Hill 2014). Trimingham describes women as more involved in "pagan" practices because "Islam provided women with little scope for ritual participation" (Trimingham 1980, 46–7). There is some truth to this claim. Throughout Muslim Africa, men dominate "official" Islam, whereas women dominate spirit possession cults and other ecstatic practices usually construed in opposition to male-dominated "orthodox"

Islam (Strobel 1979; Lambek 1981, 1993; Boddy 1989; Kenyon 1995; S.J. Rasmussen 1995; Masquelier 2001).

Many scholars have consequently described women's spiritualistic practices as feminine responses to patriarchy and Islam. Scholars have characterized such practices as a covert "Women's Liberation Movement," or "a hidden protest against both Islamic and male dominance" (Bovin 1983, 89–90); as "thinly disguised protest movements directed against the dominant sex" (Lewis [1971] 2003, 26); as "a psychodynamic response to, and expression of, [women's] powerlessness" (Bourguignon 2004, 560, see also Bourguignon 1976); and, in the Egyptian context, as a locally accepted "excuse" (Ar. *ʿuzr*) for behaviour normally inexcusable for women (Morsy 1978). Some scholars conclude that spirit possession practices fail at their presumed goal of resisting male domination and instead reinforce it (Gomm 1975; Echard 1991).

Such tendencies to define women and ecstatic religious practices in opposition to Islam and patriarchy have come under scrutiny. Janice Boddy (1989) and Adeline Masquelier (2001) concur that women's spirit possession practices are shaped by gendered needs and often find themselves in opposition to hegemonic, male-centric Islamic orthodoxies. Yet their rich accounts of women's lives reveal complex motivations and experiences that cannot be reduced to resistance to patriarchy or Islam. Resistance-centric accounts fix the meaning of an organic and "holistic reality" (Boddy 1989, 136) and "underestimate the factuality of spirits" (139) for participants. Furthermore, as Lambek (1993) has shown, even where the spheres of Islam and ecstatic religious practice are widely coded as men's and women's domains, respectively, they do not constitute diametrically opposed, gender-divided systems. As Beth Buggenhagen (2009a, 195) has pointed out, even where women are largely excluded from Islamic textual education and ritual authority, they do not generally consider themselves less pious or less devoted Muslims than men.

Like many studies of ecstatic religious practice, secular feminist studies of Islam in West Africa have often depicted Islam and women as polar opposites. Perhaps the most comprehensive of these approaches come from Callaway and Creevey, in their individual works on Northern Nigeria (Callaway 1987) and Senegal (Creevey 1991, 1996) and especially in their collaborative work examining Islam's effects on women in both countries (Callaway and Creevey 1994). Underlying their analysis is an assumption that Islam's influence varies directly with masculine domination and "discrimination" against women.

They admit that Islamic patriarchy has been compounded by indigenous and colonial patriarchies, yet they attribute misogyny in the areas they examine primarily to Islam (Callaway and Creevey 1994, 8). Using an approach reminiscent of Mernissi's pioneering feminist examination of Islam's effects on women in Morocco (Mernissi 1987), Callaway and Creevey derive attitudes damaging to women in these countries from ahistorical readings of verses in the Qur'ān and *ḥadīth* (Ar.), or reported sayings and actions of the Prophet Muḥammad. While Creevey concedes that "Islam, like all religions, adapts to the society in which it spreads" (Creevey 1991, 365), it becomes clear that this is not because Islam has always been interpreted contextually but because of different levels of "strictness" with which different societies implement Islam's hard-coded prescriptions. Callaway and Creevey envision women's liberation through attenuating Islam's influence, ideally through secular liberalism inculcated through modern, secular education (Creevey 1996, 302). It is not clear that they asked Muslim women themselves whether they perceive their religion as discriminating against them.

Feminist scholar-activists writing within Senegal have approached Islam in less essentialist ways but have generally reached similar conclusions and have similarly advocated secular activism to counteract Islamic patriarchy. Some Senegalese feminist scholars have emphasized egalitarian and matrilineal aspects of pre-colonial and pre-Islamic African societies, even characterizing them as "matriarchal" (for example, Kanji and Camara 2000). According to sociologist Fatou Sow, women in Senegal's strongly matrilineal pre-Islamic societies enjoyed a relatively high status, one that Islam challenged through concentrating religious authority in the hands of men. Nonetheless, Sow says, "Senegalese Islam" is "relatively gentle towards women" (Sow 2003, 71) because it preserves aspects of pre-Islamic matrilineality and leaves women room for informal negotiation. However, Sow warns of rising Islamic "fundamentalist" thought and advocates enacting laws to guarantee women's absolute equality, including abolishing polygamy (75). Similarly, Codou Bop describes Senegal's patriarchal institutions of Islamic authority as offering women only the possibility of "creative manipulation but not fundamental change" (Bop 2005, 1116). Holding out little hope for positive reform within male-dominated Islam, Bop instead proposes the secular state as a more fruitful venue for seeking justice. Such Senegalese feminist public intellectuals have contributed to the adoption of progressive legislation – for example, defending the controversially secular family code and advocating the *parité* (equity) law of 2010 (on this law, see Sall 2013).

As effective as secular feminists have been in securing formal human rights for women, such approaches have seldom examined concrete Muslim women's experiences and actions as religious agents and subjects. The depiction of Islam as a male sphere partly stems from researchers' focus on Islam's most visible representatives, who are typically men, while overlooking women's less visible yet considerable participation in religious life (Buggenhagen 2009a; Augis 2014). A small but growing number of scholars have heeded Boyd and Last's (1985) call to pay more attention to "women as religious agents." The West African Muslim woman discussed first and most extensively in the literature is Nana Asma'u (1793–1864), the daughter of Usman dan Fodiyo (1754–1815), the Qādirī shaykh and founder of the Sokoto Caliphate in what is now Northern Nigeria (Boyd and Last 1985; Boyd 1989; Asma'u 1997; Mack and Boyd 2000, 2013). A prolific poet, scholar, and teacher, Nana Asma'u and her corps of women teachers educated women within their homes. Her literary output and influence are exceptional, not only among West African Muslim women but among Muslim women of her period more generally, and West African women today increasingly cite her as a role model (Mack 2004; Alidou 2005). Yet even if exceptional, Nana Asma'u represents long-standing yet hidden and little-examined traditions of women's Islamic scholarship in places such as Mauritania, Northern Nigeria, and the Senegal River Valley (Mack 2008; Frede 2014). Several studies have documented the extent of women's leadership and teaching in Northern Nigeria and Niger, especially involving women affiliated with the Tijānī Sufi order (Sule and Starratt 1991; Hutson 1997, 1999, 2001; Alidou 2005).

Shortly after Boyd and Last called attention to the case of Nana Asma'u, Coulon and Reveyrand (Coulon 1988; Coulon and Reveyrand 1990; Reveyrand-Coulon 1993) introduced another exceptional woman Islamic leader, Sokhna Magat Diop. The daughter of a sonless Murid shaykh in Thies, Senegal, Sokhna Magat succeeded her father as the leader (Ar. *khalīfa*) of a religious community of both men and women. Coulon and Reveyrand cite Sokhna Magat's authority as evidence that *baraka* is inherited bilaterally among Murids, an observation that Beth Buggenhagen (2009a) confirms in her reports of men and women declaring allegiance to Aḥmadu Bamba's female descendants through ritual prostration (Wol. *jébbalu*). Buggenhagen (personal communication) also observed Murid "Sokhnas" exchanging prayers – bolstered by their inherited *baraka/barke* – for material offerings, which they redistributed to a stream of needy visitors. She did not observe them transmitting *wirds* or providing spiritual guidance. Pezeril (2008a; 2008b) suggests some ambiguity surrounding Sokhna Magat Diop's authority. Murid leaders she interviewed insisted that, as a woman, Sokhna Magat could not truly occupy the rank of *shaykh* or transmit her authority to her children. In exactly what ways and to what extent Murid women exercise Islamic authority is a question that requires more concrete ethnographic examination.

Even if they raise more questions than they answer, Coulon and Reveyrand hint at little-discussed connections between the ideal of the secluded and veiled Muslim woman and hidden Sufi power and knowledge. They suggest that, with her reclusive and elusive aura, the Sokhna is "closer to the Sufi model than most Senegalese marabouts," who are more concerned with "ostentatious demonstrations" of status (Coulon and Reveyrand 1990, 17). In chapter 3 I discuss how Taalibe Baay *muqaddamas* highlight similar homologies between normative femininity and mysticism. Extrapolating from the case of Sokhna Magat Diop, Coulon argues that mystical tendencies are better able than "reformist or fundamentalist Islam … to tackle [women's] particular problems and to give expression to their own sociability" (Coulon 1988, 118). Coulon predicts that African women will never be attracted to "fundamentalist" groups that insist on "strict moral standards for women" (1988, 117–18). His conclusion echoes Trimingham's claim that Sufism is the only Islamic tendency that accommodates women somewhat because it accepts "heterodox" practices such as visits to saints' tombs (Trimingham [1971] 1998, 18).

At some point, that generalization may have been largely accurate. Male students have often been the driving force behind reformist[7] movements in West Africa (Launay 1992; Masquelier 1999; Gomez-Perez, LeBlanc, and Savadogo 2009). Young men for whom marriage is prohibitively expensive are attracted by reformist condemnations of "wasteful" life-cycle rituals that move wealth into female-dominated reciprocity networks (Masquelier 1999, 2009; Janson 2005). In Senegal, where the male-dominated hierarchy is Sufi, Murid women have found many ways to obtain divine blessing (*baraka*/*barke*), religious merit (Ar. *thawāb*/Wol. *tuyaaba*), and prestige (Ar./Wol. *daraja*) in women's religious networks outside the masculine spaces of formal religious authority that largely exclude them (Evers Rosander 1997, 1998, 2004; Mbow 1997; Buggenhagen 2001, 2009b). Masquelier has described women's changing participation as instrumental to both the rise and the ultimate fall of a new Sufi movement in Niger (Masquelier 2009).

However, in recent years, as the Islamic scene in West Africa has diversified, women's participation in a range of Islamic movements has complicated assumptions that any tendency naturally meets women's needs. Alongside urban women's increasing visibility in the Fayḍa since the 1990s, women have participated in a range of Islamic movements throughout West Africa, including Salafī-inspired Islamist reformism (Loimeier 2003; Augis 2005, 2009; Schulz 2008), the puritanical Tablīghī Jamāʿat preaching movement (Janson 2005, 2008, 2014), Sufi revival movements (Kane and Villalón 1998; Villalón 1999; Schulz 2006; Masquelier 2009), and local movements that defy such categories (Schulz 2003; Soares 2004). Ironically, despite widespread expectations that pious women attenuate their visibility because they are *ʿawra* (Ar.) – something vulnerable that must be protected (see chapter 6) – the resulting modest dress has often made them the most visible daily signs of Islamic renewal and "public piety" (Schulz 2008; Masquelier 2009; see Deeb 2006 on Lebanon; see Göle 2002 on Turkey).

Even if participants in religious polemics often construe reformism and Sufism/traditionalism as diametric opposites (Launay 1992; Soares 2004; Masquelier 2009), women participate actively in a range of Islamic movements that tend to share several characteristics. These movements invoke textual authenticity against entrenched traditions and authority structures, emphasize individual Muslims' self-cultivation as pious subjects, preach the universal duty to seek Islamic knowledge, and actively involve men and women, while still upholding some vision of gender distinctions. The likelihood that women will commit to a movement depends less on its "liberality" towards them than on the degree to which it assumes their moral agency and actively involves them in religious life. The most "conservative" reform movements with regard to women's dress, seclusion, and patriarchy often work to expand women's education, involve them in preaching, and task them with publicly modelling pious attire and behaviour (Loimeier 1997; Umar 2001; Schulz 2008). In addition, some even exhort men to share in domestic work to provide women with opportunities to preach (Wario 2012; Janson 2014).

Hybrid Subjects and Resistance

This phenomenon – that of women actively seeking self-realization as pious Muslim subjects, one which usually entails their cultivating submissive dispositions towards men and God – has required scholars to "parochialize" liberal feminist assumptions of a universal desire for autonomy and freedom against domination (Mahmood 2001a, 203; 2005). This does not mean that pious Muslim women are unfamiliar with or reject discourses like "liberation" and "women's rights." Muslim women's experiences, struggles, and discourses are not isolated but are "intertwined" (Abu-Lughod 1998; Deeb 2006) with those of other women around the world. This is increasingly true as neoliberal institutions and liberal discourses of women's liberation and equality have globalized.

Subject to multiple, interconnected sets of norms and discourses, Muslim women situate themselves using "hybrid" discourses (Bakhtin 1981) that refract contrasting discourses or points of view through their own purposes. A hybrid utterance, Bakhtin tells us, appropriates the power of and tension between the voices it juxtaposes, refracting these voices through a potentially very different authorial purpose. Like pious Lebanese Shīʿī women discussed by Deeb (2009), many Taalibe Baay women appropriate modern "civilizational binarisms" to critique "the West" while simultaneously showing how Islam is the true path to "modernity," "progress," "equality," "development," "democracy," and "liberation." Their use of French terms signals these terms' Western origin while implicitly critiquing Western claims to realize these things better than Islam (Hill 2017a).

The *muqaddama* Sayyida Moussoukoro Mbaye told us that Islam "fights *for women's rights*"[8] (words spoken in French are italicized). She explained that the act of parading oneself naked, although touted as "freedom" (*liberté*) today, originates in slave owners' practice of parading female slaves in front of guests for their entertainment. Islam brought women's modesty, she said, to "*liberate* women" (*libérer jigéen ñi*) from sexual exploitation. A male leader speaking in a large meeting (*conférence*) in Dakar in 2005 on the topic of "Women, Islam, and Development" similarly scoffed at Western women's "*right*" to sexual liberation: "That's crazy *liberation*. That's crazy *freedom*. That's what the Westerners brought."[9] He proposed the Islamic marriage contract as what truly liberates women through guaranteeing women "rights" that no other society has given them.[10] Using French terms for concepts such as "rights," "freedom," and "liberation," both these leaders appropriated the hegemonic power of Western discourses, refracting them through the claim that "Islam" beats "the West" at its own game of liberating women. They appropriate the "universalism" invested in these hegemonic terms (Tsing 2005) towards a different universalizing project, that of Islam.

Even though women leaders I interviewed invoke discourses of "women's liberation" and "women's rights," none speak of liberating themselves from or resisting an oppressive patriarchal system. Their insights into the complexities of gender dynamics rule out that they are passively, blindly, or unwillingly upholding such a system. While they effectively challenge a male monopoly on religious authority, they do so by largely upholding existing gendered relations and conceptions of religious authority in the Fayḍa community. They perform prevalent norms of piety yet tacitly contest certain assumptions about what those norms entail. Yet to describe these women as autonomous feminist agents applying "tactics of resistance" (Certeau 1984) or "weapons of the weak" (J.C. Scott 1987) against Islamic patriarchal oppression would do violence to their own self-understanding.

For women leaders – and indeed others – in the Fayḍa, the question is not one of stasis versus change. Rather, in a time of inevitable and rapid change, the question is how to demonstrate how a particular vision of change harmonizes with the community's and Islam's values. This aspect of their new performances of authority can be understood in terms of Judith Butler's conceptualization of "performativity," or the notion that social reality is constructed, reconstructed, and potentially deconstructed through repeated communicative acts (J. Butler 1990, 1993). Although norms present themselves as stable realities, Butler tells us, they only come into being through reiterated performances that refer back to previous performances of the same norm. If norms depend on reiteration, we can imagine an imperfect or oppositional performance subverting or subtly modifying a norm. Just as Bakhtin's "hybrid utterance" (Bakhtin 1981) coopts the power of an alien discourse, a subversive reiteration of a norm coopts that norm's hegemonic power while undermining its usual implications.

Butler's theory envisions a progressive politics (Mahmood 2005), valorizing radically transgressive performances – for example, those that subvert the heteronormative gender regime. Taalibe Baay women and those around them do not seem to understand their performances of authority as transgressive, even if some observers might interpret them as such. Azam Torab has shown how Iranian Shīʿī women use performances of standardized rituals in women's spaces to various social effects, "negotiating the relationships between self, society, politics and the transcendent" in moments of social change (Torab 2007, 18). Similarly, Taalibe Baay *muqaddama*s perform Islamic leadership in new ways while presenting themselves as working entirely within a stable regime of religious knowledge and authority to realize God's timeless dictates *(sharīʿa)*[11] and knowledge of deeper reality *(ḥaqīqa)*. Through subtly reconfiguring normative practices and religious discourses, their performances accommodate practices that might once have been rejected, such as leading men as spiritual guides and chanting in meetings.

This raises the question of the utility of describing women leaders in the Fayḍa as engaging in acts of "resistance." Butler critiques liberal feminist assumptions of an autonomous agent who resists hegemonic norms from a position outside those norms. Yet she recognizes resistance as possible only in light of "the paradox of subjectivation," the notion "that the subject who would resist such norms is itself enabled, if not produced, by such norms" (J. Butler 1993, 15). Three meanings of the word "subject" intersect here: the subject of a sovereign or regime; the grammatical subject, or the subject that acts; and the subject of experience. Being subject to a normative regime, then, is what shapes our capacity to act and experience. One who resists that regime necessarily does so in ways conditioned by it, not from outside it.

While Butler – like Foucault before her (2000a, 131) – tends to assume that one is subject to exactly one normative and discursive regime, the feedback loop of the "paradox of subjectivation" seems much less deterministic when we recall that people are subject to multiple regimes, discourses, and institutions of various scales. Moreover, the normative regimes people inhabit are not monolithic, so there is no internally consistent regime of "Islam" but rather an internally diverse Islamic "discursive tradition" (T. Asad 1986). Hybrid subjects are produced by disparate yet overlapping forms of knowledge and power (Hill 2012). In turn, they creatively draw on multiple discursive and practical repertoires.

Abu-Lughod (1990) highlights such complexities in her discussion of Egyptian Bedouin girls' many forms of everyday resistance. These girls are subject to kin relationships, the attraction of modern urban lifestyles, competing religious movements, and national and international institutions and ideologies. While they sometimes stand with their community against bourgeois values or state oppression, they also sometimes resist elder kin through leveraging the power of bourgeois trappings – such as collections of lingerie – or nationalist discourses. Abu-Lughod cautions against romanticizing such resistance as a sign of "feminist consciousness" or of "the ineffectiveness of systems of power and of the resilience and creativity of the human spirit in its refusal to be dominated" (Abu-Lughod 1990, 41–2). Not all power is repressive, nor is all resistance liberating; rather, as in Newtonian physics, resistance is a necessary conjugate of power, found in every relationship of power (Foucault 1978, 95–6).

Saba Mahmood argues for recognizing forms of agency oriented not towards resistance and "(progressive) change" but towards "continuity, stasis, and stability" (Mahmood 2001a, 212). Understanding the agency of women in the Egyptian mosque movement, she argues, requires examining how "one *inhabits* norms" rather than how one's acts "resist norms" (Mahmood 2005, 16). She critiques Abu-Lughod's focus on "resistance," arguing that the term itself may "impose a teleology of progressive politics" while obscuring "forms of being and action that are not necessarily encapsulated by the narrative of subversion and reinscription of norms" (Mahmood 2005, 9).

Yet subverting and inhabiting norms, it seems to me, are merely two sides of the same coin. To inhabit, uphold, or apply a norm almost always entails resisting competing norms, alternative interpretations or applications of the same norm, or one's impulse to flout the norm. Piety movements' painstaking self-discipline, social mobilization, and rejection of secular society clearly demonstrate this. The Bedouin girls Abu-Lughod describes only resist some hegemonic norms by inhabiting and upholding others. For mosque movement women, to inhabit pious norms is to resist one's baser self *(nafs)* through engaging in struggle *(jihād)* to cultivate a more pious *habitus* through the disciplines of docility. Even if implicitly, pious women must resist their less pious kin, the secularizing tendencies of state and society, and occasionally even imams who oppose their public presence in the mosque. Although Mahmood acknowledges an element of struggle, she insists that what interests these women is not "resistance" but "positive ethics," cultivating one's habitual dispositions in line with a set of norms.

Yet struggle is not an accident on the way to piety but a central part of the experience of cultivating a pious self. Deeb clearly illustrates this principle through her account of older pious Shīʿī Lebanese women who narrated going against parents, friends, and dominant social norms to adopt pious behaviours and dress (Deeb 2006, ch. 7). Although happy that "commitment" *(iltizām)* had since become the default for young girls, some of these women doubted that today's girls could develop a deep religious "awareness" *(waʿy)* when commitment had become the norm and required no struggle to achieve. These women understood religious agency largely in terms of both the "lesser jihad" of struggling with the world and the "greater jihad" of struggling with oneself.

Perhaps one can always describe agency, then, in terms of whatever power it affirms and, as a corollary, what it resists. This is not to celebrate all women as sister resisters chipping away at monolithic patriarchal oppression; rather, it means that agency connects to everyday struggles. Instead of decoupling agency from resistance, it may be more productive to decouple both from progressive teleologies, seeing both in terms of the "friction" (Tsing 2005) and "dialogism" (Bakhtin 1981) inherent in every encounter with oneself and others.

The women discussed in this book are far from liberal feminist subjects resisting patriarchal or heteronormative regimes. Yet each woman's story illustrates numerous objects of struggle. Members of Sayyida Seynabou Mbathie's *daayira* wear black t-shirts emblazoned with an image of Baay and the slogan "Soldier of Baay,"[12] taken from a hit song of that name by Taalibe Baay rap icon Daddy Bibson. In the song, Bibson cries out "Jihad!," which he then clarifies means spreading consciousness of God. Spreading religious knowledge entails opposing "false" conceptions of Islam, whether from Muslims or non-Muslims. *Muqaddamas* emphasize the power of divine knowledge to overpower a fallen world of drugs, nightclubs, cigarettes, alcohol, and sexual promiscuity as they transform young bandits into saints. They describe combating material hardships and their own spiritual ignorance. Although these women leaders face little overt opposition from within the Fayḍa community, they are conscious of potential criticisms and anticipate them while performing and accounting for their authority.

No one's authority is automatic, as one must continually guard against the possibility of an "infelicitous," or socially ineffective, performance. In discussing "performative speech acts," or pronouncements that bring into being a state of affairs, John Austin (1962) describes a "felicitous" act as one whose execution is deemed to have followed established conventions. Far more than Austin's discussion suggests, "felicity conditions" tend to be highly contested. Still, thanks to ample historical models, many people have a clear idea of what a "felicitous" performance of masculine Islamic authority looks like. The same cannot be said of a performance of feminine Islamic authority. *Muqaddamas* necessarily confront the historical male domination of Islamic authority, improvising their own models of authority that reconcile conventionally masculine roles with norms of feminine piety. Merely asserting the possible felicity of feminine authority is a kind of struggle with a patriarchal legacy, albeit one not clearly assimilable into "liberal" feminist struggles.

Yet Taalibe Baay women leaders do not openly critique male domination and gender dichotomies. Instead, they organize their performances of leadership around aspects of feminine piety. They show that establishing newly felicitous performances may be less a matter of openly contesting the widely accepted "conditions of felicity" than of performing them in subtly different ways that implicitly suggest that alternative performances have been potentially felicitous all along. To a large extent, as Janice Boddy observed regarding Sudanese women, they "do not achieve social recognition by behaving or becoming like men, but by becoming less like men" (Boddy 1989, 56). Yet as they join feminine piety with conventionally masculine roles, invoking Sufi discourses, they also speak of the spiritually powerful woman as a "man" and even of transcending gender categories altogether through unity with the genderless Divine. Such talk of transcendence is rooted not just in Sufi texts but in the Fayḍa's particular approach to cultivating experiential knowledge, to which we turn now.

The Disciple's Ambiguous Agency

The Fayda's spiritual capital of Medina Baay, although home to one of Senegal's largest mosques (see figure I.3) and located on the edge of a regional capital of 170,000 people, felt much like a large but tight-knit village when I began my research there in the summer of 2001. One night during my first week there, I joined dozens of young men and women at their *daayira*'s weekly chant meeting (*sikkar*). Divided into men's and women's sections, disciples sat on woven plastic mats in the red-soil courtyard of a disciple's house. As they chanted, many rocked subtly back and forth with their eyes closed, as if calmly focused on inner experience. For a few disciples, inner experience erupted into ecstatic outward manifestations. Some sobbed and shrieked, and two young women convulsed and leapt as male disciples rushed to hold them down and give them water. After the chants, the *daayira*'s guiding *muqaddam*, Al-Ḥājj Baye Thioub, who had given most of these disciples *tarbiya*, gave a short speech. At one point, he addressed me, as follows:

> On the path we are on [the Tijānī Sufi path], everyone must proceed with discipline (Wol. *yar*) … You must discipline (*yar*) your hand, your eyes, your sight, your hearing – you must discipline everything in your being. You must discipline what is seen and what is unseen. To whom will you show this discipline? Not Thioub [the speaker], whom you'll leave here when you go to America. Not Ndèye Khady here, who will leave you here when she goes to Thiamène [her village]. So how will you discipline yourself, and to whom will you show your discipline? *Bāṭin* (what is not seen).

Figure I.3 The Medina Baay Great Mosque, Kaolack, Senegal, 2010. The mausoleum of Shaykh Ibrāhīm and his deceased sons and close followers is on the right.

> When you are on your own, and you're not with anything, God, who is never absent, sees you. Even if you don't see him, he sees you.[13]

Thus, the Sufi path provides tools to discipline oneself to behave correctly when no one else is present. Thioub obliquely references a famous *ḥadīth* in which the Prophet Muḥammad defines excellence (Ar. *iḥsān*) as worshiping God as if one saw him, "for though you do not see him, he sees you." Anyone constantly aware that God sees all will never misbehave.

This passage came in a larger discussion of *tarbiya,* which one could translate as "education," "upbringing," "discipline," or "training." At times, Thioub referred to mystical realizations one makes through the "discipline" of *tarbiya:*

> If everything is here, God is the one who is here; if everything goes away, God is what remains. We know that if Thioub here is at home and goes out and meets Thiam [the family name by which I am known in Medina Baay], he knows he has met himself.

Although I am the apparent addressee, Thioub references experiential truths that only the other attendees, young *tarbiya* initiates, could have tasted. Those who go through *tarbiya* sometimes speak of "seeing" God, meaning both that they transcend physical sight to intuit God's being and that everything in the mundane world appears as a manifestation of God.[14] Realizing that both the self and others are manifestations of God, Thioub suggests, one experiences an encounter with the other as an encounter with oneself and with God. *Tarbiya,* then, suggests a shortcut to cultivating excellence *(iḥsān),* as one now "sees" God constantly.

When I heard speeches like this, I immediately perceived resonances between the Fayḍa's cultivation of religious knowledge through litanies and chants and theories approaching religious practices as disciplines seeking to inculcate embodied ethical dispositions (see Hill 2007, ch. 6 for my own application of such theories). *Tarbiya* seemed to exemplify what Foucault calls a "technology of the self," a set of "operations" people carry out "on their own bodies and souls ... so as to transform themselves" (1997, 225). Following Foucault (1979, 2000b), Talal Asad (1986, 1993) examined medieval Christian and Islamic practices as forms of "disciplinary power" over the self that internalize dispositions and feelings. The *muqaddam*'s speech cited above similarly seems to present *tarbiya* as a clear example of this "disciplinary power," with God's all-seeing eye acting as Foucault's disciplinary "panopticon" (Foucault 1979).

Analysing Islamic piety movements in Egypt, Saba Mahmood (2001a, 2001b, 2005) and Charles Hirschkind (2001, 2006a, 2006b) build on these theories to conceptualize "ethics,"[15] understood as the deliberate internalization of a "habitus"[16] through embodied practice. Mahmood shows how women in the Egyptian mosque movement seek to internalize moral qualities such as humility *(khushūʿ)* and awe *(taqwā)* before God through routine actions such as regular ritual prayer *(ṣalāt)* (Mahmood 2005, ch. 4). Mahmood describes her approach to "habitus" and "positive ethics" not just as an analytical construct but as a reflection of how the pious Muslims she studied described their own religious self-cultivation. Indeed, she suggests that her own conception and these pious Muslims' conception of religious ethics may share an Aristotelian genealogy (2005, 137).

Others have more recently explored how Sufi and traditional Islamic learning practices in Senegal transform people into repositories of Islamic knowledge through reiterative disciplinary practices. Rudolph Ware has argued that Muslims throughout history have understood that "Islamic knowledge is embodied knowledge" (Ware 2014, 4), something that lies not in books but in human beings – "walking Qur'āns." He contrasts this epistemological approach, which remains dominant in Senegal's Qur'ānic schools and Sufi orders, to "modernist" approaches exemplified by reformists who reduce Islamic knowledge to a collection of "disembodied" texts. Elsewhere, I have similarly discussed how traditional Islamic education, Sufi mystical training, and esoteric healing and divination in Senegal all involve ritually receiving sacred texts from an authority and then repeating them to embody hidden attributes (Hill 2007, ch. 5). In a more recent study of the Senegalese Fayḍa community, Zachary Wright (2015) has proposed that Bourdieu's notion of "habitus" is nearly equivalent to the Islamic notion of "*adab*," or religious knowledge embodied – or "actualized," as he prefers – through discipline. Wright draws special attention to the master-disciple relationship and face-to-face interactions as indispensable to actualizing knowledge and piety in the Fayḍa.

At times, Shaykh Ibrāhīm's texts explicitly describe Sufism as essentially a system of discipline. Around the age of twenty, he wrote the poem *Rūḥ al-Adab*, officially translated as *The Spirit of Good Morals* (Niasse 1998), although a more literal translation might be *The Spirit of Discipline*.[17] The poem outlines the behaviours and thoughts the disciple should focus on while reciting the daily Tijānī litanies (*wird*) in order to bring about correct attitudes and experiences. Shaykh Ibrāhīm instructs the disciple to submit completely to the shaykh, who will then perform potentially painful operations on his or her soul. Foundational Tijānī texts (e.g., Al-Sā'iḥ 1973; Al-Fūtī [Taal] 2001; ʿAlī Ḥarāzim 2002) also detail the ideal postures and attitudes disciples should cultivate during their meditative litanies.

However, disciples emphatically do not speak of *tarbiya* as a process of cultivating embodied dispositions in oneself through repeated disciplinary practices. Although the Tijānī *wird* and *tarbiya* involve repeating sacred formulae hundreds or thousands of times while (ideally) in a state of focused meditation, disciples do not attribute their transformation into a "knower of God" primarily to this repetition. The agent of transformation is not oneself but God, often described as acting through Baay, whose agency often comes to be assimilated with that of the subject. In this way, religious agency as experienced by Taalibe Baay parallels the "expansive agency" that Simon Coleman describes among European charismatic Christians. Noting the simultaneity of individualistic "self-empowerment" and "internalised spiritual forces" in charismatic personhood, Coleman asks: "to what extent … can the believer claim the authorship of externalised actions and language that are perceived to derive their power from a transcendent, generic source?" (Coleman 2000, 205–6). To clarify how this question relates to Taalibe Baay, I will summarize widespread practices and attitudes surrounding *tarbiya* and spiritual agency.

It is important to stress that *tarbiya* – although sometimes glossed as "education" or "training" (e.g., in Niasse 2010) – is not primarily a process of "teaching" doctrines or visibly "training" a disciple. Before receiving *tarbiya*, a disciple must ritually receive the Tijānī *wird* from a *muqaddam*. When bestowing the *wird*, the *muqaddam* usually gives only minimal instructions or explanations. She or he briefly explains the conditions of the *wird:* to perform the pillars of Islam such as praying and fasting, to respect one's parents, never to abandon the *wird*, and never to submit to a non-Tijānī shaykh or perform non-Tijānī litanies. Then the *muqaddam* tells the disciple which words to recite at which times of day. When transmitting the *wird*, the *muqaddam* usually glosses the Arabic terms into the vernacular but does not elaborate further. An assistant may provide the disciple with a written, photocopied, or even e-mailed text in Arabic, which most disciples can read thanks to Qur'ānic education.

Although spoken of in the singular, the Tijānī *wird* actually consists of three litanies: the *wird lāzim* (Ar. "obligatory litany"), recited individually and silently morning and afternoon; the *waẓīfa*, preferably recited after sunset and in a group; and the *ḥaḍrat al-jum'a*, recited on Friday afternoon, also preferably in a group. The individual *wird lāzim* consists primarily of repeating *"astaghfiru Llāh"* (Ar. "I seek God's forgiveness"); the *Ṣalāt al-Fātiḥ* (Ar. "Prayer of the Opener"), a prayer for the Prophet Muḥammad; and *"Lā ilāha illā Allāh"* (Ar. "There is no divinity but Allāh"), each a hundred times. The other two litanies are variations on these three elements. Each litany normally takes between seven and fifteen minutes if recited individually. Group litanies are usually recited more slowly. Disciples count each formula on a *kurus* (rosary, Ar. *misbaḥa, tasbīḥ*, or *subḥa)* designed specifically for Tijānī litanies, with one hundred prayer beads divided into several sections. From one long, central bead dangle two shorter strings with ten beads each for counting hundreds and thousands. Some Taalibe Baay youth told me they could recognize one another in the street because they always carried beads, some of them conspicuously around their neck, although wearing them is controversial (see chapter 7).

Soon after taking the Tijānī *wird,* disciples in the Fayḍa usually ask to receive *tarbiya,* which *muqaddams* may reserve for at least a month after the disciple begins to practice the Tijānī *wird*. Then the *muqaddam* "plunges" (Wol. *sóob*) the disciple into *tarbiya* by instructing the disciple to perform longer litanies at various times in the day. These *tarbiya* litanies generally take several hours per day. Although some continue their studies or work during this time, they often cannot do so at full capacity, and many reserve *tarbiya* for a vacation period.

Tijānī books prescribe long lists of *"ādāb"* (Ar. disciplined behaviours) disciples should observe while reciting *wird,* such as sitting in a particular position in a dark room on a prayer mat facing Mecca (e.g., Al-Fūtī [Taal] 2001). Yet disciples do not necessarily receive or follow these instructions. I have often observed disciples performing *wird* in rooms full of other people with a television on, sometimes briefly engaging in some task with one hand while counting on their prayer beads with the other. Some recite *wird* while walking to work or school in the morning. Speaking out loud generally breaks one's *wird,* although disciples may briefly pause to answer questions through gestures and wordless vocalizations. Some say that more concentration and potentially even seclusion are desirable for the *awrād* of *tarbiya* to have their desired result, although disciples vary widely in the degree to which they modify their daily activities during *tarbiya*.

According to observations and conversations I have had with many disciples about their *tarbiya*, the *muqaddam* generally explains little to nothing about the spiritual knowledge the disciple is supposed to attain through reciting the litanies. One *muqaddama* encouraged me to undergo *tarbiya* but lamented that my numerous interviews about mystical knowledge might lead my conscious thoughts to impede the natural flow of the process. I often heard that youth in their mid-teens – especially those who have not studied significantly – "arrive" (Wol. *àgg*) at God more quickly than older initiates because they have fewer "obstacles" (Wol. *kiiraay*). The handful of disciples I encountered who took months or years to complete *tarbiya* were all older adults, although adults do not necessarily take longer. The disciple periodically checks in with the *muqaddam*, who may ask the disciple questions both to provoke deep reflection and to gauge changes in spiritual state.

On the surface, then, *tarbiya* is an individual – although not socially solitary – activity with minimal conversation and instruction regarding what one is to discover. Yet disciples do not describe themselves as individual agents of *tarbiya*. Instead, they are emphatic that God gradually transforms them as they recite. Many describe experiencing the presence of the Prophet Muḥammad and Baay before ultimately experiencing fusion with God. Many disciples tell of a moment during *tarbiya* when Baay becomes present and effects their transformation. One disciple told me he had begun his *tarbiya* without even knowing that it had anything to do with Shaykh Ibrāhīm, yet at a certain moment he suddenly felt overpowered, even frightened, by the presence of Shaykh Ibrāhīm.

When a disciple attains *fatḥ* ("opening"), she or he enters an unusual state of consciousness that manifests itself in various ways. Some wander around blankly, approaching bystanders to make inscrutable pronouncements while fellow disciples smile knowingly. Some have convulsions and have to be restrained and given water, especially when they hear *dhikr* chanted. Disciples are not to be left in this state for long, and as soon as possible, the *muqaddam* "brings her/him down" (Wol. *wàcce*) through giving her or him further litanies to recite. Unlike adherents of certain charismatic Christian movements, where ongoing ecstatic behaviour may be perceived as the sign of "spiritual gifts" (Coleman 2004), Fayḍa adherents generally consider such behaviour a likely yet preferably temporary by-product of experiencing spiritual growth while a spiritual novice. A person may attain *fatḥ* without any obvious manifestations at all. A *muqaddam* assesses one's spiritual state through questioning, not through observing outward behaviour. Masquelier describes *bori* spirit devotees in Niger as progressing over the course of their lives from undergoing occasional bouts of ecstatic possession to embodying their spirit's attributes in their everyday lives (2001, ch. 4). The rarity of obvious possession incidents, she tells us, indexes "their maturity and a measure of their knowledge and confidence" (130). Similarly, Fayḍa disciples are expected to suppress outward manifestations of their spiritual state (Ar. *ḥāl*) and instead demonstrate their assimilation with God through exemplary everyday behaviours.

After *tarbiya*, a disciple enters the process of *"sayr"* (Ar. continuation or walking), a lifelong process of seeking further spiritual knowledge through one's spiritual guide, fellow disciples, and personal reflection and litanies. The degree to which a disciple remains engaged in *sayr* after *tarbiya* varies. Many disciples told me that, following *tarbiya,* they were perturbed with burning questions. Some reported finding answers to these questions entirely through personal meditation (Wol. *xaatir*, from Ar. *khāṭir*) while reciting the *Ṣalāt al-Fātiḥ* thousands of times daily. Others required additional assistance and visited a *muqaddam,* who addressed these questions through a combination of discussion and transmitting further *awrād*. These *awrād* may include some of the ninety-nine names of God, each of which is prescribed to allow experiential understanding of some aspect of God's being. Some call this process of reciting various names of God as "walking in God's presences" (Wol. *dox ci péey i Yàlla yi*) or "walking in God's names" (Wol. *dox ci tur i Yàlla yi*). In contrast to *tarbiya*, during *sayr* a disciple may seek knowledge not only through performing litanies but also through "talking about God" (Wol. *waxtaan ci Yàlla*) with the spiritual guide or fellow disciples as well as attending meetings and listening to speeches by leaders.

As many narratives in this book illustrate, the *Ṣalāt al-Fātiḥ* is a key part of the Tijānī *wird, tarbiya,* and ongoing *sayr*. Every day, a disciple should recite it 250 times as part of the obligatory Tijānī litanies, in addition to, ideally, 1,000 or more additional times individually as is recommended after *tarbiya*. A supplication for the Prophet Muḥammad, this formula includes a description of attributes of the Prophet that are relevant to helping the supplicant attain any given goal: "the opener of what was closed; the seal of what preceded; the one who makes the truth victorious through the truth; and the guide to Your straight path." Many interviewees emphasized that repeating this prayer gave them "opening," especially spiritual and intellectual, helping them attain knowledge of God and understand truths that mystified them. Numerous Taalibe Baay rappers told me that repeating this supplication opened them up to receiving lyrics through inspiration, while one biologist told me he was currently meditating to the supplication daily in order to intuit the esoteric meaning of certain scientific discoveries. My interlocutors credited any person's unusual level of spiritual knowledge or power to having pronounced this supplication often. As important as the textual meaning and one's meditative frame of mind may be, they insisted that these results depended both on the efficacy divinely invested in the *Ṣalāt al-Fātiḥ* and on ceremonially "receiving" the prayer from an authorized source. Thus, a non-Arabic-speaking Taalibe Baay who has not mastered classical pronunciation of Arabic or the prayer's meaning might attain esoteric knowledge and power through reciting the *Ṣalāt al-Fātiḥ*. Meanwhile, a native Arabic speaker who repeats precisely the same words the same number of times without a spiritual chain of transmission may earn divine merit (Wol. *thawāb*, Ar. *tuyaaba*) through praying for the Prophet but will not benefit from the prayer's "secret."

Nearly all the *muqaddamas* discussed in this book describe Baay as intervening in their lives through dreams, through which he transmits knowledge, authority, and spiritual power. Several months into my research in Medina Baay, disciples expressed surprise that Baay had still not appeared to me in dreams. Dreams are recognized as legitimate sources of religious knowledge not only among Sufis (Ewing 1990, 1994; Mittermaier 2011) but even among Salafi jihadis (Edgar 2007, 2011). Sufi disciples have sometimes given authorial credit to a shaykh for poetry revealed to them posthumously through dreams (Frishkopf 2003). Shaykh Mūsā Kamarā's biography of Shaykh Al-Ḥājj ʿUmar Taal is based partly on knowledge the long-departed shaykh had given to him in dreams (Kamarā 2001). Twelfth-century Persian philosopher Suḥrawardī not only attributed factual knowledge to true dreams – for example, a conversation with Aristotle – but derived much of his speculative philosophy from ecstatic experience. He declared that, although his claims could not be demonstrated logically, others with a certain level of mystical experience could confirm them (Suhrawardī 1999). Islamic knowledge, then, comes not just from reading texts or even embodying them through discipline. It also comes through dreams, visions, and intuition, all of which presuppose that personhood and experience are not circumscribed by the body but emerge between multiple entities.

Studies of spirit possession in Africa have raised the question of how to conceptualize agency and responsibility for acts and statements attributed to ecstatic states and invisible actors. As mentioned above, accounts approaching such practices as resistance to or psychodynamic responses to patriarchy reduce them to individual intentionality. Yet it is not necessarily more helpful to assume a dichotomy between the displaced medium's agency and that of a spirit. Masquelier's account of *bori* spirit possession complicates both individualistic and dichotomous views. From a participant perspective, a spirit inhabits – rather than completely takes over – a host's body, and a host's "personhood is continually reconfigured" (Masquelier 2001, 155) over the course of her life as the boundary between her own self and that of the spirit becomes more fluid.

The discipleship narratives discussed in this book are, of course, very different from spirit possession, yet they similarly complicate the boundedness of personhood and agency. Like spirit hosts, disciples tell of encountering other agents – especially Baay and God – and experiencing themselves as increasingly coextensive with them. Although Baay died in 1975, his disciples continue to describe him as the central agent in their spiritual journeys, a being inseparable from themselves. Several interlocutors likened Baay to a glass that shattered when he died, leaving each disciple as a shard of that glass. As Baay's being merges with disciples' being, he ambiguously shares responsibility for their actions. In these narratives, Baay chooses his disciples; he transforms each into a "knower of God" (Ar. *'ārif bi'Llāh)*; he reveals the mission he has assigned to them through what I have called a "hermeneutics of mission" (Hill 2017a); and he realizes each development in the Fayḍa community through his many instruments.

All this suggests that, for Taalibe Baay, producing spiritual knowledge, power, and selfhood is not entirely analogous to cultivating one's body and mind through modern yoga classes, meditation, or weightlifting. Here it is instructive to recall anthropological discussions of "partible" or "dividual" personhood in Melanesia (Strathern 1988; Mosko 1992, 2010) and Africa (R. Werbner 2011a; 2011b). Building on Mauss (2000), anthropologists have explored reciprocity understood not merely as an exchange of things and labour but also as an exchange of parts of the person. Disciples typically perceive Baay as the one initiating the relationship through presenting an unlimited gift – choosing them and transmitting spiritual consciousness and blessing to them. In turn, they present themselves as countergifts to Baay and his representatives (cf Coleman 2004). At religious gatherings, disciples not only collect monetary and in-kind offerings (Ar. *hadiyya,* Wol. *àddiya*) for any descendants of Baay who are present, but they pronounce supplications that they then "give" (Wol. *àddiyaal*) to Baay. Such offerings cannot be explained entirely in terms of quid-pro-quo exchanges, a "prayer economy" (Soares 2005), or even attempts to knit social ties. On a deeper level, they are attempts to fuse the disciple's being with Baay, and ultimately with God. In this case, perhaps it would be more fitting to speak of personhood as "additive" or "expansive" rather than "partible" or "dividual." Disciples still describe themselves as individuals in a *ẓāhir* sense while describing hidden and interconnected layers of personhood that are not bounded by their bodies.

Although this book explores Sufi approaches to personhood and agency in particular, I would suggest that the models of agency prevalent even in non-Sufi piety movements (e.g., Mahmood 2005) also exceed explanations in terms of ethical disciplines. I have often heard non-Sufi Muslim preachers in Egypt and elsewhere exhort believers to seek virtues such as humility (Ar. *khushū'*) and God-consciousness (Ar. *taqwā*) while also reminding them that God alone can implant these virtues in their hearts. The idea that one must work hard to cultivate piety yet that the outcome of one's practices depends entirely on divine agency is widespread among Muslims, Sufi or non-Sufi, having roots in the Qur'ānic teaching that God guides whom he wills.

In short, understanding religious practice requires taking seriously practitioners' claims that non-corporeal actors influence them (Chakrabarty 2000) and not assuming that personhood, agency, and the body are coextensive. Here I am not asserting a metaphysical status of such conceptions (as do Stoller 1989, and E.B. Turner 1993). Rather, I ask how we might adapt our approaches to accommodate spiritual experiences and narratives. My telling of Taalibe Baay narratives preserves the ambiguities surrounding agency without pronouncing on their authenticity. Such ambiguities are essential to women leaders' performances of authority. Although male leaders and disciples similarly attribute happenings to Baay, I have found women to emphasize Baay's posthumous agency more consistently. As feminine piety requires self-effacement and humility, presenting Baay as the guide and even author of one's actions provides an alibi for potentially questionable activities.

Wrapping Authority

Women leaders' performances of feminine piety and authority revolve around acts of "self-wrapping." Much of the talk about Muslim women today focuses on how women attenuate their presence through "veiling" their bodies, voices, and social person. Liberal critics, whether Muslim or non-Muslim, often oppose such norms as intrinsically misogynistic. Certainly, such norms have often served to exclude women from public spaces and restrict their behaviour. Yet I complicate "veiling" by subsuming it under the larger field of semiotic acts of "wrapping." While "veiling" suggests a negative act of concealing, "wrapping" is a productive process that represents, labels, and constructs – or, alternatively, misrepresents, mislabels, and misconstrues.

Wrapping is associated not only with feminine piety but also with many other phenomena, which can thus be potentially iconically associated with feminine piety. Susan Rasmussen has argued for going beyond discussing "women's veiling and modesty … to include more extended meanings of 'covering' the person" (S.J. Rasmussen 2013, 54). Disrupting the relationship between "covering" and Muslim women, she describes how matrilineal Tuareg in Niger, unlike most other Muslim communities, hold men to a higher standard of modest restraint or shame *(takarakit)* than women, expecting them to veil their faces and attenuate their behaviour towards women. My discussion of "wrapping" extends beyond men's and women's acts of self-covering, also examining the wrapping of other things to which the wrapped person can be metaphorically linked. For example, a performance of feminine wrapping can connect pious "interiority" (Boddy 1989; Masquelier 2009) with inner *(bāṭin)* mystical realities and the dignified restraint or shame (Wol. *kersa,* roughly equivalent to Tuareg *takarakit)* conventionally associated with high status. *Muqaddama*s' acts of self-wrapping can thus contribute to their authoritative personae, revealing moral qualities through performing concealment.

Paradoxically, if women Sufi leaders are to perform moral authority, they must make apparent their possession of hidden mystical knowledge and reserved feminine piety. The *muqaddama*s I have interviewed not only internally cultivate but outwardly accentuate the "interiority" and submissiveness conventionally associated with women's piety. Inner-oriented moral qualities in turn become "icons" (C.S. Peirce 1955) of hidden knowledge, while feminine deference iconizes submission to God, the literal meaning of "Islam." Rather than seek to compete with men in visibility, these women leaders accentuate latent homologies between norms of feminine piety and mystical knowledge and authority. In addition to linking women's self-wrapping to inner *(bāṭin)* mystical truths, they assimilate motherhood with the nurturing process of spiritual tutelage. They consecrate cooking as a devotional activity through which they establish relationships with major leaders, learn from these leaders, and perform religious authority. They wrap their own actions in narratives assimilating their actions with Baay's agency.

Yet interiority, submission, motherhood, and devotional cooking can only heighten moral authority if differentiated from mere shyness, subservience, and routine housework. As women leaders outwardly index hidden knowledge and wrapped piety, they navigate between and even mobilize tensions between multiple oppositions – the apparent *(ẓāhir)* and the hidden *(bāṭin)*, the distinctions of God's law *(sharīʿa)* and the unity and equality of mystical reality *(ḥaqīqa)*, humility (Wol. *suufe bopp, oyof*) and prestige (Wol. *daraja*), a sense of restraint/shame (Wol. *kersa*) and showing oneself (Wol. *wonewu*). Throughout this book, we see women self-wrapping in ways that demonstrate religious leadership without appearing to show off.

The first two chapters of this book contextualize the emergence of visible women leaders in the Fayḍa in Dakar and introduce some prominent "new *muqaddamas*." Chapter 1 describes the Fayḍa's transformation since the late 1990s from a marginalized and largely rural group of disciples into a massive and largely urban movement of young women and men. It also discusses local, national, and global factors contributing simultaneously to the Fayḍa's growing popularity and to women's greater prominence in many roles, including in religious leadership since 2000. Chapter 2 illustrates the paradoxes of women's leadership through biographical sketches of three new *muqaddamas* in the Dakar area. Each story highlights similar tensions and harmonies between a woman's religious authority and her roles as a pious Muslim daughter, wife, and mother.

Chapter 3, "Wrapping," returns to the semiotics of showing through concealment, illustrating how wrapping can link feminine piety with nobility, mystical knowledge, and divinity. Through exploiting these connections, Sufi women can cultivate a wrapped mystique in ways not easily accessible to male leaders. Yet whether a woman's performance of wrapped piety contributes to her aura of moral authority as opposed to being interpreted as mere subservience depends on a match between the context and her performance piety.

Chapters 4 and 5 discuss two specific domains in which Taalibe Baay women leaders reconfigure conventionally feminine roles – mothering and cooking – to transform them into a basis of Islamic authority. Chapter 4, "Motherhood Metamorphosis Metaphors," centres on one *muqaddama*, Sayyida Moussoukoro Mbaye, whose chiastic life narrative suggests a metamorphosis. Starting with exemplary biological and foster motherhood, she describes passing through a liminal period of anti-motherhood metamorphosis and emerging as a spiritual mother of spiritual children and spiritual foster children. For all *muqaddamas*, motherhood is a central "metaphorical concept" (Lakoff and Johnson 1980) that not only naturalizes their authority but profoundly shapes how they exercise it. This chapter places such new uses of metaphors in the context of gender metaphors of authority in the Fayḍa and Sufism more broadly.

Chapter 5, "Cooking Up Spiritual Leadership," illustrates how four Taalibe Baay women leaders link acts of cooking to religious practice and authority. For nearly all Taalibe Baay women, "devotional cooking" is at some point central to their religious experience, their membership in the religious community, and their relationships with leaders. For many women leaders, devotional cooking has brought them to the attention of central leaders, ultimately leading them to religious leadership positions.

Chapter 6, "They Say a Woman's Voice Is *'Awra*," examines how women wrap their voices in order to make themselves heard, whether directly or indirectly, in religious gatherings. Women's voices have often been excluded from such gatherings, largely due to the belief that "a woman's voice is *'awra*" (Ar.) – something to be protected from public access. This chapter introduces another category of religious authority, *sikkarkat*s, or those who perform Sufi chant (*sikkar*) in public meetings. Even more than women's speaking, the notion of a woman publicly performing chant can seem contradictory, as it demands violating the very notion of reserved piety necessary to perform any such role of religious authority. Yet some of the best-known Taalibe Baay *sikkarkat*s today are women, two of whom are discussed in this chapter.

The final chapter, chapter 7, presents the singular case of a husband-wife team, Baay Mokhtar Ka and Yaay Aïcha Sow, who act as an indivisible leadership unit. Within the larger Fayḍa community, Baay Mokhtar Ka is a preeminent – if sometimes controversial and marginal – leader. Yet within their disciple community he and his wife seem to operate inseparably, and Yaay Aïcha often seems to be the one in charge. In some ways, Baay Mokhtar and Yaay Aïcha reverse prevalent gender roles and oppositions: she acts as a wrapper that protects, represents, and mediates her husband's inner spiritual power, and she stays by his side constantly to direct his every move. However, the two present their exceptional and arguably subversive performance of authority as following Islamic principles and historical models on a deeper level. Like the women who reimagine pious wrapping, motherhood, and cooking as essential aspects of their religious authority, this couple demonstrates the power of performatively adapting existing norms to bring about sometimes strikingly new social realities.

Chapter One

An Emerging Urban Youth Movement

From Margin to Masses in Dakar

> Someone like me, I would sit and, and, and think … For example, now, I'd sit and say, God, why do they say God is above the heavens? I would say, why this [and that]? I asked myself a lot of questions. And in general, that's the type of person – truly – that Baay comes to. They're the ones that Shaykh Ibrāhīm gathers. Because, the people who wonder about a lot of questions, sit in their room and think, wondering, asking themselves questions – what's, what's God? Who is God? Why this, why that, why the other? It gets to the point that, within, within their lives, they experience *fànnaawu* [Wol., from Ar. *fanā*ʾ, self-annihilation, here an altered state of consciousness]. Now, people like this go and search and search. So when I started saying "Baay Niasse," I didn't even know him. I hadn't even seen his picture.
>
> – Moustapha Diop ("Emdi"), 9 August 2014

When he started asking the questions to which he ultimately accepted Baay Niasse as the answer, Moustapha Diop – an underground rapper better known in the hip hop community as Emdi – was living in his family's home in the arid northern town of Louga. His grandfather, who established that house, was a *muqaddam* of Al-Ḥājj Mālik Sy, founder of Senegal's largest Tijānī branch in Tivaouane, to which the family remains committed today. While in junior high school in Louga, he hung the photo of a Tivaouane leader in his room, suggesting allegiance to him. Yet when he heard talk of this leader's preoccupation with limousines, Moustapha took down the photo, telling the absent leader "You're no longer my friend." For reasons he himself did not understand, he began telling everyone, "Now Shaykh Ibrāhīm is my leader." He had heard Shaykh Ibrāhīm mentioned in passing, he told me, but had no idea what he looked like or even whether he was still alive.

In 1998 while he was still in junior high school (sixth class), Moustapha started coming to Dakar occasionally on weekends and vacations. Seeing photos of Baay around Dakar, he could finally picture the man he had inexplicably chosen as his leader. He had been writing poetry in Wolof, and after befriending some of Dakar's rappers, he adapted his poetic efforts to writing rap lyrics. Moustapha's uncle was a member of Senegal's pioneering hardcore rap group Rap'Adio, and Moustapha would attend the group's practice sessions. Later that year, Rap'Adio's most prominent member, Daddy Bibson, went through *tarbiya*. Bibson was soon performing songs about Baay and mystical knowledge (Hill 2017b and 2016b). Like many young hip hop followers, Moustapha was profoundly influenced by Daddy Bibson and was intrigued by his mysterious lyrics.

In the early 2000s, after Moustapha left his high school studies, his mother told him to go to Dakar, as Louga offered no opportunities. Renting a small room in Dieupeul, the same neighbourhood where Baay's Dakar house is, Moustapha completed an information technology training program while performing rap in small concerts and soirées. Yet neither his technical training nor his rap has provided a dependable income. Although he sometimes makes pocket money from appearing in concerts and from providing computer advice to people who ask, most of his income comes from unrelated odd jobs. His most stable recent employment was selling clothing at a Spanish-owned store.

Several of the rappers Moustapha befriended after moving to Dakar were Taalibe Baay. When he discussed his deep questions with them, they repeatedly told him, "Go *tarbiya*, man," because *tarbiya* would answer his questions and help him write better lyrics. They said he was crazy when he insisted on receiving *tarbiya* only from Shaykh Ibrāhīm himself. His closest rapper collaborator, Baye Loks, had received *tarbiya* from a woman, Sayyida Ndèye Maguète Niang. In 2005 Baye Loks was attending Qur'ān lessons with another nearby *muqaddam*, Shaykh Ibrāhīm Diop. Moustapha began attending with him, and in 2006 the *muqaddam* told Moustapha to come and receive *tarbiya*. Although not in the way he had imagined, Moustapha told me, he had gotten what he had prayed for – "Shaykh Ibrāhīm" had indeed given him *tarbiya*.

After *tarbiya*, the most conveniently located litany circle was held at the house of Shaykh Boubou Sy, where one fellow disciple was Ndèye Seynabou Mbathie. Starting in 2007, impressed by her love for Baay and her deep spiritual state, Moustapha and a group of friends started visiting Ndèye Seynabou regularly. Later that year, Shaykh Ibrāhīm's son Shaykh Aḥmad Daam appointed Ndèye Seynabou as a *muqaddama*, and she independently started her career in divination. Soon she began giving *tarbiya*, and Moustapha was present when she formed her own *daayira*. Before emigrating to Austria, the *muqaddam* who gave Moustapha *tarbiya* encouraged him to participate in her *daayira*. Moustapha has been a devoted disciple of Sayyida Seynabou ever since. He says her disciples see her not just as their spiritual leader but as "the mother who birthed them." In 2013, Moustapha agreed to marry a female *daayira* member who had approached Sayyida Seynabou and asked her to approach him about marriage. Although his family thought he was too young and financially unstable to marry, he convinced them that being married was an important part of worshiping God without temptation. A few months before I first interviewed him in 2014, his wife had given birth to a son at the new clinic of Rokhaya Thiam, a midwife-entrepreneur and well-known philanthropist in the Fayḍa community (Hill 2017a). I will revisit Sayyida Seynabou Mbathie and her disciples in chapters 2 and 6.

In many ways, Moustapha Diop's story is typical of young Dakar men and women who, since the 1990s and especially since 2000, have transformed the once-marginalized Fayḍa movement into a mass phenomenon. Although diverse, Taalibe Baay youth in Dakar tend to fit a certain profile. Economically, regardless of neighbourhood, the vast majority come from what one might call Senegal's "average" class, just getting by from day to day yet sufficiently connected to family and social networks that they are not the most marginal or at-risk. Most recent *tarbiya* initiates I have met in Dakar (although not necessarily in rural areas), whether men or women, are high school or university students or recent graduates. Moustapha's story of pursuing technical training only to scrape by on odd jobs is common. Even disciples who are not currently students generally have a strong intellectual bent and value deep discussions about worldly and spiritual questions.

Taalibe Baay youth generally heed leaders' insistence on "correct" appearance and strict adherence to Islamic practices such as fasting, praying, and abstention from drugs, alcohol, and sexual promiscuity. Many, but not all, of the women routinely wear a dress with some kind of head covering – although rarely the modern *ḥijāb* (Ar.) worn by reformist women – while most men wear neatly pressed modern attire such as a button-down shirt or clean t-shirt – often Fayḍa themed – with jeans or slacks. During our first interview, Moustapha wore one such t-shirt – black, with a picture of Baay stenciled in neon-green on the front and the slogan "Soldier of Baye" (a reference to a Daddy Bibson song) and the name of the *daayira* on the back. In Friday meetings, many men wear a robe (Wol. *xaftaan*) associated with Friday prayer and feast days.

In their emphasis on neat and proper dress, seeking knowledge, and rigorous Islamic practice, committed Taalibe Baay resemble the young men and women who participate in Islamic reform movements (Augis 2005), even if they understand these values differently. In striking contrast, as Kingsbury (2014, 2016) has described, the hugely popular Murid leader Sëriñ Modou Kara actively recruits and socially reintegrates young men from Dakar's streets and prisons, many of them runaways and orphans. Kara does not insist on regular prayer, following a dress code (except among his security corps), or abstaining from alcohol, and young disciples are known for ostentatious displays of abject devotion to him.

The growing number and visibility of women leaders in the Fayḍa in Dakar coincides with the Fayḍa's own growing numbers and visibility in Senegal. Women had played important roles as disciples and organizers in the Fayḍa community since the Fayḍa's rural beginnings in the 1930s and since its inchoate organization in Dakar from the 1950s. Until recently, the Fayḍa was marginalized, little known, and even stigmatized in Dakar and on Senegal's national stage. Only in the late 1980s did the Fayḍa begin to develop a unified public face linked to what have come to be called national Islamic "brotherhoods" (*confréries*). This organizational process was led by members of the *daayira* Naḥnu Anṣār Allāh, of which Diarra Ndiaye (encountered in the introduction) was a co-founder. Yet only since around 2000 has the movement become a massive urban youth movement. Around the same time, several other Sufi movements came to prominence through recruiting youth in Dakar, including the *Mustarshidīn* subgroup of the Tivaouane-based Tijāniyya (Kane and Villalón 1998; Villalón 1999; Samson 2005) and followers of Murid leaders Shaykh Béthio Thioune (Havard 2001, 2016; Kingsbury 2016) and Sëriñ Modou "Kara" Mbacké Noreyni (Dozon 2010; Buggenhagen 2012b; Kingsbury 2016). Some youth have also been drawn to non-Sufi Islamic reform movements (Augis 2005, 2009), although such movements remain less influential in Senegal than in many other West African countries.

The Fayḍa's young women and men come from diverse socio-economic backgrounds and live in every neighbourhood in Dakar. Most of the early *daayira*s were formed in Dakar's densely populated northern and eastern suburbs, whose extended family households maintain strong connections to Senegal's interior. Full of unpaved roads and houses that grow upward over the years, this remains the area of the Fayḍa's most rapid growth. Yet the Fayḍa has also grown rapidly in the band of middle-class neighbourhoods within Dakar proper that stretch across the middle of the Cap Vert peninsula. Most of these neighbourhoods have been built by the colonial housing authority, Société immobilière du Cap Vert (SICAP) since the late colonial period (1950s). In practice, these neighbourhoods house people from a wide range of economic backgrounds, even if the houses and neighbourhoods were conceived primarily as "middle-class" dwellings for government and business employees. Most of the young disciples I met in these neighbourhoods were living with extended families or renting rooms from strangers. The Fayḍa's Dakar headquarters, Shaykh Ibrāhīm's house in Dieupeul (see figure 1.1), is in the eastern part of this area. The Fayḍa also has *daayira*s in other parts of greater Dakar, including the old colonial "native quarter" of Medina near the city centre, Gorée Island, and Rufisque. Nearly all the disciples I met in Dakar were born in other parts of Senegal, where they maintained family connections.

The influx of urban disciples into the Fayḍa has occasioned a demand for a large number of spiritual guides to initiate these new disciples and advise their *daayira*s. Although many male *muqaddam*s in Dakar today have extensive Arabic and Islamic education, a growing number of new *muqaddam*s are simply devout men and women with little formal education, religious or otherwise. Like their disciples, most of these leaders are from modest socio-economic backgrounds. These men and women have not simply stepped into existing leadership roles but have carved out new leadership roles that require mystical knowledge but little formal Islamic education.

A number of factors at various scales have enabled the emergence both of the Fayḍa as a mass youth movement in Dakar and of women as leaders within it. On the global level, discourses on women and Islam have proliferated, and neoliberal economic conditions have made families more dependent on women's earnings and have accustomed many to seeing women in more prominent roles. On the national level,

Figure 1.1 Friday *ḥaḍra* (group litany) at Baay Niasse's house, Dieupeul, Dakar, 22 August 2014. Top: Men sit in the overflow section on the busy street. Bottom: Women sit in the courtyard. The house's ongoing renovation is visible in both photos.

Senegal's young men and women are rapidly urbanizing, the Fayḍa has gained wider recognition through increasing integration into national media and political networks, and the mass media landscape has become liberalized and diversified. Taalibe Baay women's emerging leadership is also connected to the Fayḍa's particular approach to mystical knowledge and to Shaykh Ibrāhīm's precedent in insisting on his daughters' education and in appointing many women as *muqaddamas*. The Fayḍa's promise of divine knowledge has struck a particular chord with urbanizing youth seeking personal fulfilment and community. In Dakar, *muqaddams*' primary tasks are to initiate young recruits into *tarbiya* and to advise these disciples' *daayiras*. Women easily harmonize these roles with their experience as mothers and household managers.

Neoliberalism and the Globalization of "the Muslim Woman"

When I asked the current president of the Dakar Anṣār al-Dīn Federation, Malaw Camara, to explain the increasing visibility of women leaders like his wife Sayyida Awa Cissé, he answered simply: "Times change" (Wol. *jamano dafay dox*).[1] He attributed these changing times not to modernity but to Baay's continued presence in unfolding the Fayḍa. Baay's teachings and his accomplished daughters' examples already contained the seeds of these changes, he told me, but only now had Baay seen fit to realize them. Malaw Camara's wife Sayyida Awa Cissé further explained why most *muqaddams* are men: "Perhaps … women's behaviour is still lacking" or "they don't have the initiative."[2] Also, she said, perhaps they're too busy managing their households and "don't have time."

These are reasonable explanations from a certain perspective. Many of Shaykh Ibrāhīm's teachings are invoked today to support women's spiritual equality to men, their equal ability to receive and transmit spiritual knowledge, and their suitability to act as spiritual guides for men and women. Regarding Sayyida Awa's claims about women's personal behaviour, today's women leaders in Dakar indeed seem a different kind of woman from older village women I interviewed, who, when I asked them to tell me about their experiences, insisted that I ask their husbands. The problem was not that they objected to sitting and talking with a strange man. Rather, to speak authoritatively about the Fayḍa and family matters would contradict their performance of deferential piety. Women leaders in Dakar did not hesitate to speak openly about their experiences and views.

Yet the realization – or recontextualization – of Baay's teachings and these changes in women's behaviour has become thinkable against a background of changing conditions. A number of these conditions are interrelated and global in scope: neoliberal changes in Senegal's (and the world's) political economy; the resulting collapse of agriculture and of previously central kinship and influence networks; urbanization; a global "resurgence of religion"; and hegemonic transnational discourses on women, gender, and development.

One consequence of structural adjustment and the neoliberal economy has been a state of ongoing financial crisis since the 1980s, most spectacularly felt in the 1994 devaluation by half of the West African CFA Franc. These crises have negatively impacted women's well-being in many ways, compelling many women to work a "double shift" (Hochschild and Machung 1989), managing children and the household while also supporting their families economically. Yet an indirect outcome is that Muslims in Dakar have become more habituated to seeing women play more visible economic, social, and religious roles. The end of household-head-centric state agriculture programs, the collapse of state education, and the decline of formal middle-class employment have robbed male household heads of prestige, as youth and women surpass them in education and earnings (Mustafa 2001, 2006; Sow 2003; Perry 2005, 2009). Not only do women increasingly head their own households (Diaw 2004, 235), but globalizing labour markets have made many women de facto household heads in the absence of transmigrant husbands (Buggenhagen 2004). Other women have themselves become transmigrant workers, often earning authorities' trust and therefore travelling more easily than men (Bava 2000). Transmigrant women, many of whom run hair-braiding salons in North America or Europe, gain prestige by contributing financially to kin networks, religious leaders, and religious associations back home (Evers Rosander 2004; Kane 2011). Although *muqaddama*s describe their spiritual leadership as a divine mission that one cannot choose or strategize, in many ways they resemble non-*muqaddama* entrepreneurial women. Their ability to raise money from disciples for communal religious projects significantly boosts their prestige in the Fayḍa community. Alongside being spiritual leaders, some *muqaddama*s are successful entrepreneurs and philanthropists widely respected for personally contributing to Fayḍa projects.

Coincident with economic changes affecting women's relative status, everyone – from secular nationalists to international organizations and puritanical Islamist movements – invokes women as a "barometer" of civilization and progress (Deeb 2009). "Saving" Muslim women from their burqas even became a pretext for the U.S. invasion of Afghanistan (Abu-Lughod 2002, 2013; Hirschkind and Mahmood 2002). International development programs sponsored by the United Nations, the World Bank, and the International Monetary Fund have allied with state policies, local non-governmental organizations, and the news media to place women at the centre of development policies (Rathgeber 1990; Razavi and Miller 1995; Klenk 2004). Since the 1970s, these international institutions have mandated that all development projects be planned and evaluated in terms of their effects on women and gender relations in the affected community. The "Gender and Development" paradigm[3] has brought discourses on women's empowerment to popular awareness, especially since the 1990s, when international institutions, following neoliberal privatization policies, turned to non-governmental organizations (NGOs) to implement development programs.

As global resources became available through NGOs, many West African Islamic leaders founded NGOs focusing significantly on women's issues, such as girls' education, maternal health, domestic abuse, and microcredit for women.[4] In some areas, Muslim women have created spaces of women's sociality and authority through creating Islamic NGOs (LeBlanc 2014). Since 2000, I have attended or heard about dozens of meetings organized by Islamic leaders and associations in Senegal dedicated to such topics as "Women, Islam, and Development" (Hill 2012, 2017a). Talks at such meetings invariably take aim at Western stereotypes of Islam's oppression of women, often claiming women's "liberation" and "equality" as authentic Islamic values and criticizing Western associations of liberation with sexual libertinism. Women-headed Taalibe Baay *daayira*s and religious associations increasingly resemble NGOs. Many organize microcredit, rotating credit, health programs, and vocational training for women in the name of "development" (see chapter 5 on Sayyida Aïda Thiam and also Hill 2017a).

While I was in Senegal in June 2010, the country was abuzz with the newly passed "equity" *(parité)* law that would guarantee women equal representation in government. I often heard Taalibe Baay leaders deride the buzzword. At the 2010 "Mame Astou Diankha Day," a meeting in Kaolack organized by Shaykh Ibrāhīm's daughters and dedicated to the question of women in Islam, a male leader dismissed the "equity" agenda as something "the Westerners have planned to combat Islam."[5] He explained that Islam was already the best system for women.

Another male leader speaking at the same 2010 conference said, "Now in our country … [people keep saying] *equity*, *equity*, yet Islam brought *equity* long ago … Everything that men have, women have too."[6] As the *muqaddama* Sayyida Awa Cissé (see chapter 2) told us, "You know, they say women are calling for *equity*, *equity*. That's all true, but Islam gave women their *independence* long ago." Later, Rokhaya Thiam, founder of a women's health clinic and a charitable association of Taalibe Baay women (see Hill 2017a), told me that

> *Sometimes* when they say "women's liberation," "*the promotion of women*," and talking about "equity" and the like, as a Taalibe Baay I just laugh. Because, I say, these people are talking about *equity* but they don't even know it. Baay Niasse is the one who knows it. Baay Niasse is the one who knows what *equity* is. He's the one who *applied* it. He *applied* it *to the letter*.

She cited Shaykh Ibrāhīm's daughters as evidence that he believed in educating women equally with men.

Yet even while contesting Western hegemony, these hybrid discourses reaffirm the hegemony of the "Muslim woman question." As Malaw Camara says, "times change," and one index of keeping up with the times is demonstrating a progressive position on this question.

Religion as Personal Venture

Neoliberal economic conditions have further contributed to a collapse of agriculture, an erosion of traditional social networks and authority, and a globalization of labour. Rural and small-town youth have flooded into cities around the world, including Dakar. Especially since the 1990s, many things that formerly inspired hope in a better future – nationalism, state education, employment in the formal economy, political reform, connections with powerful elites – have failed to deliver on their promises. Throughout Africa, people have increasingly turned to alternative paths to success and personal fulfilment, leading to the emergence of diverse economic, social, and religious entrepreneurs (Banégas and Warnier 2001; Röschenthaler and Schulz 2016).

One result of this worldwide dislocation is what many scholars have called a "resurgence of religion" (Antoun and Heglund 1987; Kepel 1994; Westerlund 1996). Scholars who earlier spoke of the "disenchantment" (Weber 1958) or "secularization of the world" (Berger 1967) have more recently spoken of "desecularization," as religion takes an increasingly prominent place in public life (Berger 1999). In reality, Western elites' assumption that modernity seriously threatened religion's existence was never realistic. Yet these elites were likely right that "religion" in the Durkheimian sense of the sacred organically connected to a stable community (Durkheim 1995) – to the extent that such a thing has ever existed – has largely disappeared. Any "resurgence of religion" entails not the return of older ontologies of the sacred – whatever revivalist movements may claim – but a refashioning of the sacred in line with modern subjectivities and situations.

If one can speak of a "resurgence of religion" in Senegal, it is not a matter of less religious people becoming more religious. Since colonial times, personal identities and even political participation in Senegal have hinged on association with charismatic Islamic authorities (Cruise O'Brien 1971; Copans 1980; Coulon 1981; Villalón 1995; Robinson 2000). The French colonial regime bequeathed to the Senegalese state not only its secular model but also its dependence on the mediation of powerful religious elites. Islamic leaders and their disciple constituencies occupy a place analogous to "civil society" in middle-class Western societies (Villalón 1995; Hill 2013b). However, despite the continued dominance of several long-established Sufi obediences, new religious movements have proliferated in Senegal since the 1990s. This proliferation can be seen throughout West Africa, where newly liberalized and technologized "mediascapes" (Appadurai 1996) and economic neoliberalization have led to intense competition among increasingly diverse Islamic movements (Schulz 2006, 2012a; Soares 2006). Young men and women especially, disillusioned with secular politics and established elites, have turned to everything from Middle East-influenced piety movements (LeBlanc 2000; Kane 2003; Schulz 2008; Augis 2012) to "unconventional" charismatic Sufi leaders (Soares 2010).

For many, religious adherence is not an inherited link to one's birth community but a personal path to moral and social fulfilment that one must discover for oneself. One must validate one's path through personal study, attending meetings of potential religious communities, discussions with peers, and interpreting dreams and visions. Many Taalibe Baay thus exemplify what I call "charismatic discipleship," a paradoxical combination of humble submission to the shaykh and discovery and execution of one's unique mission (Hill 2017a).

Dislocated youth who have poured into Dakar from Senegal's villages and small towns have turned to diverse and dynamic religious movements that provide a sense of personal fulfilment, community, and moral order. Most of these youths are not discovering Islam for the first time. Most studied in Qur'ānic schools in their early childhood and come from families affiliated with some Islamic lineage (*kër u diine*). Some youth have joined "Sunnite" reformist movements (Augis 2005, 2012; Gomez-Perez, LeBlanc, and Savadogo 2009) that view entrenched Sufi elites as corrupt and Sufi practices as backward and heterodox. Others have joined reform-minded or populist segments of existing Sufi orders (Kane and Villalón 1998; Villalón 1999; Samson Ndaw 2009; Kingsbury 2014).

In a neoliberal era that demands individual achievement, the Fayḍa has become a popular destination for young women and men, thanks to its emphasis on personalized experience of God, its flexibility concerning modern education and material success, and its opportunities for promotion for both male and female disciples. When I first conducted research in Senegal in 1998, I found that the terms "Fayḍa" and "Taalibe Baay" were practically unknown in Senegal. Shaykh Ibrāhīm's followers were usually described as forming a small, rural, allegedly low-caste "brotherhood" called the "Ñaseen" (on the Ñaseen's disputed "blacksmith" caste origins, see Seesemann 2004, 2011; Hill 2007). Over subsequent trips I found the Fayḍa increasingly well known, and by 2009 I found that it had rapidly transformed into a highly dynamic and visible urban movement.

Like the Fayḍa, and likely due to the same conditions, non-Sufi Islamic reform movements in Senegambia began in the 1930s yet remained little known for decades (Loimeier 1994, 1996, 2000; Gomez-Perez 1998), only becoming more visible and popular since the 1990s during times of great socio-economic change (Augis 2005, 2009, Janson 2008, 2014). While reformist movements and the Fayḍa have often presented themselves as antitheses in Senegal (in other parts of Africa much earlier – see Hiskett 1980; Loimeier 1997; Seesemann 2000; Kane 2003), both have become popular with diverse urban youth through their shared emphasis on universalizing religious knowledge, cultivating individual piety, involving women, and meritocracy. Several Taalibe Baay *muqaddam*s in Dakar participated actively in the "Sunnite" Jamā'at 'Ibād ar-Raḥmān (JIR, "Association of Servants of the Merciful," popularly called "*ibaadu*") movement before entering the Fayḍa. These include two women we interviewed, Sayyida Bousso Dramé (see chapter 2) and Sayyida Moussoukoro Mbaye (see chapters 4 and 5). Like Sunnite reformists in Dakar (Augis 2005), Taalibe Baay hail from all educational and social backgrounds and are found everywhere, although they are most concentrated in Dakar's outskirts populated mostly by newcomers, such as Parcelles Assainies, Guédiawaye, and Pikine.

An Emerging Urban Youth Movement

The rate of appointments of *muqaddama*s correlates directly with the Fayḍa's urban growth, with several being appointed during the movement's rise to prominence in the 1990s and new appointments accelerating as the Fayḍa became a mass youth movement starting in 2000. Many of the *daayira*s I visited in Dakar's suburbs were ethnically mixed groups of youth who had recently migrated from Senegal's regions. Many were Pulaar speakers from the Senegal River Valley to the north and Wolof and Serer speakers from Siin and Saalum to the south, where the Fayḍa began but remains a minority. Most active *daayira* participants had undergone *tarbiya* at some point within the previous two or three years, often shortly after arriving in Dakar. The vast majority of these *daayira*s in Dakar have been founded since 2000. Only a few pioneering *daayira*s with older memberships date to the 1990s or before.

Young and new initiates predominate in Taalibe Baay *daayira* life both because of the movement's exponential growth among this demographic and because disciples tend to devote less time to *daayira* activities as they marry and have children. By all accounts, the Fayḍa's growth and dynamism has from the beginning been fueled by youth, starting with Shaykh Ibrāhīm's juniors while he was in his twenties and thirties. Yet the currently widespread phenomenon of the *daayira* composed primarily of unmarried and recently initiated youth seems to date to the late 1990s. Weekly *daayira* activities have become an alternative to nightclubs and *sabar* dances for young women and men seeking sociality and marriage partners. *Daayira*s previously tended to bring together disciples of various ages, even if the most active members were often young. Mature members typically do not so much drop out as participate less frequently as they take on more family and career responsibilities, often still participating in larger monthly or yearly gatherings. Nearly all *daayira*s I visited included at least a few active older, married members, many of them playing leadership roles.

In a time when religion is widely seen as a personal venture, the idea that anyone can "know God" through *tarbiya* has resonated with vast numbers of young people. This is evidenced not only in the Fayḍa's growth itself but also in some unaffiliated Sufi groups' subsequent adoption of similar *tarbiya* practices.[7] The Fayḍa's rapid growth has required the deputization of certain outstanding foot soldiers to lead other foot soldiers. Women's increasingly visible participation in the economy, combined with the globalization of discourses and policies regarding women, has led to a broad acceptance of women's leadership under certain constraints.

These factors, all of them connected to global material and discursive developments, are necessary but not sufficient conditions for the phenomenon of women's leadership in the Fayḍa. Subsequent chapters examine in more detail the extensive practical and symbolic work that women leaders do to harmonize their religious leadership with their performance of feminine piety. The remainder of this chapter outlines the emergence of the Fayḍa as a mass youth movement in Dakar.

The Inchoate Period

Writing a history of the Fayḍa in Dakar is a bit like writing a history of people in a marketplace. One might mention some major personalities, dates of infrastructural changes, or demographic figures, but this would say little about how people ended up there and how they experience it. The Fayḍa's growth has been multi-centred, such that participants in different parts of this rhizomatic network differ in which events and figures they perceive as significant. Here I will only summarize a few general observations, milestones, and central figures.

I divide the Fayḍa's history in Dakar into three main periods. During the first, from around 1950 to the early 1980s, the Fayḍa had little organized presence in Dakar, although Taalibe Baay would later realize they had been more numerous than anyone had assumed. During the second period, from the mid-1980s to the mid-1990s, the Fayḍa community in Dakar began a long and uneven process of centrally organizing itself and establishing links to state and national media to reflect and promote the Fayḍa's growth. This involved reorganizing the Dakar Anṣār al-Dīn Federation, which groups all Taalibe Baay in the region, as well as insisting on state support and media coverage of large Fayḍa events commensurate with what other Islamic groups were receiving. During the third period, since the late 1990s and especially since 2000, the Fayḍa has become a mass urban youth movement, and its organizational structures have undergone further reorganization. During all three periods, women have been at least as numerous and active as men in terms of attending and organizing meetings, making financial contributions, and recruiting, even if they have not always occupied the positions of greatest formal authority.

In a 1948 poem, Shaykh Ibrāhīm described the prosperous merchant Al-Ḥājj ʿUmar Kane as "the first person [he] met from Dakar" and his "*muqaddam*" there (I. Niyās [Niasse] 1993a, 118). In 1949, Al-Ḥājj ʿUmar married Shaykh Ibrāhīm's daughter Maryam (b. 1932), who was finishing her Islamic studies in Medina Baay and would join her husband in Dakar in 1952. She soon started teaching Qurʾān in her home, starting with the children of her co-wives, then neighbourhood children, then the children of her father's disciples throughout West Africa who sent their children to live with her. She has expanded her teaching operations over the years, now overseeing three Qurʾānic schools and a large Islamic institute in Dakar. Although she held an *ijāza,* or appointment as a *muqaddama,* from her father through much of her adulthood, Shaykha Maryam only started giving *tarbiya* after her husband's death in 1985. She explained to me that she did not want to challenge his position as *muqaddam* and was too busy teaching the Qurʾān. Although many Taalibe Baay are unaware that she is a *muqaddama* who has given *tarbiya* and appointed *muqaddams*, she is Baay's oldest child residing permanently in Dakar and as such is treated in some sense as the Fayḍa's senior representative there (Hill 2013a).

At a grassroots level, the Fayḍa's numerical growth and vibrance in the Dakar region had less to do with major figures than with ordinary disciples' face-to-face encounters and disciple-initiated neighbourhood *daayira*s. Early disciples in Dakar told me that Shaykh Ibrāhīm had never had much interest in the colonial city of Dakar and preferred to spend his time in villages and in historic Muslim cities of Northern Nigeria. Some told me, moreover, that Shaykh Ibrāhīm considered Dakar the turf of the Sy family of Tivaouane and the Mbacké family of Touba and had remained aloof to respect their authority. Before 1960, Shaykh Ibrāhīm normally only came through Dakar when on his way to the airport to travel abroad. Yet as his disciples in Dakar grew more numerous, they entreated him to appear there more regularly, and in 1960 he bought a small house on the busy street separating the new middle-class Dieupeul and Castors neighbourhoods (see figure I.2). Today the house overlooks a constant stream of honking taxis, *cars rapides* (shared transport vans), city buses, and roving salesmen. Originally of the same floor plan as many other single-level family homes in the neighbourhood, this humble colonial-era bungalow consisted of a few rooms around a courtyard. As the Fayḍa's Dakar headquarters, the house lodges occasional disciples and *muqaddams* who come through Dakar, and it fills with disciples during the Friday afternoon litany *(ḥaḍra)* (see figure 1.1).

In 1964, Shaykh Ibrāhīm wrote a letter instructing his disciples around the world to organize themselves into chapters of a worldwide organization that would be called *Anṣār al-Dīn* ("Champions of the Faith").[8] Although he had instructed his disciples to organize under that banner as early as the 1940s, the organizations of that name had never effectively grouped together all disciples. This widely circulated letter is now remembered as setting in motion the slow creation of an organizational structure for Shaykh Ibrāhīm's disciples. Three *daayira*s in the Dakar area joined together to form the Dakar Anṣār al-Dīn Federation. By 1980, the number of *daayira*s had increased to five or six. The Dakar federation's headquarters was and remains Baay's house in Dieupeul. The federation's major yearly activity has always been organizing the Dakar *gàmmu*, which many still refer to as the "Dieupeul *gàmmu*" even though it outgrew its original location and moved outside Dieupeul during the 1990s. While the Anṣār al-Dīn Federation has become more organized over the years, it still exists largely through organizing such yearly events. The Fayḍa community's day-to-day activities overwhelmingly take place in local *daayira*s.

"We Are God's Champions": Localizing and Nationalizing the Fayḍa in Dakar

Only during the 1980s did the Fayḍa community expand beyond the few small founding *daayira*s of the Dakar Anṣār al-Dīn Federation. The leaders of this expansion of the federation were members of a new *daayira* called Naḥnu Anṣār Allāh ("We are God's Champions"), whose name is the motto Shaykh Ibrāhīm designated for Anṣār al-Dīn.[9] "Naḥnu," as its members often call it, was founded in 1981 by disciples in the up-and-coming middle-class neighbourhoods of Mermoz and Fann.[10] Most of Dakar's previously existing *daayira*s had been on Dakar's northern outskirts and comprised disciples from agricultural areas. In contrast, Naḥnu was more centrally located and had a more middle-class membership, including government functionaries, military officers, and others educated in the francophone system. It was thus better positioned to introduce the Fayḍa onto the national scene. Naḥnu emerged from several nuclei of disciples who had met informally in these neighbourhoods for several years before becoming aware of one another. Several women played key roles in organizing the *daayira*, which became responsible for organizing and providing the large meals for the Fayḍa's main events.

Multiple interviewees described themselves as the *daayira*'s founder. As each of them independently had taken steps to form a *daayira* before joining with the others, all can be said to be correct in this claim. Due to the Fayḍa community's inchoate organization, several key members only came to know one another after making efforts to found a *daayira*. One of these founders, Muḥammad "Papa" Maḥmūd Niasse, was a student at the University of Dakar when the *daayira* was founded. Both a son of Shaykh Ibrāhīm's only full brother and the first person from Medina Baay to pursue a francophone university degree, Papa Maḥmūd was uniquely positioned to mediate between the religious leadership and national institutions and media. Although *daayira* members sometimes refer to him as the "*sëriñ*" out of respect for his genealogy, Papa Maḥmūd insists that he has always been a mere disciple who is uninterested in being a religious leader.

Another founding member, Modou Niang, was the son of Baay's early disciple from Kaolack, Al-Ḥājj Ibou Niang, with whom Baay would often stay when in Dakar. Baay personally initiated Modou Niang's *tarbiya* and then had his right-hand man, ʿAlī Cissé, complete it. Once while staying at the Niang house during the 1950s, Modou Niang told us, Shaykh Ibrāhīm instructed Ibou Niang to form a *daayira* at the house and call it Naḥnu Anṣār Allāh. In addition to these personal ties to Baay, Modou Niang reported vivid dreams in which Baay revealed that he was the one to organize his disciples in Dakar. But the *daayira* of this name would only form decades later in 1981, when Modou Niang was appointed as its founding president. Several years later, he became president of the Dakar Anṣār al-Dīn Federation as well. He served as president of the Dakar Anṣār al-Dīn until 2004 and as president of "Naḥnu" until his death in March 2015 (which I heard of while writing this chapter). He was also a *muqaddam* and, he told me, gave *tarbiya* to many people. Yet his role as a *muqaddam* is less known, and he is best known as a passionate and effective organizer.

Another disciple with a claim to Naḥnu Anṣār Allāh's founding is Malaw Camara. Then a military officer, he lived in Fann Hock, the same middle-class neighbourhood where Modou Niang lived, although the two only came to know each other through their attempts to found the *daayira*. Like Modou Niang, Malaw Camara reports spiritual experiences telling him to found a *daayira*. His wife Sayyida Awa Cissé, described below, is now a well-known *muqaddama*. She describes herself as her husband's ardent supporter in founding Naḥnu but not as its founder. Later, in 2003, she founded a separate *daayira* for her own *tarbiya* initiates. In 2013, Malaw Camara became president of the reorganized Dakar Anṣār al-Dīn Federation. He is also officially a *muqaddam,* although he is not known to act as a spiritual guide and his appointment is widely perceived as a formality intended to avoid the impression of raising his wife's position above his own.

During the late 1970s, as the Fann Hock disciples were becoming acquainted, another nucleus was forming just to the north in the new Mermoz neighbourhood. The leading member of this nucleus was Sayyida Diarra Ndiaye. The other key organizers of the nucleus were her husband, Ma Samba Fall (d. 2013), and her close friend and neighbour Astou Diop. After Diarra Ndiaye took Astou Diop to Mbaye Bitèye to receive *tarbiya* – Astou Diop told me this would have been around 1975 – the two women began to meet every evening for the *waẓīfa* litany inside either of their houses. They would hold the Friday afternoon litany *(ḥaḍra)* in the open space in front of Diarra's house, where a major highway now runs. After sundown and *waẓīfa,* they would chant *sikkar* together until the early morning hours. At first it was usually just those two women and sometimes a neighbouring Catholic woman who enjoyed their company. Diarra's husband joined whenever his schedule permitted. Performing *sikkar* in an open space soon drew the attention of passersby. Existing Taalibe Baay from surrounding neighbourhoods joined them, and passersby drawn by their chanting also joined them and sought *tarbiya*. As their numbers grew, they decided to form a *daayira*. Modou Niang's younger brother lived nearby and suggested joining forces with his brother, who had also spoken of starting a *daayira*. Just before these disciples met to form Naḥnu Anṣār Allāh, Sayyida Diarra received an *ijāza* (an appointment as *muqaddama)* from Shaykh Ibrāhīm's close disciple Cerno Ḥasan Dem. Although she kept this appointment secret for several years, she would eventually initiate hundreds into the Fayḍa, some of whom became influential members of the Fayḍa community. Sayyida Diarra describes herself and her husband as Naḥnu's founders. Like Malaw Camara, her husband held what many describe as a courtesy appointment as a *muqaddam* but never acted as a spiritual guide.

Unlike most *daayira*s today, Naḥnu was not under a single *muqaddam*'s spiritual guidance. Rather, it was a collection of disciples who had received *tarbiya* from various leaders but reported directly to Medina

Baay's leadership. Many of its members received *tarbiya* from Mbaye Bitèye, reportedly the only *muqaddam* active in Dakar proper during the 1970s and early 1980s. Yet even if he was the common denominator for many disciples in Dakar, he actively refused the role of religious leader, and those who received *tarbiya* from him often did not end up knowing one another. A leather tailor, he would often change his work location to prevent disciples from coalescing around him. Although those who knew him praise his modesty and simplicity, several told me this approach restricted disciples' continued spiritual progress *(sayr)* and their ability to organize themselves (see chapter 4).

After founding Naḥnu in 1981, the *daayira*'s members organized one large *sikkar* meeting each month in addition to their Friday litanies. Members in neighbourhoods all over Dakar took turns hosting. Loudspeakers carried the distinctive tonality of Taalibe Baay chant through Dakar's soundscape, drawing both existing and new Taalibe Baay wherever they held their meetings. After discovering the Taalibe Baay community, some of these disciples joined Naḥnu while others formed their own neighbourhood *daayira*s.

During the same period, members of Naḥnu also organized monthly "conferences," meetings where a keynote speaker addresses some theme. Each conference featured a different son or close companion of Baay. As a classificatory son of Baay, Papa Maḥmūd Niasse was able to entice many of Medina Baay's leaders who might otherwise have had little interest in Dakar. These meetings had several important effects. They brought Dakar's previously marginalized Taalibe Baay community to the attention of leaders in Medina Baay who had paid little attention to the city. They also created ties between leaders and members of the disciple community in Dakar, especially the women who hosted and cooked for the leaders. In addition, these high-profile events drew previously uninvolved disciples into action and attracted potential new disciples. Dakar was changing from a marginal transit point to a central node in the Fayḍa's growing global community.

According to Papa Maḥmūd Niasse, the event that put the Fayḍa on the national stage was a "cultural week" organized at the University of Dakar by the Union Culturelle Musulmane (UCM) in 1986 honouring Al-Ḥājj ʿAbdallāh Niasse. The UCM had already organized similar events for Shaykh Amadou Bamba and Al-Ḥājj Mālik Sy. The choice to honour Shaykh Ibrāhīm's father rather than Shaykh Ibrāhīm himself was a political compromise that allowed followers of non-Fayḍa members of the Niasse family to share the event. On the one hand, this choice cemented the inaccurate perception of a "Ñaseen" identity while keeping terms relevant to community members, such as "Taalibe Baay" and "Fayḍa," hidden from outsiders. Yet on the other hand, the event raised awareness of Taalibe Baay both among themselves and among government and media representatives.

Papa Maḥmūd thus described the cultural week as the start of a Taalibe Baay "boom" in Dakar. Politicians began currying the Fayḍa leadership's favour by giving them government posts. Papa Maḥmūd, Modou Niang, and representatives of the larger "Ñaseen" family approached Radio and Television of Senegal (RTS) to negotiate news coverage of Taalibe Baay and other Ñaseen groups' annual religious events. They negotiated state support for these same events, borrowing the stands where leaders sit in such events and arranging for dozens of city buses to form a caravan transporting Dakar disciples to the annual Medina Baay *gàmmu*.

Events such as these established Naḥnu Anṣār Allāh's core members as effective organizers who were not only organizing the Fayḍa community in Dakar for the first time but were bringing the Fayḍa into the national public sphere. By the mid-1980s, core Naḥnu members occupied the key positions in the larger Dakar Anṣār al-Dīn Federation. After becoming the *daayira*'s president, Modou Niang was appointed as the federation's president. Similarly, the president of the *daayira*'s Women's Commission, Astou Diop's uncle's wife, Rosalie Diop, took on the same title within the federation. The women's president is often called the "vice-president." Diarra Ndiaye became the treasurer of the federation's Women's Commission and then its president in 2004 after Rosalie Diop's passing. In 2013, Diarra Ndiaye resigned to take care of her ailing husband, and Astou Diop replaced her. Although a non-Naḥnu member replaced Modou Niang as president of the Dakar federation during a controversial reorganization in 2004, during the federation's later reorganization in 2013 Naḥnu founding member Malaw Camara took over.

The Dakar Anṣār al-Dīn Federation's primary activity was to organize the annual Dakar *gàmmu*. This event's size is one important index of the movement's growing publicity. When disciples in Dakar initiated this event during the early 1960s, a few dozen attendees fitted comfortably into the street in front of Baay's house in Dieupeul. During the 1990s the event outgrew the street and moved to a nearby public square that could accommodate several thousand people. After 2010 it relocated to the sports terrain behind Shaykha Maryam Niasse's Islamic Institute, a space several times larger. The event now garners significant media attention and is attended and sponsored by many political leaders.

Although media attention focuses on who speaks on the main stage, much of the work and resources related to the *gàmmu* go into the collective meal. The women of Naḥnu prepare the meal, supplementing federation members' dues with their own considerable monetary and in-kind contributions. For three decades, Naḥnu's women were responsible for organizing the "reception" (cooking) at the Fayḍa's three major events in Senegal: the *gàmmus* of Dakar ("Dieupeul"), Medina Baay, and Taïba Niassène. I will discuss women's involvement in cooking at these and other events in chapter 5.

Women's centrality to the Fayḍa in Dakar is reflected in the fact that, although several men from Naḥnu Anṣār Allāh were appointed as *muqaddams*, the only core Naḥnu members widely reputed as spiritual guides are women – Sayyidas Diarra Ndiaye and Awa Cissé (see figures 1.2 and 1.3). Appointed in 1980, Sayyida Diarra Ndiaye was probably the first Taalibe Baay woman in Dakar to give *tarbiya* and to lead a *daayira*.[11] Here I will zoom in from this general picture of the Fayḍa in Dakar to narratives of these two women and the people around them. These women's shift from participating in Naḥnu to heading their own *daayiras* after 2000 echoes broader shifts in the Fayḍa, including the emergence of the "new *muqaddamas*," a phenomenon I elaborate on further in chapter 2.

Sayyida Diarra Ndiaye, Astou Diop, and the Mermoz Nucleus

In 1974, Astou Diop and her husband moved into a house around the corner from Diarra Ndiaye and her husband, Ma Samba ("Maas") Fall, in the Mermoz neighbourhood, then on the edge of developed Dakar. Although Sayyida Diarra was the one destined for appointment as *muqaddama*, her story is intertwined with that of Astou Diop, her partner in starting the Mermoz nucleus, her constant companion in organizing events, and the one who made known her spiritual stature and first guided disciples to her.

Diarra, from an early Taalibe Baay family from Medina Baay, had married at the age of thirteen and moved to Dakar with her husband. She was seven months pregnant with her daughter when she received *tarbiya* around 1975 from Mbaye Bitèye, who also gave *tarbiya* to her husband and her mother. Diarra Ndiaye's elder by several years, Astou Diop was born in 1942 to a family that followed the Tijānī family of

Figure 1.2 Sayyida Diarra Ndiaye in 2014.

Figure 1.3 Sayyida Awa Cissé and a daughter of her leader, Shaykh Nadhīr Niasse, 2010.

Al-Ḥājj Mālik Sy of Tivaouane. Her husband did not adhere to any Sufi order. Although it was Diarra who took Astou Diop to Mbaye Bitèye to receive *tarbiya*, Astou already had connections in the Fayḍa community. Her uncle Babacar Ndiaye had befriended Shaykh Ibrāhīm and his second son, Aḥmad Daam, in the 1960s while on the boat to Mecca. Although this uncle remained affiliated with the Tivaouane branch, the families developed a close friendship. After Diarra Ndiaye gave Babacar Ndiaye's daughter Sophie Ndiaye *tarbiya*, Sophie Ndiaye became a wife of Aḥmad Daam.

Witnessing the moment when Diarra attained *fatḥ* ("opening") – the point of *tarbiya* when one "knows God" – had a profound effect on Astou. Astou would walk in front of Diarra's house early every morning on her way to work at the airport as an airline customer-service representative. While Diarra was undergoing *tarbiya* in 1975, Astou would find her every morning outside her house reciting the *wird*s assigned for *tarbiya*. Astou would tease Diarra, saying, "You're still looking for God! When you see him, tell me, ok?" Then one morning she called out to greet Diarra, who simply replied: "*Allāh!*" Although she had heard people mentioning God every day, Astou told me, the way Diarra said it was unlike anything she had ever heard. She immediately knew that she, too, had to know God. Soon after this, Diarra took her to Mbaye Bitèye, and Astou took a temporary leave from her airport work to undertake *tarbiya*. Astou was the first of her family to undergo *tarbiya*, and most of her family – aside from her husband – followed.

In 1981, the same year that Naḥnu Anṣār Allāh was founded,[12] Shaykh Ibrāhīm's close deputy Cerno Ḥasan Dem appointed Diarra Ndiaye as a *muqaddama*. Diarra's aunt had married this Islamic scholar, a Pulaar-speaking *muqaddam* who had moved to Medina Baay during the 1930s from the Mauritanian side of the Senegal River Valley. After moving from Kaolack to Dakar, Diarra would often return to Medina Baay to visit relatives and had opportunities to talk with Cerno Ḥasan. During one of these visits, as she was getting up to leave, she told us, Cerno Ḥasan told her to stay. He said he could see that she truly loved God. While her peers were out pursuing worldly things, she was always pronouncing litanies and praising God. He presented her with an unlimited *ijāza* that he told her he had been holding onto for several months. Her husband, Ma Samba Fall, received an *ijāza* two years later but never acted as a spiritual guide.

According to Sayyida Diarra, the possibility of receiving an *ijāza* had never occurred to her before her appointment. Besides, she said, one does not ask for such things. Like most *muqaddam*s I interviewed, she reports following the general rule that one does not reveal oneself (Wol. *feeñal boppam*) but instead lets God do the revealing.

The person who recognized her spiritual gift was Astou Diop. In 1982, Astou's husband was transferred to the Senegalese embassy in Paris, and Astou accompanied him and started a restaurant there. She and her daughter Mame Diarra Ngom were among the leading organizers of the Paris Anṣār al-Dīn Federation, and Astou Diop only relocated back to Senegal in 2013. While living in Paris, she continued to travel to Senegal at least once a year to help with the food preparations for the Medina Baay and Dieupeul *gàmmu*s.

During one of these stays in Senegal in the 1980s, Astou Diop contributed to outing Diarra as a *muqaddama*. Diarra told us that others had begun to recognize in her the attributes of a spiritual guide, seeing their own knowledge of God grow just from being in her presence. She recounts an occasion when she left her friends inside her house, which was hot and full of frivolous talk and loud music, and went outside for fresh air and meditation. Astou followed her out and remarked, "I can see you are someone who knows God." As they talked about God, Astou became increasingly convinced of Diarra's mystical knowledge *(ma'rifa)*. Her possession of an *ijāza* seems to have been revealed at this time.

Astou desired strongly to share her knowledge of God with her family and friends. After she had conversations with six younger members of her uncle's family, all of them asked for *tarbiya*, and she proposed taking them to Diarra for *tarbiya*. One of these cousins was Sophie Ndiaye. Not only was Diarra Ndiaye likely the first woman to give *tarbiya* in Dakar, but she was among a small handful of people there, men or women, who was giving *tarbiya* at all.

Since then, Diarra Ndiaye has initiated hundreds of disciples, including the mothers of Sophie Ndiaye and Astou Diop. Yet only in 2001 did she form her own *daayira*, comprising primarily young people she herself had initiated. Shaykh Ibrāhīm's oldest son, Al-Ḥājj 'Abdallāh Niasse, the Khalīfa at the time (who would die just three days later), authorized the *daayira* and provided its name, "Ahlu al-Sabqi," which, he explained, means "those who take the lead" (*ñu raw*). Although Diarra Ndiaye continues to be active in Naḥnu Anṣār Allāh, which is now officially headquartered in her home, the older *daayira* is less active and no longer actively recruits new members. She has shifted much of her attention to the younger *daayira*, which conforms to the newer model of the *daayira* composed primarily of young women and men initiated by the *daayira*'s focal *muqaddam*. I will return to Sayyida Diarra Ndiaye's and Astou Diop's involvement in devotional cooking activities in chapter 5.

Sayyida Awa Cissé and Malaw Camara

While the Mermoz nucleus was forming, Sayyida Awa Cissé (figure 1.3) and her husband, Malaw Camara,[13] joined with neighbours, including Modou Niang, Papa Maḥmūd Niasse, and a woman named Ami Kolle Diop, to form another nucleus in nearby Fann Hock. Malaw and Awa's house in Fann Hock was Naḥnu's first headquarters. *Daayira* members elected to move the headquarters to Sayyida Diarra Ndiaye's house some time around 2000 after Malaw Camara retired and the couple moved farther north to the Ouakam neighbourhood. Malaw Camara was the *daayira*'s first general secretary. Sayyida Awa describes herself as working hard to realize her husband's vision, although she was not one of Naḥnu's main officers. Both have also been active members of the larger Dakar Anṣār al-Dīn Federation, although once again Malaw Camara has been the most visible leader in that organization. Malaw Camara was the president of the Dakar federation's Cultural Commission in its 2004 iteration, and he then led the 2011–13 reorganization of the Dakar Anṣār al-Dīn Federation and became its president in 2013. Like Sayyida Diarra Ndiaye's husband, he also holds an appointment as *muqaddam* but has apparently never acted as a spiritual guide. Both husbands have actively supported their wives' leadership and *daayiras*.

Although Sayyida Awa was first appointed as a *muqaddama* in 1990, she only started acting as a spiritual guide shortly before founding her own *daayira* in 2003. Their house acts as her new *daayira*'s headquarters. Malaw Camara divides his time between their house in Ouakam and the house where his second wife lives in another neighbourhood, leaving Sayyida Awa in charge of the Ouakam house much of the time.

Sayyida Awa descends from a line of leaders (*sëriñ*) of the Qādiriyya, the first Sufi order to become widespread in West Africa.[14] Her ethnically Mandinko family has roots in the Gambia, although she was born and raised in a village in Saalum (east of Kaolack). Her marriage to a fervent Taalibe Baay during the mid-1960s may seem sufficient explanation for her switch to the Fayḍa a decade later. Yet her narration of her spiritual journey to Baay asserts a deeply personal trajectory while minimizing her husband's influence.

One night in 1975, she told us, while she visited her parents in their Saalum village, she took refuge in her mother's room from a heavy storm. After it cleared, she emerged into the courtyard and saw a star "as big as the sun" falling. Her brother turned to her and said, "Someone great has left the world today." The next day she was listening to the radio and heard that Shaykh Ibrāhīm had died in London. Although not a disciple, she was immediately filled with a profound love for Shaykh Ibrāhīm and collapsed in tears. For three days she fell ill and could not eat or drink. She went to Medina Baay and sat with many other wailing disciples in Shaykh Ibrāhīm's tomb next to the great mosque. A daughter of Baay came and told all the mourners to stop crying, for Baay had gone to receive his pay for his life's work. Sayyida Awa was immediately consoled. Yet she could not be truly at peace until she went through *tarbiya* the following summer. Like her husband and many others in Dakar then, she received *tarbiya* from Mbaye Bitèye.

As discussed above, in 1981, Sayyida Awa and her husband joined with disciples in Mermoz and Fann Hock to form Naḥnu Anṣār Allāh. Through their leadership in this influential *daayira*, they established close relationships with Shaykh Ibrāhīm's sons and other leaders from Medina Baay who came to Dakar to speak at the *daayira*'s meetings. Malaw befriended Shaykh Ibrāhīm's son Shaykh Nadhīr (d. 1998), then the director of Shaykh Ibrāhīm's Islamic Institute in Kaolack. Shaykh Nadhīr ended up staying at the couple's house whenever he was in Dakar, where Sayyida Awa would cook for him.

In 1990, Shaykh Nadhīr opened an Islamic school in the neighbourhood of Benn Braque in the remote suburb of Yeumbeul. One evening, Shaykh Nadhīr came to the school to lead *waẓīfa* litany, which Awa attended. After the meeting, Shaykh Nadhīr wrote her an *ijāza* appointing her as a *muqaddama*.

Like most *muqaddama*s, Sayyida Awa tells of waiting over the next few years before God made her known. In 2003, another leader, Sayyidinā ʿUmar Cissé (d. 2008), gave her a second appointment as *muqaddama*. A son of Shaykh Ibrāhīm's right-hand man, ʿAlī Cissé, Sayyidinā had often accompanied Shaykh Nadhīr when he stayed with Sayyida Awa and her husband.[15] After Shaykh Nadhīr passed away, Sayyidinā continued to stay with them when in Dakar, and Sayyida Awa continued to cook for him. During one of his visits, she revealed to him that Shaykh Nadhīr had given her an *ijāza*. He was happy to hear this, she says, and gave her an *ijāza* himself. He told her that he had been able to observe her behaviour night and day, both at home and out in the community. He said to her, "'Get going – don't sit there any longer! You have all this and you're just sitting. You should have been working with this long ago but you're just sitting.' That was when I got up and started giving *wird*." He instructed her not only to give *wird* and *tarbiya* but to form a *daayira*, which she soon did, naming it "Anṣār al-Fayḍa" ("Champions of the Fayḍa") following Sayyidinā Cissé's instructions.

Daayira members who live nearby meet each evening for group litany *(waẓīfa)* at her house, something I saw multiple times during my visits. On Saturdays, all members meet for a nighttime *sikkar* meeting at her house. Disciples also take turns hosting a larger *sikkar* meeting one Sunday each month. In 2014, the *daayira* organized its first annual *gàmmu*, which featured several prominent speakers from Medina Baay and a grandson of Baay performing *sikkar*.

Sayyida Awa exemplifies the roles that new *muqaddama*s tend to play for their overwhelmingly young and financially struggling disciples. Her disciples are mostly students or recent high school or university graduates who do not have full-time jobs. However, she says, they make valiant efforts to raise money to pay the regular *daayira* dues and to contribute to the various projects of the larger Fayḍa community, often contributing more than much older and better-established disciples. When I interviewed her in 2014, she told me that since our 2010 interview, nine disciples had gone to study at Western universities and that all continue to call her regularly and to send their financial contributions. Several *daayira* members who live nearby raise chickens at home and use part of the income to sponsor *daayira* activities. Inspired by their success, the *daayira* itself has started a chicken coop project to raise money for its own and the larger community's activities. (Seynabou Mbathie's *daayira,* discussed in the next chapter, has a similar project.) Shortly before our 2014 interview, Sayyida Awa had built a coop on her own house's roof, and the *daayira* had begun raising money to buy chicks for it. They ultimately hoped to expand to a larger area outside her home.

The stories Sayyida Awa told me during our 2014 interview about some of her disciples highlighted her maternal relationship to her disciples. As we spoke, a young woman came and spoke to her quietly for a few minutes. Afterwards, she told me that this young woman exemplified the sincere devotion typical of her young disciples. The young woman was born to a Muslim mother but raised a Christian by her father. When she insisted that she was Muslim and tried to practise Islam at home, her Christian siblings gave her all kinds of problems. The family had turned one room into a speakeasy and insisted that the girl cook pork and sell alcohol to customers. Some of her friends were *daayira* members and took her to see Sayyida Awa for guidance. The girl took *wird* and *tarbiya,* but when she pronounced the *wird,* her family assumed it was an evil incantation designed to harm them. They expelled her from the house, and she would sleep in the street or at Sayyida Awa's house. Sayyida Awa declined the girl's friends' suggestion that the girl move in with her, explaining that people would say that Baay Niasse's people are taking others' children and keeping them in their houses. She could bear having people say bad things about her but not about Baay. Instead, she suggested that the young woman try to work things out (*maslaa*) with the family, selling alcohol if necessary, knowing that God would help her. This is what happened. Police soon showed up and shut down the speakeasy. The family gradually accepted her religious path. Then a young man saw her and wanted to marry her, and the girl told him that she should speak to her *"Zéydaa" (Sayyida).* Sayyida Awa approved and sent the young man to speak to the young woman's parents, who also agreed. Less than two weeks before our interview, the couple had married at Shaykh Ibrāhīm's house in Dieupeul.

Sayyida Awa prefaced the next story by commenting that young people who have legal or family problems "don't dare go to men to receive *wird* ... but when they see a woman, they say, she's a mother, if I come she'll talk to me." One night, she told us, "the leader of the bandits" in the nearby beach drug scene was sleeping and heard a voice telling him, "Get up and go to Baay's people [*kër* – lit. household]." The voice told him that the first stranger he met would take him there. When he told his companions that he was going to take *wird* from Baay's people, they laughed. He went out and stopped a young stranger, telling him that he was to take *wird* from Baay's people but did not know where to go. The stranger, who happened to be a member of Sayyida Awa's *daayira*, answered, "I'm one of Baay's people." When the bandit came to Sayyida Awa, her son warned her that this man was an "aggressor" and would attack her sooner or later if she let him in. She calmly replied that Baay would not let her be attacked while doing his work.

Sayyida Awa asked the young man why he had come. He replied, "God brought me to you." He had prayed that a woman would be the one to guide him, as he knew that no man would accept him in his state. When he asked her for *wird*, she told him to go away, remove his bracelets, shave his dreadlocks, dress nicely, and then return. He did as instructed, but she still sent him away four times, always telling him to come back the next day. The fourth time, continuing to test him, she rebuffed him once more, but he told her he wouldn't leave without receiving the *wird*. She gave him *wird* and *tarbiya*. After his *tarbiya*, his mother visited Sayyida Awa to thank her. She said her son was now living in her house, not smoking, not drinking, and not doing anything bad. He had legitimate work and regretted his past actions. Sayyida Awa repeatedly described her disciples as "children" or "youth" (*xale*) who needed not just gentle nurturing but assertive intervention to solve their problems.

New *Muqaddama*s and an Urban Youth Movement since 2000

I heard countless similar stories of how young men's and women's problems with family, the law, drugs, and alcohol were solved through Baay's intervention at the hands of a maternal spiritual guide. Such stories take place against the backdrop of the Fayḍa's reinvention since around 2000 as a popular youth movement led by hundreds of charismatic *muqaddams* throughout Dakar. Sayyida Diarra Ndiaye and Sayyida Awa Cissé have seen a shift between two models of *daayira*. In the first model, represented by Naḥnu Anṣār Allāh, the *daayira* is a collection of disciples who share a geographical area but may have received *tarbiya* from various *muqaddams*. In the second model, represented by the newer *daayiras* surrounding both women, the *daayira*'s focal point is a single *muqaddam* from whom most *daayira* members have received *tarbiya*. While both models have coexisted from the beginning of the Fayḍa, the latter model has become ubiquitous as young women and men have poured into the Fayḍa since 2000, while *daayiras* following the former model have dwindled.

Since Naḥnu Anṣār Allāh's heyday from the 1980s to the 1990s, both Sayyidas Diarra Ndiaye and Awa Cissé have shifted their energy from Naḥnu to their own *daayiras*. While Naḥnu was once a cutting-edge *daayira* dominated by dynamic young people, its most active members remain those who founded it more than thirty years ago. They seldom meet other than to coordinate cooking for the large yearly *gàmmus*. Even the Medina Baay and Taïba Niassène *gàmmu* receptions that Naḥnu was famous for organizing were recently reassigned to a group of young intellectuals, Groupe de réflexion Ansaroudine (GRAD). Significantly, even though Sayyidas Diarra Ndiaye and Awa Cissé were appointed well before the other new *muqaddamas* discussed in the following chapter, both only founded their own *daayiras* after 2000 as the newer youth *daayira* model emerged during the Fayḍa's rapid expansion among youth.

This expansion is increasingly visually and aurally palpable. Once-rare reproduced images of Baye Niasse and other Taalibe Baay leaders have become widespread on storefronts and in taxis and buses. Market stalls selling cassettes, CDs, DVDs, and audio and video recordings of Taalibe Baay sacred chants and speeches have sprung up alongside those selling recordings of Murids and other Tijānī groups. Starting around 2000, many of Senegal's foremost rappers became Taalibe Baay and soon began to communicate mystical teachings through their most popular songs, attracting many young men into the Fayḍa (Hill 2016b, 2017b). Taalibe Baay *sikkar* meetings can now be heard at night throughout the Dakar area, especially in the northern suburbs, broadcast to the whole neighbourhood over loudspeakers.

The Fayḍa has always spread far more through word of mouth and small neighbourhood disciple circles than through any centralized recruitment efforts. However, the Fayḍa community has recently made significant strides in creating institutional structures, organizing large events, and keeping track of the proliferating *daayira*s. In 2004, a major and controversial reorganization of Anṣār al-Dīn replaced Modou Niang with a younger man, Abdoulaye Thiam, who owned a printing business and whom many considered better equipped to manage a newly liberalized and technologized media landscape.

Yet the federation's organization continued to lag behind the community's growth. In 2011, the current Khalīfa in Medina Baay, Shaykh Tijānī Niasse, ordered a more drastic reorganization. He dissolved all previous Anṣār al-Dīn structures globally and implemented an entirely new organizational structure that was in place by 2013. Whereas Anṣār al-Dīn in Senegal had previously been made up of fourteen federations corresponding to Senegal's fourteen regions, it now had one federation in each of Senegal's forty-five departments.

Anṣār al-Dīn's projects also became more ambitious. Previously, the Dakar Anṣār al-Dīn had primarily existed to organize a few events such as the yearly Dakar *gàmmu*. When I was in Dakar in 2014 and 2016, the most active project was to renovate and expand Shaykh Ibrāhīm's house in Dieupeul to include a new upper floor with guest quarters, a larger prayer space, and a library. After remaining largely unchanged for more than fifty years, the humble bungalow was now an active construction zone. The huge mango tree in the courtyard had been removed as this open area was transformed into an enclosed ground floor (see figure 1.1). Several prominent women I had interviewed, *muqaddama*s and others, were widely hailed as the most generous financial contributors to this project. When I returned in 2017, the house was unrecognizable. Almost the entire ground floor had been consolidated into a sizable mosque space, while new rooms were being constructed on two upper floors.

The newly organized Anṣār al-Dīn Federation conducted a census of all *daayira*s throughout Senegal to link them into the central organization. It also created a centralized system of membership and dues. Malaw Camara, who became president of the new federation in the Dakar department, visited *daayira*s throughout Dakar in 2011 and 2012. In 2011, he said, 55 *daayira*s were affiliated with the Anṣār al-Dīn Federation throughout the department of Dakar proper. By the time of our latest interview (August 2014), he had enlisted 88. Together, the federations for each of the four departments in the Dakar region (Dakar, Pikine, Guédiawaye, and Rufisque) include over 500 *daayira*s, not counting the handful that have chosen not to join the Anṣār al-Dīn Federation.

Malaw Camara contrasted this situation to 1981, when the Dakar region had around four *daayiras*.

The Dakar Anṣār al-Dīn Federation's expansion is more an index than a motor of the Fayḍa's more locally driven numerical growth. Each *muqaddam* occupies a paradoxical position. From their disciples' and their own perspective, they are charismatic leaders with a unique mission revealed through dreams and mystical experiences. Yet in relation to the Anṣār al-Dīn Federation's bureaucratic structures and Medina Baay's leadership, they are functionaries and foot soldiers whose role is subordinated to the larger Fayḍa movement. The next chapter presents three of the charismatic women behind the Fayḍa's recent growth in Dakar, illustrating both their diversity and the similar paradoxes they face and solutions they have found as they reconcile womanhood with Islamic leadership.

Chapter Two

The New *Muqaddamas*

A New Kind of Woman Leader

Getting to Sayyida Bousso Dramé's house in Dakar's remote northeastern suburb of Thiaroye (see figure I.2) can be a challenge. Many Dakar taxi drivers refuse to enter the area, whether during the dry season when the deep sand can trap their cars or during the rainy season when many roads in the area become impassable canals. Dakar's ubiquitous, bright yellow and blue *car rapides* (transport vans) can only get you to the main road nearly a kilometre away. Then you either have to walk or take a run-down, local "clando" (an unlicensed "clandestine" taxi), whether sharing one with other passengers heading in the same general direction or paying a little more to hire one to go directly to the house. Sayyida Bousso's friend Sayyida Aïda Thiam's apartment in nearby Yeumbeul is even more remote but is on one of the few paved roads in the area.

Living in the area for well over twenty years, both women have watched it transform from an expanse of swamp, sand, and squatters to one of Dakar's fastest developing neighbourhoods. Over the same period, the area has gone from zero Taalibe Baay *daayiras* to dozens, which take turns organizing large *gàmmu* meetings about once a month. Along with Dakar's other northern neighbourhoods and suburbs, this is the area of the Fayḍa's most rapid growth in Senegal in recent years, attracting primarily young men and women. Out of more than 500 Taalibe Baay *daayiras* in the Dakar region in 2014, 88 were in Dakar proper, including the northern borough of Parcelles Assainies, while the rest were in the three suburban departments of Pikine, Guédiawaye, and Rufisque.[1] In the early 1980s, each of these suburban departments had only one Taalibe Baay *daayira*, while more remote neighbourhoods like Thiaroye and Yeumbeul had none at all.

Like Yeumbeul and Thiaroye, many other areas of the northern Cap Vert Peninsula were until recently swampy and sparsely inhabited. These include parts of today's Parcelles Assainies ("Reclaimed/Sanitized Lots"), Guédiawaye, Malika, and Keur Massar. As the government has gradually built roads to the area and canals to divert rainwater into reservoirs, floods of water have given way to floods of people from Senegal's villages and towns as agriculture has declined. In 2013, a fast new toll road opened, making the northern peninsula more accessible from Dakar, even though large parts of it still lack taxis, *car rapides*, and general infrastructure. New development has somewhat raised the standard of living and infrastructure, although most residents still struggle to get by from day to day. All but a few main roads remain unpaved, and encroaching sand often covers even the paved ones.

With little organized presence throughout most of these northern neighbourhoods, the Fayḍa's emergence there depended on the initiative of enthusiastic disciples in organizing the disciple community and spreading news of the Fayḍa to others. Sayyida Bousso Dramé and Sayyida Aïda Thiam were among the earliest and most effective disciple organizers, both founding *daayira*s and sponsoring Qur'ānic schools years before receiving authorization to act as spiritual guides. Their enthusiasm, organizational effectiveness, and ability to speak about religious matters brought them to the attention of leaders who appointed them to represent the Fayḍa where there were few or no other *muqaddam*s. Both have become well-known and respected figures in the Dakar area's Fayḍa community.

Their lives and personalities are in many ways very different. Sayyida Aïda Thiam is from a long-standing Taalibe Baay family, whereas Sayyida Bousso Dramé, after passing through the anti-Sufi reform movement Jamāʿat ʿIbād al-Raḥmān, was the first of her Murid family to become Taalibe Baay. Sayyida Aïda is far better known as a community organizer than as a public speaker. Sayyida Bousso's powerful oratorical skills are facilitated by her significant – even if informal – Islamic textual education, something uncommon among the new *muqaddama*s I have known. Yet both perform and explain their religious authority in similar ways. They highlight their roles as both biological mothers and spiritual mothers, yet also speak of transcending gender to become spiritual "men." Both live without a husband and head their own household.

Sayyida Bousso is one of three women profiled in this chapter, and I will return to Sayyida Aïda Thiam in chapter 5. Most of the other *muqaddamas* I interviewed live to the south, in Dakar proper. Wherever they live in Dakar, *muqaddamas* face similar paradoxes of being a woman Islamic authority. This chapter draws from interviews with more than twenty *muqaddamas* in Dakar and elsewhere, although I focus here on narratives of three of the seven new *muqaddamas* featured in this book. While each *muqaddama*'s story and views are rich enough to fill a book, as Flueckiger (2006) did for a remarkable Sufi woman in India, I only have room in this chapter for three abridged sketches. By presenting the three women in separate sketches, I aim to highlight not only each woman's uniqueness but also her similarities with other woman leaders. My collaborators and I interviewed all three women multiple times between 2009 and 2014, and observed their interactions with disciples and their participation in religious gatherings. In retelling these women's stories, I am not concerned with the factual completeness or accuracy of the mystical experiences and historical details they narrate. Rather, I am interested in how these women's narratives and social performances contribute to a gendered exercise of authority.

Like their disciples, the new *muqaddamas* in the Dakar region come from a wide range of educational, social, economic, religious, and ethnic backgrounds. Most have formally studied little beyond the basic Qur'ānic memorization that nearly all Senegalese Muslim children receive. Yet one, Sayyida Khadi Fall, holds five university degrees. Diénaba Seck is a francophone schoolteacher. Sayyida Moussoukoro Mbaye diligently taught herself the francophone curriculum and has become a highly literate leader of university students. Only Sayyida Bousso Dramé has pursued extended traditional Arabo-Islamic education, albeit informally from within her own home. Yet even if she is the most proficient in citing Arabic texts, all the new *muqaddamas* I interviewed quote Arabic texts and interpret them in Wolof to some degree.

Like the youth who tend to be attracted to the Fayḍa, the new *muqaddamas* come from a range of socio-economic classes. Of those we interviewed, one was born into relative economic privilege – Sayyida Moussoukoro Mbaye – while one was born to parents with significant Western education – Sayyida Khadi Fall. Both have managed to amplify these advantages. The two pioneers of the Fayḍa in Dakar – Sayyidas Diarra Ndiaye and Awa Cissé – became associated by marriage with the emerging postcolonial functionary class. The rest, however, come from the same socio-economic background as the bulk of Taalibe Baay – Senegal's "average" class of struggling yet not entirely marginalized families. Such families themselves are usually internally differentiated, with some members still scraping by on farms and others working in government offices, market stalls, or in hair salons in New York. Most *muqaddamas* tell stories of humble beginnings in Senegal's small towns and villages, and some tell of being expelled by their families and sleeping in the streets or being taken in by similarly indigent disciples. If some are now surrounded by "middle-class" trappings and seem better off than their average young disciple, this has less to do with birth class than with their life trajectory. What now look like "middle-class" homes often began without electricity or plumbing. Perhaps through their husbands' salary and/or through their own renown as spiritual figures, several *muqaddamas* have gradually added upper floors to their homes, filled in a dirt courtyard with bedrooms, and upgraded furniture and décor. In short, there does not seem to be a significant correlation between economic privilege and the likelihood of being appointed a new *muqaddama*.

All the new *muqaddamas* have spent most or all of their lives in Wolof-dominant environments, although they come from a number of ethnolinguistic backgrounds. Two (Sayyida Khadi Fall and Diénaba Seck) are ethnically Haal-Pulaar and another (Sayyida Awa Cissé) is Mandinko. The rest identify as Wolof, even if at least two of these are from families with Haal-Pulaar roots. Aside from the *Dakaroise* Khadi Fall, nearly all were born in the region of Kaolack and moved to Dakar during their youth, either as children or when they married during their mid-teens (see table 2.1).

Most new *muqaddamas* have full-time jobs apart from their work as spiritual guides. Sayyida Khadi Fall is a full professor of German at the University of Dakar and an official in the Ministry of Education and was briefly a government minister. Sayyida Moussoukoro Mbaye, the spiritual guide of Taalibe Baay university students, is better known as the owner of a thriving skincare-product business. She often appears on television programs discussing fashion or Islam. Both these women own spacious homes in upper-middle-class neighbourhoods. Other *muqaddamas* work outside the formal sector. Sayyida Seynabou Mbathie works full-time as a spirit medium, advising clients with the help of a friendly *jinne*, or spirit. She is married to a bank employee who divides his time between his own house, where another wife lives, and the house Sayyida Seynabou bought using income from her divining practice. Sayyidas Diarra Ndiaye and Bousso Dramé have run humble restaurants and food stands.

Table 2.1. Dakar-based *muqaddama*s interviewed who have given *wird*/*tarbiya*. Titles are omitted. One, Maryam Niasse, does not fall into my category of "new *muqaddama*s." This table omits *muqaddama*s interviewed inside or outside Dakar who are based elsewhere.

Name	Residence in Dakar	Birthplace	Parents' *ṭarīqa* affiliation at birth	*Tarbiya muqaddam*	Year of *tarbiya*	Place of *tarbiya*	*Ijāza muqaddam*	Year of first *ijāza*	Year est. *daayira*	Other Occupation
Aïda Thiam	Yeumbeul	Keur Tapha (Saalum)	Tijānī (Fayḍa)	(Unnamed)	?	?	Makkī Ibrāhīm Niasse	2008	c. 2002	Religious organizer
Awa Cissé	Ouakam	Rural Saalum	Qādirī	Mbaye Bitèye	1976	Dakar	Seydina Cissé	1990	2003	
Bousso Dramé	Zamzam II Thiaroye	Rural Saalum	Murid	Aḥmad Daam Ka	1985	Kaffrine	Aḥmad Daam Ka, Ḥasan Cissé	late 1990s, 2003	2002	Food stand owner
Diarra Ndiaye	Mermoz	Kaolack	Tijānī (Fayḍa)	Mbaye Bitèye	1975	Dakar	Cerno Ḥasan Dem	1980	2001	Restaurant owner
Diénaba Seck	Guédiawaye	Thiès	Tijānī ('Umarī)	Nūr al-Dīn Sall	1996	Libreville (Gabon)	Nūr al-Dīn Sall (from Shaykh wuld Khayrī)	?	N.A.	Schoolteacher
Khadi Fall	SICAP Sacré Coeur	Dakar	Tijānī (Tivaouane)	Ibrahim Diallo	1991	Dakar	Shaykh wuld Khayrī	2000	N.A.	Professor/ author/ government
Maryam Niasse	Mermoz	Kossi (Saalum)	Tijānī (Fayḍa)	Alioune Cissé	?	Kaolack	Ibrāhīm Niasse	1960s?	N.A.	Qur'ān teacher
Moussoukoro Mbaye	Maristes	Kaolack	F: Tijānī (Fayḍa) M: None	Mbaye Bitèye	1992	Dakar	Moustapha Ka	c. 1998	c. 2001	Entrepreneur
Ndèye Maguète Niang	Cité Conachap	Kaolack	Tijānī (Tivaouane)	A *muqaddam* of Ibra Fall	1988	Kaolack	Ibra Fall	1990s	?	
Ndèye Seynabou Mbathie	SICAP Derklé	Kaolack	Tijānī (Tivaouane)	(Unnamed)	1994	Rufisque	Aḥmad Daam Ibrāhīm Niasse	2007	2007	Diviner/healer

Only two of the nine Senegalese new *muqaddamas* I interviewed in Dakar (Sayyidas Aïda Thiam and Diarra Ndiaye) grew up in Taalibe Baay households. One (Sayyida Moussoukoro Mbaye) had a Taalibe Baay father but only discovered Baay as an adult. The remaining six, including all three discussed in this chapter, had no Taalibe Baay parents and discovered the Fayḍa only as adults after marrying and having children. Four come from families affiliated with the Tivaouane branch of the Tijāniyya, while one each come from Murid and Qādirī families. Two spent several years actively participating in the anti-Sufi reformist group Jamāʿat ʿIbād al-Raḥmān before becoming Taalibe Baay.

Despite their diversity, all the "new *muqaddamas*" I interviewed share important similarities. Two important characteristics make these women unusual and novel as women leaders both in West Africa and in Islam more broadly. First, unlike most women Sufi authorities discussed in the literature (Coulon 1988; Boyd 1989; Coulon and Reveyrand 1990; Sule and Starratt 1991; Mack and Boyd 2000; Alidou 2005; Flueckiger 2006; Pemberton 2006), none of these women derive religious authority, knowledge, and/or divine blessing (*baraka, barke*) from male kin. Like many Senegalese not involved in religious work, several describe themselves as descendants of Qurʾān teachers and Sufi *muqaddams*, although none are daughters or wives of Islamic teachers or Sufi leaders. Far from continuing a family vocation, several of them described experiencing serious problems with their families, in some cases separating from parents or their husband after becoming Taalibe Baay. The only woman discussed in this book whose authority depends on her relationship with her husband is Yaay Aïcha Sow (see chapter 7), although I do not include her in my count of "new *muqaddamas*" because the disciples she leads are formally considered her husband's disciples. I have also included Shaykha Maryam Niasse in my table of Dakar-based *muqaddamas*, although she also differs from the new *muqaddamas* in having been educated and appointed by her father, Shaykh Ibrāhīm.

The second unusual characteristic is that these women are openly and uncontroversially recognized as the spiritual guides of both men and women. Acting Tijānī *muqaddamas* in other times and places have led women within gender-segregated spaces (Hutson 1999, 2001, 2004; al-Idrīsī 2010; Frede 2014). More generally, women Islamic leaders around the Muslim world have most often led and taught other women (Mahmood 2005; Kalmbach 2008; Islam 2012; Le Renard 2012; Rausch 2012; Omar 2013). In contrast to Northern Nigeria, where there is a long tradition of women teaching other women, Senegal's relative lack of routine gender segregation seems to have contributed to a lack of urgency in appointing women as spiritual guides. Yet when women were appointed as leaders, the same limited segregation meant that men saw no barriers in approaching them for spiritual guidance. Both male and female *muqaddam*s generally attract similar numbers of male and female disciples. A *muqaddama* may have somewhat more male or female disciples, but none have overwhelmingly one or the other. As there is nothing unusual about men sitting with a female leader, my male assistants and I were not out of place sitting with these women, who were usually surrounded by both men and women.

These new *muqaddama*s are a subset of the broader phenomenon of "new *muqaddam*s," which includes both men and women leaders and appeared as the Fayḍa gained prominence as an urban youth movement starting around 2000. Like new *muqaddama*s, their male counterparts come from diverse backgrounds, do not inherit religious authority, and may have limited formal Arabo-Islamic education. Whether man or woman, these leaders act primarily as leaders of young women and men, spiritually guiding disciples and their gender-mixed *daayira*s. Because they are perceived as close to God, people may also approach them seeking prayers and blessings. In general, these leaders have distinguished themselves through recruiting and organizing disciples and have received appointments from Baay's sons and other major leaders, who are hereditary and formally trained Islamic specialists. As "religious entrepreneurs" (Haenni 2002; Haenni and Holtrop 2002; Kane 2003; Lubeck 2011; Hill 2016a), these exemplary disciple-leaders creatively carve out new roles for themselves under changing circumstances. Although part of a routinized hierarchy, each *muqaddam* more or less acts as a charismatic leader within his or her own community and speaks of a direct relationship with Baay through dreams, miracles, and ecstatic states.

Paradoxes of Women's Leadership

In a context where men have long dominated Islamic leadership and learning, women's leadership is riddled with paradoxes. However, a paradox is not necessarily an insurmountable obstacle. On the contrary, a common thread weaving together these women's stories is their embrace of the productive tensions in these paradoxes, an approach strikingly at home in a Sufi tradition that describes reality as paradoxical from top to bottom. Nothing is more paradoxical than gender itself. My Taalibe Baay interlocutors agreed that, to some extent, social reproduction and organization require distinct and opposite male and female social roles. Moreover, drawing on ancient Sufi thinkers such as Ibn ʿArabī (see Murata 1992), male and female leaders often described masculine and feminine as complementarity principles inherent in any dynamic process, from God's gendered creation of the universe to the transmission of spiritual knowledge (see chapter 4 and Hill 2014). Yet, at the same time, they perceived gender distinctions as illusory, melting away in the cognizance of divine unity.

Muqaddamas simultaneously approach their gender in three apparently contradictory ways. First, they locate moral authority and leadership qualities in conventionally feminine qualities such as mothering and humble wifehood. Second, they cite the ancient Sufi saying that a spiritually powerful woman is in a deeper sense really a "man" (ʿAṭṭār 1966, 40; [Niasse] 1969, 1:131; Schimmel 2003, 19). And third, they speak of transcending "masculine" (*góor*) and "feminine" (*jigéen*) altogether through unity with a genderless God.

Motherhood is the central metaphor of authority for perhaps all the Senegalese *muqaddamas* I interviewed. All have had children and describe themselves as spiritual "mothers" to their disciples, sometimes even suggesting detailed parallels between their maternal roles and spiritual leadership (see chapter 4). However, despite motherhood's metaphorical power, literal motherhood involves potentially overbearing husbands, sexuality, and ritually impure reproductive processes. Janice Boddy has described numerous practices in which Sudanese women engage to accentuate the high status of motherhood through denying its inherent sexuality (Boddy 1989). Likewise, all these *muqaddamas* manage in one way or another to distance themselves from the potential limitations of actual female reproduction and wifely submissiveness. Whether currently married or not, nearly all new *muqaddamas* – and all three discussed in this chapter – have managed to establish their own household independent of husbands. Only one new *muqaddama* – Diarra Ndiaye, discussed in the previous chapter – was an only wife who lived full-time with her husband in his house throughout her married life. The only new *muqaddama* who gave birth while acting as a spiritual guide describes miraculously transcending the ritual impurity of menstruation and postpartum bleeding.

Far more often than male leaders and disciples whom I have interviewed, women leaders minimize personal responsibility for their spiritual trajectories through emphasizing the influence of powerful spiritual states on their actions. All Taalibe Baay ideally go through a liminal stage during *tarbiya* in which they lose themselves in divine unity before being "brought down" (*wàcce*) by their initiating *muqaddam*. Both men and women describe their entrance into the Fayḍa not as a personal choice but as something Baay thrust upon them through dreams and mystical states. Yet most *muqaddamas*' narratives go a step farther, telling of long periods both before and after *tarbiya* during which they were "mixed up" and were driven by external spiritual forces. Few of my male Taalibe Baay interlocutors have described such extended periods of spiritual wayfaring. Two of the three women featured in this chapter – along with several others – recount an extended liminal period during which they were unable to fulfil family obligations or obey husbands or fathers. Yet none describe disobedience as an individual choice – they only disobeyed when compelled inexorably by involuntary absorption in God. Their return to productive membership in family and society required some shaykh to "fix" them through proper spiritual guidance. The disobeyed husband or relatives eventually either abandoned them or joined their divine mission. In short, women leaders simultaneously accentuate and deny their gender. I will return to the question of women's paradoxical Islamic leadership after illustrating with three biographical sketches.

Sayyida Bousso Dramé

Sayyida Bousso Dramé's life narrative clearly illustrates this balance between accentuating femininity and transcending it through esoteric experience and discourse. An imposing presence and a skilled orator, Sayyida Bousso (figure 2.1) is a major figure in the Fayḍa's recent expansion in parts of Dakar's north-eastern periphery. Her Murid parents named her after Maam Diarra Bousso, mother of Murid founder Shaykh Aḥmadu Bamba. When she entered the Fayḍa in 1985, she told me, she could find almost no Taalibe Baay in the surrounding neighbourhoods of Thiaroye and Yeumbeul. Over the past few years, she has participated actively in turning this area into one of the most important areas of Fayḍa expansion.

Sayyida Bousso's house has become a gathering place for Taalibe Baay in the area, whether her own *tarbiya* initiates or others who happen to live nearby. She has also become one of the most talked-about female Islamic leaders in Senegal. She owes her fame partly to having a close disciple who is a cameraman at the private TV2S television

Figure 2.1 Sayyida Bousso Dramé and a disciple in 2014.

station and who has influenced the channel to air interviews with her and events she has organized. In 2012, she spearheaded a conference featuring numerous Taalibe Baay *muqaddama*s in Dakar that was covered on TV2S and viewed by many Senegalese, alerting many for the first time to the existence of female Islamic leaders.

Despite having little formal education, Sayyida Bousso is the most skilled of all the new *muqaddama*s we interviewed at quoting classical Arabic texts and working them into her Wolof speeches. This contributes to her reputation as a leader possessing both mystical and textual knowledge. Her dedication to textual learning is also evidenced in the Qurʾānic school she sponsors in her own home. When we visited her in 2009 and 2010, a teacher she had hired was teaching under an improvised wood-and metal-roof structure. In 2014, we found she had just inaugurated a more permanent structure in her home, where students learned the Qurʾān and other Islamic disciplines. She also hosts regular communal prayer in her house, which an older Taalibe Baay male neighbour with an Arabo-Islamic education leads. Although not formally her disciple, he is often present and informally provides Islamic knowledge to *daayira* members. As she explained, "you can't claim to be a religious leader [*sëriñ*] if you don't teach," even if indirectly. (This was one of the few times I have heard a woman leader imply self-identification as a "*sëriñ*.")

For some Taalibe Baay, Sayyida Bousso's status as a knowledgeable leader and speaker is somewhat tempered by their objection to her and her disciples' engagement in the increasingly popular yet controversial practice of *yëngu* ("moving oneself"), which combines sacred chant (*sikkar*) with frenetic percussion and dancing (on this practice, see Hill 2016c). In interviews, she offered several defences of the practice. Just as water from the sea will always taste salty, she told us, *yëngu* will always be part of the Fayḍa for her because she entered the Fayḍa in eastern Saalum (Ndukkumaan), where *yëngu* began in the 1980s. She also credits the practice with allowing her to reach out to young people in this difficult neighbourhood, leading them away from nightclubs, crime, drugs, and bars and instead towards God.

When Sayyida Bousso became a Taalibe Baay in 1985, she had already had some connection to three other Islamic groups – the Murids, the Tivaouane Tijāniyya, and the reformist Jamāʿat ʿIbād al-Raḥmān. When she was two years old, her family moved from their village in Saalum (the area to the east of Kaolack) to Dakar. Although she has always hungered for knowledge, she says, her struggling parents were forced to end her Qur'ānic education early so she could help her mother with housework and her food stand. The food stand, in front of the downtown Dantec hospital, remains her primary source of income, although she now delegates most of the work to others so she can focus on religious leadership.

When in her teens, Bousso married a fish trader who lived in the peripheral suburb of Yeumbeul. A devoted Tijānī, who followed the Sy family of Tivaouane (the largest Tijānī branch in Senegal), her husband hired a young relative to run an informal Islamic school in his house. Bousso seized the opportunity, taking private lessons in the Qur'ān and standard texts of Islamic pedagogy. Seeking Islamic knowledge wherever she could find it, she also joined a neighbourhood study group of the anti-Sufi reform movement Jamā'at 'Ibād al-Raḥmān. She was active in this group for several years and describes becoming known for her facility in speaking and being asked to speak often in women's meetings.

While preparing her lessons, she says, she came across a *ḥadīth* saying that one must know God before serving him. She went to all the Islamic teachers she could find to ask how one could know God. All told her that this was impossible. She finally spoke to a Taalibe Baay teacher who admitted to knowing God yet refused to give her *tarbiya,* fearing it would create problems with her Murid family and Tijānī husband. She explained to us that back then the few Taalibe Baay *daayiras* in Dakar were nowhere near where she lived, and few people around her had any idea who Shaykh Ibrāhīm was. One day she heard that a Fayḍa *muqaddam,* Shaykh Daam Ka, would be speaking at a night meeting in a nearby neighbourhood. She went to hear him speak and found out that he lived in a village in Ndukkumaan, the area in eastern Saalum surrounding the town of Kaffrine, about 250 kilometres south-east of Dakar.

One day in 1985, the day that she was to host a large reception celebrating her husband's return from the pilgrimage in Mecca, Bousso left home without permission. Although she had devoted her whole life to her household responsibilities, she frantically desired to know God without delay. Arriving in Shaykh Daam Ka's village, she told him she had come from Dakar because she could find no one there to help her know God. Astonished that she would come all that way, he immediately gave her the Tijānī *wird* and "plunged" (*sóob*) her into *tarbiya.* During that time, she must have been introduced to *yëngu,* which had recently been popularized in the Kaffrine area by Shaykh 'Abdallāh Wilane, a close associate of Shaykh Daam Ka.

Sayyida Bousso stayed until she reached *fatḥ* and returned to Yeumbeul. She had entered such an ecstatic spiritual state that her family thought she had gone crazy. She was interested in nothing but repeating the *Ṣalāt al-Fātiḥ* and lost all interest in eating. Pointing out to me the bright red inside of her lips, she explained, "the heat of the *Ṣalāt al-Fātiḥ* is what did this to me." Realizing that the only reality was God, she concluded that none of the details she had read about in books were true – a conclusion she now regrets, as it unnecessarily led her to set aside her studies.

For nearly a decade, Bousso took care of her household and had little contact with Daam Ka or any local Fayḍa community. In 1993, her husband died and she moved with her daughter and son from Yeumbeul to her deceased mother's then-vacant house in nearby Zamzam 2 Thiaroye, where she still lives. She later remarried, fulfilling the widespread perception that it is more decorous for a Muslim woman to have a husband (*boroom kër*, lit. "master of the house"), even though her husband lives in another town and she rarely sees him. After moving, she suddenly went from managing a bustling household that consumed twelve kilograms of rice a day to taking care of herself and two children. Yet her new house gradually became just as busy, as the neighbourhood drew a stream of disciples from outside Dakar. Many of them were young men looking for work who needed a transitional home and a "mother" figure. By day, she continued to commute to her mother's food stand downtown.

Some time in the late 1990s, Sayyida Bousso re-established contact with Daam Ka, who gave her a verbal *ijāza* authorizing her to give the *wird* and *tarbiya* to anyone who asked. Yet she was too busy with family obligations to give the *ijāza* any thought. Still, she and a few disciples in the neighbourhood would meet for litanies every evening in her house, and in 2002 they asked Daam Ka for permission to form a *daayira*. He inaugurated their *daayira* that year while attending a conference they organized.

Bousso had kept up periodic contact with the teacher who had originally refused to give her *tarbiya*, who had since moved back to his Saalum village to teach the Qur'ān. In 2003, she visited him there. When he asked if she had an *ijāza*, she said no, apparently not ready to make her appointment known. Likely recognizing not only her knowledge but also her leadership in organizing a *daayira* where the Fayḍa was little represented, he told her he wanted to give her an *ijāza*. He took her to see his leader, Shaykh Ḥasan Cissé, then principal imam of Medina

Baay and the Tijāniyya's leading figure worldwide. Shaykh Ḥasan himself ended up giving her an unlimited written *ijāza* (which she showed me). She seems to have taken this as her signal to begin giving *wird* and *tarbiya*, which she did while continuing to organize the area's disciple community and expanding her own *daayira*. They organized their first *gàmmu* in the same year, for which the guest of honour was her original leader, Daam Ka. As she became busier with her religious work, Sayyida Bousso handed off most of the work at her downtown food stand to her daughter.

Sayyida Bousso was one of my most explicit interlocutors in elaborating on the ancient metaphor of spiritually powerful woman as man. As we discussed the possibility of women performing the same kinds of religious work as men in 2010, she quoted the same lines of Shaykh Ibrāhīm's poetry that probably all *muqaddamas* I interviewed referenced in some way: "As for the secrets *(maqāsid)*, they are the lot of the gnostic *('ārif)* ... This is the Man, female or male" ([Niasse] 1969, 1:131).[2] Speaking in the paradoxical mode common in Taalibe Baay discourse, she said, "So what is Baay saying? All his disciples are men ... There are no women *muqaddams* of Baay! There are none! There are only *muqaddams* who are men!" She explained that Taalibe Baay women do act and dress differently from men in some outward senses – for the Qur'ān does say "the male is not like the female" (Qur'ān 3:36) – and that *sharī'a* only allows men to lead congregational prayer. Yet "in *ḥaqīqa*, we don't recognize men [and women]."

Sayyida Ndèye Seynabou Mbathie

Another *muqaddama* who often invoked the mystical transcendence of gender is Sayyida Ndèye Seynabou Mbathie.[3] More centrally located in the band of middle-class neighbourhoods that bisects the Cap Vert peninsula, Sayyida Seynabou lives in Derklé, just a few blocks from Baay's Dieupeul house, the Fayḍa's spiritual centre in Dakar. The full-colour business card that Sayyida Seynabou gave me in 2010 sums up the "two jobs" (*ñaari liggéey*) that Sayyida Seynabou describes herself as performing. It shows a small photograph of herself on the right and one of Shaykh Ibrāhīm on the left. Between them, large, block letters spell out her occupation in French: "VOYANTE" (psychic or clairvoyant). Above these block letters is the motto "Working together for Baye Niasse"[4] in Wolof. By day, she performs divination for clients to help them solve problems and cure ailments, many of them caused by hostile *jinne* (spirits).[5] She does this with the help of a friendly *jinne* who began visiting her and helping her in 2007.

Her other job, which she says has no pay, is to act as a *muqaddama*, inducting young people into mystical knowledge through *tarbiya* and guiding them in her *daayira*, "Chifa Al Askham" (*Shifāʾ al-asqām*, or "healing afflictions"). In 2007, six months after the *jinne* began visiting Sayyida Seynabou, Shaykh Ibrāhīm's second son and then-*Khalīfa*, Shaykh Aḥmad Daam, appointed her as a *muqaddama*.[6] Since Shaykh Aḥmad Daam's passing in 2010, Sayyida Seynabou's leader has been Shaykh Aḥmad's son Sīdī Ḥabīb. Appointed when she was around thirty-one years old, she is the youngest *muqaddama* I interviewed. She is also one of the few who has had children while acting as a spiritual guide. By the time we first interviewed her in 2010, she already had a large and active *daayira*, and members of this *daayira* and clients of her healing practice were constantly streaming through her house. Her disciples are primarily young men and women living in the surrounding neighbourhood. Although Derklé has a more middle-class feel than Yeumbeul or Thiaroye, Sayyida Seynabou's disciples are not necessarily better off financially than Sayyida Bousso's disciples.

As Sayyida Seynabou's business card suggests, her two jobs are linked. She describes the *jinne* as not only providing guidance in working for her clients but also as guiding her in leading her *daayira*. In 2010, she even described the *jinne* as "buying" her the house she lived in, seemingly implying that his assistance in her divination provided the income to buy a house. Having her own house has provided Sayyida Seynabou with her own professional space to serve her growing number of clients without inconveniencing the rest of her husband's family. This home has also provided a headquarters for her *daayira* and a space in which to give *tarbiya* and advise her disciples. When I returned in 2014, I found that Sayyida Seynabou had moved into a new, multi-story house across the street from the smaller one she had lived in before.

Although she has established her own home and work space, Sayyida Seynabou involves her husband, a bank employee, in her religious work more than most new *muqaddama*s I met. She also makes a point of displaying the wifely deference understood to be an Islamic prescription. At *daayira* gatherings, when her husband is present she delegates to him ritual functions that only men perform, such as leading prayer and group litanies. Whenever I visited her while he was at work, she was sure to call him and have me greet him, showing that she did not speak with other men without his permission. When present, he actively participated in our conversations.

Sayyida Seynabou's house in Derklé is a few blocks from Baay Niasse's house in Dieupeul. The part where she lives is known as "Angle Baay Fall" (Baay Fall Corner) because it is dominated by Baay Faal, zealous Murid followers popularly associated with colourful patchwork attire, cannabis smoking, and claims to a spiritual level that exempts them from praying and fasting.[7] A larger-than-life painting of Shaykh Ibra Fall, the devoted follower of Murid founder, Shaykh Aḥmadu Bamba, whom Baay Faals consider their progenitor (not to be confused with Shaykh Ibrāhīm Niasse's follower of that name), overlooks the street corner from the side of a kiosk.

Sayyida Seynabou describes moving into the neighbourhood and finding it full of aggressive, pot-smoking Baay Faals who had long had run-ins with neighbours. Soon after she moved in, she says, the police inspector saw her and her small group of disciples meeting for evening *waẓīfa* and feared conflicts between them and the Baay Faals, who had driven out other religious groups attempting to establish themselves in the neighbourhood. Yet when they told him they were Taalibe Baay, he thanked God and said things would improve. Instead of fighting with the Baay Faals, they worked to establish good relations with them. They invited the group's leader to their house and, on the occasion of a large meeting the Baay Faals held, they lent the group a sound system and provided the spiced coffee (*kafe Tuubaa*) to serve attendees. When the Baay Faals prepared to travel to a large religious event, she provided money to charter a bus. She and her followers also ingratiated themselves with a nearby group of Tijānīs affiliated with Tivaouane and attended their yearly conference. She describes these good relations as inspired by Shaykh Ibrāhīm's teachings advocating peaceful coexistence.

Sayyida Seynabou's immediate family are not religious specialists, yet she tells of great-grandfathers on both sides of her family who were *muqaddam*s of Al-Ḥājj Mālik Sy of Tivaouane. She also lists ancestors on her mother's side who were closely related to Shaykh Aḥmadu Bamba. Born in 1976 in Kaolack, Sayyida Seynabou was a childhood friend of the now-famous *sikkarkat* (and *muqaddama)* Aïda Faye. (I discuss the two in chapter 6.) Her childhood neighbourhood, adjacent to Medina Baay, was dominated by recent migrants from Jolof, like her own parents.[8] Although she grew up a short walk from Medina Baay's towering mosque, Sayyida Seynabou says, her father disliked Shaykh Ibrāhīm so much that he would walk to a more distant mosque to avoid Friday prayer in Medina Baay.

Despite growing up where Shaykh Ibrāhīm had lived, Sayyida Seynabou says she only came to know Shaykh Ibrāhīm after leaving home during the early 1990s and going to live with a maternal cousin who had married and moved to Rufisque, a coastal town just outside Dakar. In 1994, at around the age of eighteen, Seynabou was living with this cousin when Shaykh Ibrāhīm came to her in a dream, bringing her a prayer mat, prayer beads, and a white ribbon. He showed her a circle of people sitting and chanting *sikkar* and told her to join them. As she ran to them, she tripped and dropped her prayer beads. When she knelt down to pick them up, someone took her arm and told her she had arrived.

When Seynabou told her cousin about the dream, her cousin offered to bring her to a woman who cooked for Shaykh Ibrāhīm's niece Rokhaya Niasse, who lived nearby. (Others have described Rokhaya Niasse as a *muqaddama* with her own *daayira*, although Sayyida Seynabou says she was not aware of her being a *muqaddama*.) The cook took her to Rokhaya, and on the way Seynabou found and picked up a white ribbon just like the one Shaykh Ibrāhīm had given her in the dream. When she told Rokhaya about the dream and showed her the ribbon, Rokhaya cried profusely in a powerful spiritual state *(ḥāl)*. Rokhaya sent Seynabou to a nearby *muqaddam*, to whom she explained that "the dream showed that Baay himself called me to the path."[9] He agreed to give her *tarbiya*.

Seynabou's family's already negative attitude towards Shaykh Ibrāhīm became worse when they saw how *tarbiya* affected her. *Tarbiya*, she says, left her "in a powerful spiritual state *(ḥāl)*"[10] that lasted at least three months. Her relatives in Rufisque, thinking she was suffering from depression, took her to a series of doctors. Unable to cure her, they expelled her from their house, and Seynabou tells of times when she slept in the streets.

In 1996, Seynabou found an older Taalibe Baay woman willing to lodge her in the Dakar neighbourhood of Grand Médine near the sprawling northern suburbs of Parcelles Assainies. Friends in Grand Médine took her to the *daayira* of the *muqaddam* Shaykh Boubou Sy, the most prominent Fayḍa *muqaddam* in Grand Médine. She participated in this *daayira* for several years, during which several fellow *daayira* members became impressed with her, eventually following her to her own *daayira*. El-Hadji Moumine Dia, her *daayira*'s founding president, participated in Shaykh Boubou Sy's *daayira* after receiving *tarbiya* from him in 2004. He told me of hearing fellow *daayira* members speak of a woman who "can't be held back when she's in a *ḥāl*."[11] This suggests that she was known for powerful bouts of spiritual ecstasy nearly a decade after her *tarbiya*.

While she was still in her troublesome spiritual state in 1996, Sayyida Seynabou found her shaykh, Shaykh Ibrāhīm's second-oldest son, Shaykh Aḥmad Daam Niasse (d. 2010). Some of her fellow disciples from Dakar took her to see him at the *gàmmu* of the village of Taïba Niassène. When she spoke to him, he was impressed with her love of Baay and the troubles she had endured with her family. He told her to consider him her father, which she has ever since. During many long conversations with him in Medina Baay and at his house in Dakar's SICAP Baobab neighbourhood, he taught her many things about Baay and gave her many *wirds* (litanies) to meditate on daily to cultivate spiritual knowledge. Of her spiritual state at that time, she says, "no one could rid me of it or extinguish it or bring it down, no one, except Shaykh Aḥmad Daam Ibrāhīm Niasse."[12] The state had prevented her from making sense of and using the divine knowledge she had learned, and "Shakyh Aḥmad Daam is the one who helped me to come back, to be proper … so I could benefit from Baay, so I could benefit others, or teach someone about Mawlānā Shaykh Ibrāhīm."

In 1997, when she visited Shaykh Aḥmad Daam again in Medina Baay, he asked her teasingly, "Have you visited the leader (*sëriñ*)?" She asked: "Who is the leader?" He answered: "Sīdī Ḥabīb is the leader," referring to his oldest son. So she went and visited Sīdī Ḥabīb in his nearby house. Henceforth, Sīdī Ḥabīb became the leader she worked with most. Others familiar with Shaykh Aḥmad Daam have told me similar stories of his insistance that Sīdī Ḥabīb was the "*sëriñ*." These anecdotes reflect not only Shaykh Aḥmad's great confidence in his son but also his humble demeanour, his intensely private inclinations, and possibly his fragile health. Shaykh Aḥmad was gravely ill during most of the time he was Medina Baay's Khalīfa between 2001 and his death in 2010. During this time, Sīdī Ḥabīb represented him in most capacities.

Shortly after meeting Shaykh Aḥmad Daam, Sayyida Seynabou says, in 1997 or 1998, she met the man who is now her husband, who was at that time an adherent of the Tivaouane branch of the Tijāniyya. When they first started talking about religion, he assumed that she was an "*ibaadu*," or a strict reformist, because of her concealing dress and her meticulousness in following Islamic prescriptions. But she soon told him about the possibility of knowing God through *tarbiya* and took him to Medina Baay to see Shaykh Aḥmad Daam. He became a disciple and they married.

One late afternoon in 2007, during the month of Ramadan, Sīdī Ḥabīb called Sayyida Seynabou as she and her husband were preparing to break their fast.[13] Sīdī Ḥabīb was visiting Dakar and needed them to come to the hotel where he was staying. They said they would come as soon as they had broken their fast. But Sīdī Ḥabīb called again and told them his two assistants were on their way to bring them to the hotel. When they arrived, he told her that his father had instructed him to give her an *ijāza* and to tell her to go to work for Baay. He explained why his father had decided to give it to her and how to use the *ijāza*. In an interview in 2014 she told us of this *ijāza*: "It was a great surprise to me, and something weighty, because it was something I hadn't expected, something I hadn't thought of."[14] Yet in 2010 she had told us that part of her was actually not surprised, "because during certain periods [she] experienced a spiritual state in which [she] would see the *ijāza*" before receiving it, although she could never have predicted how and when these intimations would play out.

Sayyida Seynabou's first disciple was a Frenchman from Nantes who was in Senegal as a tourist and converted to Islam at her hands. She showed us photographs of this disciple in Senegal and of her visiting him in France. After her French disciple returned to France, several young men who had received *tarbiya* elsewhere began congregating in her house. Several of them had grown up on the island of Gorée, including the *daayira*'s senior member and president, El-Hadji Moumine Dia, who was born in the 1960s and is a decade or two older than nearly all the other *daayira* members. Growing up around the artists' community in Gorée, Moumine told me, he was more into Rastafarianism than Islam. He had worked as an account representative for the Senegalese national water company for well over a decade before his teenaged nephew underwent *tarbiya* and spoke to him of knowing God, sparking his interest in Islam.

Despite having heard of her powerful spiritual state following his *tarbiya* in 2004, Moumine only met Sayyida Seynabou three years later when some fellow disciples invited him to accompany them to see a woman who "is crazy about Baay" and "loves anyone who loves Baay." Before visiting her, they called her and learned that she was organizing a *gàmmu*. Although he had never met her in person, Moumine was impressed with her devotion and told her over the phone not to

Figure 2.2 Sayyida Seynabou Mbathie and disciples at a Friday *ḥaḍra* and *sikkar* meeting, 2010.

worry about renting the sound system, the tent, and the chairs, which he would work his connections to obtain free of charge. Only when he visited her for the first time and delivered the materials to her did his companions mention her recent *ijāza*.

After this, Moumine and his friends would often visit her together to talk about God, and if they were there at sunset, they would perform the sunset prayer and recite the *waẓīfa* litany together. *Waẓīfa* became an official activity in Sayyida Seynabou's house when Shaykh Aḥmad Daam instructed her to hold it every Thursday. For the Friday *ḥaḍra* litany, members of the group would go either to Shaykh Boubou Sy's house or to Baay's nearby house in Dieupeul, the Fayḍa's Dakar headquarters (see figure 2.2). But after Sayyida Seynabou gave *tarbiya* to several of her own disciples from the neighbourhood, she and her disciples received authorization from her leader to form a *daayira*, which he named *Shifā al-asqām* ("healing afflictions"). At their inaugural meeting, they elected the absent Moumine president. At that time, Moumine told me, there were around seven or eight *daayira* members, all young men in their teens and early twenties except him. Soon they were joined by a young woman, and eventually the *daayira* had roughly equal numbers of young men and women.

When I visited the *daayira* in 2010 and spoke with Sayyida Seynabou and several *daayira* members, they did not have regular dues or even a treasury, as most *daayira*s do. Then, they proudly told me they raised money spontaneously as the need arose. In 2014, however, Moumine told me their initial system had been lacking. The young disciples, most of them high-school students, did not have the cash flow to raise sufficient money for events, so Sayyida Seynabou herself would end up paying most of the costs. For example, she would rent a bus and buy the ingredients for the large communal meal when the *daayira* travelled to a *gàmmu*. Moumine told me that Baay's younger brother, Sëriñ Mbay (Abū Bakr) Niasse, had taught that "the disciple's increase is in giving to his/her leader (*sëriñ*)." Thus, disciples had to work to give to Sayyida Seynabou instead of taking from her.

Not long after my visit in 2010, the *daayira* radically shifted from its informal and improvised approach to an elaborate and ambitious one. They established a new dues structure – a 6,000-franc (FCFA) annual fee, a monthly fee of 500 FCFA (and later 1,000 FCFA), and a weekly fee of 200 FCFA – which they enforced carefully at weekly meetings. By the time I returned in 2014, five of the core *daayira* members I had spoken with in 2010 had emigrated, with Sayyida Seynabou's help, to Europe and one to Canada. Assumed to have more access to Western cash, these overseas members contribute 25,000 FCFA monthly. The *daayira* has used these fees not just to organize meetings but also to purchase a range of materials that most *daayira*s rent for meetings – pots and pans for cooking large communal meals, a high-quality amplification system, chairs, and so on. In 2014, I found these materials stowed in various places in Sayyida Seynabou's new and spacious house. Not only does the *daayira* use these materials in their events but they also rent them out to people in the neighbourhood for other religious events or life-cycle events.

The *daayira* also officially registered as a "groupe d'intérêt économique" (GIE) to organize projects that would raise money for the *daayira* and provide employment for some disciples. In doing so, they have joined a growing trend of Taalibe Baay religious associations engaging in "development" projects and organizing themselves on the model of an NGO (Hill 2017a). Moumine explained that they had initially intended to include all *daayira* members by default in the GIE but had decided to make membership voluntary so that members would have a greater sense of ownership and would work harder to ensure the GIE's success.

Still, most active *daayira* members have joined. *Daayira* members pay 3,000 FCFA ($6 U.S.) to join the GIE. The women decided to put their money together to buy cows to raise, the profit of whose sale would go to the *daayira*. The *daayira* also started an ambitious chicken operation, starting with 300 chickens, increasing to 500, and then sustaining some losses because of what Moumine described as ineffective management, a problem he said they had since fixed.

Like disciples of other women leaders, several of Sayyida Seynabou's disciples lovingly described her to me as a "mother," even those who were significantly older than she is. Moumine explained her helping him and many other disciples with many things beyond spiritual leadership as follows: "because she's a mother. She's a *muqaddam*, but she's a mother. We – I am familiar with her in a way I am not familiar with anyone else in the world." He stated that he can't go a day without seeing her, and when she's travelling, he has to go to her house and sit for a while just to feel her presence. He explained: "Because she's our[15] *muqaddam*, she's our mother, she's everything to us. She's even our father/ Baay" ("*mem moom mooy suñu Baay*"). Here, Moumine's poetic language outwardly describes Sayyida Seynabou as both "mother" and "father," yet the latter term – "*Baay*" – is intentionally bivalent. He clarified that, just as she had described seeing Baay himself when she looked at her leader Shaykh Aḥmad Daam, "for us, she is Baay," because "everything that comes through Baay, we'll obtain it if we go through her." Thus, he is not saying that she is a paternal figure but that she makes Baay present to her disciples.

Sayyida Seynabou describes her disciples as easily overcoming any habits that go against Islam and Shaykh Ibrāhīm's teachings, thanks both to her example and maternal role and to the unusual spiritual power she makes available to them. She told of a young Murid man who wanted to take the *wird* and *tarbiya* but had smoked since 1992 and was afraid he could not give it up as required. She told him she would give him the *wird* and see what happened. He performed the *wird* for three days and came back and said that during that time he became physically ill if he smelled cigarette smoke.[16] She also described a highly Westernized female disciple who spoke French at home, had spent several years in Italy, and enjoyed drinking and nightclubs. This young woman went through *tarbiya* and immediately gave up drinking, nightclubs, hair extensions, skin lighteners, and immodest dress. Sayyida Seynabou told similar stories about many other disciples who had also given up smoking cannabis and other un-Islamic behaviours. She emphasized that none of her female disciples wear hair extensions or use skin lighteners, both of which she describes as forbidden in Islam, and that all of them cover themselves "like an *ibaadu*."

She never has to tell a disciple to do these things, she says, but simply shows an example and uses the power of prayer and litanies. She tells of disciples who underwent *tarbiya* with other *muqaddam*s who still smoked and wore miniskirts but who changed when they renewed (*yeesal*) their *wird* with her. She describes her success in inculcating good behaviour as her reward for strictly adhering to Baay's teachings, as opposed to *muqaddam*s who talk about Baay but neglect his teachings. Also, she says, part of her success has to do with her being a woman. First, women "are better at educating, I think, than men."[17] "If we're talking about real education (*yar*)," she said, "a woman is the one who can do it well." This especially applies to teaching female disciples, who see their leader dressing according to "*sharī'a*" – in her interpretation covering herself and not using hair extensions, skin lighteners, or pants – and simply emulate her. She explains to anyone who comes to take *wird* that one of the *wird*'s conditions is following Islam, which means following *sharī'a* before following the *ṭarīqa* (Sufi path). As her disciples' mother figure, she says, a *muqaddama* has a closer relationship with both male and female disciples. "The closeness you have with a female *muqaddam*," she told me, "talking to her about many things, is something you don't have with a male *muqaddam*." For example, she talks to male and female disciples about matters like ritual purification after spousal intimacy, something that makes many male leaders squeamish.

This maternal relationship is especially apparent in the area of marriage arrangements. Moumine explained that almost all *daayira* members were unmarried when they joined but that nearly all are married now. He explained that this has been possible because, "Sayyida, you know, she's our *muqaddam*, but she's our mother. You know, you don't hide anything from your mother." By 2014, she reported, nineteen marriages had taken place between couples who had met in her *daayira*. In several cases, including those of two disciples I interviewed (Moumine and Moustapha Diop), it was the woman who first expressed an interest in the man. In some cases, Sayyida Seynabou played an instrumental role in their seeking family approval. Many disciples approached her before approaching their parents, especially those who feared their parents' disapproval because of customarily incompatible backgrounds or a financially unstable groom. If the couple could not afford the marriage, Sayyida Seynabou contributed whatever they lacked. Even though Moumine was a mature adult with a stable job when he married a fellow *daayira* member in 2011, Sayyida Seynabou still provided money and sacks of rice and onions for the marriage and then again for the couple's infant-naming ceremony. In only one case have she and her *daayira* proceeded with a marriage against a family's wishes. In that case, a family had disowned a young woman because they disapproved of her becoming Taalibe Baay. Now they disapproved of her marrying a fellow *daayira* member. Sayyida Seynabou and the *daayira* acted as the young woman's family, believing that her birth family had relinquished their authority. Disciples have used the *daayira*'s cooking and hosting equipment for their weddings, which are free for all *daayira* members to use.

When I visited Sayyida Seynabou in 2014 and 2017, she told me of numerous trips she had made to Europe, during which she had met many new and prospective disciples of various origins. In 2014, she had just returned from several trips abroad. During one trip, she had visited friends in Turkey and had then continued on to France, Germany, and Switzerland, visiting contacts in some places but in others simply arriving alone and trusting she would meet people there. She told of arriving alone at the Munich airport and happening upon a Ghanaian man whose Senegalese wife was coming to pick him up. They invited her to stay with them, and the wife became her disciple, along with her German friend. This friend ended up visiting Dakar, marrying a leading member of her *daayira*, and bringing him back with her to Germany. When in Switzerland, Sayyida Seynabou met a Frenchman who worked for the World Bank, and he ended up converting and becoming her disciple. He introduced her to several French people who became interested in converting, and she later returned to visit them. She also helped a teenaged disciple to relocate to Italy after her Dakar family had expelled her from their home for undergoing *tarbiya*. Following the disciple's problems with her birth relatives, an Italian family ended up legally adopting her, after which she married another *daayira* member and moved him to Italy. Another *daayira* member moved to Canada and another to France.

When I visited Sayyida Seynabou again in 2017, she told me she had returned to Europe several times since our 2014 conversation. She had visited Belgium, Italy, and France. In the Parisian suburbs, she had developed an especially close relationship with young North African Muslims. She had also been introduced to a group of Roma youth who now called her mother, and she told of plans to visit them again and of hopes that they would embrace Islam. With *daayira* representatives in several Western countries, including both Senegalese and Western disciples, Sayyida Seynabou has made this international dimension an important part of her self-presentation and future plans as a leader.

Sayyida Khadi Fall

Like Sayyida Seynabou Mbathie, Sayyida Khadi Fall lives in a spacious house in a middle-class Dakar neighbourhood – Sicap Sacré Coeur – that she purchased with her own income. Also, she has similarly used her income and connections to send several disciples to study or work in Europe and North America. Aside from that, perhaps Sayyida Khadi's greatest similarity with the other new *muqaddama*s we interviewed is that her life has been atypical – perhaps in many ways the most atypical. Whereas few other new *muqaddama*s have pursued significant formal education, Sayyida Khadi Fall has a distinguished academic and governmental curriculum vitae.[18] She has earned five university diplomas, the first in 1973 and the most recent in 2014. She is a full professor of German studies at the University of Dakar Cheikh Anta Diop and a high-ranking official in Senegal's Ministry of Education, even serving as a government minister from 2000 to 2001. Although she is not the only divorced *muqaddama* or the only one whose narrative minimizes married life, she is the only one who insists that she will never marry again. She is the only *muqaddama* we interviewed who was born in Dakar. She raised four children even while spending years of her life in Europe and the United States as a student and research fellow. She is by far the most familiar with feminist theory and practice, having written a doctoral dissertation on German literature using a feminist analysis and having struggled mightily to succeed in academics and government while raising her children. When she speaks, this Wolof literacy advocate alternates between a deep Wolof uncommon among Dakarois and full French sentences typical of her professional environments.

Despite her unique background, Sayyida Khadi Fall shares important similarities with other new *muqaddama*s. Like many *muqaddama*s, she comes from a family affiliated with the Tivaouane branch of the Tijāniyya and only discovered the Fayḍa as an adult. Yet she was the only one I interviewed who had already taken the Tijānī *wird* before discovering the Fayḍa. Despite teaching and writing about feminism, she maintains that *sharī'a* prescribes different behaviour for men and women, and she was among the most explicit in connecting motherhood with education and leadership. Sayyida Khadi wears the same kinds of modest clothing that other *muqaddama*s wear, generally a colourful African-style dress with an ample shawl over her head and shoulders (figure 2.3). Despite her years in the West and in international academic networks, she remains firmly grounded in her Senegalese kin,

Figure 2.3 Sayyida Khadi Fall in 2010.

social, religious, and political networks and could hardly be described as "Westernized."

Sayyida Khadi Fall was born in Dakar in 1948 to a Wolof-speaking family of Haal-Pulaar origin. Her parents encouraged their ten children to study religious and non-religious subjects and to be financially independent. After graduating from high school in Dakar in 1969, Khadi Fall studied German literature and history at the University of Toulouse, France, earning her undergraduate degree *(licence)* in 1973. She then returned to Dakar and taught German at her high school alma mater, Lycée Van Vollenhoven. While teaching, she worked on a master's degree in teaching German at the University of Dakar. On graduating in 1979, she returned to France for a doctorate in German literature from the University of Strasbourg. In 1983, she defended her doctoral dissertation, which analysed recent German novels using a feminist sociological approach. She then began teaching German studies at the University of Dakar, where she was one of three full professors of German when I interviewed her. From 1992 to 1994, shortly after becoming a Taalibe Baay, she was awarded a two-year fellowship to write her habilitation thesis *(doctorat d'état)* at the University of Hanover, Germany. She has published two novels in French (Fall 1989, 1992), a book of poetry in Wolof and English (Fall 1995), a book of literary commentary in German (Fall 1996), and a collection of essays in French and Wolof on education and culture (Fall 2008).

When I visited Sayyida Khadi in 2014, she had just finished a professional master's degree in "Decentralization and Land Development" through the University of Dakar's Geography Department while working full-time as a professor. Her thesis research for this program assessed household solid and liquid waste in Medina Baay and made recommendations for improving sanitation. Believing that she now had the practical and theoretical understanding necessary to address the problem, she enlisted disciples to help her start an association to improve sanitation, to put into practice what she was learning. Although her vision was to start in Medina Baay and then expand to other parts of Senegal, when I revisited her in 2017 she told me she had decided to start her projects in Dakar because navigating the complex networks of authority and patronage in Medina Baay had proved too difficult at that time.

In addition to her academic activities, Sayyida Khadi has been active in government and politics, although she told me she no longer involves herself in party politics, concluding that it is too corrupt. She has acted as an inspector general of national education in Senegal's Ministry of Education since 1987. For many years she was active in Moustapha Niasse's Alliance des forces de progrès (AFP) party. From 2000 to 2001, the party formed a short-lived coalition with newly elected President Abdoulaye Wade, and Moustapha Niasse was appointed prime minister. During that period, Sayyida Khadi served as Senegal's minister of decentralization and land development.[19] Just before her appointment as minister in 2000, Mauritanian *muqaddam* Shaykh wuld Khayrī gave her verbal authorization *(ijāza)* to give *wird* and *tarbiya*. About five years later, word got out that she had an *ijāza*, and young men and women started to approach her for *wird* and *tarbiya*. Yet she remains far better known in Senegal for her academic, literary, and governmental qualifications than for her religious leadership.

Finding Baay in 1991, she says, was a great surprise, especially since a non-practising Christian – a Swiss journalist – led her to him well after she had established herself as an academic. Sayyida Khadi had recently learned that she had been awarded a competitive two-year fellowship in Hanover, Germany, to write her habilitation thesis, a requirement for promotion to full professorship. Soon after receiving this good news, she received a phone call from her sister-in-law, the wife of her younger brother who lived in Switzerland, telling her that a Swiss friend of hers was going through a personal crisis. This sister-in-law had arranged for her friend to travel to Senegal on a package tour to get her mind off her difficulties, and she asked Khadi to host her friend at least once for dinner. During that dinner, the Swiss woman mentioned hearing about Senegal's holy men who use their spiritual power to solve people's problems. Khadi Fall laughed at the idea. The woman then went on her tour of Senegal and, just before returning to the airport, banged on Khadi Fall's door and exclaimed: "I found what I was looking for!" Khadi let her in and asked her to explain. She said her tour guide had seen her sitting dejectedly and had spoken to her about God in a way that made her realize that all her problems no longer existed. She was returning to Switzerland happy.

Although the woman apparently never converted to Islam, her words intrigued Khadi Fall. She called the tour guide, Abdourahmane Guèye,[20] and invited him to visit that evening after her Swiss friend had already boarded her plane. He brought along his younger brother and a friend. All were at least ten years her junior, and all turned out to be followers of Baay through the Mauritanian *muqaddam* Shaykh wuld Khayrī, who has thousands of disciples throughout Mauritania, Senegal, and other countries. She went on to invite this group and the rest of their disciple community every Saturday afternoon to have lunch and discuss God. Before long, her three lunch guests became twenty. One of the regulars was the group's spiritual guide in Dakar, Cerno Ibrahim Diallo, a charismatic *muqaddam* of Shaykh wuld Khayrī who lives in the suburb of Guédiawaye. He soon gave her *tarbiya,* and for some years he and she were married, although married life was absent from Sayyida Khadi's narrative.

In 1992, Khadi Fall was scheduled to fly to Germany for her two-year fellowship but missed her flight. Then, she told me, she discovered the reason God had ordained that she miss her flight – after a three-year border closure due to ethnic violence between Mauritanian Arabs and Black Senegalese, Shaykh wuld Khayrī had just arrived in Dakar. Two days after meeting Shaykh wuld Khayrī, she left for Germany. After returning to Senegal in 1994, Khadi Fall began travelling regularly to the Mauritanian village Shaykh wuld Khayrī founded in 1978, Bubakkar, to receive instruction from him directly and to attend religious events.

During a visit to Bubakkar in 2000, shortly before Khadi Fall's appointment as a government minister, Shaykh wuld Khayrī appointed her as a *muqaddama*. It is not surprising that Shaykh wuld Khayrī has appointed numerous women as *muqaddama*s, as he owes his own spiritual status partly to his mother, Fāṭima bt Sīdī Aḥmad. A direct *muqaddama* of Shaykh Ibrāhīm and the closest disciple of Mauritanian Shaykh Muḥammad al-Mishrī, she was known as "Dāya" (midwife or wetnurse) for her supporting role in spiritually guiding Muḥammad al-Mishrī's disciples (Frede 2014). When male or female disciples came to Muḥammad al-Mishrī for *tarbiya,* he would often delegate much of the process to Dāya. Dāya's sister played a similar role before moving to Medina Baay, where Shaykh Ibrāhīm nicknamed her "ʿAbdallāh wuld ʿAbdallāh" ("ʿAbdallāh son of ʿAbdallāh") and declared that she should never be spoken of as a woman – even through feminine pronouns – because her spiritual rank surpassed that of nearly all men of her time.[21] Aside from Sayyida Khadi, I have interviewed two other *muqaddama*s in Dakar who were affiliated with Shaykh wuld Khayrī. One was a Mauritanian woman named Maḥjūba who was visiting Sayyida Khadi. The other was a Senegalese woman in Dakar named Diénaba Seck who was appointed by Nūr al-Dīn Sall, a Gabon-based Senegalese *muqaddam* of Shaykh wuld Khayrī.

Like most *muqaddam(a)*s, Sayyida Khadi did not disclose her appointment for several years, even as she hosted regular disciple meetings in her home. She began to give *tarbiya* only five years after her appointment. She told me she suspects the first disciples to approach her for *tarbiya* had heard of her appointment from other disciples of Shaykh wuld Khayrī who had been present when he appointed her. "I didn't call anyone," she said, "people just came on their own." By the time of our interview in 2009, she had given *tarbiya* to around forty disciples, most of them male high school or university students from the surrounding middle-class neighbourhoods, and nearly all from non-Taalibe Baay families. When I returned in 2014, she told me that several of her disciples had graduated from university and were now living in Europe, and she had given *tarbiya* to many more.

In the summer of 2017, when Sayyida Khadi was only days away from retirement from the university, I interviewed her again, in addition to independently interviewing several of her disciples. I found that her disciple community had continued to grow, although I was surprised to learn that she had recently switched her allegiance from Shaykh wuld Khayrī to Muḥammad al-Amīn (Baaba Lamin) Niasse, the Niasse family's representative in Dakar. When she explained to her disciples her reasons for switching (which she refrained from discussing with me), nearly all stayed with her, although three left to follow another *muqaddam* of Shaykh wuld Khayrī. I interviewed disciples from both groups.

Sayyida Khadi depicts her relationship to disciples simultaneously in terms of motherhood and transcending gender altogether. She habitually refers to her disciples as her "children," and her description of spiritual leadership – "guiding young people, giving *wird* to young people, showing them the way" – is easily reconcilable with maternal nurturing. She describes the person through whom one knows God as one's "spiritual parent" in contrast to one's "blood parent."[22] Although she uses the gender-neutral term "parent," male *muqaddams* rarely describe themselves using parental metaphors, as explained in chapter 4. Without prompting, she volunteered that she imagines herself as a mother in everything she does and often calls her students and even her academic colleagues her children.

Although she has children and was once married to a *muqaddam* of Shaykh wuld Khayrī, Sayyida Khadi is now divorced and emphasizes that she bought her home with her own means and will not remarry. Like most *muqaddamas*, her religious authority and gender have an ambivalent relationship. Her self-description as a spiritual mother draws on her experience as a literal mother. Yet her current freedom from the perceived impurities of female reproduction and subordinate wifehood, along with her seniority, facilitates her claim to the status of honorary "man."

Womanhood and/as Leadership

Despite these women's diverse backgrounds and differing levels of education and wealth, their narratives show similar solutions to similar challenges as they accommodate or even naturalize the relationship between womanhood and leadership. Here I return to the paradox of women's leadership I discussed near the beginning of this chapter. As these stories illustrate, motherhood is a ubiquitous metaphor used to naturalize women's leadership. All the *muqaddama*s I have interviewed are mothers, most of them starting after an early marriage in their mid-teens, as is common in Senegal. Motherhood therefore became an important part of their experience and identity from early in life. The symbolic power of motherhood in society can hardly be overestimated. Mothers are culturally associated with guidance and sustenance, and one owes one's mother veneration and obedience throughout one's life. At the same time, women must minimize the practical constraints and symbolic impurity associated with literal female reproduction and sexuality. Although none of these women explicitly mentioned these negative implications, all manage somehow to distance themselves from them. Some are beyond childbearing years; others are divorced, widowed, or living apart from their husbands and have only grown children.

One widely cited explanation for why a woman cannot act as an imam, or congregational prayer leader, is that they experience menstruation and postpartum bleeding, during which they do not perform ritual prayer due to ritual impurity. *Muqaddama*s were unanimous that leading prayer was the only religious role a woman could not perform, yet they varied slightly in explaining whether menstruation affected their other religious functions. Most told me they continued to perform and transmit litanies while menstruating. One told me that, just to be on the safe side, she would tell disciples to come back later if they asked for a litany while she was menstruating, although this did not stop her from performing her own litanies. The only new *muqaddama* who gave birth while acting as a spiritual guide likened herself to the Prophet's daughter Fāṭima, who never experienced the ritual impurity of menstruation or postpartum bleeding. Shaykh Ibrāhīm cites this lack of menstruation as the reason why Fāṭima was the only exception to the rule that women cannot attain the highest level of sainthood – the "pole" *(quṭb)* that holds up creation at any given time (Niasse 2010, 261–2). Amber Gemmeke (2008, 2009) interviewed women spiritual healers in Dakar who also reported not menstruating, suggesting a broader perception of incompatibility between women's biological reproduction and spiritual power. Several leaders, male and female, told me that spiritual power can also "burn" the fragile female reproductive system, especially during the vulnerable time of menstruation. For example, menstruating women are told not to recite the "hot" prayer *Jawharat al-kamāl* ("pearl of perfection"), part of the daily *waẓīfa* litany, for fear that it can render them infertile. One *muqaddama* mentioned a *muqaddam* who refused to give her more powerful spiritual secrets because of this perceived incompatibility, although she frequented other *muqaddams* who gave her the same secrets, so it was not a problem for her. Shaykh Ibrāhīm himself declared that powerful secrets are destined for any knower of God, who is "a man, whether feminine or masculine" ([Niasse] 1969, 1:131).

Similarly, the submissive wifehood associated with feminine piety can conceivably interfere with a woman's performance of religious authority. While all these women uphold wifely submissiveness as a general norm, most of them effectively head a home that serves as their headquarters with relative independence from a husband or other male relatives. Some of those who remain married have bought or inherited their own home where their husband is essentially a guest. These women's husbands maintain a separate home with another wife, perhaps in Dakar or perhaps farther afield. One woman, Sayyida Awa Cissé (discussed in the previous chapter), does not own her home yet is in charge when her husband is with her co-wife in another neighbourhood. Only Sayyida Diarra Ndiaye, the only wife of a prominent Taalibe Baay, has long shared a single home with her husband (deceased in 2013). Both these women's husbands played or play leading roles in Anṣār al-Dīn, fostering a sense of shared mission despite the wives' more prominent spiritual leadership roles. A few *muqaddamas* are divorced and head their own households, including Sayyida Khadi Fall (discussed in this chapter) and Aïda Thiam (discussed in chapter 5). Whether or not they own their home, all the married *muqaddamas* publicly show deference to their husbands, an act of humility that accentuates their air of piety (see chapter 6).

In parallel to their relative practical independence from husbands, most women's narratives tend to minimize or even erase husbands' roles. Even in cases where I later learned that a Taalibe Baay husband had been instrumental in introducing a woman to the Fayḍa and its leaders, narratives usually attribute one's pathway to Baay and leadership entirely to dreams and providential encounters. Non-Taalibe Baay former husbands are often cast in a negative role as not understanding and obstructing a woman's spiritual mission. The result is to present a woman's path to spiritual authority as deriving entirely from a mission assigned by Baay and carried out with the support of the Fayḍa's leaders and a leader's own disciples, not as something deriving from a marital relationship.

This sense of a revealed mission is central to all these women's narratives. Each tells of mystical experiences and dreams through which Baay revealed that he had chosen her as a disciple with a unique mission. Thus, while each *muqaddama* operates with authorization from one or more male leaders in the larger Fayḍa community, each also claims charismatic leadership connected directly to Baay. Several women (including two discussed in this chapter and Sayyida Moussoukoro Mbaye, discussed later) described liminal periods during which their all-consuming ecstatic state *(ḥāl)* led them to lose interest in sleeping, eating, social relations, and other worldly things. Such periods disrupted each of these women's family and social life, leading family members to think they had gone insane and sometimes leading them to separate from husband or family. Each required the intervention of some enlightened leader to "fix" them. Whether or not a woman's narrative features such a liminal phase of social disconnection, each woman attributed her mission as leader not to herself but to forces larger than herself. Although men also describe their religious authority as coming not from themselves but from Baay, I have found women far more likely to emphasize the role of overpowering spiritual experiences in accounting for their path to religious authority.

The themes linking womanhood to religious authority that are illustrated in this chapter are further developed in the remaining chapters. These include feminine modesty and self-concealment, something I explain in terms of the concept of "wrapping"; motherhood as a metaphor for authority; cooking as a devotional act; the ambiguity surrounding the woman's voice; and wifely devotion as its own basis of religious authority. Now I turn to one of this book's central concepts, the relationship between women's acts of "self-wrapping" – whether through clothing or otherwise – and spiritual power and authority.

Chapter 3

Wrapping

Wrapping Up Muslim Women

Sayyida Moussoukoro Mbaye, a *muqaddama* and successful entrepreneur in Dakar, once explained to me how she successfully teaches her female disciples to dress and act modestly. She tells them, for example, to imagine being offered two bowls of food, one open and the other covered, as meals are normally presented in Senegal. She asks her disciples: Which would you prefer? Certainly the covered one and not the open one, which may have been picked at by people and flies. So it is with women: a woman who covers herself and maintains her purity is more desirable than the one who exposes herself. Many men pretend to like women who dress or behave immodestly, but they don't respect them. If a man calls out in the street that he loves you and that you're beautiful, he is merely playing with you. If a man really respects you, he will come to your house and ask your father. During another conversation, Sayyida Moussoukoro reported asking her female disciples whether they would prefer a wrapped piece of candy or an unwrapped candy that may have been swarmed by flies and ants.

I have come across the candy metaphor many times before and since that interview, including in several viral images appearing on many Muslims' Facebook feeds. One shows two lollipops, the first wrapped and the other unwrapped and covered with flies. In an English version, the wrapped lollipop is labelled "Woman wearing a veil," while the other is labelled "Woman without a veil," and the flies are labelled as "males." Similar images compare women to jewels so precious they must be kept in a safe or to meat that must be wrapped and not dangled before cats and dogs. Some of the Muslim men and women I have seen re-post such images on social media to endorse the message. Yet just as often, liberal and progressive Muslims re-post these same images with satirical comments ridiculing both the patriarchal objectification of women as candy, jewels, or meat and the expectation that men have no more self-control than flies, cats, dogs, and petty thieves. In early 2014, a Facebook page called "A Man's Hijab" satirized such tropes by applying them to men's beards.[1]

Rather than seeking to critique or defend such images, this chapter contextualizes them in the broader field of semiotic acts of "wrapping."[2] Examining many kinds of work done by such processes, I suggest that opposing interpretations of such tropes cannot be reduced to a question of misogyny versus egalitarianism. Throughout the Muslim world, feminine piety is strongly connected to acts of wrapping. On the other hand, many non-Muslims as well as liberal Muslims have used "female coveredness" as "a barometer for gauging female subjugation" (Afsaruddin 1999, 7). Yet wrapping is also part of many domains other than women and Islam. If we look beyond the ubiquitous cliché of "the veiled Muslim woman," we see that discourses and practices of wrapping extend to religious truths, male leaders, high-status men, and even God. In the anecdote above, the *muqaddama* connects wrapping objects with women's concealing dress, with their social wrapping through their father, and with high social status, equating nakedness to slavery.

Senegalese women leaders in the Fayḍa Tijāniyya movement embrace whole-heartedly the discourses and practices of pious feminine wrapping that liberal critics dismiss as misogynistic and prejudicial to women's full membership in modern society. These leaders iconically connect women's pious self-wrapping with other wrapped things, including hidden truths and social prestige. Central to this book is the point that, although acts of wrapping can serve to marginalize women from decision making and opportunities, a performance of self-wrapping may also associate a woman – or man – with forms of power. Like any signifying act, the meaning and outcome of any act of wrapping is not predetermined but depends on its performance and reception in a particular context.

As the anecdotes that opened this chapter suggest, my use of the term "wrapping" is inspired by metaphors and acts of wrapping used by my interlocutors and by many other Muslims. The term "wrapping" literally translates some of the locally relevant terms used in Fayḍa contexts. For example, a growing number of pious Senegalese women, including many of the *muqaddamas* I interviewed, have adopted the long, colourful, full-body "wrapper" (*malaḥfa* in Arabic, Wolofized as *mëlfa*) traditionally worn by Mauritanian Arab women. Yet "wrapping" as an analytical category does not gloss a single folk term but designates a range of semiotic acts, including physically wrapping bodies or things as well as words, voices, social presences, truths, mystical realities, feelings, actions, social relations, and more. It encompasses "veiling," a term that, whether championed or demonized, has become a fetishized symbol of Muslim womanhood worldwide. At the same time, "wrapping" exceeds the strongly feminine, visual, and negatively concealing implications of "veiling." Most Senegalese Muslim women, including many committed adherents of the Fayḍa movement, do not in fact routinely wear headscarves. Still, they engage in non-sartorial forms of pious self-wrapping. "Wrapping" also encompasses the feminine habitus that Boddy (1989) calls "interiority" or "enclosure," which shapes Sudanese women's spatial movements, tastes, and selves. However, in addition to internalizing, enclosing, concealing, and safeguarding, a wrapper can also represent, translate, display, assert, advertise, decorate, allure, and even mislead. Wherever veiling has become widespread as a means to preserve Muslim women's modesty, women have used veiling as a marker of distinction, a fashion statement (Schulz 2007; Masquelier 2009, 2013; Tarlo 2010; Buggenhagen 2012b; Fair 2013; Rabine 2013), and even a means of seduction to expand their potential pool of marriage partners (Wiley 2013).

Returning to the image of the candy wrapper, we can imagine this wrapper as performing many functions beyond protecting the candy from filth and insects. Even while concealing the candy, it also announces this candy as strawberry-flavoured. Its designer has taken pains to present the candy as more appetizing than the competing brand, whether through pure opacity or through tantalizing transparency. Such *indexical* functions of the wrapper – that is, its act of marking and identifying its contents – often depend on the suggestion that the wrapper's qualities *iconically* represent qualities of the candy itself. An elaborate, rare, high-quality, and pristine wrapper depicting strawberries suggests that its contents embody the same qualities.

Of course, the wrapper may not perform all these functions as one might hope. Ants and dirt might sneak through. A prankster may have replaced the candy with something else. Its claim that the candy tastes like fresh strawberries may be a lie. A lollipop hidden behind three colourful layers emblazoned with glittery stars may disappoint compared to the competition in plain wax paper. A ten-pack may actually only contain nine. Yet even though we may lack total confidence in a wrapper, the Facebook meme is correct to suggest that we would only buy a lollipop that had one, preferably one marked with a name we trust or at least one embodying the quality we expect of its contents.

Just as a lollipop wrapper can perform an act of deception or decoy through overestimating, underestimating, or altogether mislabelling what is inside, debate and doubt often surround whether persons, doctrines, movements, and claims are presented in the correct wrapper. While I conducted research in Kaolack in 2004, a *muqaddam* who ran a business downtown recounted discovering that an employee had siphoned off several thousand dollars worth of revenue over the past few months. Shaking his head with amazement, he told me no one would ever have suspected that a woman who wore an "*ibaadu*" (pious Sunni reformist) headscarf and prayed regularly and visibly could do such a thing. This "*ibaadu*"-branded wrapper had clearly been marking the wrong contents. Yet despite abundant stories like this, we can never completely live by the old adage "don't judge a book by its cover." Instead, we seek to develop intuitions and methods to judge whether a wrapper is doing what we think it should do. Despite proverbs warning not to send away the angel in beggar's clothing or buy all that glitters at the price of gold, we still do both. To "know" is to have the power to discern the subtle clues that mark the site of buried treasure, that separate the real from the fake, or that hint at deeper meanings of a text or narrative.

In at least one crucial way, a social performance of wrapping differs from the physical act of wrapping a candy. While both acts can do all the instrumental and signifying work mentioned above, a performative social act does not merely wrap a pre-existing object but constitutes its object, both during that particular act and through the sedimentation of many acts (J. Butler 1990, 1993). Even if one can falsely index one's social identity, one's "actual" social identity is also largely constructed through indexes (Ochs 1992; M. Silverstein 2003). Thus, the authoritative selves of Taalibe Baay *muqaddama*s hinge on acts recognized as indexing their piety and knowledge.

The performance of feminine piety is the domain of wrapping most central to this book. The connection between wrapping and women's piety is not merely an unexamined *habitus* (Bourdieu 1977) but a set of consciously cultivated and discussed practices of religious disciplines (*ādāb*) explicitly informed by religious scholars' interpretations of the Qur'ān and *ḥadīth*. Although sometimes associated with women's "nature" *(fiṭra)*, many religious discourses throughout this book present wrapping less as a natural disposition than as an index of feminine piety and dignity. Men also participate in wrapping women to show respect for a woman as pious and close to God. When I mentioned to a research assistant that I had recently heard of a woman leader I might want to interview, he told me he had known of her too but had not mentioned her to me to avoid bringing a pious woman's name out into the open. Now that I had unmasked this woman without his help, he agreed to take me to her.

This practical tendency is supported by speeches that male leaders give at public meetings and is confirmed in numerous writings and recorded speeches of Shaykh Ibrāhīm and other Islamic leaders. I will cite just one example from a compilation of Shaykh Ibrāhīm's Qur'ānic exegesis *(tafsīr)*. Commenting on a verse from the Sūra of Women (Qur'ān 4:1) that describes God as creating from a single person *(nafs)* "many men and women,"[3] Shaykh Ibrāhīm notes that "many" only explicitly describes "men" (coming after it in the Arabic) but is omitted for women, "showing that what is right for women is concealment [*tasattur*]" (I. Inyās [Niasse] 2010 [1964], 358).[4] That is, women are protected from being described openly, and it is only through a description of men that we can deduce that women are many too. On its own, this interpretation may seem a stretch to someone not already inclined to read the text in this way. Yet it follows the Sufi practice of seeking hidden meanings wrapped up in literal language. Indeed, the grammar of this phrase mirrors a tendency throughout the Qur'ān to refer to women obliquely through men, often in the possessive ("tell your women") and the third person.[5] Shaykh Ibrāhīm's writings repeatedly affirm women's equality in spiritual matters while calling for indirection and concealment, which are ultimately connected to maintaining women's sexual purity.

Yet the semiotics of wrapping applies to many things other than women's modesty. Processes of wrapping and unwrapping are central not only to gendered piety but also to the Fayḍa's approach to truth, authority, and community. Fayḍa adherents exemplify in their own particular ways the widespread Sufi focus on "apparent" *(ẓāhir)* realities that wrap "inner" *(bāṭin)* realities. Preserving the tensions and ambiguities between outer and inner truths often plays into strategies to accommodate competing imperatives and avert potential crises (Hill 2007, 2013b). The dialectic between wrapping and unwrapping, the apparent and the hidden, connects performances of gendered piety to other domains of wrapping, contributing to the construction and deconstruction of gender differences.

Throughout this book we see how women leaders foreground the paradox of gender: that gender appears simultaneously as an essential cosmic principle and as an arbitrary, artificial, and evanescent distinction. These women highlight pious feminine wrapping as an iconic representation of inner, mystical truths; yet they also deconstruct gender as an essential category. They preach the practical necessity of adhering to gendered roles in a social world that depends on a gendered division of responsibilities; yet they insist that such outward distinctions lose their transcendent appearance through mystical religious experience and contemplation. They use gendered metaphors to explain mystical concepts and to imagine their own roles, yet they also use metaphors to deconstruct gender.

This paradox, I think, is central to the semiotic power of gender more generally. Gender is constituted largely through naturalizing metaphors. In turn, gender provides naturalizing metaphors for constituting other things (see chapter 4 and Hill 2014). Male Sufis have for centuries used the image of the wrapped woman as a metaphor for God's hidden nature as an object of longing (Murata 1992). Although men have usually used such metaphors for their own purposes (see Bouhdiba 1985; Tourage 2007), the women discussed in this book connect wrapped feminine piety with wrapping in domains such as mystical truths and nobility, performing power and authority through performing humble feminine piety.

This chapter contextualizes the semiotics of Taalibe Baay women leaders' acts of self-wrapping in relation to three main domains of wrapping. First, I discuss Sufi discourses of wrapped truths prevalent in the Fayḍa. I then relate wrapping to traditional Senegalese notions of "*kersa*" – shame or dignified restraint. Finally, I compare and contrast men's and women's patterns of bodily covering in Senegal. I show that for both men and women, bodily covering can embody the meaningful quality or "qualisign" (C.S. Peirce 1955) of wrapping, linking them to intangible virtues and mystical knowledge perceived as embodying the same quality.

Truths Wrapping Truths

> When you give birth to your baby – I'll give you an allegory – in the clinic or hospital, when she[6] is born she is born completely naked. She has no shirt or pants! Is that not true? When she dies too, she is returned

> naked – they wrap her up and put her in a hole. You understand? The time that she is living in between she wears clothing. She pays respect to the body by wearing clothes! That is how *sharīʿa* (God's law) is to *ḥaqīqa* (Divine Reality). Today when one is born one is naked, they cover her, give her, wrap her and play with her to make her happy. But now if she is ten or twenty years old and stands in the street naked they will yell out that she is crazy! And yet when she was born no one said she was crazy, and yet she arrived completely naked! Hmm? So that's how *sharīʿa* and *ḥaqīqa* are to each other. *Sharīʿa* is just a robe that they put over *ḥaqīqa*. But what is really really true is *ḥaqīqa*.[7]

This is how Sayyida Seynabou Mbathie, a *muqaddama* in Dakar, characterized the relationship between God's law and the Divine Reality that it envelops. A male *muqaddam* in Dakar[8] used similar imagery of sartorial decency in explaining how someone carried away *(majdhūb)* by self-extinction *(fanāʾ)* in God must then "come down" (*wàcc*) to a state of "persistence" *(baqāʾ)* in God's law *(sharīʿa)*.[9] Although experiencing God transforms one's perception of reality, one continues to "wear the same robe (*mbubb*), which is *sharīʿa*."

If one can generalize at all about Sufism in its many forms, one might describe it as an endeavour to go beyond "apparent" *(ẓāhir)* realities to pursue the "inner" *(bāṭin)* realities wrapped by the Qurʾān and other phenomena in the sensory world (see Burckhardt 2008). Senegal's various Sufi groups share an emphasis on making available the power of *bāṭin* realities (Roberts and Roberts 2000; Buggenhagen 2013), and Fayḍa adherents have their own elaborate set of discourses and practices surrounding this opposition. Indeed, the coexistence of *ẓāhir* and *bāṭin* is central to nearly all the conversations and observations reported throughout this book.

Shaykh Ibrāhīm quotes Qādirī Shaykh Sīdī Mukhtār al-Kuntī, writing as follows:

> Those who explain the prophetic traditions draw the analogy of a nutshell and a kernel: the shell being the sacred law *(sharīʿa)* and the kernel being the Reality (*ḥaqīqa*). A kernel without a shell becomes rotten and putrid, and a shell with no kernel inside is worthless. (Niasse 2010, 153)

I have found this nut-and-shell metaphor widespread among Sufis I have spoken with in other Sufi orders as well. Extending the nut metaphor, one might say that, just as a nutshell bears signs signalling to the informed what it contains and where to open it, the language of the

Qur'ān provides clues to the inner reality of God and oneself. Answering critics who accuse them of introducing unlawful innovations *(bid'a)* to Islam, Taalibe Baay and other Sufis proclaim that they have simply followed the signs on the shell of *sharī'a* indicating how to get to the nut, while their critics see Islam as nothing but shell.

In his magnum opus, *Kāshif al-ilbās* (translated as "The Removal of Confusion" in Niasse 2010), Shaykh Ibrāhīm argues that the Tijānī path is the most excellent path because it combines the inside and outside perfectly: "Its exterior is the noble virtues of the sacred law *(sharī'a)*, and its interior is the product of the divine Reality *(ḥaqīqa)*. There is nothing found in its practices or arrangements of litanies except something explicitly commanded by Allah in His Mighty Book" (Niasse 2010, 143). While insisting on adherence to God's explicit commands, the same work explains how following these commands leads one to hidden truths that can be tasted but not stated. The title *Kāshif al-ilbās*, published in English as *The Removal of Confusion*, alludes to dispelling misunderstandings about the Fayḍa's teachings. Yet the term *"kāshif"* is also the active participle of *"kashf,"* a Sufi term usually translated as "unveiling," especially in the sense of perceiving beyond God's "veils" (see below). The title thus could be literally translated as "unveiler of the confusion," invoking an established Sufi concept of going beyond the confusion of appearances to unveil "the Real" – *al-Ḥaqq*, the name of God used to refer to God's hidden reality.

The coexistence of seemingly contradictory *ẓāhir* and *bāṭin* truths is often rife with paradox and tension. Among Sufis themselves and between Sufis and their critics, continual controversy surrounds which if any mystical teachings can be reconciled with *sharī'a* and whether one should ever speak openly about hidden realities. The history of Sufism presents abundant cases of mystics carried away *(majdhūb)* into an ecstatic state in which they make pronouncements that even Sufis admit literally violate the law. The most famous example is the ninth-century Persian mystic Manṣūr al-Ḥallāj, who accepted his execution for declaring "I am the Real" (Massignon 1994). When the Fayḍa emerged in the 1930s, even fellow Tijānīs bitterly objected to similar statements made by Shaykh Ibrāhīm and his followers (Seesemann 2011), such as declarations of being or seeing God and claims that Shaykh Ibrāhīm was the Prophet. As I wrote this chapter in 2015, news broke that nine Northern Nigerian followers of Shaykh Ibrāhīm had been condemned to death for blasphemy for reportedly proclaiming in a *mawlid* meeting that Shaykh Ibrāhīm outranked the Prophet Muḥammad (Muhammad

2015). Such claims tend to be attributed to a state of mystical rapture in which words express not literal beliefs about individuals but intuitions comprehensible only within that mystical state.[10]

Shaykh Ibrāhīm's mystical approach, like that of many Sufis, revolves around a verse in the Qur'ān (57:3) that describes God as "the First and Last, the Seen *(Ẓāhir)* and Unseen *(Bāṭin),*"[11] all four attributes being counted among Allāh's ninety-nine names. As a *ḥadīth* quoted by the Qādirī shaykh Sīdī al-Mukhtār al-Kuntī elaborates, "You [God] are the Manifest, and nothing can obscure You; and You are the Hidden, and nothing can unveil You." Sīdī al-Mukhtār interprets this to mean that God "appears in every visible object" yet that God's true nature is hidden "by the negation of definition and explanation" (quoted in Niasse 2010, 135). God, then, is simultaneously the wrapper and the wrapped, the veil and the one behind the veil.

Many Sufis describe all of known existence as a series of veils between human perception and God. The multifarious existents conceal God's unity yet provide signposts potentially leading the seeker to discover God's hidden nature. In connection to the Sufi concept of *kashf* ("unveiling," see above), an oft-cited *ḥadīth* states, "God has 70,000 [or 70, or 700][12] veils of light and darkness; were He to lift them, the glories of His Face would burn up everyone whose sight perceived Him" (Treiger 2007, 10). In a well-known explanation of this *ḥadīth,* Al-Ghazālī interprets these veils as the light of partially correct belief and the darkness of disbelief and worldliness (al-Ghazālī 1998). Only "the elect among the elect" penetrate God's veils to perceive divine reality through the annihilation *(fanā')* of all existents and ultimately of the self in divine unity (Treiger 2007, 15–16). Similarly, in *Kāshif al-ilbās,* Shaykh Ibrāhīm cites the image of the aspirant becoming conscious of his own veil as being rendered "threadbare" by remembrance of God *(dhikr),* permitting the aspirant to "hear the call of the Real" *(al-Ḥaqq)* (Niasse 2010, 224).

Despite the imagery of God's "unveiling" to the aspirant, one does not definitively remove God's veils but rather has a glimpse of penetrating beyond them, for the hidden would cease to be what it is without its veil. The Sufi literature is replete with gendered metaphors of the aspirant as a suitor who ultimately gains admission to the bridal chamber, where the bride finally removes her veil (Malamud 1996; see also chapter 4). This suggests a selective unveiling that is only possible to one who has been admitted to an inner space. This image of God's nested veils illustrates the principle that what is wrapped can in turn wrap a yet deeper reality. Shaykh Ibrāhīm and other Sufis sometimes describe the Prophet Muḥammad himself as a veil whose outward existence cloaks God yet whose mystical existence provides an entrance to gnosis (e.g., Niasse 2010, 140). *Ẓāhir* and *bāṭin*, then, designate not two opposing realms but a relation between more and less visible, outer and inner, from some viewpoint. In his 2013 *gàmmu* address, Taalibe Baay shaykh Baay Mokhtar Ka said, "There's *ẓāhir*; there's *ẓāhir* of *ẓāhir;* ... and there's *ẓāhir* of *ẓāhir* of *ẓāhir*. There's *bāṭin;* there's *bāṭin* of *bāṭin;* ... and there's *bāṭin* of *bāṭin* of *bāṭin*."[13]

The contrast between *sharīʿa*'s outer dictates and *ḥaqīqa,* which transcends and often seems to contradict *sharīʿa,* is ever-present in Taalibe Baay religious discourse. Although a source of perpetual controversy for Fayḍa adherents, this productive tension is central to the paradoxical aesthetics and rhetorics of Fayḍa discourse. Fayḍa adherents differ in the degree to which they openly speak or condone open speaking about mystical secrets. Some insist on only speaking of uncontroversial *ẓāhir* Islamic teachings openly, while others veil mystical speech sufficiently to make it incomprehensible to the uninitiated. In my experience, high-profile leaders familiar with the controversies surrounding mystical doctrines tend to be reticent about or even to deny many mystical teachings, while local leaders more often speak enthusiastically about such doctrines to promote the distinctiveness of the Fayḍa.

Like al-Ḥallāj, a Fayḍa disciple who is initiated through *tarbiya* (spiritual training) to the point of experiencing *fanāʾ al-nafs,* or obliteration of the self or individual soul, declares that he or she "sees" God or even "is" God. On several occasions I have witnessed a *muqaddam* quizzing an initiate in this state who is feverishly repeating *"Lā ilāha illā Allāh"* ("There is no divinity but Allāh"). When asked, "Who are you?" the disciple answers, "I am God." "Who is asking you?" "God. There is nothing but God." In *Kāshif al-ilbās,* Shaykh Ibrāhīm discusses the necessity for the *shaykh* to question the Sufi aspirant to establish that such claims derive from a genuine obliteration of the self in divine unity (Niasse 2010, 231). Many disciples who narrated their life stories to me spoke of this moment during their *tarbiya* as the moment when they "saw God" or "knew God."

Fayḍa leaders whom I have asked about "seeing God" have given me contradictory answers. One son of Shaykh Ibrāhīm insisted that it is impossible to see God, while other prominent leaders have told me that through *tarbiya* one sees God constantly. Although one might wonder whether this difference signals a fundamental disagreement in the

Fayḍa community, both the denial and the defence of claims of seeing God are found in Shaykh Ibrāhīm's writings, especially in *Kāshif al-ilbās*, which dedicates a whole chapter and an appendix to the question of seeing God. Shaykh Ibrāhīm also wrote a separate treatise on the question.[14] While affirming that no one can see God with the eyes as one sees other things, he qualifies that "the one seeing does not lay claim to ocular perception. He does not notice the eyes *(abṣār)*, or anything else" (Niasse 2010, 131). When God "enraptures" (*yajdhabu* [literally, "pulls"]) the one who draws near to Him, Shaykh Ibrāhīm continues, the aspirant "becomes absent from his personal witnessing *(shuhūd)*," and

> In this state, he witnesses the divine Presence *(haḍra)*, as before the world and after the Hereafter, as before the before and after the after ... The lover becomes extinct in his Beloved. And he becomes extinct to his own extinction *(fanā')*. Nothing remains except the divine Selfhood *(al-huwiyya)*.
>
> Words may emerge from the one entrusted with this (state), which those with no spiritual experience consider preposterous claims. Nonetheless, his conduct in this is perfect in the sight of Allah. (Niasse 2010, 132)

Shaykh Ibrāhīm goes on to cite numerous Sufi scholars who support the possibility of "seeing" God.

He also cites several Sufis' statements concerning the famous case of Abū Yazīd al-Bisṭāmī, whose followers heard him say "Glory be to Me! How exalted is My affair!" When Abū Yazīd returned to his senses and his followers told him what he had said, he replied, "I was not aware of anything of this. Why did you not kill me in that condition? If you had killed me, you would have been warriors in Allah's way, and I would have died a martyr" (Shaykh Aḥmad al-Tijānī's account, quoted in Niasse 2010, 237–8). Certainly, neither Abū Yazīd nor the Sufis relating this anecdote considered him worthy of Ḥallāj's fate. Rather, his retort rhetorically highlighted the paradoxical disjuncture between *ḥaqīqa* and *sharīʿa* – that the lover and knower of God appears guilty according to God's own law. This account exemplifies paradoxical language pervasive in Fayḍa discourse, which achieves "edification through puzzlement" (Fernandez 1980). Shaykh Ibrāhīm's approach is neither to dismiss nor to reinterpret *sharīʿa* but to show that *sharīʿa* wraps transcendent principles that, from some vantage point, seem to negate it.

For all his reliance on Sufi scholarship, the Qur'ān, and *ḥadīth* to legitimize his and his disciples' practices and pronouncements, Shaykh Ibrāhīm insisted that knowledge of God transcended language and could only be experienced through the heart and "tasted." As I have mentioned, the *tarbiya* process usually lacks any explanation of Sufi concepts. Shaykh Ibrāhīm's oldest grandson and most prominent representative until his death in 2008, Shaykh Ḥasan Cissé, quoted him as saying, "Secrets are in the hearts of the distinguished folk *(rijāl),* not in the bellies of books," meaning that they can only be transmitted spiritually, not explained (Niasse 2010, xii). The more profound a truth is, the less amenable it is to direct representation through language and rational comprehension. Yet language, an outer truth, is necessary both to conceal inner truth from the unprepared and to lead the aspirant to inner truth through sacred litanies, metaphors, riddles, and chanted poetry.

The role of language in Shaykh Ibrāhīm's Sufism, then, resembles its role in Wittgenstein's philosophy – that of a ladder providing "steps" to "climb beyond" it (Wittgenstein 1953). Yet instead of throwing the ladder away as Wittgenstein suggests, Fayḍa adherents climb back down and continue to play the "language games" as if they were not games. The *muqaddam* mentioned above who spoke of the need to "come down" from *fanā'* told me that once one has done so, one sees all individual creations (*mbindéef*) as cinema. Yet even if one knows it is all *"mise en scène,"* one goes along with it as if it were reality. For Taalibe Baay, it would be irreverent – even impossible – to unwrap and expose *ḥaqīqa;* instead, they seek to penetrate it while respecting its eternal hiddenness. (See chapter 4 on gendered metaphors that are used to depict this penetration.)

When I asked Sayyida Seynabou Mbathie to explain why, if women were equal in Islam as she insisted, they do not lead prayer, she lowered her voice and said,

> You know, in the *Fayḍa* of Shaykh Ibrāhīm, if we were to talk about, as they say, the *"bāṭin,"* it would be a bit surprising. But we keep the best behaviour, in that we follow *sharī'a* and take women and place them behind [in prayer]. Because *sharī'a* has placed women behind … That's how we make [our behaviour] beautiful [*taaral*], how we give it a pleasing form [*rafetal*]. But [leading prayer] is not something women *can't* do. Everything that a man can do, a woman can do too … A woman, if we are talking about the true, true, true, true "reality" [*ḥaqīqa*] – God – truly – a woman can be an imam. Because once you've gone to the point of hitting your chest and reaching God, there is no man or woman there.

Here Sayyida Seynabou explicitly describes adherence to *sharīʿa* – God's prescriptions for correct practice – as a performance of gendered roles that God has commanded despite the illusory nature of those distinctions. This is not to say that Sayyida Seynabou sees gender roles as false performance. Like other *muqaddamas*, she also describes such roles as necessary for cultivating piety and maintaining social cohesion. Instead, she maintains the apparently contradictory coexistence of apparent truths and hidden truths common in Taalibe Baay discourse.

Just as *sharīʿa* wraps inner *ḥaqīqa*, the Prophet Muḥammad was an individual human with a social identity and lifespan whose tangible personhood indexes a deeper reality. In Sufi thought, the Muḥammadan Reality *(Ḥaqīqa Muḥammadiyya)* or Muḥammadan Light *(Nūr Muḥammadī)* is the first of God's creations from which all other creations derive.[15] As the wrapper is the tangible handle for the intangible and unnamable, Fayḍa adherents' references to Muḥammad are often bivalent, slipping between referring to the tangible person and the deeper realities he wraps.

Ancient metaphors presenting God as the veiled beloved woman suggest potential iconic connections between wrapped truths and actual wrapped women. Yet any iconic relationship exists only through being actively shown and recognized. Women leaders alchemically consecrate performances of self-effacing womanhood as icons of egoless mystical knowledge and authority. In addition, in the Senegalese context, Sufi doctrines of outer and inner truths converge with local attitudes that associate performances of self-wrapping with elevated social status. Women leaders' performances of dignified, pious authority emphasize these associations, which apply to both men and women, albeit in gendered ways.

Cultivating Interiority, Piety, and Shame (*Kersa*)

A mother repeatedly scolds her small daughter "Sit! Girls don't stand!" The girl sits, her arms clasping her folded knees, on the courtyard floor next to several other women, neither up on a chair nor with legs extended like the boys. Another mother chides her daughter, "Kneel when you bring your father water!" I observed women who far surpassed their husbands in economic and social capital repeat the same behaviour for them. Janice Boddy (1989) observed that Sudanese women embodied a largely tacit and stable *habitus* (Bourdieu 1977) of "interiority" or "enclosure" that shaped their practices, preferences, and discourses (on femininity as interiority, see also Hirschon 1981; Laqueur 1990; Young 1990; Morris 1995). Anthropologists elsewhere have observed similar habitual spatial associations between the oppositions of male/female and up/down (Gilmore 1996). From a young age, both urban and rural Taalibe Baay women embody "feminine" behaviours of interiority – or what I call self-wrapping – that profoundly yet subtly shape their inclinations, including their speech, bodily mannerisms, and use of space.

Just as some have shown how veiling can act as a form of "portable seclusion" (Papanek 1971, 1973), a woman's home can act as an immobile veil, and her male guardians as social wrappers. The further a woman strays from the home, the greater the need for other forms of wrapping. Girls in almost every Taalibe Baay household I visited spent much of their time inside the home performing domestic tasks. Both boys and girls might walk similar distances from home while running errands (see Katz 1993 on Sudan). Yet boys are typically allowed much more free time to play and socialize with friends, often outside the home, while girls are constantly reminded not to dawdle in the street. As mentioned in chapter 1, Shaykh Ibrāhīm sent his sons to study abroad yet had his daughters study in Medina Baay under family protection. His daughter Shaykha Maryam (b. 1932) told me that, more recently, after she returned from a 1986–7 tour of the Middle East promoting Qur'ānic education, her older full brother instructed her to limit her travels, explaining that it was indecorous for her to travel without male guardianship. Although her entourage had included her grown sons as well as teachers and students from her schools, her husband had recently passed away, and she had not travelled with an older male who qualified as her guardian. She obeyed out of respect for her brother's seniority yet resumed touring after his death in 2001. Her increased social maturity by that time may have contributed to her ability to resume touring without criticism. However, she was already quite senior throughout this period, suggesting that a more important factor was her contrasting interpretation of a pious Muslim woman's need for social cover.

Senegalese Muslims widely understand the Qur'ān to prescribe that the husband go out and work to support the family while the wife stays home to take care of domestic matters.[16] In practice, sharing domestic work with several other women in an extended, often polygynous household makes working outside the home easier for many Senegalese women than for many middle-class Western women in nuclear families. Moreover, a husband's inability to provide may demand it. Many women travel alone frequently to buy and sell at markets or to attend relatives' and friends' life-cycle events. Especially during the daytime, one often sees as many women as men on long-distance buses, many of them travelling alone and carrying a child in their lap. Yet these ideals of opposite gender roles and ways of relating to space still seem nearly universal among Senegalese Taalibe Baay regardless of status or background. Even women who earn far more than their husbands oversee all the cooking, cleaning, and childcare, although they tend to delegate most of this work to maids or daughters.

Despite its strong associations with feminine piety, self-wrapping is not a uniquely feminine moral or social virtue, just as self-exposure is not a positive masculine virtue. Respectable men and women both must cultivate the moral quality of *kersa,* which scholars have glossed variously as "honor" (Heath 1990; Buggenhagen 2009b), "restraint" (Heath 1990), "docility" (Buggenhagen 2004), "reserve" (McLaughlin 1997), and *"sangfroid"* (Irvine 1995).[17] Perhaps most generally, *kersa* means "shame": "to have *kersa*" (*am kersa*) can mean both "to have a sense of shame" and "to feel ashamed." One aspect of *kersa* is showing *sutura,* which can mean "discretion" or, more generally, "decency." Deriving from the classical Arabic word *"sutra"* – a cover such as a curtain or cloak – *sutura* suggests that decency and shame require revealing only what must be revealed. Similar notions can be found throughout the Muslim world – for example, in Ottoman Turkey, where "inaccessibility" was a sign of high status for both men and women (L.P. Peirce 1993).

Kersa demands a degree of interiority of both men and women, requiring them not to put themselves "out there" – for example, through speaking too loudly and openly or dressing revealingly. Still, the bar of *kersa* is higher for women than for men: behaviour that is acceptable for a man may show a lack of *kersa* in a woman. Also, an older or richer woman may be freer to show less restraint in dealing with a younger or poorer woman. Even so, the same woman would more clearly demonstrate her dignity and piety through freely electing to preserve exemplary restraint. It is important to remember that the social consequences of *kersa* as "condescension" – an elective performance of humility through which one benefits simultaneously from one's high status and from appearing to deny that status (Bourdieu 1991) – are fundamentally different from those of *kersa* that is demanded of subordinates. In religious contexts, people with a more pious and mystical persona tend to exhibit a high degree of self-wrapping, whatever their gender or ascribed status. Many charismatic male Taalibe Baay *muqaddams* wear the same level of concealing clothing in public that pious women do, albeit in styles marked as masculine. They make elaborate shows of submission to their own leaders, albeit not to their wives. They often sit close to the ground and speak quietly through an animator (*jottalikat*), someone of lower status – often a griot, or praise singer – who broadcasts to an audience the speech of someone of higher status.[18] All of this enhances their aura of piety, mysticism, and aloof nobility.

Beyond the direct wrapping of one's body, voice, and social presence, many forms of technological mediation can come to act as wrappers, representing one's inner or outer characteristics to the world while preserving one's *kersa*. A microphone can stand in for a *jottalikat* (see chapter 6; Irvine 1974; Heath 1990), allowing a subdued voice to be heard – perhaps clothed in distortion – by an assembly or an absent audience. Photo portraiture can act as an extended "social skin" (T. Turner 1980), or a frontier between the person and society that projects a certain kind of person. Discussing Senegalese Murid women's photo albums, Beth Buggenhagen compares the portrait photographer to the griot, explaining that both "hold the power to make or break reputations" through associating a person with signs of social and economic value (Buggenhagen 2014, 91). These women's portraits can invoke the Sufi conceptions of *ẓāhir* and *bāṭin*: they both reveal and conceal; they can highlight a person's "inner essence" or foreground material possessions; and they may include iconography that associates the subject with a saint's *baraka* (*barke*) (94).

Most mature Senegalese women I have photographed have insisted on being photographed in "proper" attire, including with a prayer shawl over the head, even though most of them only wear such a shawl during prayers. *Muqaddamas*, however, generally keep themselves photo-ready throughout the day, as their homes become "inner public spaces" (Cooper 1997a) where disciples regularly request to take cell-phone photos with them. Thus, *muqaddamas* seldom insist on significantly changing their appearance for photographs, although – like many Taalibe Baay – they may reposition themselves to ensure that an image of Shaykh Ibrāhīm appears in the background. When photographed with leaders, disciples usually sit beneath the leader with their palms up as the leader models praying for them. Through both dress and bodily actions, then, the photograph can act as a wrapper, outwardly indexing moral qualities and relationships of discipleship.

Both male and female Sufi leaders confront the paradox of having to show enough to be recognized without being perceived as "showing oneself" (*wonewu*), "lacking shame/restraint" (*ñàkk kersa*), or being a "person of appearances/the world" (*nitab zaahir*). Any ostentatious show of piety risks appearing as the opposite of piety (Niasse 1998; Soares 2004). Both male and female *muqaddams'* authority depends on recognition of their ability to transmit hidden (*bāṭin*) truths; yet those perceived as unduly publicizing their esoteric knowledge may be castigated as false Sufis. *Muqaddama*s face this paradox doubly: whereas a man might show *kersa* by not appearing to show himself, a woman will more likely show it by appearing to hide herself. For women, then, the question is not merely how much to show but how to show through performing acts of concealing.

Separating Humility from Humiliation

Even if women's dispositions throughout life are shaped by inward-oriented habits tacitly embodied from an early age, such virtues are not entirely tacit but are the object of constant talk and disciplinary practices designed to refine one's piety and good behaviour. That is, interiority is *habitus* both in Bourdieu's (1977) sense of a permanent disposition learned from a young age and in the Aristotelian sense of an ethos cultivated through self-discipline (Mahmood 2005; T. Asad and Scott 2006; Hirschkind 2006a). In his earliest work, *Rūḥ al-Adab* (Niasse 1998, 53–4), Shaykh Ibrāhīm exhorts the disciple as follows: "Be God fearing, a man of humility"[19] for "you will not by humility be in abasement." To illustrate, he contrasts several "low-pitched" Arabic words for desirable things (knowledge, wealth, fertility) with their "high-pitched" opposites (ignorance, poverty, infertility), and states that floods settle in low places.

The potential conflation of humility and abasement engenders a dilemma for Sufi women leaders: their expected social roles involve submission, domesticity, and withdrawal from publicity, yet they must differentiate these behaviours from social inferiority, servitude, and a lack of confidence. Like Muslim women in many other communities (see, for example, Mahmood 2005; Augis 2009), Taalibe Baay women leaders describe acts of wifely submissiveness as expressions of submission to God's law *(sharīʿa)*[20] and of their sincere desire to care for husband and family.

Sayyida Khady,[21] a *muqaddama* in Dakar, demonstrated that negotiating these opposing principles is an ongoing process. During an interview in 2009, she described her frustration when, as she was busy helping a client while at work, her idle husband told her to bring him water. She complied. Sayyida Khady's initial explanation of this practice suggests a conscious "patriarchal bargain" (Kandiyoti 1988) – a pound of flesh she agreed to give in exchange for peace and autonomy. Her first husband, she explained, was "liberated." He forbade kneeling before anyone but God and did not allow these provincial ("*Saalum-Saalum*") behaviours, and she agreed with him. However, despite recognizing that kneeling or curtsying while serving men water is not an Islamic prescription, she advises disciples to comply if they are in a context where such behaviours are viewed as part of showing good manners (*yar*). What matters is the intention, which should be to show respect – not veneration – for the person.

In a conversation a year later, Sayyida Khady seemed less resigned than committed to distinctions between men's and women's roles. Modern society's problems, she said, would go away if everyone played their role, especially if women focused on giving their children a proper upbringing. Her business was still growing, yet she described dividing her attention equally between three tasks – God, her family, and her business – emphasizing especially her attention to serving and pleasing her husband. Her insistence on playing one's role well in whatever situation one may find oneself, potentially including kneeling when serving water, suggests that cultivating a single set of pious dispositions may sometimes be less important than adjusting one's behaviour to the context and assigning it a proper meaning.

Some may perceive Sayyida Khady's position as a mere bargain with or capitulation to patriarchy. Yet in myriad ways, she and other *muqaddamas* signal that in a deeper (*bāṭin*) sense an outward performance of lowering oneself might reveal an opposite reality. The notion of "patriarchal bargain" suggests that the women give up something they value – for example, equality – in exchange for something they value more – for example, autonomy in some area. Yet it is not clear that *muqaddamas* see themselves as giving something up through performing submission, which only superficially concerns husbands and fathers. To these women and those who see them exercise authority while showing "good behaviour" (*adab*, *yar*) towards often less remarkable husbands, this behaviour wraps a deeper submissive relationship with God. Some *muqaddamas* explicitly describe acts of submissiveness and interiority as ritual performances demonstrating obedience to God's prescriptions, highlighting the opposition between the performance's apparent (*ẓāhir*) meaning and the hidden *(bāṭin)* truth behind it. Such a "performance" is neither a disingenuous charade nor a naive reproduction of social roles but rather an act presented *as* an act intended to have multiple interpretations.

Of course, whether such a performance successfully raises a woman's moral standing and religious authority depends on its "felicity" (Austin 1962) – that is, on whether viewers perceive and accept its hidden meaning. As a vignette about Sayyida Seynabou Mbathie and Aïda Faye described in chapter 6 shows, *muqaddama*s present feminine *kersa* and related practices of submission and interiority as indexes not of "abasement" but of moral authority. The success of these performances depends not only on disciplined mastery of a pious *habitus* but also on a larger performative stage whose public is aware of a woman's status.

The "publics" in question are not necessarily the highly visible, external spaces this word might conjure. Indeed, women leaders often seem the very opposite of public: few speak in large Taalibe Baay meetings held in streets and city squares; many do not even address their own *daayira*s' outdoor weekly meetings; and most are not recognized by the government and news media as religious leaders – although all these areas are beginning to change as the idea of women Islamic leaders becomes more widely known. Yet their domestic spaces become "internal public spaces" (Cooper 1997a) where disciples assemble to learn about and discuss religious and other matters. *Muqaddama*s use such spaces to influence and sometimes move into "external public spaces" – for example, by organizing *daayira* meetings and conferences or running Qur'ānic schools, Islamic institutes, and economic projects.

In short, the outcomes of women's performance of the norms of self-wrapping are complex and ambiguous. These norms can distance women from the circuits of Islamic knowledge and authority, yet they can also bring them closer than many men to the ascetic and reclusive "Sufi model," as Coulon and Reveyrand suggest of the female Murid leader Sokhna Magat Diop (Coulon and Reveyrand 1990, 17). Understanding how this can be possible requires an examination of which aspects of self-wrapping are particular to women and which they potentially share with men. This starts with a discussion of Muslim women's "veiling," which I understand as any form of dress that obscures one's bodily form and reveals at most one's face and hands.

The Iconic Veiled Muslim Woman

In 2004, a French law designed specifically to eliminate Muslim girls' headscarves from public schools banned all "*signs* and dress through which students openly *show* religious adherence" (République de la France 2004; emphasis mine). Public debate leading up to the law had widely assumed that a veil's primary function was to signify Islam (Bowen 2006). More particularly, to borrow Charles Sanders Peirce's (1955) terminology, veils were construed as conventional *symbols* of Muslim identity and as *indexes* of community membership, piety, and – to opponents – even women's oppression and extremism. As veiling practices have become more widespread around the world, they have become politically charged signs with many conflicting meanings (see, for example, El Guindi 1999; Bowen 2004, 2006; P.A. Silverstein 2004; J.W. Scott 2007; Ahmed 2011). In addition to the veil's function in indexing religious identities or moral qualities (Göle 1996; El Guindi 1999; Ahmed 2011), some scholars have emphasized its instrumental uses, such as increasing women's mobility (Papanek 1971; Hoodfar 1997).

As Saba Mahmood (2005) points out, discussions of veiling that privilege its significations or instrumental uses tend to overlook what it *does* for women who wear it. For the pious Egyptian women Mahmood studied, veiling contributes to disciplinary practices aiming to internalize a pious subjectivity and experience (Mahmood 2005). As Masquelier puts it, veiling "is not simply expressive but is *constitutive* of the pious integrity it is often assumed to represent" (Masquelier 2009, 214). While the question of how veiling embodied practice shapes subjective experience is worthy of further discussion, I want to focus here on how the veil's "constitutive" nature is inseparable from its semiotics, or its signifying work, in gendered performances of piety and authority. Much of the talk about the meaning of veiling has focused on its role as an index or symbol – Peirce's (1955) second and third modes of signification. Less invoked is Peirce's first mode of signification: the icon, or a sign that invokes something through sharing a perceived intrinsic quality with it. Pictures, metaphors, and diagrams all act as icons through sharing some visual or logical property with their object. Beyond being a conventionalized symbol and index of pious Muslim womanhood and Islam, the veil provides ways to embody – and thus become an icon of – inward-oriented moral qualities. The meanings and effects of women's veiling stem partly from iconically connecting women with things that also embody the quality of wrapping.

More specifically, the veil exemplifies a category of icon that Peirce calls a "qualisign," an embodied quality that bears "a privileged role within a larger system of value" (Keane 2003, 414; see also Munn 1992, 414; Chumley and Harkness 2013). Disagreements over the veil's meanings derive largely from contrasting interpretations of qualities understood to be embodied through veiling. In liberal Western contexts, democratic participation is often construed as requiring each individual's outward and direct expression, transparency, and sometimes sexual self-determination, values that clash with concealing and opaque attire (J.W. Scott 2007). Here a Muslim woman's concealed body comes to represent iconically not only her own separation from the public sphere but the larger Muslim community's presumed separation and secrecy, qualities perceived as especially dangerous since 9/11 and the appearance of the self-styled Islamic State. Yet in Senegalese Sufi contexts, sartorial self-wrapping can iconically depict an inward orientation towards contemplation, separation from mundanity, knowledge of inner *(bāṭin)* truths, and dignified reserve (*kersa*) and inaccessibility – all prerequisites for exercising religious authority. Consequently, men and women associated with Sufi authority tend to exhibit a similar degree of self-wrapping.

The question of whether any man's or woman's particular form of self-wrapping contributes to a "felicitous" (Austin 1962) – or socially effective – performance of mystical knowledge and authority is complex and context-specific. While men's and women's styles of dress are shaped by similar attitudes towards *kersa* and spiritual principles, the norms for men and women are somewhat different. Here I detail some of these similarities and differences.

Veiling and Not Veiling Women

As in Senegal, throughout much of the Muslim world veiling and seclusion are not universal but have often been a mark of social distinction for women who need not go out to work or engage in manual labour (Papanek 1971; Tucker 1993; Cooper 1994, 1997b; Meneley 1996; El Guindi 1999). Only recently have strict reformist movements promoted universal veiling for women. Many women in such movements today struggle to observe dress codes while performing housework and other manual tasks (e.g., see Janson 2014). Most Senegalese women, including most Taalibe Baay women, only completely cover their heads and shoulders during ritual prayer and other religious activities. Aside from a small minority of Islamic reformists, only female Islamic authorities and relatives of male authorities are known to cover their heads routinely (although not their faces) and may practice a certain level of seclusion. Even then, current conventions of rigorously wrapping the head and shoulders seem to be recent adoptions, possibly through increased contact with the Middle East and reformist movements. Photographs show women of Shaykh Ibrāhīm's own household around the 1950s wearing modest dress, including head ties, but not systematically covering their neck and shoulders.

Many unmarried, urban Senegalese women today prominently wear long, braided hair extensions. Only upon marrying do most women begin to tie their hair with a multi-coloured cloth that does not cover the neck, ears, and shoulders as a headscarf does. Many of these women only cover themselves completely – aside from their face and the palms of their hands – during ritual prayer and other religious activities such as performing litanies or attending meetings. Even then, Taalibe Baay women do not typically fasten an opaque headscarf with pins, a style that West African reformist women have borrowed from Egypt. Instead, they loosely wrap a large and often thin, brightly coloured, and slightly translucent prayer shawl (*kaala*) over their head and shoulders. Some, especially older women, may don such a shawl whenever they leave the house to go to the market or on social calls, or whenever posing for a photograph.

The minority of Senegalese women who adopt typically Middle Eastern veiling styles such as the modern *ḥijāb*, *ʿabāya*, and *niqāb* are widely assumed to adhere to Salafi-inspired reform movements such as the Jamāʿat ʿIbād al-Raḥmān or Al-Falāḥ. Many Senegalese refer to anyone who veils in these ways as an *"ibaadu"* (from ʿIbād ar-Raḥmān), whether or not she adheres to this organization. As is often the case in controversies over correct practice (Launay 1992; Horvatich 1994), differences between Sufis' and conservative reformists' veiling practices are less about clearly different beliefs than about different priorities and imaginations of religious community. Senegalese Sufis widely accept the notion that Islam requires or strongly encourages women to cover all but the face and palms. Drawing on Mālikī *fiqh* (Ar. jurisprudence), leaders have long instructed their disciples to veil, although they did not necessarily assume that this meant adopting the same rigour in covering advanced by today's reformists. In her short work of counsel for Muslim girls, Shaykh Ibrāhīm's daughter Sayyida

Ruqayya Niasse describes in detail how a Muslim girl should dress in the morning, including covering all but her face and palms (R. Inyās [Niasse] 1964, 43).

Perhaps influenced by reformist movements, many Senegalese Muslims I have spoken with acknowledged to me that the letter of Islamic law *(sharīʿa)* at least recommends veiling. In urban areas since 2000, I have encountered a growing number – yet still a minority – of women in Sufi groups who rigorously cover themselves. Yet rather than adopt Middle Eastern veiling styles as reformist women do, most wear either the multicoloured Mauritanian *malaḥfa* (*mëlfa*) or a West African-style dress with a thin, loose-fitting prayer shawl.

Taalibe Baay do not generally insist that every woman follow what they describe as the *"sharīʿa"* position. In practice, they more often treat a woman's bodily covering as an index of her spiritual status and an icon of her spiritual attributes than as a universal imperative. I have seldom heard Taalibe Baay justify veiling as necessary to prevent men's sexual lust or harassment, a justification I have often heard in the Middle East. Some rank-and-file disciples explained to me that strict rules of dress and gender segregation were mostly intended for Arab men, who cannot control their lust when they see a woman. Some young Taalibe Baay women I spoke with aspired to achieve a level of spirituality that would make them comfortable with veiling but said they would feel presumptuous doing so now. Unmarried Taalibe Baay men sometimes told me they would prefer to marry a woman who follows *sharīʿa* by covering herself (*muuru*), yet those who have since married seemed not to object when their wives continued to dress like most other Senegalese women.

Male and female *muqaddam*s I interviewed consistently described veiling as prescribed by *sharīʿa*, yet only women leaders have told me they insist that their female disciples practise it. Even then, it is not clear that their female disciples veil as consistently as these leaders suggest or that there is significant pressure to do so. One male *muqaddam* I interviewed agreed that Islam taught women to cover themselves, yet he told me he had never told a woman to do so because he considered one's dress trivial compared to inner modesty, which he called "veiling your heart" (*muuru sa xol*). When I asked a son of Shaykh Ibrāhīm why Senegalese women do not typically veil, he shrugged, saying that Senegal is a hot country. He did not mention that Saudi Arabia, where Islamic prescriptions were recorded and where women must veil by law, is hotter.

All the *muqaddama*s I interviewed, regardless of age, covered themselves whenever in the company of non-kin, wearing either the prayer shawl or the Mauritanian *malaḥfa*. One of them, Sayyida Moussoukoro Mbaye, told me she insists that her female disciples cover themselves at all times. Although I cannot verify her claim that all her female disciples cover themselves even when not in her company, they did cover themselves when in her presence, and far more of the Taalibe Baay university students whose federation she oversees cover themselves daily with prayer shawls than is typical in Senegal. Sayyida Seynabou Mbathie told me that her female disciples all cover themselves "like *ibaadu*s," following her example, and that her husband had assumed she was an *ibaadu* when they met because of her dress and her commitment to Islamic prescriptions.

In short, despite widespread agreement that "*sharīʿa*" prescribes Muslim women's covering, bodily wrapping among Senegalese Taalibe Baay women tends to be semiotically primarily connected to indexing spiritual rank and iconizing hidden knowledge.

Wrapping Men and Women

El Guindi has argued that, to understand Muslim women's veiling, we need to account for the fact that many Muslim men cover their bodies and heads to a similar degree and for similar reasons as women (El Guindi 1999, ch. 7). In Senegal, bodily wrapping has similar semiotic functions for men and women yet follows different patterns. The same term in Wolof, *kaala*, refers to any scarf worn by men or women, whether around the head or the shoulders. Beyond certain material uses, such as protecting the wearer from sun and wind, such a scarf worn around the head suggests some kind of social reserve, which can in turn imply piety, an Islamic identity, religious authority, mysteriousness, and charisma. For both men and women, wrapping one's head is not universal and often implies high spiritual status. Just as most women do not routinely cover their heads when young and then only wear a head tie when they mature and marry, most young men normally go bareheaded, wearing a *mbaxana* (an embroidered fez-style cap) to Friday prayer and perhaps more regularly as they mature. For both men and women, wrapping oneself more than one's peers do may signal a more religious identity but may also be perceived as pretentious or overly strict. Yet at the same time, men's and women's covering are associated with somewhat different conventions and meanings.

Many male religious figures wear multiple layers of highly concealing clothing, even in sweltering heat, obscuring their bodily form and in many cases their heads to the same degree as pious Muslim women. This is especially true of charismatic leaders reputed for mystical knowledge and power. Just as many say that distinctions like gender lose their reality as one rises in spiritual knowledge, men and women tend to converge around highly concealing dress as they approach the ideal of the charismatic Sufi leader. This principle applies to the Fayḍa community, whether in Senegal or in other West African countries, as well as to other Sufi movements.

Examples of holy men who cover themselves can be found throughout the history of Islam and especially Sufism. The Almoravids *(Al-Murābiṭūn),* the mystical Islamic revival movement that ruled Northwest Africa and Iberia during the eleventh and twelfth centuries, were also known as "The Veiled Ones" *("Al-Mulaththamūn")* because the men veiled their faces. The Almoravids emerged from the Berber-speaking Ṣanhāja (Znaga), many of whose male descendants today in Mauritania, especially those recognized as religious scholars, continue to cover their heads and often much of their faces with a black turban. The charismatic Moroccan resistance leader Sīdī Muḥammad al-Kattānī (1873–1909) similarly veiled his face, which "added to the aura of sanctity and mystery that surrounded him" (Munson 1993, 63). Susan Rasmussen (2013) has described how, among the matrilineal Nigerien Tuareg, men are held to a higher degree of modest shame (*takarakit,* roughly equivalent to *kersa*) than women, "covering" their faces and social persons more.

Some stories even explicitly connect humble asceticism with taking on the form of a veiled woman. When his companion's wife demanded a servant, the great Moroccan Sufi ascetic Abū Yiʿzzā disguised himself as a veiled slave woman to serve her. When the companion's wife found out that her slave was the great saint, she repented and agreed to do the work herself (Cornell 1998, 70).[22] This story highlights the ascetic's spiritual stature through depicting interiority and humility. Simultaneously, it reconfirms male hegemony by presenting absolute abjection through the slave woman and housework as women's work.

In rituals of several Sufi orders I have attended in Cairo, the presiding *shaykh* has similarly worn loose-fitting robes and wrapped his head in a white turban. This contrasts with the official uniform of Islamic scholars *(ʿulamāʾ)* trained at Al-Azhar University in Cairo: a sleeved robe *(jalabiyya)* accompanied by a red fez cap *(tarbūsh)* with a small white turban *(ʿimāma)* wrapped snugly around it. This dress properly covers the body and top of the head but does not obscure the bodily form to the same degree as the ample robes *(faḍfāḍa, mbubb bu réy)* and turbans that in many contexts mark a charismatic Sufi shaykh.

In West Africa, turbans have many implications depending on the context and style of tying. Although Fulani herders throughout West Africa wear turbans for protection from sun and wind, sedentary Wolof speakers in Senegal have little instrumental use for turbans and reserve them for religious leaders of a certain status and mystique. In Wolof-speaking villages in western Saalum where I conducted research, the turban was customarily worn only by male Islamic scholars certified as Qurʾānic exegetes bearing the title of *Tafsīr* (Arabic for "exegesis," usually Wolofized as *Tamsiir*). Such men may be ritually fitted with the turban during a public ceremony. Even if the turban is not always or only worn by someone of this title, among Wolof speakers it always seems to mark an Islamic figure.

Of course, each article of clothing can have multiple meanings both within a context and across many West African contexts. Yet the fact that Sufi figures throughout the world are often photographed wearing many layers of concealing clothes suggests that the iconic relationship between self-wrapping and esoteric knowledge and power spans cultural contexts. These figures' clothing wraps them just as they wrap their secret. Less concealing bodily covering can, in contrast, suggest lower status within a mystical path, a display of humility, or a specialty in non-mystical topics such as Islamic law.

The founders of the major Sufi lineages during the early twentieth century in colonial Senegal are almost always pictured wearing an ample robe *(grand boubou)* and with a scarf or turban obscuring the head area. The only part of the body they exposed more than women was their ankles, which certain *ḥadīth* suggest that men should expose.[23] The most widely reproduced picture of any Sufi leader in Senegal is the single extant photograph of Murid founder Shaykh Aḥmadu Bamba Mbacké (1853–1927) (figure 3.1), which shows his head and face mostly obscured by a white scarf, his few visible facial features washed out by the harsh sunlight or obscured in deep shadows.[24] The ubiquitous artistic representations seen all over Senegal further stylize and obscure his features (Roberts and Roberts 2000, 2002). Reportedly, this was how the reclusive Aḥmadu Bamba habitually dressed, and few people saw his face (Babou 2007). The abiding appeal of this image certainly has much to do with the mystique suggested by the shaykh's self-wrapping. Photographs of the Tijānī leader Al-Ḥājj Mālik Sy of Tivaouane also show him with a scarf encircling his head although not obscuring his face (figure 3.1).

Nearly every photograph I have seen of Shaykh Ibrāhīm has shown him with a white turban wrapped either around the upper part of his head or, occasionally, around his whole head and neck. These two styles reflect his dual persona as the bearer of *ẓāhir* and *bāṭin* religious knowledge – as a scholar of the Qur'ān and *sharī'a* and as the bearer of "the greatest secret."[25] Likewise, nearly all male Fayḍa *muqaddams* I have encountered cover their heads in some way when in public or in the company of guests. Their deliberate choice of covering projects a particular kind of religious persona informed by prevailing conventions.

When in public, most imams and *muqaddams*, from lesser-known leaders to Shaykh Ibrāhīm's own sons, wear an ample outer robe (Ar. *dirā'a, faḍfāda,* Wol. *daraa, mbubb bu réy,* Fr. *grand boubou)* over an inner, sleeved robe (*xaftaan*), with a scarf around their shoulders and a *mbaxana,* which is often taller than the kind most men wear to Friday prayer. The ample robe is typical of male religious authorities, elders, and notables. When presiding over a large meeting or leading Friday prayer, most religious leaders cover their outer robe with at least one other layer, often the kind of gold-trimmed white or black robe worn by Middle-Eastern imams. On their heads, they wear either a *mbaxana,* a small turban covering the upper head, or a cap designed to look like a turban. In short, the higher a man's spiritual rank, the more likely his body is to be obscured.

Most *muqaddams* do not tie or drape a scarf over their heads and instead don a less concealing *mbaxana*. Leaders who do wear a turban, especially in a way that obscures the head, neck, and shoulders, tend to be those considered by their disciples to occupy a special mystical status. Yet doing so can be risky. I have heard many criticisms of *muqaddams* who "wear a big turban" (*sol kaala bu rëy*) in an attempt to be big shaykhs when even Baay's sons are supposed to be mere "disciples of Baay" ("Taalibe Baay"). A few *muqaddams* who cultivate the image of a humble ascetic servant do not cover their heads at all, especially in the presence of one of Baay's descendants. Ironically, then, both a draped turban and bareheadedness can contribute to a man's saintly image: the

Figure 3.1 Shaykh Aḥmadu Bamba Mbacké (above); Al-Ḥājj Mālik Sy (facing page) (from Marty 1917).

Figure 3.2 The Friday litany *(ḥaḍrat al-jum'a)* at the Medina Baay mosque, 25 August 2014. Imam of Medina Baay Shaykh Tijānī 'Alī Cissé (centre) leads, while Mauritanian *muqaddam* Shaykh wuld Khayrī sits to his right (viewer's left).

turban can iconize reclusive asceticism and mystical knowledge, while bareheadedness can index an ascetic lack of concern with the social distinction implied by a turban.

Among Mauritanian Arabs, most mature men wrap a turban around the upper part of their head, while a young man who does so may be considered pretentious. Thus, wearing a turban in Mauritania marks seniority more than religious authority. The charismatic Mauritanian *muqaddam* Shaykh wuld Khayrī, who has many disciples in Senegal, distinguishes himself from most Mauritanian men by wrapping his head in a more concealing way (see figure 3.2). His distinctive look matches the distinctive rank many of his disciples attribute to him as God's hidden *Khalīfa* after Shaykh Ibrāhīm.

One of Shaykh wuld Khayrī's *muqaddams* in Dakar, Babacar Ndiaye, was nicknamed "Sang Ndiaye" (Noble Ndiaye) after declaring that it was actually he who occupied this rank. When I interviewed

Sang Ndiaye in 2004 at his second-hand television shop in the Parcelles Assainies neighbourhood, he was bareheaded. When I returned to his shop in 2014, after he had become more public about this controversial claim, I found he had adopted a new look, with an ample white robe and a turban covering his head and wrapped around his chin. This concealing dress iconized what he told me was his unique access to the innermost meanings of Shaykh Ibrāhīm's poetry.

Shaykh ʿAbdallāh Wilane, the major Fayḍa *muqaddam* of eastern Saalum, also often wraps his head. I have seen him drape it in such a way as to cover much of his face while speaking before disciples. Yet when in the presence of Shaykh Ibrāhīm's sons, he bares his uncut tufts of hair and prostrates himself (*jébbalu*) in a sign of absolute submission, an act common among Murids but uncommon among Taalibe Baay. This change parallels his shift between his role as charismatic leader to his disciples and his absolute dependence on Baay, whom he describes as present through Baay's sons.

In an interview, Sayyida Diarra Ndiaye, the first well-known *muqaddama* in Dakar,[26] criticized *muqaddams* who go around "wearing their big robes and their big turban."[27] All Taalibe Baay are merely disciples, she said, including *muqaddams*. Another widely respected *muqaddam* and teacher I interviewed in a Saalum village in 2004 emphasized his role as a disciple and worker rather than a "big *muqaddam*." He pointed to his scarf, which he wore around his shoulders like someone working the fields, not around his head like a shaykh. Shaykh Tijānī Cissé, current imam of Medina Baay, once told me, "Being a *khalīfa* in Senegal is easy: just sing praises of your father's lineage, wear a big turban."[28] One cannot read this as a criticism of wearing ample clothing, something Shaykh Tijānī Cissé himself tends to do. Rather, he seems to suggest that such forms of dress can assert a higher status than one actually has.

I witnessed one arguably infelicitous "big turban" performance at a small *daayira* meeting a friend invited me to attend in 2009. The presiding *muqaddam*, who follows a trend in the Fayḍa associated with what one might call a liminal Sufi aesthetic (see chapter 7), left his unkempt hair uncovered, suggesting abject discipleship and detachment from material appearances. A young visitor who looked no older than twenty made sure to announce his *muqaddam* status to anyone he met. During the meeting, he wore an ample blue *grand boubou* and a billowy white turban and gave a meandering speech about arcane mystical secrets. My host afterwards confided in me that he found the young *muqaddam*'s tone boastful. Many young *muqaddams*, he said, think being a *muqaddam* is about putting on a big turban and talking big.

In addition to the question of covering too much or too little, both men and women navigate between aesthetically wrapping themselves too humbly or too ostentatiously. Shaykh Aḥmad al-Tijānī and then Shaykh Ibrāhīm after him taught the importance of being concerned with God alone and not the world, even while presenting oneself decorously. Some *muqaddam(a)*s have explained to me the need to live a material life that reflects God's blessings, for the Qur'ān says, "You shall proclaim the blessings from your Lord" (93:11). I have known several *muqaddam*s whose unkempt hair and clothes match their inclination towards otherworldly, *bāṭin* truths over superficialities. When given a shiny new robe, money, or cell phone, they promptly give it away. Although such figures may be revered for rare spiritual power, they tend to be socially marginal among Taalibe Baay (see chapter 7).

At the other extreme are a few *muqaddam*s who wrap themselves not only in ostentatiously expensive clothing but in layers of protocol, guards, and the tinted windows of luxury cars. Of course, such displays are not arbitrary symbols but are material indexes of wealth, which is only possible if a clientele believes in these leaders' spiritual power and seeks to gain access to it through giving them offerings. Speaking of Senegalese Islamic leaders who tour the United States exchanging divine blessing (*barke/baraka*) for honoraria, Ousmane Kane has remarked that leaders who draw large honoraria are noted not just for their piety or their saintly descent but, especially, for displays of material prosperity that show divine favour (Kane 2011, 163–4). Kate Kingsbury (personal communication; see also Kingsbury 2016) describes Sëriñ Modou Kara Mbacké as cultivating a divine mystique by appearing in a stretch Hummer with tinted windows wearing an Armani suit, then almost instantaneously and miraculously reappearing in a luxurious Islamic robe and then in another ensemble.

Among Taalibe Baay, while ostentatious religious figures wrapped in shiny robes, tinted windows, and layers of protocol have their disciples, they tend not to be the ones with the largest followings. There has been increasing talk about a cohort of young men trained as Islamic leaders in Medina Baay who have suddenly become rich, closing themselves off in mansions and wearing the most expensive Islamic and European fashions. Whenever I asked where these young men had obtained their money, I usually heard a sardonic explanation that they had been "striking the hammer" (*dóor marto*), or making money through abusing people's confidence. Most commonly, this term refers to receiving money from rich Gulf Arabs on the (likely false) pretence of distributing sacrificial meat to the poor or investing in Islamic education. Yet even if some people's wealth is perceived as obtained and displayed in an antisocial fashion, the line between good and bad ostentation is ambiguous. Paradoxically, worldly wealth remains widely perceived as evidence of divine favour bestowed on those who transcend the world (Weber 1992). Hence the increasing popularity of $500 gemstone prayer beads (*kurus*), the very tool through which one comes to understand that nothing in this world matters.

In short, the most ostentatious forms of wrapping may signify antisocial wealth accumulation and false pretenses, while the humblest forms of wrapping – or a lack thereof – may suggest insufficient attention to social decorum. Religious figures occupying the whole range of the abjection-ostentation continuum have their followers. Shaykh Ibrāhīm and his sons and daughters are often held up as a yardstick of moderation, neither showing off nor letting themselves go to seed, neither exposing themselves in the public square nor walling themselves off with protocol. They honour important events and guests by dressing nicely, yet their everyday dress is relatively simple. Although most of them have at least one large house, these houses consist mostly of bedrooms occupied by family and guests and perhaps a Qur'ānic school and prayer space. Several of Shaykh Ibrāhīm's senior sons have a comfortable four-wheel-drive vehicle that facilitates long-distance travel on Senegal's back roads, although none has anything like a stretch Hummer as some popular leaders do.

The *muqaddama*s I interviewed, whatever their economic condition, generally espoused the same principle of moderation. Rather than either abjection or ostentation, they emphasized demonstrating measured social decorum. Sayyida Ndèye Maguète Niang told of going through a liminal period during which she wore cast-off clothes and dreadlocks. She described this as a sign that she had not found what she was looking for and cautioned against judging any other liminal Sufi who has not quite settled into a decorous state. Eventually, however, she came out of that liminal phase and dressed nicely, following Shaykh Ibrāhīm's example of "purity" (*sell*). Sayyida Moussoukoro Mbaye has made a handsome living selling fashion and skincare products, a blessing she told me she must embrace through maintaining a beautiful house and presenting herself well. As Sayyida Seynabou Mbathie told me, the naked truth of *ḥaqīqa* must always be wrapped in the decorous robe of *sharīʿa,* which here is understood to include aesthetic self-presentation.

The Gender of Wrapping

In short, these principles of self-wrapping, including norms of concealing dress, are both different and similar for men and women in the Senegalese Fayḍa community. On the one hand, for both men and women, concealing dress can index a religious persona and can iconically suggest social prestige and concealed spiritual qualities. While much of the talk about women's veiling assumes that concealing attire indexes Muslim women, in the context examined here, men and women often show a similar degree of covering, and both male and female religious figures cover more than other Senegalese. On the other hand, norms of dress are shaped by highly gendered prescriptions of Islamic jurisprudence *(fiqh),* notions of propriety, and local practices. The same degree of bodily wrapping that may be necessary for a woman's performance of piety and authority may seem presumptuous for a man. Yet what indexes gender is not the quantity but the kind and configuration of fabrics (cf Ochs 1992). What male and female leaders' bodily covering shares is the meaningful quality – the "qualisign" – of enclosing or wrapping, even if this quality is interpreted through many discourses and norms.

Although the norm that pious women are to veil according to *sharīʿa* does not effectively compel Senegalese women to do so, one result of the norm is to make it easier for women than men to get away with a highly enclosed Sufi self-presentation. Coulon and Reveyrand imply this iconic relationship between pious feminine interiority and Sufism when they describe Sokhna Magat Diop as closer to the "Sufi model" than most male leaders. They describe her as lacking concern for "outward demonstrations" of authority and instead making her existence "the mirror of an internal world" (1990, 17). As men's covering is less strictly regulated by understandings of *sharīʿa,* men may have more options with respect to how and how much to self-conceal, including the option of going bareheaded. Yet on average, men and women religious leaders contrast more in how than in how much they self-wrap.

Taalibe Baay women leaders' self-wrapping practices and the discourses surrounding them are certainly informed by the global politics of Islam and veiling, including a global Islamic revival perhaps most visibly symbolized by women's veiling (El Guindi 1999; Augis 2009, 2014; Ahmed 2011). What the ubiquitous talk of women's veiling tends to neglect is how its meanings and effects are shaped by their coexistence with other domains of wrapping. My shift to "wrapping" moves beyond the fixation on articles of clothing, women, and concealment to examine a range of wrapping processes that not only conceal but mark, depict, protect, represent, and so on. The authority of Senegalese Taalibe Baay *muqaddama*s is profoundly shaped by their ability to draw iconic connections between pious feminine self-wrapping and wrapping in other domains, such as social prestige and hidden knowledge. These women highlight these iconic connections through their performances of piety and authority. The next two chapters illustrate more specifically how women leaders derive religious authority from the conventionally feminine roles of motherhood and cooking.

Chapter Four

Motherhood Metamorphosis Metaphors

True Myth-Making

Sayyida Moussoukoro Mbaye (figure 4.1) leads a religious association (*daayira*) consisting of several hundred young women and men she, or a *muqaddam* representing her, has initiated into the Fayḍa Tijāniyya Sufi community through spiritual education (*tarbiya*). In addition, she is the official "mother" and spiritual guide of "Dahira des Étudiants Talibés de Baye Niasse" (DETBN), the association representing Taalibe Baay at Dakar's university and other institutions of higher learning. Beyond the Fayḍa Tijāniyya community, she is better known as the face of Établissement Moussoukoro Mbaye, a successful distributor of skin-care products. She has long appeared regularly in her own television advertisements and on popular fashion programs, and more recently she has begun to appear in televised discussions of Islam.

I visited Sayyida Moussoukoro in 2004 at her home, then in the Parcelles Assainies neighbourhood, accompanied by student members of DETBN who were collaborating with me on my research project.[1] During that visit, she welcomed us warmly and sat across from us in her well-appointed living room. A dark, gold-embroidered scarf draped over her shoulders framed her kind face, and her measured and calm voice exuded confidence and gentleness. She told us how, during the late 1990s, she had received written authorization (*ijāza*) from a male religious leader to act as a *muqaddama*, or a spiritual guide representing the Tijānī Sufi order. Although some of her family members knew of her appointment and received spiritual enlightenment through her then, she kept her appointment from public knowledge for several years, she says, until God "revealed" (*feeñal*) her by guiding disciples to her.

Figure 4.1 Sayyida Moussoukoro Mbaye in 2010.

I have continued to visit her over the years and brought my wife to visit her in 2014. During my visits, I have encountered many young disciples at her home who had come to receive *tarbiya,* to attend occasional group litanies, or to prepare for their *daayira*'s upcoming activities. Soon after our first visit in 2004, as her *daayira* grew, she appointed several men from her *daayira* as *muqaddam*s to help initiate new disciples and lead meetings. In 2009, she gave an *ijāza* to her own mother, a clairvoyant who received *tarbiya* from Sayyida Moussoukoro and became a Taalibe Baay only in her old age. When I first met Sayyida Moussoukoro, her disciples – or "spiritual children" as she calls them – would meet weekly at her house for the Friday *ḥaḍra* and to chant the name of God (*dhikr, sikkar*). Her *daayira* soon split into several chapters that met regularly in various neighbourhoods of Dakar rather than in her home. When I visited her in 2009, I found that she had moved to an apartment in the elite Maristes neighbourhood, and since then she has bought her own spacious house there. Since this neighbourhood is remote and is not easily accessible by public transportation, her associated *daayira*s only gather there occasionally for special Friday *ḥaḍra* meetings.

During a visit in 2009, a young man studying at the national nursing school who had accompanied me greeted her and said, "You are our spiritual guide, you are our mother, you are our everything." During a Friday meeting held by the nursing students at her home during the following year, the male *daayira* leader gave a short speech in which he addressed her as "Mama" (*Yaay-bóoy*) and said, "Pray for your children, pray for your disciples."[2] These disciples' words expressed sentiments I found widespread among Taalibe Baay students, who often described her as their spiritual mother, a personal and professional role model, and an exemplar of wisdom and generosity.

During my first interview, I asked Sayyida Moussoukoro whether anyone had ever opposed her playing the typically masculine role of spiritual guide. She shook her head. On the contrary, she answered, prominent male *muqaddam*s often send young people to her to be initiated into the secrets of divine knowledge. She told us that these leaders recognize that, like childbirth, the perilous process of Sufi initiation requires a guide who is naturally inclined to nurture and care for new initiates, as they are most often young people in particular need of guidance. "A *muqaddam* is your spiritual parent," she told me. Other Taalibe Baay *muqaddama*s I met in Dakar unanimously described spiritual leadership as naturally growing out of motherly qualities, and disciples consistently described *muqaddama*s as their spiritual mothers.

One challenge that women leaders like Sayyida Moussoukoro face is that the novelty of their leadership roles provides them with few female models. *Muqaddama*s often employ the ancient Sufi trope equating a spiritually powerful woman to a "man," which allows them to follow in some limited sense paths traced by men. They quote a fatwa by Shaykh Ibrāhīm declaring that the "knower of God" (*'ārif bi'Llāh*) is "the man, feminine or masculine" ([Niasse] 1969, 1:131). They also speak of transcending all distinctions, including gender, through unity with the Divine. Yet these claims are largely limited to the hidden (*bāṭin*) side of spiritual knowledge. In day-to-day matters, no one seems to question that *sharī'a* – the divine law governing social relations and religious practices – still recognizes natural differences between men and women, prescribes contrasting social roles, and requires some degree of gender segregation. Even if mystical truths conditionally abrogate certain distinctions, in matters of visible (*ẓāhir*) kinship relations, norms of sociality and piety, and ritual practice there is no such thing as an unambiguous "honorary man."

While many holy women both within and beyond the Islamic tradition have sought to overcome limitations on women by denying motherhood and wifehood, contemporary Taalibe Baay *muqaddama*s integrate both into their performances of piety and authority. Today it is common for female religious leaders around the world, including Muslims (Alidou 2005; Flueckiger 2006; Schielke 2008) and Christians (Crumbley 1992; A.D. Butler 2007), to be nicknamed "Mother" and to be described in terms of motherhood. Schielke points out that in Egypt, male Sufi leaders are often called "Uncle," while the holy woman he discusses is more intimately called "Mother" (Schielke 2008). For Sayyida Moussoukoro, motherhood is not just a fictive kinship term but provides a highly elaborate "metaphorical concept" (Lakoff and Johnson 1980) for speaking about and enacting religious authority. Such metaphors significantly reconfigure the en-genderment of Islamic authority, nonchalantly picturing historically masculine roles as naturally growing out of women's maternal roles.

Sayyida Moussoukoro told me her spiritual life narrative over several interviews between 2004 and 2014. She was among my most frank and eloquent interviewees, engaging in friendly discussions that sometimes went on for hours and would range over many topics: the influence of television and the Internet on young people; her successful business importing skincare products and clothing; changing social attitudes towards marriage and childrearing; and ways of managing the potential conflicts between these different roles. The theme to which her accounts of herself returned continually was that of motherhood. Her narratives of how she came to be a disciple and religious leader were remarkably focused on her inner religious transformation, referencing others only when they were directly relevant to this experience and completely omitting important life events such as marriage, divorce, and her business activities. During these parts of the discussion, she assumed an oratorical "footing" (Goffman 1981) similar to what I had heard her and other religious leaders take during more public speeches. These personal narratives were organized around a process of metamorphosis from biological to spiritual motherhood.

The resulting story takes the form of a myth, in the sense not of something non-factual but of a coherent narrative that anchors the timely in the timeless, thus "naturalizing" a state of affairs (Barthes 1972). Although Sayyida Moussoukoro plays many, often competing roles (see chapter 5), the underlying binary oppositions, syntagmatic relations, and transpositions displayed in her myth seem to be perfect candidates for Lévi-Strauss's graphical representations of myths (Lévi-Strauss 1963, 1979). Many scholars have noted that autobiography and other forms of self narration, especially narratives of conversion and other spiritual transformations, are mythical performances that contribute to constituting a credible self.[3] Yet Sayyida Moussoukoro's self-narration is mythic on yet another level, not only naturalizing her own authoritative self but naturalizing new metaphors that reconfigure prevalent notions of gender and power more generally. Such metaphors present potentially controversial activities as flowing seamlessly from what has always been.

As important as this mythic narrative's structural elements and metaphors may be, they are only effective as part of a performance of religious authority in relation to a particular set of goals and historical circumstances. Like any communicative action, Sayyida Moussoukoro's narrative is performative, both in John Austin's (1962) sense of creating a social reality through socially recognized utterances and in the theatrical sense of convincingly playing social roles before an audience (Goffman 1959; J. Butler 1988). Her mythic metaphors of leadership as motherhood do not liken two contrasting things but rather establish the two as two names for the same thing, engaging in what Bourdieu calls the ultimate performative speech act – the "power to name" (Bourdieu 1991, 105) – or what Kenneth Burke (1962) calls "entitlement." Motherhood, Sayyida Moussoukoro suggests, is only superficially distinguishable from religious leadership. Her wide acceptance as an effective spiritual guide among young people and the movement's central leadership suggests that her equation is part of a socially effective – or "felicitous," to use John Austin's term – performance. If myth and metaphor, as anthropologists have long maintained, are performative in that they naturalize and uphold a particular social order, then we must consider the telling of new myths and metaphors as meta-performative acts that reconfigure the social order.

In Sayyida Moussoukoro's narrative of metamorphosis from biological motherhood to spiritual motherhood, the pivotal episode is the liminal phase when her mystical state *(ḥāl)* overwhelmed her and negated her conscientious efforts to be a good mother and wife. During this time, she became an anti-mother and anti-wife, dropping out of these roles and instead participating in a *communitas* of "men of God" who would sit for days at a time aware of nothing but God. She emerged as a spiritual mother. Like many conversion and spiritual enlightenment narratives, including dozens of narratives Taalibe Baay have told me, her metamorphosis narrative provides a textbook example of the liminal phase described by Arnold van Gennep (1960) and then Victor Turner (V. Turner 1967, 1995). Yet unlike conversion narratives that describe a passage from abject sin to salvation, her metamorphosis is a more symmetrical, chiastic structure depicting the transubstantiation of one kind of good motherhood into another. This parallelism prepares the hearer to accept women's religious leadership as naturally extending maternal roles inherent to their God-given nature, reversing perceived contradictions between womanhood and religious authority.

By characterizing her narrative as hinging on a metaphor, I do not mean that she intends her claims to "spiritual motherhood" to be taken less than literally. We too often think of metaphor as a "merely" figurative way to liken one thing to something that is actually different. Yet metaphors and other tropes do not merely embellish literal reality but constitute how we experience and practise reality at every level (Whorf 1941; Fernandez 1974, 1991; Lakoff and Johnson 1980). Indeed, the power of metaphors derives from their slippery place between the actual and the imagined, the same and the merely similar.

Metaphors such as those used by Sayyida Moussoukoro can only effectively reconfigure the relationships between motherhood and religious authority if other conditions facilitate a performance's acceptance as felicitous. In Sayyida Moussoukoro's case, these conditions include her skills in speaking and leading, her social and economic connections, as well as a confluence of larger political and economic changes leading to a demand for women's religious leadership. During the period I interviewed her, the Fayḍa Tijāniyya was in the process of transforming itself from a largely rural and stigmatized religious community into a global mass movement attracting especially urban youth looking for moral community and religious self-realization (see chapter 1). Under these conditions, motherhood metaphors have acted as meta-performatives helping to establish not just a single act but a whole new class of acts – women's Islamic leadership of both men and women – as felicitous performances of authority. For women leaders themselves, these metaphors draw not only cognitive but practical connections, applying mothering skills to the exercise of religious authority.

En-Gendering Authority through Metaphor

As I have argued elsewhere, Islamic authority is gendered not only because opportunities to exercise it are gendered but because it is largely imagined through gendered imagery (Frede and Hill 2014; Hill 2014). Whether knowingly or not, Sayyida Moussoukoro reiterates classical Sufi tropes that have for centuries served to humanize the cosmos through gendering it and, in turn, to naturalize gendered social roles through invoking gendered cosmic principles. Such gendered metaphors have long served to concretize intangible Sufi truths and relations of authority among men. Before turning to Sayyida Moussoukoro's narrative, it is worth summarizing these classical Sufi traditions that Senegalese Taalibe Baay both reproduce and modify.

Kinship and reproduction metaphors in classical Sufi literature connect to broader conceptions of masculinity and femininity as opposite, complementary, and omnipresent principles. These principles clearly derive from men's sometimes contradictory ways of experiencing women. On the one hand, women were objects of profound desire and beauty, and one's mother was one's initial source of existence and sustenance. On the other hand, women were understood to play a passive/receptive role in procreation; their overwhelming attraction could lead to a man's downfall; and their reproductive functions (menstruation and childbirth) rendered them weak and ritually impure. Masculinity represented initiative, visibility, penetration, magnificence *(jalāl)*, and the subject of action or desire, while femininity represented passivity, invisibility, receptivity, beauty *(jamāl)*, and the object of action or desire. This may seem to contradict Mernissi's claim, based on Sufi scholar and jurisprudent Al-Ghazālī, that the Islamic tradition construes women as "active" and men as "passive" in matters of sexuality (Mernissi 1987, ch. 1). Aside from the problems with assuming a single Islamic approach to gender (Keddie 2007, 298), what Mernissi presents as women's "active" nature has little to do with what we understand as "agency." If men's preoccupation with women's seductive power makes women "agents," this can only be in the same sense as "chemical agents," their potentially destructive effects construed as arising not from their own intentionality but from the reaction provoked by their mere existence. Thus, even if women's inherent sexual allure was described as acting on men, gendered imagery far more often presented femininity in passive terms, reflecting women's perceived passive roles in sex, reproduction, and other domains, as, for example, in the ubiquitous procreative metaphor of the seed and the soil (Delaney 1991).

While masculine and feminine principles are often presented as complementary and equally necessary, they nonetheless tend to be ranked hierarchically. Yet what is consistent is not that one is ranked above the other but that the feminine is always cast as the "other" – whether exalted or abject – in relation to the masculine "self."[4] Jamal Elias aptly divides these opposing "others" of classical Sufism into the ideal "feminine" and the lower "female." The "feminine" is represented by a few untouchable women – Maryam, Fāṭima, and the mythical beloved who represents God or the Prophet – while actual women are more often depicted as "female," denoting a being whose animal attributes "prevail over her spiritual nature" (Elias 1988, 220). The same opposition is found in European Enlightenment thought – for example, in Goethe's transcendent "eternal feminine," which coexists with fallen temptresses and witches (Goethe 1998).

Drawing on the association between femininity and sublime beauty, Ibn ʿArabī's doctrine of love presents God as the beautiful beloved hidden behind many veils that must be penetrated. Ibn ʿArabī also mobilizes the associations between motherhood and primordial origins – "*umm*" in Arabic can mean both "mother" and "origin," and its derivative "umma" means "nation" or "community." God encompasses everything, including the masculine and feminine principles, yet for Ibn ʿArabī the feminine is the most transcendent creative principle that gives birth to all of existence and encompasses the more immanent masculine principle (Corbin 1969). Sufi poet Rūmī describes the beloved woman as "a ray from God" who is "creative" rather than created (Rūmī 2004, 150). Yet some argue that this exaltation of "the feminine" in the Sufi literature does not accompany heightened respect for actual women. On the contrary, Bouhdiba (1985) argues, the Sufi doctrine of love devalues love for actual women as something to be transcended in favour of union with the transcendent feminine principle.

The same Sufi writers who associate the feminine with the divine also associate effeminacy with passivity, weakness, and animality. Sometimes using overtly phallic imagery, Rūmī presents the spiritually powerful Sufi as a "man" who possesses the spiritual strength to penetrate the veils of ignorance between man and God. His foil is the spiritual "effeminate" *(mukhannath)*,[5] who is incapable of penetrating the veils of spiritual knowledge (Tourage 2007). Yet Rūmī exhorts the Sufi aspirant to seek the transcendent feminine even while fleeing any female attributes in himself. He instructs the aspirant to "court" the Qur'ān and serve it from afar – that is, to obey the outward prescriptions of *sharī'a* – so that, like a bride on her wedding night, it will "show you its face" and allow you to penetrate its inner secrets (Tourage 2005).

Even if feminine and masculine principles are often hierarchized, the classical Sufi literature sometimes calls more attention to their complementarity, which, as Murata (1992) points out, closely resembles the gendered complementarity of yin and yang in Eastern philosophy. Ibn 'Arabī's doctrine of love holds that all of existence is at every moment (en)gendered through the "marriage" of masculine and feminine principles of active creation and passive nurturing. Thus, heaven casts God's commands "into the earth, just as the man casts water into the woman through intercourse" (quoted in Murata 1992, 143).

Medieval Sufi writers depicted shaykh-disciple relationships using elaborate gendered imagery of lineage, penetration, conception, active and passive roles, gestation, birth, nursing, incubation, maternal nurturing, and wifely and filial devotion (Malamud 1996). These texts assumed a male religious subject, yet they depicted both shaykhs and disciples using feminizing and masculinizing metaphors. The actively seeking disciple was sometimes masculinized while the shaykh and God were feminized as objects of desire. The shaykh could also figure as the disciple's mother or wetnurse to emphasize his role as a passive conduit for God's more active, masculine role (Malamud 1996, 96). The same writers might also masculinize the shaykh when highlighting his initiative, his role as "father" of a spiritual lineage, or the absolute obedience due to him from a wifelike or sonlike disciple. Fakhr Al-Dīn Al-Rāzī described himself as his disciples' "Wetnurse" *(Al-Dāyā)*, nurturing disciples on behalf of the Prophet. Yet he also described disciples as his obedient wives. Through transmitting *dhikr*s, the shaykh would impregnate them to conceive the "fruit of sainthood" (quoted in Malamud 1996, 95).

In striking contrast, biographies of early women saints and spiritual guides lack such kinship metaphors (see, for example, the accounts in Ibn Al-Jawzī 1278; Nūrbakhsh 1983; as-Sulamī 1999). Early Muslim Sufi women tended to eschew literal or metaphorical connections to kinship and reproduction. Most remained unmarried, reserving their love and devotion for God only, while the few who did marry presented their marriages as asexual (Nūrbakhsh 1983; Dakake 2007; Silvers 2010). Some even engaged in ascetic practices apparently intended to prevent menstruation and its ritual pollution (Elias 1988). Significantly, both women held up by Islamic scholars as having attained the highest spiritual status, Maryam (Mary) and Fāṭima, gave birth while avoiding these pollutions, the first through virgin birth and the second through escaping menstruation and postpartum bleeding.[6] Reproductive metaphors, then, seem to have been most useful to men, who risked no association with the impurities of female reproduction.

Ancient metaphors return in many forms among Senegalese Fayḍa adherents, both because they resemble concepts already prevalent in Senegal and because of Fayḍa scholars who are familiar with earlier texts. Shaykh Ibrāhīm often quoted Ibn ʿArabī (see, for example, Niasse 2010), filtering the latter's gendered imagery into his disciples' speech.[7] Echoing Ibn ʿArabī's concept of the "creative feminine" (Corbin 1969), some Taalibe Baay *muqaddams* describe the Prophet Muḥammad's transcendent hidden reality *(Ḥaqīqa Muḥammadiyya)* as a feminine principle. In response to my suggestion that some people underestimate women, Sayyida Ndèye Maguète Niang told me that "woman represents the Muḥammadan Reality."[8] She explained that existence depends on Muḥammad's mystical Reality or Light in the same way that a foetus depends on its mother, or that a mango, once fertilized, ripens on a female tree. Muḥammad's hidden being is thus the mother of existence, whose sustenance depends on the female principle.

I encountered the gendered heaven/earth relationship articulated by Ibn ʿArabī when I attended a *gàmmu* in 2014 presided over by Baay Sokhna, a *muqaddam* of Baay whose name, it happens, can be translated literally as "Father Woman/Wife." The man introducing the *muqaddam* offered an esoteric reverse etymology of the *muqaddam*'s name:

> Baay Sokhna's being includes father [*baay*, which here also invokes Shaykh Ibrāhīm] in it, and it includes woman [*soxna*] ... The father is the heaven, whereas the woman is the earth. Everything is encompassed between

> those two. What the man preaches [i.e., all-encompassing mystical reality] resembles him.

Both in interviews with me and in speeches to disciples, I have often heard Sayyida Moussoukoro herself declare that everything in existence is the result of "marriage" or "coupling" (*séy*). As we spoke, she told me, the sound of her voice was coupling with my ear, while the rays of light were coupling with our eyes. Everything happens through that complementarity, which is why God has ordained complementarity between men's and women's roles. Although her performance of authority embodies the transcendent feminine through her emphasis on spiritual motherhood, she continues to speak of the masculine principle as the spark of *élan vital* that projects the cosmos and the human microcosmos forward. In a speech to nursing students in 2010, she fused this ancient complementarity with the scientific principles her auditors were studying:[9]

> The human being [child of Adam] originates in initiative. Those of you who study *medicine*, on the day the *couple couples*, when the *sperm* scatter and run, they are racing, they are jostling, they are rushing, Each one says "It's me! it's me! it's me!" When it *seizes* and takes hold, it starts to *express* itself. It has *eliminated* all the others. This one, he's the victorious one. That [desire for] victory is what is in every human being [child of Adam]. That's why everyone has his/her *"me."* Everyone has his/her own *fingerprints*. No one is like any other. Each one is unique. God is unique. And when the human being is born and lies in the *cradle*, its initiative is to sit. When he sits, what does he want? To go crawl. When he crawls what does he want? To walk. When he walks what does he want? To run. When he runs what does he want? He wants to know where, and even when he was born, he wants to *discover*, wants to know. Any moment you see a baby, he'll show you something new. Every day he'll show you a new action. He's just *expressing* himself. Thus we continue, we continue, we continue, we continue, which is why the *nurse* sitting and facing me now, when he was a baby lying in the *cradle*, where was his *nurse* [current self]? He was there sleeping. He just hadn't appeared. Thus is the being *(jëmm)* of God and the Prophet.

Thus, every stage of human life is defined by the masculine initiative to know and become, which is represented at its most atomic and originary moment in the sperm that strives to become the human being. This atomic representation of active masculinity, as in many Western medical descriptions (Martin 1991), is an active force that "seizes and takes hold." This masculine principle of initiative, the unique will to realize and express the self, is what makes each human unique. Ultimately, the *élan vital* of the tiny sperm that originates human life through a female medium is the same principle as the all-encompassing initiative of God, who creates through the medium of the Prophet.

A few years before this speech, in 2004, I had heard another *muqaddam* in Medina Baay, Doudou Bitèye, similarly invoke semen as representing the divine principle of creative initiative. He described the dot under the first letter of the Qur'ān (*bā'*, ب) as representing the primordial drop of semen that penetrates the second letter (*sīn*, س) to give birth to the third letter (*mīm*, م), which stands for Muḥammad, the light from which God created all other things. Muḥammad's name takes the shape of a human (محمد), because humans are the one creation that encompasses the rest of creation. (I have discussed this account in more detail in Hill 2014.) For Sayyida Moussoukoro, Sayyida Ndèye Maguète Niang, and this *muqaddam*, gender is not a culture-bound interpretation of subtle biological variations. Rather, gender is a metaphysical principle of complementarity that integrates every scale of existence, from microscopic particles and dots on letters to the human being and, ultimately, to the complementary forces behind the universe's creation and sustenance.

The social consequences of this metaphysical observation, as is often the case in Sufism, are ambiguous and open to interpretation. On a *bāṭin* level, all beings contain both masculine and feminine principles, and thus metaphors that masculinize and feminize the same person need not be understood as contradictory. Yet on a *ẓāhir* level, one never transcends one's gender, for gender complementarity is hardwired into God's law *(sharī'a)*, which governs day-to-day life.

While these discourses of gender largely elaborate on imagery found in early Sufi texts, which generally assumed a male subject, Taalibe Baay use kinship and procreation metaphors to describe both men and women. The central kinship metaphor in the Fayḍa, of course, is that of Shaykh Ibrāhīm himself, described as "Baay" ("Father"). Yet narratives also commonly describe Baay as his disciples' milk mother. Accounts of Baay's mother, Maam Astou Diankha, asking for *tarbiya* sometimes discursively reverse her generational and gender relationship with Baay. Sayyida Ndèye Maguète Niang described her as telling him, "This spiritual knowledge (*xam-xamu ma'rifa*) that you have brought, Baay [Father] – that is what I want to suckle from."[10] Others describe her as asking Baay if she, too, should call him "Baay," to which he reportedly answered, "I am the father of all creatures."[11] *Sikkarkat* Baye Amadi Diouf alludes to this statement in a song praising Maam Astou Diankha: "Astou gave birth to the father of [all] creatures"[12] (A. Diouf 2004). Shaykh Ibrāhīm's closest companion, ʿAlī Cissé, reportedly described himself as absolutely obedient to Shaykh Ibrāhīm as a wife is to her husband (Hill 2014). As we have seen above, all of these kinship metaphors were widely applied to shaykhs in early Sufism. Yet Taalibe Baay use these metaphors in particular ways.

First, the fatherhood metaphor tends to be reserved for Baay himself. Disciples may refer to the *muqaddam* who gave them *tarbiya* as the one who "raised" (*yar*) them, but they rarely refer to him as their spiritual "father," a role occupied by Baay. Other prominent leaders' names are affectionately accompanied with titles of a similar meaning, whether "Baay" itself (especially leaders of Baay's generation) or "Pàppa" (especially those of the next generation). Yet, as I have heard many leaders say, "There is only one Baay." Many disciples refer to the *muqaddam* they follow as "Baay," yet when I have asked them about this they have always explained that it was because their *muqaddam* manifests Baay to them. Similarly, some Taalibe Baay may refer to Baay as "our Prophet" (*suñu Yónent*), yet once again this is a proper noun that means that Baay is not *a* prophet but manifests *the* Prophet, Muḥammad.

While a household has room for only one father, multiple female leaders can be imagined as mothers in their own right, especially in a context of widespread polygyny. Where Senegalese Taalibe Baay *muqaddama*s differ radically from early Sufi women is that they invariably present themselves as spiritual mothers. As the narratives in chapter 2 show, they distance themselves from biological reproduction yet simultaneously present spiritual leadership as a transposition of maternal roles. Shaykha Maryam Niasse surrounds herself with children, emphasizing her motherly persona, even while presenting herself as a "spiritual man." Indeed, these *muqaddama*s tend to infer from the metaphysical doctrine of marriage that motherhood is an inescapable part of a woman's destiny and piety. Thus, Sayyida Moussoukoro told me that, while she looked up to the early Sufi saint Rābiʿa al-ʿAdawiyya as a spiritual role model, she could not emulate her in every respect because Rābiʿa saw her relationship with God as excluding the divinely ordained roles of wifehood and motherhood.

Here I turn to Sayyida Moussoukoro's self-narrative to show how literal and metaphorical motherhood fit into her performance of feminine

Islamic authority. I stress that, in identifying claims of "spiritual motherhood" as metaphorical, I am not reducing these claims to mere figures of speech. Since language is constitutive and not merely referential, to highlight a deeper *(bāṭin)* shared quality between things of different apparent *(ẓāhir)* categories profoundly changes those things as phenomena, making them differently intelligible and accessible.

Motherhood

Sayyida Moussoukoro was born in 1960 in Kaolack, where Shaykh Ibrāhīm lived and is now buried. Her father was a prominent businessman and a disciple of Shaykh Ibrāhīm, and her parents established a close relationship with the shaykh despite her mother's formal membership in a different Sufi group. Her mother told me that when she was pregnant with Sayyida Moussoukoro the couple visited Baay. He gave her an amulet, telling her to wear it until the child was born and then to tie it to the new baby. She did so, and on the night of the *gàmmu (mawlid)*, her newborn came down with a cold and turned a glowing white, and since then she knew that Baay had "done something to her." Since then, her mother says, Sayyida Moussoukoro "sees nothing except Baay."

Sayyida Moussoukoro did not herself mention this episode, although she did describe feeling an inexplicable love for Shaykh Ibrāhīm even during the decade when she played a leading role in an anti-Sufi Islamic reform movement. She married a conservative reformist Muslim in 1974 at the age of fourteen, had her first child at sixteen, and had her seventh and final child at thirty-one. She describes her early motherhood as "good fortune" *(chance)* because it allowed her to finish raising her family early and to devote the rest of her life to religious and business pursuits. Her early marriage led her to leave her secular and religious studies. Her husband encouraged her to pursue an informal education at home, although he forbade her from working and studying outside the home. While raising her family, she studied at home to earn her high school equivalency diploma and went on to join a program by correspondence in typing and medical secretaryship.

When she finished her correspondence program in 1980, just after having her third child, she wanted to work in an office, but her husband forbade it. So, she says, "I stayed home but I didn't just sit … *All that time* I was *cultivating* myself wherever I was." Looking back, she says she does not regret staying home and focusing her thirst for knowledge on learning things that would make her a more effective mother, for if she had worked outside the home, "perhaps my children would not have had the *education* they have today." She read voraciously, especially books of child and family psychology, and strove to apply what she was learning about childrearing.

Every Friday morning after the daybreak prayer, Sayyida Moussoukoro held "self-critique" sessions with her own seven children along with, over the years, thirteen other children sent by relatives and acquaintances for to her to raise. During these sessions, each person would take a turn listening as everyone else told what he or she had done well or badly over the previous week, and each had to accept responsibility and commit to doing better. She says she never resorted to corporal punishment or found the children fighting with one another. She treated the children with such fairness and equality that her neighbour of six years, a Lebanese woman, stopped her one day and asked, "Ma'am, which ones are your own, the light ones or the dark ones?" Sayyida Moussoukoro replied, "Why do you ask, Mother?" The woman answered, "I've seen that the darker ones cling to you more; the lighter ones look like you; and they all say *'Mother.'*" Sayyida Moussoukoro replied – clearly speaking of effect rather than fact – that she had borne all of them.

In 1987 the family hired a Qurʾānic teacher to come to the house to give her and her children private lessons on the Qurʾān and other Islamic topics. Up until that point she had had little Qurʾānic education. She says all she knows about Arabic and the Qurʾān she learned as an adult. Although she cannot write or converse in Arabic, she says, "Whatever you say I can understand." She has memorized many passages from Arabic religious texts that she regularly quotes and comments on in Wolof during interviews and speeches to disciples. She sums up this time of home education saying that she spent all this time "at home, getting pregnant, having children. *But* I was studying *all along* – I always wanted *to cultivate* [myself] and study ... *but* I have never, never accepted just *staying at home*, just to take care of children, go to sleep, eat, sit – *no, no*. From the day I was born I have never accepted that."

Sayyida Moussoukoro began her informal Islamic education during a period when, from 1983 to 1992, she was active in the Islamic reform movement Jamāʿat ʿIbādu ar-Raḥmān ("Association of Servants of the Merciful"), known in Wolof as the *ibaadu* movement, in which her husband had become involved. Although members of this movement oppose Sufism as a blasphemous innovation, she now portrays her life and beliefs during this period in largely positive terms, describing the people she knew as close friends and the beliefs she held as largely consistent with her beliefs today. As someone who had always been intensely curious and religious, Moussoukoro embraced the *ibaadu* community, which encouraged her to seek knowledge, to perfect herself as a Muslim woman, and to preach and lead. She describes both her husband and herself as "leaders" (*kilifa*) in their local *ibaadu* community and as close friends of the chapter's director and his wife. She was often asked to speak at their meetings.[13] She described taking a theme, such as "women and *education* in Islam," quoting the Qurʾān, *ḥadīth,* and Arabic sayings – for example, "The woman is the first school in life" – which she would gloss into Wolof and illustrate. After she recalled to me the kinds of things she taught in such a speech about women, motherhood, and education, she agreed with me that it sounded much like what she teaches today.

Yet she describes being powerfully and increasingly drawn to Shaykh Ibrāhīm even while active in this movement. She says, "You cannot avoid your *destiny* … You reach a point where you yourself don't know what is *motivating* you. God himself is *guiding* you." In 1982, a year before joining the *ibaadu* movement, she already felt inexplicably drawn towards Shaykh Ibrāhīm. She went to Kaolack to attend the large Medina Baay *ziyāra* (Ar.; Wol. *siyaare*) meeting. When she entered Shaykh Ibrāhīm's mausoleum, "without knowing what I was crying about … I cried until my heart was calm and then came home [to Dakar]. I didn't know what it was." Even during her *ibaadu* period, if she ever visited her parents in Kaolack and did not go to the Medina Baay mosque for Friday prayer and to visit Baay's mausoleum, she would feel guilty.

Metamorphosis

After many such experiences, Sayyida Moussoukoro developed a consuming desire to take the Tijānī *wird*. In 1992, she approached Ustādh Ibrāhīm Maḥmūd "Barhām" Diop (d. 2014), a close friend of her mother and eminent Taalibe Baay leader whom she describes as her uncle (*nijaay*), and asked him to give her the *wird*. He recommended that she instead seek the *wird* from the person with the highest authority to give it, the imam of Medina Baay, Shaykh Ḥasan Cissé. He had his daughter take Sayyida Moussoukoro to the imam, who gave her the *wird*. She returned to Dakar and told her husband that she had received the *wird*.

Stunned, he asked why *("Pourquoi?")*, and she answered, "'Because it pleases me – my heart wants it. I don't know what it is.' *Thus the war began* (Fr.). [pause] *Praise God* (Ar. *Al-ḥamdu li-Llāh)*." Although she says she now has a good relationship with her then-husband and other members of her former religious community, at the time things were difficult for everyone. Members of the community would push her husband to intervene, telling him she was "ascribing equals to God, that [she] had left the Sunna, that [she] was in a state of *shirk* [Ar. idolatry]."

Taking the Tijānī *wird* was only the first step in quenching Sayyida Moussoukoro's spiritual thirst, and she continued to visit the movement's leaders in Kaolack. During one visit, a son of Shaykh Ibrāhīm asked her to deliver a letter to a disciple who directed a transport company in Dakar. Four disciples accompanied her to the recipient's office, where the recipient "just started talking about Baay. He talked about Baay, talked about God, and just kept talking and ended up crying." The fact that he would allow himself to speak so openly and cry in front of business associates *"impressed"* her and she herself began to cry. At that moment "a mystical state entered [her]" (*ḥāl dugg ma*). The director asked her companions if they had gone through *tarbiya*, and they all said yes. She answered that she considered herself a disciple of Baay but had not done *tarbiya*. Taken aback, the man said he had assumed from her speech that she was a "knower of God" (Ar. *'ārif bi-Llāh*).[14] It pained her when he told her, "then you are not a 'Taalibe Baay'; you're just a *sympathizer* [Fr.]." Immediately, she could think of nothing other than receiving *tarbiya*.

This was the beginning of a mystical state (*ḥal*) lasting anywhere from five to seven years – she says she lost track of time but she usually describes it as five years. During that time, Sayyida Moussoukoro was "burning hot" (Wol. *tàng jirr*) and "no one could talk to [her]," including her husband and children. That her accounts of this period sometimes seem contradictory may reflect her state of mind at that time. Her friends and family often found her crying inexplicably. She had asked Barhām Diop to help her find someone to give her *tarbiya*, but he went on a trip to Morocco before being able to do so. A Taalibe Baay friend came to visit Sayyida Moussoukoro and asked her why she was crying. She answered that she needed to have *tarbiya* and know God. Her friend took her to see the itinerant and reclusive tailor and *muqaddam* Babacar (Mbaye) Bitèye.

Mbaye Bitèye was the only *muqaddam* widely known to give *tarbiya* in Dakar during the 1970s and early 1980s. He initiated hundreds, including many future male and female leaders of the Fayḍa in Dakar (see chapters 1 and 2). When Sayyida Moussoukoro did her *tarbiya* with Mbaye Bitèye in 1992, he was working in central Dakar out of Shaykha Maryam Niasse's house, which still has a tailor's shop today. Sayyida Moussoukoro had hoped that *tarbiya* would bring her peace and calm, yet knowing God only opened up more questions and put her in a state of even greater perplexity. Mbaye Bitèye was a "man of God, a Sufi [Wol. *suufiyanke*]" who shunned attention to the point that "whenever he stayed someplace long enough that people started gathering around him, he would move." If you came to him, he would give you *tarbiya*, then "he would be finished with you." She came out of her *tarbiya* "mixed up" (*jaxasoo*), in need of being "fixed" (Fr. *réglée*), and continuing to feel an "intense thirst."

Not getting what she needed from her *shaykh tarbiya*, Sayyida Moussoukoro "visited the men of God" to pursue her *sayr* (spiritual progression). During this period, a frenzied *ḥāl* would often "captivate" (Fr. *capter*) her. A question about the nature of God would occur to her and she could not rest until "someone who had more knowledge than me about that" resolved her question. During these stretches, she would not eat, drink, sleep, or use the bathroom. Instead, she says, she would sit in her room feverishly reciting the *Ṣalāt al-Fātiḥ*, first five thousand times a day, then ten thousand, and finally fifty thousand times a day. Her mother, daughters, and nieces all recall keeping her company and supporting her during what she describes as "extremely difficult times" but being unable to communicate with her. Sayyida Moussoukoro alternates between describing this time as a time of "great anguish" and a time of "serenity" *(sérénité)* despite what appeared as anguish to others.

While she was in her "mixed up" spiritual state, one *muqaddam* she had frequented for spiritual instruction had a week-long *dhikr* retreat at his home, and she attended the closing session with a group of university students she had befriended. She told me: "[The host] saw me in that hot *ḥāl* that I was experiencing, with that *love (maḥabba), passion (shawq)* that I was experiencing, and he gave me an *ijāza*." In our first interview she told us that she kept her appointment secret for years before agreeing to give *wird* or *tarbiya*, and in a later interview she reiterated, "that *ijāza* did not make me to go off and say I'm going to go *tarbiya* someone"; instead she kept visiting the men of God to expand her spiritual knowledge. Yet in a later interview, when I mentioned her earlier statements about waiting to give *tarbiya*, she said, "Actually, those were the days I gave *wird* most," along with *tarbiya*. Indeed, she describes being in such a state that someone only had to touch her to attain *fatḥ*.[15]

Sayyida Moussoukoro's narratives about this period almost completely abandoned any talk of motherhood, which she continually referenced when we discussed nearly any other topic. Her only references to motherhood in connection with this liminal phase have to do with her inability to be a mother and, in later interviews, the presence of certain daughters (biological and foster) at her side supporting her through this difficult time, reversing the direction of nurturing. She told of losing her ability to act as both mother and wife, roles she normally described as being her highest priorities. During our first interview with her in 2004, she recounted sleeping alone for at least five years on a thin mattress on the floor of her bedroom. In later interviews she clarified that her husband, trying to correct what he considered rebellious behaviour, had become furious, had removed all the furniture from her room, and had ceased to spend the night there.[16] She says:

> He tried by every *means*! But it seemed that the *means* that he *applied* just made me stronger. Because you know, when you come to fear God you no longer fear someone God created. You only fear God. And God becomes your *security*, he becomes your support.

Sayyida Moussoukoro's husband pressured her for at least five years to give up her mystical pursuits and resume her duties as wife and mother, but she was beyond his or her children's reach and "loved nothing but God."[17] He divorced her, and she moved back in with her mother, who had been by her side during this process and would herself soon take *tarbiya* from her, another case of spiritual reversal and transfiguration of biological relationships. Sayyida Moussoukoro repeatedly told us that she did not blame her husband and that he has since come to respect her path.

A friend took her to see a *muqaddam* named Al-Ḥājj Aada Kundul who would sit daily to help disciples with their *sayr* at his corner store next to Shaykha Maryam Niasse's house after late afternoon prayer (Wol. *tàkkusaan;* Ar. *ʿaṣr).* This *muqaddam* "fixed" *(régler)* her one day "between the late afternoon and sunset prayers."[18] Being "fixed" in a single afternoon did not stop her from continuing her *wird* sessions with the "men of God." She would sit at the *muqaddam*'s store with other disciples, sometimes for twenty-four hours at a time, pronouncing *wirds* without any of them feeling the need to eat, drink, sleep, or even use the restroom.

Metaphors

Over numerous interviews, Sayyida Moussoukoro consistently came back to the metaphor of the *muqaddam* as mother, the new disciple (*taalibe*) as a baby, *tarbiya* as a gestation process leading to spiritual birth through the *muqaddam*, and continued spiritual progression *(sayr)* as a child's upbringing. The *muqaddam* who gives you *tarbiya*, she told me, is "your *bāṭin* parent."[19] She habitually referred to those she had guided through *tarbiya* as her *"spiritual children"* (Fr. *enfants spirituels*). During her liminal phase, and before receiving authorization *(ijāza)* to birth her own spiritual children, Sayyida Moussoukoro tells of being designated as a spiritual foster parent for disciples spiritually born elsewhere.

In 1994, shortly after Sayyida Moussoukoro's *tarbiya*, a group of university students approached her for help. These young men had invited a senior son of Shaykh Ibrāhīm, Shaykh Nadhīr, to deliver the speech at their inaugural university *gàmmu*. When they asked her to prepare a special meal for him, she gladly accepted. When she presented the meal to Shaykh Nadhīr, he said to her,

> "I entrust you with this family of Baay at the University. I must tell you, though, that accompanying student disciples is difficult, because a student disciple owns nothing and has many needs." He said, "But I tell you that you will see the day when you become the mother of the doctors, the mother of the engineers, the mother of the presidents, the mother of ministers, the mother of ambassadors." He told me, "You will see a time that will be very pleasant. However, the journey will be difficult."[20]

Ever since, Taalibe Baay students at the university, and eventually at Dakar's other institutions of higher learning, have called her "Mother" and have held occasional meetings in her home. She confirmed that Shaykh Nadhīr's prediction has come to pass. During earlier interviews in 2004 and 2005, she told us that although disciples sometimes brought her small monetary offerings (*àddiya*), she spent far more of her own money to help struggling students with their problems. In an interview in 2010, she said that now whenever she goes out to take care of paperwork, almost always "there is someone there who recognizes me and comes and says, 'You were my mother when I was in the student *daayira*'" and takes care of whatever she needs. If she is sick, she says, she does not need to go see a doctor. Instead, some doctor who used to be a member of the students' *daayira* will visit her and someone else will buy any prescribed medicines.

Sayyida Moussoukoro presents her own difficult *tarbiya* as a cautionary tale showing the need for a more methodical approach that gives disciples the right amount of spiritual guidance at the right time so they "neither ruin or get ruined." Another *muqaddam* helped her develop a methodical system for guiding a disciple through *tarbiya* "without ruining him/her."

On the one hand, such maternal metaphors are unsurprising in Senegal, where people refer to any elder as "mother," "father," "aunt," "uncle," or "grandparent." Yet Sayyida Moussoukoro's motherhood metaphors go far beyond suggesting fictive kinship to draw highly specific parallels between spiritual guidance and childbirth and childrearing. Both culturally and biologically, a mother is not just a female father, and Sayyida Moussoukoro's metaphors suggest that women are not only capable of spiritual guidance but are in fact uniquely suited to it because it is identical to motherhood but not to fatherhood.

The period during and immediately following *tarbiya*, she told us, is a most perilous time for disciples spiritually, and if a *muqaddam* does not continue to guide disciples and help them channel their knowledge in productive ways, it is as if they "just gave birth and threw away" (*jur rekk sànni*) the child. She often used the term "born" to describe attaining *fatḥ* through *tarbiya:* "As I have *always* told you, the disciple, *as long as*, when he/she has just been born into the community [of those who know God], he/she is at the level of drinking milk. You know, whoever is at the level of drinking milk, if you give him/her a piece of meat, if they choke you've brought him/her a problem." This problem of giving disciples the appropriate dose of spiritual knowledge for their particular state so as not to damage them is a central problem that she has sought to resolve through developing an increasingly methodical approach to giving *tarbiya*. She at first gave limited authorization *(ijāza muqayyada)* to her son and another disciple so that, by delegating some of the spiritual guidance duties to them, she could make the process more collaborative and systematic. In a striking parallel to her Friday meetings with her biological and foster children, she meets every Wednesday with these apprentice *muqaddam*s to "fix" *(régler)* new initiates, discussing their progress and making sure they are getting the right dose of spiritual instruction.

The connections Sayyida Moussoukoro draws between being a mother and being a *muqaddama* and between giving birth and giving *tarbiya* go much further than the common practice of addressing any esteemed elder as "Mother" or "Father." Like mystical Sufi discourses more generally, her talk of spiritual motherhood walks a thin line between the metaphorical and the literal. Once, as we discussed the possibility of a disciple's "making up" (Wol. *sos*) an ostentatious display of ecstasy (Ar. *jadhb*), Sayyida Moussoukoro explained that "those who know what a *ḥāl* is" know whether "it's a real *ḥāl*" or whether a disciple "is trying to put on *his/her show (cinéma)*." More particularly, a *muqaddam* can tell when a disciple undergoing *tarbiya* is merely pretending to reach *fatḥ*. She explained as follows, with what seemed more than a metaphor to her:

> AM: Can a child be born in its mother's absence? Have you ever heard of such a thing?
> JH: (laughing) can be born in its mother's absence?
> AM: Hmm? Have you ever heard of that? …
> JH: (laughing) I've never heard that.
> AM: Its father was travelling and the child was born in his absence, we've heard that one.
> JH: Yes, that can be.
> AM: But the mother was travelling and the child was born in her absence, that has never happened. So, could you be born while I, who carried you, am not aware that you were born? That's impossible! I would tell you, "Take your prayer beads and go back! Stop putting on your *show* and go *wird*! If God is really what interests you, go and don't hurry. It will come."

She then explained that during *tarbiya*, the *muqaddam* literally feels the disciple's spiritual state *(ḥāl)*, because this state is literally passing through the *muqaddam* like electricity and then to the disciple. (Electricity is another metaphor that she sometimes used to describe spiritual energy.) When she first started giving *tarbiya*, the *ḥāl* that came through her when a disciple reached *fatḥ* was so powerful that she would have to go and lie down in her bedroom, she says, "because I could not withstand it myself. And whenever that *ḥāl* comes, that person has *fatḥ*. So whatever comes to him/her goes through you [the *muqaddam*] in order to go down to him/her." She only gradually learned to "control" *(maîtriser)* this. The striking similarities between the physically incapacitating experience of giving spiritual birth and the labour pains of childbirth, which Sayyida Moussoukoro experienced seven times, are surely not accidental.

Her description of literally acting as the medium through which disciples are spiritually born draws on but reconfigures a long tradition of Sufi literature dealing with the transmission of mystical knowledge. Both male and female Taalibe Baay *muqaddams*, referring to the same tradition, describe *tarbiya* as effective not just through the disciple's repetition of *wirds* but through the emanation of the shaykh's (in this case Shaykh Ibrāhīm's) spiritual energy *(himma)* and mystical state *(ḥāl)* (see Seesemann 2011, 79–81). I never heard male *muqaddams* describe *tarbiya* in terms of such an intimate spiritual connection that might be compared to giving birth. Yet when I mentioned the parallel to a son of Shaykh Ibrāhīm, he told me that the comparison made sense, as the *muqaddam* might feel Baay's spiritual energy flowing to the disciple.

Motherhood metaphors are not just feminine versions of fatherhood metaphors but suggest different attributes and relationships. In Wolof traditional thought, one inherits certain things from one's father, especially one's lineage identity, public status, and hard tissue. Yet other things, like moral qualities, more nurturing personal relationships, and soft tissue, come from one's mother (Diop 1985). As Sayyida Moussoukoro's own difficult experience with *tarbiya* and her consequent emphasis on nurturing illustrate, she sees mothers as particularly nurturing and able to guide these overwhelmingly young disciples. With its labour pains, giving *tarbiya* is like a woman giving birth but is not like a father procreating. Partly for the sake of unity and partly because of how *tarbiya* is understood to work, a prevalent discourse insists that all Taalibe Baay are directly disciples and spiritual children of Baay, not distant spiritual descendants through the chain of *muqaddams*. A *muqaddam* administers *tarbiya*, but Baay is said to be directly responsible for all disciples' *fatḥ*, and many leaders fastidiously avoid suggesting that those they initiate are "their" disciples. Sayyida Moussoukoro can much more easily claim to be her disciples' parent than a male *muqaddam* can, because claiming to be their spiritual mother does not challenge Baay's role as spiritual father.

Another striking parallel between Sayyida Moussoukoro's description of motherhood before her *tarbiya* and her spiritual motherhood afterwards is that both included both her own progeny and foster children who were "entrusted" to her. Her kin and acquaintances brought

Biological motherhood   Spiritual motherhood

Foster motherhood   Spiritual foster motherhood

Liminality/metamorphosis

Figure 4.2 Chiastic structure of Sayyida Moussoukoro's motherhood metamorphosis.

their children to her to raise, and her neighbour could not tell the difference between them; and Shaykh Ibrāhīm's son entrusted her "with this family of Baay at the university," which forms one larger *daayira* in addition to the *daayira* of disciples she has personally initiated.

Embodied Tropes

Although this retelling of Sayyida Moussoukoro's life narrative is a composite assembled from numerous conversations over ten years, it reflects a mythic story persisting more or less intact behind every telling of her story. While we often discussed mundane topics in more conversational registers, her life narrative consistently returned to a mythic register centred on motherhood as an alibi for her performance of what many around her assume to be men's roles. The shift into a mythical register and time-space is significant in that it naturalizes her leadership in terms of apparently timeless ideas. Yet even more, these mythic metaphors provide a charter not only for her own performance of self but also for a whole new category of women's leadership.

Sayyida Moussoukoro's narrative coalesces into a chiastic mythic structure (although no single telling of her story took on that structure in a linear fashion) that presents two parallel yet in some ways opposite periods in her life marked by two contrasting forms of motherhood (see figure 4.2). During a liminal phase between these two parts, her motherhood role negates itself: she becomes incapable of being a good mother, is supported by her own daughters, and gives spiritual birth to her own mother (along with her daughters). This liminal phase transfigures her from a biological mother – she has finished childbearing at this point – into a spiritual mother who in many details parallels her earlier self as a biological and foster mother. As both biological and spiritual mother, she develops a systematic way of teaching, has many of her own (biological and spiritual) children, and because of her reputation for nurturing young people, is entrusted with an even greater number of other people's children. Just as she becomes a foster mother to the children of relatives, she later becomes a spiritual foster mother to university students who have already been initiated by other *muqaddams*.

Up to here, my point may sound like a structuralist one, and indeed her story may seem to confirm cross-cultural claims of organizing binary oppositions and liminality. Whether or not Sayyida Moussoukoro is consciously aware of organizing her own experience according to these forms, at some level it is undeniable that the structure of her narrative is extremely effective in highlighting the parallels – not unknown before her but rarely mobilized on behalf of women – between motherhood and Sufi religious authority. Certainly, presenting her experience according to this metaphor heightens her narrative's rhetorical persuasiveness.

Yet what may look like a primarily rhetorical strategy, I would argue, arises more from what some have called "motherhood as experience" (Rich 1977; Nnaemeka 1997). Sayyida Moussoukoro's transposition of motherhood into the field of religious authority works largely because she has implicitly recognized its fit with her long, embodied experience with motherhood. Moreover, others have recognized her conscientious mothering as a potentially important skill in an urban environment where many young people live far from their families and need maternal guidance. In short, one of the many conditions of Sayyida Moussoukoro's felicitous performance of religious authority is the fact that both she and others implicitly recognize the practical similarities between what mothers do and the responsibilities of spiritual leadership today. As the following chapter discusses, similarly to motherhood, Sayyida Moussoukoro and other women leaders mobilize their ability to cook to demonstrate their religious devotion and their leadership skills as they organize cooking for leaders and large religious events.

Chapter Five

Cooking Up Spiritual Leadership

While biographical details about Senegalese *muqaddamas* appointed by Shaykh Ibrāhīm are scarce, it is striking that nearly all accounts mention their involvement in acts of devotional cooking. I once asked Shaykh Ibrāhīm's daughter Shayhka Maryam Niasse to tell me what she knew about women her father had appointed as *muqaddamas*. The first example she mentioned was a woman in Kaolack – whose name she could not recall – who had often cooked sumptuous meals for Shaykh Ibrāhīm. Like most of the women Shaykh Ibrāhīm appointed, this woman seems not to have acted openly as a spiritual guide during his lifetime. Several other interviewees described four *muqaddamas* in the village of Darou Mbitéyène near the beginning of the Fayḍa as spiritual guides who gave *tarbiya* to women. These women had distinguished themselves through organizing women to cook lunch for Shaykh Ibrāhīm and for fellow disciples on work days in Shaykh Ibrāhīm's fields. These women's appointments only make sense if we understand devotional cooking as a deeply religious practice for many Senegalese Taalibe Baay women. The two previous chapters foregrounded how women leaders consecrate conventionally feminine practices such as self-wrapping, submissiveness, and motherhood as grounds for religious authority. To that list, this chapter adds cooking, which becomes a devotional activity for nearly all Fayḍa women at some time. For some women, devotional cooking becomes an investment in "religious capital" (Bourdieu 1971) that results in formal or informal religious authority.

Commensality and culinary offerings are central to Taalibe Baay activities. Likewise, one could hardly overstate the importance of cooking to Taalibe Baay women's religious sociality and devotional practice. Even the highest-profile and highest-status women value participating in this devotional act, to which they attribute great material and spiritual rewards. Most currently active Taalibe Baay women participate in devotional cooking during major religious events such as *gàmmus*. Some also do so throughout the year for religious leaders. Although younger women perform most of the manual food preparation for large religious gatherings, older women remain involved through contributing financially to food offerings, procuring ingredients, and supervising the cooking. When a woman says she "cooked" a meal, the extent of her physical involvement in preparing it is often ambiguous. However, as the story of Diarra Ndiaye and Astou Diop below illustrates, even older and higher-status women often insist on physically participating in cooking as an act of religious devotion, even if the same women are also entrepreneurs who contributed significantly to purchasing the ingredients. In contrast, when organizing a family-centred gathering, many of the same women delegate cooking to paternal cross-cousins (jokingly referring to them as their "slaves") or to griot clients.[1] Still, throughout this chapter, one should keep in mind that women's narrations of "cooking" may refer ambiguously not just to physically cooking but also to organizing the labour of junior women.

Producing and sharing food, of course, is of great importance in many religious traditions, including in Sufi Islam more broadly. In Cairo, for example, some male and female Sufi adepts organize *khidma*s ("services"), spaces that provide food, drink, and shelter to pilgrims and passersby, whether permanently or during periodic *mawlid* gatherings. Amira Mittermaier has shown how *khidma*s provide "a taste of alternative modes of togetherness," embodying an "ethics of immediacy" (2014, 55). During Taalibe Baay *mawlid* (*gàmmu*) events, every Taalibe Baay home in the vicinity becomes a *khidma*, welcoming honoured leaders, *daayira*s, and a stream of anonymous pilgrims. The women who organize meals at such events thus invite a liminal moment of "pure possibility" for an undifferentiated "communitas" of known and unknown disciples (V. Turner 1995). Yet they also present special offerings to religious leaders, who are in a sense proxies for Baay and ultimately for God. They thus uphold a hierarchy of religious authority while earning divine blessings and potentially even a place for themselves in that hierarchy.

After introducing the phenomenon of devotional cooking, this chapter tells the stories of three *muqaddama*s and one non-*muqaddama* for whom devotional cooking contributes significantly to their leadership status in the Fayḍa community. These women's narratives illustrate this book's recurring theme that a performance of conventional feminine roles – in this case, cooking – can reorient these roles to myriad ends. For example, on the surface, cooking a special meal can index devotion to the person cooked for. Yet certain performances transfigure such acts to show devotion to and cement a spiritual connection with Baay and ultimately to God. Furthermore, cooking is not just a signifying performance but is a materially grounded activity through which participants can invest and augment their economic, social, symbolic, and religious capital. Outstanding participants in devotional cooking activities are either entrepreneurs with their own financial resources or are effective community organizers who inspire others to make financial contributions. Yet rather than reduce this religious practice to capital investment, my ultimate aim is to situate such investments in a spiritual economy with quantitatively and qualitatively transcendent rewards.

Devotional Cooking

Despite their different socio-economic backgrounds, all the women featured later in this chapter place acts of devotional cooking at the centre of their narratives of religious authority. Scholars long ago recognized the central place of culinary offerings and commensality in religious practices around the world (e.g., W.R. Smith 1894; Hubert and Mauss 1899). Many have explored the symbolic connections between what people eat and refuse to eat and their conceptions of self, society, and cosmic order (Douglas 1966, 1972; Lévi-Strauss 1969; Bourdieu 1984; Fischler 1988). Yet beyond commensality and consumption, the meanings and consequences of food offerings for their producers – overwhelmingly women – have widely been overlooked. It is all too easy to dismiss cooking as a menial chore rather than recognizing it as a potential means of achieving prestige, power, meaning, and community. For most Senegalese women, cooking is at some point a central activity, whether for their households, clients, kin and neighbourhood networks, or religious leaders and fellow disciples.

Penda Mbow has observed that Senegalese women are tasked with serving the meal at religious events and that this often prevents them from participating in the ceremony itself. Yet she also recognizes that, from their point of view, doing so provides "an opportunity to demonstrate their faith," not only by cooking the meal but by contributing more to it financially than men (1997, 155). Transmigrant Senegalese Murid women abroad raise their status back home and deflect accusations of immoral wealth accumulation through giving large offerings *(àddiya)* to religious leaders and contributing to organizing religious events (Evers Rosander 2004). Beth Buggenhagen (2012b; 2012a) has shown that Senegalese Murid women's explanations of food offerings emphasize different religious motivations than those emphasized in the malecentric literature. Women she interviewed described food offerings to religious leaders more as a means of earning religious merit (*tuyaaba*) directly from God than of earning spiritual blessing (*barke*, from Arabic *baraka)*, a quality most often transmitted through and emphasized by men. Although the Fayḍa women I interviewed did not make the same distinction (see the story of Diarra Ndiaye and Astou Diop below), they did celebrate devotional cooking as a source of immense social and divine rewards. For the women discussed in this chapter, investing time, money, and social capital in cooking contributes significantly to religious authority.

In every Senegalese Fayḍa household I have visited, women have been responsible for preparing meals, and even senior women who delegate the work to hired servants and juniors insist that, as pious Muslim women, they are ultimately responsible for the state of the house and the food served in it. To explain women's natural connection to the home, many women leaders quoted the Qur'ānic verse commanding women as follows: "And stay quietly in your houses, and make not a dazzling display, like that of the former times of ignorance" (Qur'ān 33:33).[2] Even internationally known *shaykha*s (senior religious leaders) and successful businesswomen insist that their domestic responsibilities are their first priority even if they perform little of the actual domestic work. Indeed, as Hoodfar (1997) found among working-class Cairene women, many of whom earned more than their husbands, I found that the busier a woman is with economic pursuits the more likely she is to insist on her dedication to running her house. The short biography on the website of Shaykha Maryam Niasse, Shaykh Ibrāhīm's world-renowned daughter who runs four Qur'ānic schools and a large Islamic Institute in Dakar, tells how she became a well-known teacher "without ever neglecting her domestic tasks" (Dar Al Quran Al Karim 2011). Shaykha Maryam told me her father described her as a son when she was born and predicted that she would never do "women's work." Yet she repeatedly emphasized her deference for her late husband and the fact that he worked outside the home while she taught and ran her schools from within her bedroom while overseeing the home.

Many women find ways to profit socially and economically through their cooking. A woman's efforts at offering hospitality through good cooking bring praise from guests, who may offer her a monetary gift to thank her. The practical knowledge of food markets and cooking and the social networks that women develop through group cooking for life-cycle rituals and religious events serve as economic and social resources. I have known many women who have converted culinary knowledge and networks into commercial activities, selling raw ingredients or prepared meals at tables in the street or market. Such work can dovetail with their domestic duties, as they can use unsold merchandise to feed their families.

For Taalibe Baay women, cooking has religious significance far beyond feeding the household and making a living. Since the Fayḍa's beginning, women's culinary expertise has provided ways for them to participate in religious activities, distinguish themselves as devoted disciples, and gain access to divine rewards. Many elder women who joined the Fayḍa movement during its early days fondly recalled how their village organized work days in fields whose produce was consecrated as an offering to Shaykh Ibrāhīm, who himself would visit the village during those days and pray for the disciple community. Some women would hoe weeds alongside the men while others would stay behind to cook lunch for the rest. A few would cook a special meal for Baay and his companions. Several rural women I spoke with placed these meals for Baay at the heart of their discipleship narratives, retelling the words with which Shaykh Ibrāhīm blessed the cooks and how his prayers were later realized. As mentioned above, interviewees from the early Fayḍa village of Darou Mbitéyène described four rural women during the 1930s as "leaders of women" appointed by Baay as *muqaddamas*.[3] Their primary responsibilities were to organize women for these work days and to oversee the production of meals for workers and the special meal presented to Baay. Today, disciples in some villages continue to organize similar work days for Shaykh Ibrāhīm's sons and other major leaders, although monetary offerings have overshadowed agricultural work in recent years.

Women's cooking remains indispensable to the large meetings that *daayiras* and *daayira* federations organize in Dakar and throughout Senegal. Nearly every *daayira* has a male president and a "President of the Women's Commission" *(Présidente de la commission féminine)*, sometimes called "Women's President" or "Vice-president." The women's president participates in the *daayira*'s general organizational meetings, but her primary responsibility is to coordinate the production of collective meals at large meetings. At smaller *gàmmus* associated with a single *daayira*, the organizing *daayira* usually prepares one meal, usually dinner, for all attendees and guests. At major meetings like the Taïba Niassène *gàmmu*, most of the visiting *daayiras* are responsible for preparing their own meals, while one prominent *daayira* – until recently Naḥnu Anṣār Allāh – prepares a larger central meal for prominent leaders and their guests. For many years, whoever was the women's president of Naḥnu Anṣār Allāh was also the women's president of the Dakar Anṣār al-Dīn Federation, and her largest task every year was to take money raised by hundreds of *daayiras* and organize the production of meals for thousands of guests at the Fayḍa's main annual events in Kaolack and Dakar. In addition to collective meals prepared by the women of various *daayiras* for *daayira* members and leaders, some women individually cook special meals for leaders, either at large events or during leaders' visits to a community. Visiting leaders and their companions may eat a little from each bowl, pronouncing a blessing on the women who cooked the meal. Leftovers will then be distributed to other meeting attendees, who receive blessing *(baraka)* through eating from the same bowl as a leader.

In 2010, I accompanied a *daayira* from Kaolack to attend the *gàmmu* in Shaykh Ibrāhīm's birthplace of Taïba Niassène and observed a division of labour identical to what I have seen at numerous other events. The *daayira* prepared three meals: a lunch before the meeting began, a dinner between the afternoon and night portions of the meeting, and a simple breakfast after the all-night meeting just before *daayira* members boarded their chartered bus to return to Kaolack.

Before the meeting, male and female *daayira* members had each paid 5,000 CFA (around U.S. $10) to the *daayira*'s treasurer to cover transportation, food, sound system, and commemorative t-shirts emblazoned with their shaykh's photo and the name of the *daayira* and the event written in French. The *daayira*'s women's president had distributed some of this money to *daayira* women to buy rice and vegetables, while male *daayira* members procured several sheep. The morning of the *gàmmu*, *daayira* members gathered in Medina Baay in front of the house of their shaykh, a grandson of Shaykh Ibrāhīm. When the bus arrived, an hour late, the men tied the food, the sheep, a folded canvas tent top, and a sound system to its roof. *Daayira* members boarded the bus, distributed the t-shirts, and throughout the two-hour trip to Taïba Niassène chanted *sikkar* in unison.

Nearly every house in Taïba Niassène was hosting at least one *daayira* and a number of individual guests, including family, friends, and a stream of unfamiliar pilgrims. This *daayira* had arranged to set up its tent in the spacious courtyard of one of the two village heads. As soon as the bus parked in front of the compound, male *daayira* members unloaded it and set up the canvas tent and some woven plastic mats where *daayira* members could relax inside the courtyard. Some men set up a sound system under the tent for the *daayira*'s smaller meetings before and between the main sessions held in the village square. Other men of the *daayira* butchered the animals while the women gathered around large bowls, chopping vegetables, picking debris out of rice, and then stirring huge cauldrons (*mbana*) of rice and meat sauce (*ceeb u yàpp*) for the collective lunch. The women, mostly schoolmates from high school, engaged in light-hearted conversation as they cooked. They sent a special bowl to the daughter of Shaykh Ibrāhīm staying in the same compound with her *daayira* and another bowl to a son of Shaykh Ibrāhīm with whom they had an ongoing relationship. Both leaders surely had many other bowls to eat from but might be expected to take a handful of rice from the bowl the *daayira* sent and give the rest to their many guests. Each of Shaykh Ibrāhīm's senior sons has a house in Taïba Niassène, and disciples gathered around them in the early afternoon before the main meeting began, some bringing them bowls of food and monetary offerings (*àddiya*).

After lunch, the *daayira* held a short meeting in its tent and then broke for the large afternoon meeting in the adjacent village square. Some women stayed behind to prepare dinner: bowls of millet couscous with meat stew (*cere ak ñeex u yàpp*) and plates of salad with meat and bread. Shortly after midnight, following a short *sikkar* meeting in the *daayira*'s tent and then dinner, many *daayira* members returned to the main square to attend the main *gàmmu* meeting while others rested in the courtyard on the plastic mats and listened to the amplified speeches and chants. After sunrise, the meeting ended, and some *daayira* women prepared a breakfast of buttered baguettes, coffee, and kinkiliba (*sexaw*) tea with powdered milk and sugar. The disciples then got back onto the bus and headed back to Kaolack.

In this context, where cooking is central to women's social, economic, and religious activities, it is not surprising that nearly all the *muqaddamas* I interviewed place acts of cooking at key points in their narratives of becoming religious leaders. Two male leaders Sayyida Awa Cissé hosted and cooked for ended up giving her *ijāzas*; Sayyida Ndèye

Maguète Niang cooked for Baay Mokhtar Ka; Sayyida Bousso Dramé earns income from a food stand she inherited from her mother and uses these skills to organize dinners for disciples and guests. Similarly, the women featured in this chapter transfigure acts of cooking into spiritual authority, redirecting hegemonic notions of womanhood towards Islamic leadership.

The Women of Naḥnu Anṣār Allāh: Sayyida Diarra Ndiaye and Astou Diop

In April 2004, while I was living in Medina Baay, Kaolack, members of the local high school *daayira* invited me to travel to Dakar with them to attend the annual Dakar *gàmmu*. Several dozen students rode for more than five hours on a chartered bus to Shaykh Ibrāhīm's house in the middle-class Dieupeul neighbourhood of Dakar, arriving around 2:30 in the afternoon. Congregating in the large reception room, we were treated to a rousing speech by Modou Niang, longtime president of both the Dakar Anṣār al-Dīn Federation and the Naḥnu Anṣār Allāh *daayira*. Then the legendary *sikkarkat* Babacar Thiam, who would lead chants that night, gave a short speech, interspersed with sung poems by Shaykh Ibrāhīm. After the speeches, women emerged and placed dining cloths on the floor and on them large bowls of rice with meat sauce (*ceeb u yàpp*). Approximately eight *daayira* members knelt on the cloths around each large bowl, eating with their right hands. Before and after serving the food, the women brought pails of soapy water for hand washing, and then they collected the bowls and cloths and swept the area. We then moved from the reception room to the courtyard to make room for another wave of *daayira*s who enjoyed the same treatment. The courtyard in Shaykh Ibrāhīm's house became more crowded as the afternoon wore on.

In the late afternoon everyone walked several blocks to the large field next to the Liberté 6 roundabout, where an enormous tent top had been set up, to hear speeches by several major leaders during the evening "conference" portion of the event. When this meeting ended, at around 11:30 at night, those of us being hosted at Shaykh Ibrāhīm's house walked back. We were treated to dinner – Senegalese millet couscous with meat sauce (*cereek ñeex u yàpp*) – in the courtyard, once again served in several waves. At around 1:00 a.m., we returned to the tent for the main *gàmmu* event. Several thousand people sat inside the well-lit tent in plastic chairs, and an even larger number sat outside listening to the proceedings over loudspeakers, some brewing tea. The *gàmmu* ended at around 7:00 in the morning. Our chartered bus arrived back in Kaolack by noon.

I would later learn that the food at the *gàmmu* had been cooked and served by the women of the *daayira* Naḥnu Anṣār Allāh. Even though this meal had been cooked for hundreds of people, I was impressed that it was not the simplified, rushed food often served at large gatherings but showed the effort and expense of a meal for honoured guests. Along with the *gàmmu*s of Medina Baay and Taïba Niassène, the Dakar *gàmmu* is one of the Senegalese Fayḍa community's three largest annual events. Soon after Naḥnu Anṣār Allāh was founded in 1981, Shaykh Ibrāhīm's oldest son, Al-Ḥājj ʿAbdallāh, tasked the *daayira* with organizing each year's "reception" at all three events. This primarily involved preparing and serving vast quantities of food for hundreds of guests. The *daayira*'s women also cooked for other major events, such as the laying of the first stone of the new Taïba Niassène mosque.

Even though Naḥnu's membership was aging and recruiting momentum had shifted to newer, youth-dominated *daayira*s, the *daayira* stayed in charge of all these *gàmmu*s until 2011. After Shaykh Aḥmad Daam passed away in 2010, his younger brother, Shaykh Tijānī, became the community's Khalīfa and drastically reorganized the Anṣār al-Dīn Federation (see chapter 1). He assigned a newer organization of younger, university-trained professionals, Le groupe de réflexion Ansaroudine (GRAD), to cook for the Medina Baay and Taïba Niassène *gàmmu*s. The women of Naḥnu still officially cook for the Dakar *gàmmu* and unofficially cook large quantities of food for the Medina Baay *gàmmu*.

As the women's leader and long-time organizer of receptions at the Fayḍa's major events, Rosalie Diop became a well-loved figure in the Fayḍa community. In 2004, a year after she died, a large conference was held in her memory at the Islamic Institute in Dakar featuring Shaykh Ibrāhīm's son Shaykh Muḥammad al-Amīn (Baaba Lamin) and the major *muqaddam* Shaykh ʿAbdallāh Wilane. The following day, the Dakar Anṣār al-Dīn organized a well-attended group Qurʾānic recitation (*wàcce kaamil*) at Rosalie Diop's house. Diarra Ndiaye replaced Rosalie Diop in 2004 as leader of the women of both organizations. In 2013, when her husband fell ill, Diarra Ndiaye handed both positions off to her friend Astou Diop, who had recently returned to Senegal from more than three decades in Paris.

These three women presidents were tightly connected. As discussed in chapter 1, Diarra Ndiaye went through *tarbiya* in 1975 and influenced her friend and neighbour Astou Diop to do the same. The family of her uncle Babacar Ndiaye followed her into the Fayḍa, including his wife Rosalie Diop and his daughter Sophie Ndiaye, who received *tarbiya* from Sayyida Diarra Ndiaye and later married Shaykh Ibrāhīm's son Shaykh Aḥmad Daam. The only one of these three officially appointed as a *muqaddama* is Sayyida Diarra Ndiaye.

For many years, both Sayyida Diarra Ndiaye and Astou Diop ran restaurants, using their cooking skills to make extra money, much of which they invested in the *daayira*'s cooking activities, supplementing funds raised by Dakar's *daayiras*. Sayyida Diarra Ndiaye's restaurant was in front of her house, and she eventually entrusted it to others. Astou Diop opened a Senegalese restaurant in Paris, where her husband had been transferred to the Senegalese Embassy in 1982. She agreed to relocate to Paris only on condition that her husband, not a follower of any Sufi order, allow her to return to Senegal several times a year to help organize the cooking for the three major annual *gàmmus*. The restaurant provided enough income to allow her to contribute to numerous devotional cooking activities. She often made the majority contribution to *gàmmu* meals.[4]

In addition, whenever leaders from Medina Baay came to Paris, Astou Diop would cook for them in her house on her own dime. In this way she became a close friend of several of Shaykh Ibrāhīm's children, especially Shaykha Maryam, who also lives in the Mermoz neighbourhood. When I interviewed her during Ramadan in 2014, Astou Diop would walk to Shaykha Maryam's nearby house every evening to break her fast with her. Her interactions with Shaykh Ibrāhīm's children have provided opportunities for her to continue her "spiritual progression" *(sayr)*, deepening the knowledge of God she began through *tarbiya*.

While in Paris, Astou Diop participated in founding a Paris chapter of Anṣār al-Dīn. For five years (ending in 2014), her daughter, who was born in Paris, was president of the Paris Anṣār al-Dīn *daayira* – not as president of the Women's Commission as is usually meant when one refers to a woman as *daayira "présidente."* Yet Astou Diop still describes her daughter's role in terms of hospitality. Since her daughter "was the one in charge of Anṣār al-Dīn," whenever any guest visited the Paris community, "she would receive you – she would host you." In late 2012, Astou Diop relocated to Dakar, although she still returns to Paris often and has children who live there.

The night before the Dakar *gàmmu*, Astou Diop explained to me, the women of Naḥnu gather to cook in the open space in front of their headquarters, Diarra Ndiaye's house. Meanwhile, the *daayira*'s men put up the main tent at the *gàmmu* site. That night, the women stay up all night roasting the chickens for the next night's dinner. At 8:00 the next morning, they move the cooking operation to the *gàmmu* site, which for the past few years has been the large space behind Shaykha Maryam's Islamic Institute in Patte d'Oies. They cook the rice and meat (*ceeb u yàpp*) – seven or eight enormous cauldrons (*mbana*) of rice – and throughout the day they serve the guests who arrive, as I myself saw in 2004. When lunch ends, they immediately proceed to dinner preparation. They cook Senegalese couscous (*cere*), roast chickens, roast meat, and salad. Serving dinner until well after midnight, they have little time to catch any of the all-night *gàmmu* meeting. After the meeting ends, they prepare breakfast for anyone who hasn't gone home yet. After breakfast, they gather the copious cooking equipment and transport it back to their owners' homes. This means at least three days with practically no sleep, ending the afternoon after the *gàmmu*, when they finally return home and rest.

For the Medina Baay *gàmmu*, every year the women would gather contributions from their own and other *daayira*s of the Anṣār al-Dīn Federation, buy all the ingredients, go to Shaykh Aḥmad Daam's house in Medina Baay to cook, and divide the food up to send to the houses of all the *muqaddam*s for their guests. According to my own observations, in addition to this official meal, each private house in Medina Baay also hosts dozens of guests and is responsible, sometimes along with a visiting *daayira*, for feeding any visitors. Many households slaughter a cow for their guests, who typically do not give anything in return. The *gàmmu* thus represents a large financial sacrifice for each household and an opportunity for many women to engage in devotional cooking.

Even after responsibility for the Medina Baay and Taïba Niassène *gàmmu*s shifted to GRAD, the women of Naḥnu have continued unofficially to cook a large meal for Medina Baay's guests. Hundreds of thousands attend the *gàmmu* each year, so there is always a need for more food. Now the house of Astou Diop's cousin Sophie Ndiaye has become the *daayira*'s base in Medina Baay. The women cook the same things they cook for the Dakar *gàmmu, sending* bowls to Medina Baay's leaders (*sëriñ si*) and to neighbouring houses, and invite any guests they find to eat in the house. Early the next morning, as the *gàmmu* is wrapping up, the women prepare breakfast and begin to prepare lunch – usually onion sauce (*yaasa*) with chicken. After lunch, the guests and the *daayira* members pack up their things, climb onto their chartered buses, and head home.

The Medina Baay *gàmmu*, Astou Diop told me, is for the thousands of guests who come from foreign countries, while the people of Medina Baay (by which she means Senegalese disciples) serve them. Whenever Astou Diop attends the Medina Baay *gàmmu*, instead of dressing up and going to the main tent she works non-stop in Sophie Ndiaye's house. She can hear the speeches over the loudspeakers but is too busy cooking to sit and listen. However, a week later, there is another meeting designed for Senegalese disciples themselves, the "*gàmmuwaat*" ("*gàmmu* again") or "*ngénte*" (infant naming ceremony), so called because it happens one week after the birthday, like a *ngénte*. This meeting follows the same format as the main *gàmmu* but is far less crowded.[5] She and other *daayira* members return to Medina Baay, this time not cooking but dressing up and sitting in the main tent to listen.

In an interview in 2014 with both women,[6] I remarked that when people talk about *gàmmu*s they usually mention male leaders who spoke or chanted there, yet there would be no *gàmmu* without the food women cook for the many guests. Both concurred, saying that female disciples always contribute more to events than men, whether in the form of money, work, or attendance. "People talk about the men, but the women work even more than the men,"[7] Astou Diop told me. She explained that when they are preparing the Dakar *gàmmu*, the men bring the basic contribution *(cotisation)* required of all members and say "this is what we have" (*lii lañu am*). This is enough to buy the chickens. The women bring the same contribution but then add whatever other food items they have on hand – homemade Senegalese couscous (*cere*), sacks of potatoes and onions, salt and pepper, garlic, more money, cows, and so on. They add whatever money they have earned through their own economic activities. For women, these activities tend to be largely informal, such as selling fabrics, vegetables, and prepared foods from their own homes. If the men give 500,000 FCFA, she said, the women give 2 million, and on top of that they cook and serve everything. Diarra Ndiaye commented that women used to lag behind men in participation, but that now they are doing what Baay told them to do – to "compete" (*rëjrëjluleen*) with men in excellence.[8]

I told them that I had observed many times during *gàmmu*s that women work several days straight doing the cooking and serving while most of the men lounge around and socialize. Women must be exhausted after all this, I concluded. Astou Diop agreed but added,

"But they do it with *pleasure* [Fr.]." Diarra Ndiaye told of going to Taïba Niassène and spending three whole days cooking without sleeping. When the women were finished they would take a catnap on the plastic chairs set up in the courtyard because men were filling all the floor space in the house. She explained:

> Yet we couldn't do that at home – if we did that at home we would become ill. That's why working for a saint of God is more beneficial than everything else, because you don't get the fatigue. We even finish all that work and ask, "Are we really the ones who did all this?" Because there's a lot of work, but before the time comes God makes everything complete.

They do not perceive cooking and serving food, then, as a matter of serving other people but as a matter of serving Baay and, through Baay, God.

As Astou Diop explained, "It's hard but ... it's pleasant for us!" Diarra Ndiaye added, "It's pleasant because we're working for God. We know the one we're working for. And we know that he will reward us." For example, she said, a woman who needs to steam something tears a strip of fabric off her dress to seal the steaming pot (*inde*). The next year, all the women remember this and compete to tear their own dresses to seal the pots, because they see that "Baay paid her back in endless dresses."

Unlike Sayyida Moussoukoro Mbaye and Aïda Thiam, discussed below, neither of these women describes a particular act of devotional cooking as directly leading to an investiture with authority. What their accounts highlight is the continual importance of cooking to women's devotional activities. For these women, cooking is not a mere supporting activity for men's events but is a religious activity in itself with tangible *ẓāhir* and *bāṭin* rewards. Women in the Anṣār al-Dīn leadership and community come to prominence largely through organizing and sponsoring cooking activities.

Some scholars have reported that Murid women distinguish between *barke* (Ar. *baraka,* divine blessing), something one can gain access to through a connection with a saint, and *tuyaaba* (Ar. *thawāb,* divine reward), a reward one earns directly from God through good deeds. Although *barke* has been a central term in the male-centric literature on Muridism, Buggenhagen (2009a, 2012b; 2012a) and Evers Rosander (1998, 2003) have reported that Murid women emphasize *tuyaaba* more. Earning *tuyaaba* directly from God, these scholars suggest, may appeal more to women because they have less access to the spaces and networks through which *barke* is transmitted. In the shared interview, I asked Diarra Ndiaye and Astou Diop whether the same distinction was relevant to their cooking activities. Diarra Ndiaye immediately responded that, "*Tuyaaba* and *barke* are the same thing! It's all just the same thing!" Almost simultaneously, Astou Diop answered, "They're the same!" (*Benn la!*)

An Islamic scholar who had stopped by during the same interview explained how the two terms are technically different, even if they may refer to the same things. While these women's answers do not reflect doctrinal differences between Taalibe Baay and Murids, they hint at widespread Taalibe Baay attitudes surrounding their relationships with leaders, Baay, and God. Although, like Murids, Taalibe Baay may describe visiting a leader in order "to seek blessing" (*barkeelu*), I have never heard Taalibe Baay describe following a leader because that leader possessed *barke*. Rather, Taalibe Baay report following a leader for knowledge and guidance. Although knowledge must normally be transmitted through a living intermediary, as shown throughout this book, many disciples describe receiving guidance and blessings directly from Baay. Still present and accessible to all, Baay continues to be described as God's hidden representative even after his bodily death. Therefore, being blessed by one's connection to Baay (*barke*) and being rewarded by God (*tuyaaba*) may be experienced as the same. Sayyida Diarra Ndiaye and Astou Diop's accounts of being rewarded for cooking illustrate that they see divine reward as directly tied to serving Baay through serving his representatives and community. While women may have their own avenues, such as cooking, for obtaining God's blessing and reward, it is not clear that they feel less capable than men of gaining access to them.

Sayyida Moussoukoro Mbaye

One might wonder whether a successful entrepreneur like Sayyida Moussoukoro Mbaye might dispense with conventional women's tasks such as cooking as she establishes herself as a religious authority. However, in addition to the centrality of motherhood to her narrative, she traces her induction into religious leadership to a moment of culinary sacrifice that she was able to subsidize through her independent income. She has repeated such culinary offerings many times over the years, bringing herself to the attention of many major leaders and helping university students for whom she is the official *daayira* "mother" to organize collective meals at their religious events. She has thus invested resources from her successful economic entrepreneurship into her religious entrepreneurship, often through engaging in or overseeing acts of cooking.

One day in 1994, not long after Sayyida Moussoukoro had received *tarbiya,* a group of Fayḍa students at the University of Dakar knocked on her door seeking help. They were forming a new student *daayira* of fewer than ten members, mostly men living in dormitories far from their families. They were organizing their first annual conference and had invited their preferred keynote speaker, Shaykh Nadhīr, a senior son of Shaykh Ibrāhīm. Known as an intellectual and patron of learning, Shaykh Nadhīr had been appointed by Shaykh Ibrāhīm to run his Islamic Institute in Kaolack. Although they had made all the arrangements for the venue, the amplification, and the chairs, the students could not cook a meal worthy of such an esteemed guest. A junior daughter of Shaykh Ibrāhīm who was studying at the university recommended approaching Sayyida Moussoukoro. The students brought her the money they had raised for the meal – 18,000 CFA francs (at the time, shortly before devaluation, around U.S. $70). Sayyida Moussoukoro thanked God that they had been sent to her and prayed for Shaykh Ibrāhīm's daughter for making the suggestion. She then told them to keep the money they had raised and to use it to buy juices and soft drinks for the event. She would take care of the meal herself. From her own coffers she took twice the amount they had raised, bought a large ram and had it slaughtered, and cooked an "exquisite lunch" for the conference attendees and their honoured guests.

The students presented the meal and drinks to the shaykh. After he had eaten they introduced Moussoukoro to him as the one who had provided the meal. As recounted in chapter 4, she describes this as the moment when Shaykh Nadhīr designated her as the "mother" of the students, a role that the *daayira* of student disciples still recognizes. In addition to offering students spiritual guidance, she offers female students the use of her kitchen, expertise, and cooking materials to prepare sumptuous meals for attendees and special guests at the now large meetings they organize.

Sayyida Moussoukoro has since repeated many such acts of devotional cooking. Over the years since I first visited Sayyida Moussoukoro in 2004, I often found her hosting important religious leaders visiting from Kaolack or Mauritania, and she often sent plates of food to leaders staying in other houses. While Shaykh Ibrāhīm's then-eldest living son,

Ahmed Daam Niasse (d. 2010), was ill and was spending time in Dakar to be treated, she would send him and his family a nice lunch every day. A prominent Mauritanian *muqaddam* and his entourage would sometimes stay in her apartment, and on other occasions when they stayed elsewhere she would still send them daily meals.

In addition, Sayyida Moussoukoro allows the young women of the *daayiras* associated with Dakar's various institutions of higher learning to use her kitchen and her extensive cooking materials to prepare meals for their *daayiras*' annual events. When students have organized large meetings in Dakar, I have found the *daayira*'s women at her apartment before the meeting to cook the collective meal. The men and women of the *daayira* would then coordinate to transport Sayyida Moussoukoro's large pots full of cooked food to the conference venue and then back to her apartment afterwards.

Although Sayyida Moussoukoro tends to present her acts of culinary devotion as part of a purely spiritual narrative, these acts of course depend on her culinary skills and personal financial resources. Not only does she come from a well-to-do family – she says her father owned around a hundred rental properties in Kaolack and many cattle, while her first husband was a successful trader – she also started her own business ventures and became financially independent during the 1990s, around the time she joined the Fayḍa. When I met her in 2004, she was running a successful clothing import business. In fact, the person who took me and my collaborators to see her was the manager of one of her clothing shops and a *muqaddam* himself who actively participated in organizing her *daayira*. Soon after this visit, she travelled to Dubai and shipped back large quantities of clothing to sell at her shops.

Sayyida Moussoukoro has since shifted her attention from the clothing business to acting as the sole licensed importer, distributor, and public face for a line of beauty products manufactured in Côte d'Ivoire. Her products are now widely distributed throughout the Dakar area, and her company has a presence on Facebook and on television. During an interview in 2010, Sayyida Moussoukoro calmly paused our conversation and switched on the flat-screen television to the private TV2S station. The fashion program "Actumode" appeared, showing Sayyida Moussoukoro in her office telling the station's fashion reporter about the benefits of her collagen-based skin-care products. Wearing a white, gold-embroidered dress and an elegant white headscarf similar to the one she wore during our interview, Sayyida Moussoukoro described the anti-aging benefits of these products and gave tips on how to use the products to reverse the damage caused by "aggressive" skin lighteners (*xeesal*). Sayyida Moussoukoro's business ventures are formally separate from her religious activities, and many of her employees are not Fayḍa adherents, although she employs some graduates she met through the university *daayira*.

In short, Sayyida Moussoukoro became the "mother" of the university students and a prominent and well-connected disciple at least in part through investing economic capital into social and religious capital (Bourdieu 1971, 1984). Most notably, she has subsidized acts of devotional cooking, helping her to establish and maintain relationships with key leaders. Her business and religious activities are intertwined in numerous ways: her religious networks feed into her employment network; she earns enough to personally sustain her own devotional cooking and to help students organize their events; and she maintains her own home in Dakar (plus a recently finished home in Medina Baay) where she can host important leaders, hold meetings for her disciples, and invite *daayira* women to cook for large student meetings. Lately, she leaves most of the house's cooking work to maids and daughters, although she sometimes goes to market to locate the best ingredients, and she carefully supervises to make sure meals are up to her standards. Of course, Sayyida Moussoukoro's religious leadership depends not only on cooking and entrepreneurship but also on her uncommon ability to communicate religious knowledge and guide young people. Her cooking activities combine with many other resources she can marshal to satisfy students' and other leaders' needs.

Sayyida Aïda Thiam

With few of Sayyida Moussoukoro's (even if informal) educational or economic opportunities, Sayyida Aïda Thiam (figure 5.1) demonstrates an opposite flow of investment between economic and religious capital. Yet the two women's stories show many parallels. Both were raised in Kaolack and claim a long ancestry of Islamic educators, even if neither inherited religious knowledge or authority from her father. Although Sayyida Aïda was born into a more solidly Taalibe Baay family, neither describes her relationship to Baay as an automatic matter; instead both describe being inexorably led by God through Baay to the mission they now carry out. Both were entrusted with many children in addition to their own children and are called "Mother" by disciples of all ages. Most importantly for this chapter, Sayyida Aïda also also traces her

Figure 5.1 Aïda Thiam (centre) at a *gàmmu* in 2014.

investment with religious authority to a moment of devotional cooking, and her religious activities continue to feature food preparation.

Soft-spoken and modest in demeanour, Sayyida Aïda is better known as an enthusiastic and effective community organizer than as a public speaker or scholar. Her quiet and unassuming speech more closely resembles that of a rural housewife than of a typical urban elite or Islamic leader. Since I first interviewed her in 2009, Sayyida Aïda's reputation as an enthusiastic and successful organizer has grown. When the international Anṣār al-Dīn Federation was reorganized in 2013, she was appointed as co-president of the Women's Commission for the federation in the Department of Pikine, which includes Yeumbeul. When I visited her in 2016, she had recently been reappointed for a second three-year term.

Unlike most new *muqaddamas*, Sayyida Aïda was born into a committed Taalibe Baay family, although she speaks of her relationship to Baay as a matter of ongoing dreams and miracles. She continues to struggle economically despite her success in organizing the Fayḍa community in Dakar's periphery. In her youth, Sayyida Aïda and her parents moved to Yeumbeul, which was then one of Dakar's most economically and geographically marginal neighbourhoods. After marrying young and divorcing a few years later, she raised many children on her own, including her only son, who died in an accident in 2011, and her deceased sister's seven children. Her younger widowed sister also lives with her along with her own six children. Each year I have visited her, I have found that new children have come while others have returned to their parents.

Sayyida Aïda founded a *daayira* in Dakar's remote suburb of Yeumbeul around 2002, six years before Shaykh Ibrāhīm's son Muḥammad al-Makkī appointed her as a *muqaddama*. The *daayira* has the distinction of being the first of many organizations named after Shaykh Ibrāhīm's little-known mother, Maam Astou Diankha (see Hill 2017a for another example). Although gender-specific *daayira*s are the norm among Murids (Mbow 1997; Buggenhagen 2012a, 78–80), the Maam Astou Diankha daayira is the only Taalibe Baay *daayira* I have encountered that was founded as a women's *daayira*. Also, whereas younger men and women have initiated and dominated most recent *daayira*s, mature women founded and remain core members of this *daayira*. However, men also figured prominently in the *daayira* from its beginning, and over time the *daayira* has come to resemble other *daayira*s, as many young men have joined. In 2010, it incorporated a youth *daayira* in nearby Thiaroye that lacked a local leader, further converging with the dominant Taalibe Baay model of a gender-integrated youth *daayira*. Yet the *daayira* continues to organize women-specific activities, including vocational training in food and craft production, areas in which Sayyida Aïda personally has training and experience.

Since I met her in 2009, Sayyida Aïda has moved between several rented or borrowed homes, and she often speaks of her prayer to own her own house to act as *daayira* headquarters and Qur'ānic school. Sayyida Aïda repeatedly told me that everything she has comes from Baay, which in a material sense means that she has no livelihood other than what comes to her through her work for Baay, including occasional support from people who recognize her religious community work or gifts in return for her prayers. She told me many stories showing that Baay was constantly opening the way for her – for example, when she left for a long trip without a coin in her pocket yet arrived at her destination easily with the help of strangers along the way.

When I interviewed her in 2009 and 2010, Sayyida Aïda was sponsoring a Qur'ānic school, paying its teacher a monthly stipend and hosting him in her house; yet when I returned in 2014 she had closed the school because of a lack of resources. Her father and grandfather, she says, were Qur'ān teachers descended from the scholarly lineages of the Senegal River Valley related to nineteenth-century Tijānī reformer Al-Ḥājj 'Umar Tall. While this narrative situates her authority in terms of a longer family tradition, her only schooling is the same basic Qur'ānic education most Senegalese children pursue.

Sayyida Aïda's accounts do not mention her former husband. But the *daayira*'s vice-president, Assane Niasse, told us that she and her husband had led the effort to form a small, mixed-gender *daayira* in the late 1990s. Assane Niasse moved into the neighbourhood in 2000 and joined with them to organize the disciples throughout Yeumbeul. Sayyida Aïda confirmed these details later.

When Sayyida Aïda first told me her own story, she skipped these previous initiatives and began her account with founding the Maam Astou Diankha *daayira* after her divorce. She told of living in Yeumbeul as an adult with her devout Taalibe Baay mother when Shaykh Ibrāhīm spoke to her in a series of dreams. He told her to organize the women in the area into a *daayira* named after his own mother, Maam Astou Diankha. Like many households I encountered, her own household was made up of several women relatives, including her widowed sister and mother, along with their dependents. All these women were Taalibe Baay, and she had met several other Taalibe Baay women in the neighbourhood. In 2001, she called these women together and proposed forming a *daayira*, and they then scoured the neighbourhood to find other Taalibe Baay.

After she had recruited around eight women, the group decided to approach Shaykh Ibrāhīm's sons for official authorization to found a *daayira*. They raised 30,000 CFA (around U.S. $60) and went to the annual *gàmmu* in Taïba Niassène, where they cooked a meal that they named "the lunch of Maam Astou Diankha" (*añ u Maam Astu Jànqa*). They presented bowls of rice and meat to several of Shaykh Ibrāhīm's senior sons. They told each of these leaders of their desire to found a *daayira* named after Shaykh Ibrāhīm's mother. Sayyida Aïda describes each leader as replying that Shaykh Ibrāhīm himself had foretold this but that they were the first to realize it. Shaykh Ibrāhīm's son Shaykh Makkī said to them, "Thank God, praise God. Perhaps the person meant to do this or the time hadn't come yet, so may you all work hard." Shaykh Makkī agreed to become the *daayira*'s "*wāṣila*" or link to the headquarters of Medina Baay, Kaolack. Since then, he has been the keynote speaker at their annual conferences. Shaykh Makkī is accustomed to seeing women play leadership roles and often visits his full sister, Umm al-Khayrī Niasse, who has become an influential leader with many thousands of disciples in her marital country of Niger.

Sayyida Aïda's *daayira* grew to the point where it had hundreds of members, including a growing number of men. According to Assane Niasse, the new *daayira* absorbed the previous one. In 2008 Makkī Niasse appointed Sayyida Aïda as a *muqaddama*, and since then she has initiated many new disciples into the Fayḍa movement. Two years later, Sayyida Aïda's *daayira* incorporated another *daayira* in nearby Thiaroye that had previously lacked a resident *muqaddam*, making her the spiritual authority for a much larger number of young people.

Although men participate in its religious activities, the *daayira*'s economic activities remain specifically designated for women. Sayyida Aïda had long been involved in women's economic issues before founding the *daayira*. Before moving from Medina Baay to Dakar, she had received training in cloth dyeing and commercial food processing and had started a women's centre to teach women these skills. When I first interviewed her in 2009 and 2010, Sayyida Aïda told of the *daayira*'s plans to organize economic activities for women, such as vocational training and rotating credit. When I returned in 2014, I found that they had made great progress in organizing these projects. Sayyida Aïda was hosting training and work sessions in her home where female disciples learned a number of skills. Women were coming by every week to learn to process millet into dry porridges (*laax*, *caakri*) on commercial scales. She was raising money to buy an electric grain mill. Women were meeting to learn other crafts, such as making decorative baskets (one of which she gave to my wife) and embroidery. All these skills were customarily associated with women.

When I visited the *daayira* on the afternoon of the Taïba Niassène *gàmmu* in 2010, I found the women of the *daayira* busy preparing their lunch (see figure 5.2). They soon dished out several bowls of rice with meat, one of which Sayyida Aïda personally delivered to Shaykh Makkī's crowded house, accompanied by me and some of the *daayira*'s leading women. He received us and conversed at length with Sayyida Aïda.

At one of the *daayira*'s annual conferences, in 2007, Shaykh Makkī inaugurated the *daara* (Qur'ānic school) after they had asked him for authorization to open it. In the neighbourhood, Sayyida Aïda had noticed an unfinished and unroofed house in which garbage had been accumulating over the past two years. She located the absentee owner

Figure 5.2 Sayyia Aïda Thiam (top left) and women of her *daayira* preparing lunch at the Taïba Niassène *gàmmu*, 2010.

and asked him and the neighbourhood head for permission to open a Qur'ānic school there. Whenever a son or close companion of Shaykh Ibrāhīm visits, it is customary to raise "offerings for Baay" (*àddiya Baay*), so at the conference, *daayira* members raised 50,000 CFA (U.S. $100) and presented it to Shaykh Makkī. Responding that he had not come to collect *àddiya* but to dedicate the school, he returned the money to her in addition to 50,000 CFA of his own. They used the money to finish a room and build a roof over it, and to hire a teacher. At the *daayira*'s 2008 conference, Shaykh Makkī appointed her as a *muqaddama*.

One difference between Sayyida Aïda most of the other *muqaddam(a)*s I interviewed is that she has no source of livelihood beyond her religious activities. As with most *muqaddama*s, her home doubles as her *daayira*'s headquarters. Yet she has been unable to realize her dream of buying a house to act as a stable *daayira* headquarters and Islamic school. Until not long before I met her in 2009, she had lived in her mother's nearby house, where the *daayira* would meet in her own bedroom. The *daayira* soon outgrew this single room. Nearby was a neighbourhood for military officers (Cité Comico Yeumbeul) where many new houses were being built but were not yet inhabited. She located one of these unfinished homes (much as she had done for the Qur'ānic school) and convinced the owner (not a Fayḍa adherent) to rent it for use as her home and the *daayira* headquarters at a nominal rate.

In 2010, she moved out of the officers' neighbourhood back next to her mother's house, where she and the *daayira* rented another house, and when I returned in 2014, I found that she had moved yet again to a more suitable apartment, where she has remained since. When I asked how she pays the rent, she said God provides it. Although the *daayira* members do their best to support her, most of them are young students who have no stable income of their own, and she describes much of the support she gets for her school and the *daayira* as coming not from her own religious community but from neighbourhood benefactors who value her provision of religious education and a sense of moral community to at-risk young people who may otherwise lack guidance. Also, some people approach her to pray for them, giving her a monetary gift in return. She depends, therefore, on her reputation for saintliness among both disciples and non-disciples and on her ability to teach and guide young people.

Like Sayyida Moussoukoro Mbaye, Sayyida Aïda occupies formal leadership roles typically occupied by men yet redefines these roles to make her own set of experiences and expertise relevant to the needs of urbanizing young people and neighbourhood leaders. Also like Sayyida Moussoukoro, Sayyida Aïda expresses her relationship with young people living far from their families through the idiom of motherhood and interacts with major leaders through culinary offerings. An important difference between the two is that Sayyida Aïda does not invest her own economic capital into her religious mission but, on the contrary, subsists economically – if humbly – through her religious mission.

Investing in Cooking

As different as the life stories of the four women discussed in this chapter may be, each woman performs acts of cooking that contribute in various ways to her religious authority. Like the many practices of self-wrapping and submission associated with women's piety, the meanings and outcomes of any act of cooking depend on its performative context. Regardless of their economic or educational background, none of the many women who mentioned cooking in interviews described it as an unwanted chore or as indicating secondary status. Especially when speaking of devotional cooking, women spoke with pride and excitement, describing joy from cooking for the community and honoured leaders, the resulting divine blessings, and the positive social relations fostered through cooking.

In addition, these women leaders consecrate acts of cooking as part of their performances of religious authority and leadership. Their roles in organizing and individually performing devotional cooking have brought each of them to the attention of fellow disciples and leaders, especially Shaykh Ibrāhīm's senior sons. Yet these women's acts of cooking are not identical social acts. Their different economic circumstances accompany different strategies of investing in religious capital and demonstrating leadership.

For Sayyida Diarra Ndiaye and Astou Diop, commercial cooking provides economic capital to invest in devotional cooking. In addition to showing their religious devotion through material contributions, these two show leadership in organizing the other women of Naḥnu Anṣār Allāh and the Dakar Anṣār al-Dīn in their cooking activities. Both have occupied the highest-ranking female position in the Dakar Anṣār al-Dīn Federation, which has allowed both to cultivate close relationships with many leaders. They both describe cooking not just as a core leadership responsibility but as a great source of pleasure and divine blessing.

Similarly, Sayyida Moussoukoro's successful non-religious business provides economic capital to invest in devotional cooking and other religious activities. This has allowed her to cultivate close relationships with religious leaders through devotional cooking and to invest in long-term reciprocal relations with future professionals and leaders in the student *daayira*s. Whether she materially profits from her religious roles is less important than the prestige, influence, and fulfilment she realizes through investing in religious activities.

Sayyida Aïda's initial act of devotional cooking showed less an ability to invest her own economic capital than an ability to organize Taalibe Baay women in an area where the Fayḍa was just emerging. In fact, her livelihood depends on others who recognize the value of her religious activities, such as leading the neighbourhood's potentially at-risk youth, attempting to start an Islamic school, and praying for people who come to her with a need. Others' contributions allow her to carry out her religious projects and take the place of a formal income, husband, or working kin who can support her.

What all of these women share is that, in a booming spiritual market, they have carved out new leadership roles that are well matched to the maternal nurturing and household management skills they have learned from a young age. Whether they primarily invest income in or derive income from religious activities, all have increased their religious capital through cooking. My purpose in expressing these women's roles partly in economic terms is not to reduce their actions to economic logic but to highlight that, however transcendently they experience their spiritual journeys, they lead in a material environment that demands the kinds of leadership they can provide.

These acts of devotional cooking simultaneously reproduce hegemonic norms of feminine piety and resignify the meaning and consequence of those norms. Routine cooking is often understood as an act of care and devotion towards family and guests. Taalibe Baay women transfigure this devotion, reorienting it to Baay and ultimately to God. Furthermore, these women connect leadership of women's cooking to religious authority more generally and demonstrate their readiness to give everything to God. Ultimately these acts of cooking have brought these women recognition both as pillars of the Fayḍa community and, in their role as *muqaddama*s, as authorities leading men and women.

Chapter Six

"They Say a Woman's Voice Is *'Awra*"

Senegal's Sacred Sufi Soundscape

As Fatou prepared our lunch of *maafe* (peanut stew served with white rice), her phone rang. I immediately recognized the ring-tone: a virtuosic *sikkar (dhikr)* performance by Aïda Faye, currently the most popular Taalibe Baay *sikkarkat* (religious singer, literally "one who performs *dhikr*"). After she hung up, I complimented her on her ring tone. Smiling proudly, Fatou replied, "I have many, many more *sikkar*s." She held up her aging phone, its low-resolution, low-colour screen displaying a photograph of Baay Niasse. She brought up its media library and scrolled down a list of mp3 recordings, having me read out their names, which were written in a mixture of Arabic and French spellings. Some were contemporary *sikkarkat*s like Muḥammad Ndaw of Kaffrine and Muḥammad Kébé of Sokone. Others were grainier recordings of the two blind Qur'ān teachers appointed by Baay Niasse to lead *sikkar* at all major Taalibe Baay gatherings, Babacar Thiam (d. 2010), and his teacher, Sëriñ Omar Faati Diallo Niasse.

This list showed that, by "*sikkar*," Fatou meant not only *sikkar* strictly speaking – from the Arabic phrase "*dhikr Allāh*" ("remembrance of God" or "mentioning God"), or repeating God's names or sacred formulas – but a range of genres of sacred chant and song.[1] These included performances of Shaykh Ibrāhīm's panegyric poems *(qaṣā'id*, sing. *qaṣīda)* in Arabic about the Prophet Muḥammad and songs in Wolof praising Shaykh Ibrāhīm composed by his close followers. Throughout this chapter, I refer to this collective repertoire as "sacred chant," and I follow local practice in calling a person who performs this body of sacred chant a *sikkarkat* ("one who engages in *sikkar*/*dhikr*").

Earlier that year (2014), Fatou had paid a man at a market stall 1,000 FCFA to copy these recordings from his own computer. A few years earlier, I had bought many such recordings from a market stall crammed with cassette tapes. These tapes had included a recording of a major gathering just the previous weekend as well as faint copies of copies of recordings made in the 1960s. Today, one no longer readily finds cassettes in the market or working cassette players. Instead, nearly everyone carries a library of low-bitrate recordings on their cell phone. Although Aïda Faye and a handful of others have recorded studio albums, far more of these recordings are from meetings that permeate Senegal's sacred soundscape nearly every night. A growing number are made using meeting attendees' cell phones and iPads.

Since 2001, I have attended dozens of such meetings, ranging from a handful of attendees to hundreds of thousands, in towns and villages throughout Senegal. Although between 2001 and 2005 I had occasionally seen a young woman leading a single song at a small youth *daayira* meeting,[2] before 2009 I was unaware of any woman acting as a primary chant leader in any meeting. Yet in 2009, I was astonished to hear the voice of one Taalibe Baay woman, Aïda Faye, daily through people's ring tones, telephone media libraries, computers, and stereo systems. In 2010 and 2014, I saw Aïda Faye lead *sikkar* at several meetings, from weekly neighbourhood *daayira* meetings to larger *gàmmus* (*mawlids*) attended by thousands of disciples and by major leaders, including Shaykh Ibrāhīm's descendants. I also found several male *muqaddams* teaching female disciples to lead *sikkar* and to perform the repertoire of Arabic and Wolof sacred chant. In several Taalibe Baay evening meetings I attended in 2010, amplification systems carried women chant leaders' powerful, melismatic voices throughout the neighbourhood, and by 2014 the phenomenon seemed even more widespread. In 2014, I also saw many more women speaking in meetings than ever before, although they still did not give the keynote speech at large meetings.

How had women's voices erupted without apparent controversy – indeed with widespread acclaim – into a Sufi soundscape where the very notion of a woman's powerful voice leading religious chant seemed to contradict local norms of reserved feminine piety? While there seems to be no explicit teaching among Fayḍa adherents forbidding women from speaking and singing publicly, their voices have largely been excluded from Senegal's sacred soundscape. Senegalese Fayḍa adherents typically understand the pious Muslim woman as reserved, quiet, and deferential, one who shields herself from public gaze and keeps some distance from men, especially in religious activities. Not just a pious woman's bodily form but also her voice is often described as *'awra* (Ar.). The term "*'awra*" has many usages and translations, often being rendered as "imperfection," "pudendum," and "weakness" (Wehr 1994, 769). In Islamic jurisprudence, it usually refers to the parts of men's and women's bodies to be covered. Based on its uses in the Qur'ān, El Guindi translates "*'awra*" as "inviolate vulnerability" (1999, 142), suggesting something requiring special protection.

In this context, women who lead sacred chant may seem more intrinsically contradictory than the women spiritual guides discussed in previous chapters. Unlike performing musical entertainment, performing sacred chant at public meetings is an act of religious authority and power that presupposes exemplary piety. Yet reconciling the visibility and powerful singing style involved in sacred chant with performances of demure, self-concealed feminine piety is complicated. In contrast, a *muqaddama* can spiritually guide disciples while still wrapping her body, voice, and social presence in public. Moreover, part of the sacredness of such religious meetings stems from their apparently unchanging spatial and temporal structure, which includes separate men's and women's spaces. Today, microphones are usually located in a leaders' area deep within the men's section. Although homes, schools, and workplaces in Senegal show little normative segregation, gender segregation is a relatively stable feature of Islamic ritual activities.

Shaykh Ibrāhīm's writings and precedent ambiguously support the norms of propriety that have usually prevented women from publicly engaging in sacred chant. Yet those who support women's inclusion in Senegal's sacred soundscape cite the same writings and precedent. This chapter addresses how some women have made their voices powerfully heard in religious publics that had previously excluded their voices. Several factors, I suggest, have limited, enabled, and otherwise shaped women's voices in a ritual context. These include the Senegalese notion of *kersa* (shame) in relation to social status (*daraja*) (see chapter 3); the widespread juridical and cultural notion that not only a woman's bodily form but also her voice require veiling as part of her *'awra*; mystical views of gender transcendence and divine mission; and social and economic changes that have subtly accustomed members of the community to seeing and hearing women engaging in high-profile activities. Then I discuss the cases of the two best-known female Taalibe Baay *sikkarkat*s: the pioneer Khady Ndiaye and the current star of the *sikkar* scene, Aïda Faye. First, I begin with a discussion of the history and centrality of *sikkar* and other sacred chant genres in Fayḍa gatherings.

Sacred Chant as Cultural Performance

Nocturnal gatherings in which the repertoire of Taalibe Baay sacred chant comes to life are the primary "cultural performances" (Singer 1955; V. Turner 1987) through which the Taalibe Baay community organizes, enacts, and imagines itself at various scales. These meetings also highlight the Taalibe Baay community's relationships with its various others, both through the presence of government and religious delegations (Hill 2013b) and through the distinctiveness of a community's discourses and chant repertoire. The concentric levels of Taalibe Baay organization exist largely through such meetings (see chapters 1 and 5), which can occasionally become "social dramas" (V. Turner 1957) through which community relations are broken, reconfigured, or healed (Hill 2013b, 2016c).

Indeed, the Fayḍa's moment of inception is usually traced to one such social drama, the 1929 *gàmmu* in Léona Niassène, the *zāwiya* (religious centre) established by Shaykh Ibrāhīm's father, Al-Ḥājj 'Abdallāh Niasse, near Kaolack's city centre. Since his father's death in 1922, young Ibrāhīm himself had acted as the lead *sikkarkat* at the annual *gàmmu,* while his father's oldest son and successor, Muḥammad "al-Khalīfa," took over his father's role of delivering the central *gàmmu* narrative speech. Some accounts of that night say that Ibrāhīm led the chants throughout the night and at one point introduced his new sung poem in praise of the Prophet, "Muḥammad al-Muṣtafā," which has its own melody and is central to large Fayḍa *gàmmus* today. At some point – some say while reciting this poem – he entered a strong *ḥāl,* abruptly jumped up, thumped his chest, and declared himself the successor of Shaykh al-Tijānī and the one through whom anyone who desired to know God must pass.

This social drama established publicly that Shaykh Ibrāhīm claimed an authority higher than that of his elders, occasioning a rift between his followers and followers of his older brother. After Shaykh Ibrāhīm and his followers founded the spiritual centre of Medina Baay in 1932, one of the clearest signals that they were founding a new religious community was that they would henceforth have their own annual *gàmmu,* complete with a new repertoire of sacred chant largely composed by Shaykh Ibrāhīm himself. This included new and distinctive *sikkar* melodies and a series of poetic anthologies *(dawāwīn*, sing. *dīwān)* composed by Shaykh Ibrāhīm in Arabic and sung to his own melodies.

As the leader of the new religious community, Shaykh Ibrāhīm himself would now provide Medina Baay's central *gàmmu* narrative, an account of the miraculous side of the Prophet Muḥammad's life delivered in a sing-song recitative style in Wolof. He left the task of performing *sikkar* to a corps of disciples that included accomplished Islamic scholars. He had them spend the month before each year's Medina Baay *gàmmu* together in a house to practise the texts and melodies of the poems he taught them to sing.

The body of poetic texts and melodies composed by Shaykh Ibrāhīm himself remains the most prestigious and central part of the Taalibe Baay sacred chant repertoire. In addition, many *sikkarkat*s in the community, from his senior sons and prominent deputies to young *sikkarkat*s in local *daayira*s, have contributed new texts and melodies over the years. Each annual *gàmmu* has a slightly different repertoire that includes standards, new compositions, and adaptations of *sikkar* melodies from Nigerian Hausa and Mauritanian Arab disciple communities. Whereas Shaykh Ibrāhīm's own *sikkar* and poetry melodies are indispensable to Senegalese disciples' performances, disciples in these other countries sing the same texts to very different melodies that favour pentatonic rather than Senegal's heptatonic scales.

In a context in which singing, public speaking, and highly animated communication styles have largely been associated with socially stigmatized praise singers (griots or *géwal*) (Irvine 1985), the association of assertive vocal performance with high status may seem surprising. Yet there are numerous genres of high-prestige Islamic sacred chant and oratory. Some of these genres do not require significantly raising one's voice – for example, low-intensity group litanies (called *waẓīfa* and *ḥaḍra* among Tijānīs) and speeches pronounced almost inaudibly then relayed by a lower-status animator (*jottalikat*). Other genres require vocal exertion, such as full-throated renditions of *sikkar*, sung panegyric poems in Arabic praising the Prophet Muḥammad, Wolof songs praising leaders such as Baay,[3] and impassioned religious oratory. Traditions of sacred chant are connected to larger traditions of "sacred audition" *(samāʿ)* among nearly all Sufi communities worldwide.[4] Senegalese Sufis share some sung texts with Sufis around the world – for example, those of the thirteenth-century poet al-Būṣīrī. Many performers of sacred chant and oratory thus have a high social status not shared by non-religious verbal and vocal performers in the Senegalese context. Indeed, the founders of all the major Sufi spiritual lineages in Senegal, including Murid founder Aḥmadu Bamba Mbacké and Tijānī leaders Al-Ḥājj Mālik Sy, Al-Ḥājj 'Abdallāh Niasse, and Muḥammad al-Khalīfa Niasse, composed vast bodies of sung poems in Arabic praising the Prophet Muḥammad. Their close disciples, some of *géwal* heritage and some not, in turn composed songs in Wolof expounding these leaders' unique spiritual characteristics (see Babou 2007). Regardless of their hereditary status, many singers emphasize their devotion to praising their shaykh by dubbing themselves their shaykh's "*géwal*."

Among Taalibe Baay, as among Sufis elsewhere (see, for example, Waugh 2005), sacred chant repertoires are not merely modes of personal artistic expression but are associated with esoteric knowledge and power on at least three levels:

First, their authors are considered to have written them in an inspired spiritual state, encoding profound spiritual teachings and in some cases even predictions directly from God. Even *muqaddams* not fluent in Arabic make a point of memorizing Shaykh Ibrāhīm's poetry along with its Wolof gloss in order to quote it and comment on its mystical teachings while addressing disciples. A prominent *sikkarkat* I interviewed described Ibou Diouf, the best-known composer of Wolof songs about Shaykh Ibrāhīm, as the hidden *(bāṭin)* embodiment of the secret Shaykh Ibrāhīm represented visibly *(ẓāhir)*.[5] Ibou Diouf's poetry thus conveys the imponderable reality made concrete and manifest in Shaykh Ibrāhīm's form. This *sikkarkat* and others approach Ibou Diouf's texts as an inspired reference for mystical truths. They even cite a song Diouf wrote in the 1940s as predicting Shaykh Ibrāhīm's death in 1975 in London.[6] As Aïda Faye said to me, "If you listen very well ... to one word of Ibou Diouf, you can continue your spiritual progression for a long, long time."[7] His songs express "deep mystical knowledge" (*ma'rifa yu xóot*), she said, for "what he is saying is the Qur'ān." "Baay himself would inspire what he said."

Second, performing or listening to sacred chant is essential to cultivating mystical experience. In many meetings, I have seen listeners exhibiting all the behaviours of someone who has fallen into an uncontrollable *ḥāl*, or altered state of mystical experience. Speaking of Babacar Thiam, for many years the best known Taalibe Baay *sikkarkat*, one *muqaddam* declared that "when he does a *gàmmu*, he does it in a *ḥāl*" (Nata Ndiaye, quoted in Hill 2007, 263). His performance is therefore not a form of personal artistic expression but a manifestation of the Divine.

Third, as holy texts, sacred chant texts have talismanic uses, much like Qur'ānic verses. As most Senegalese Taalibe Baay do not understand Arabic, these texts' spiritual power – as distinct from their literal meaning – has particular importance. I have seen manuscripts in some Taalibe Baay religious specialists' homes with instructions on medicinal uses of al-Būṣīrī's verses. Similarly, I have seen dedications that Shaykh Ibrāhīm's descendants have written in his poetry books granting the recipient authorization to "use" the "secrets" found in the text. Although members of a *sikkar* troupe's chorus (the *awukat*s) are often economically and socially marginal, many well-known *sikkar* leaders are considered spiritually powerful religious authorities in their own right. In addition to embodying the esoteric knowledge and power of the texts they master, they may have been directly empowered by Shaykh Ibrāhīm and/or other prominent leaders. Many are also esteemed *muqaddam*s and Qur'ān teachers. Many prominent *sikkarkat*s, such as Babacar Thiam and Omar Faati Diallo Niasse – both of whom were blind yet memorized the Qur'ān and other books of learning – combine all these sources of spiritual potency.

While a few prominent *sikkarkat*s owe their fame largely to their personal connection to Shaykh Ibrāhīm, far more become known – and in some cases earn part of their living – through the local *daayira* meeting circuit. Some work their way up to larger *gàmmu*s and become famous through the viral circulation of recordings of these events. In nearly every *daayira* I have visited, at least one member acts as its *sikkar* leader. In *daayira*s that lack a competent *sikkarkat*, the presiding *muqaddam* may assign one disciple to learn the extensive Wolof and Arabic repertoire of sacred chants, something that requires a considerable investment of time.

Daayira leaders may also invite *sikkarkat*s from outside the *daayira* to help lead their weekly meetings. Attendees sometimes show appreciation by giving a *sikkarkat* a small amount of money. At larger and longer meetings, such as *gàmmu*s, a larger number of *sikkarkat*s take turns leading, sitting around a table and sharing at least two microphones between them. Depending on seniority and audience appreciation, each *sikkarkat* typically makes some money during these larger meetings, both from individual attendees' contributions and from a portion of the event budget allocated to *sikkarkat*s.

Although most *sikkarkat*s derive little or no income from performing sacred chant, for some it becomes a profession and perhaps even a stepping stone towards recognition as a religious figure more generally, as is shown in the story of Aïda Faye below. One well-known *muqaddam* in the Dakar area, Pape Amadi "Baay" Diouf, began his time in Dakar as a *sikkarkat* who would make the rounds of *daayiras*' weekly meetings. Starting in 1999, he released a series of cassettes combining *sikkar* with praise songs for Baay and members of his family, including Baay's mother, Maam Astou Diankha. He was soon appointed as a *muqaddam* and started his own *daayira*. Now his renown is bringing him a clientele as a spiritual healer. Despite not coming from a *géwal* family, he described himself to me in 2004 as "the *géwal* of Baay," highlighting his role as humble praiser, although his self-deprecating performance of discipleship has raised his status in the religious community.

The Islamic ritual sphere has long been an exceptional space in which engaging in high-intensity vocal performance does not suggest low status but, on the contrary, can be associated with the highest-status leaders, including Shaykh Ibrāhīm and his sons. At least this has been the case with men. Women have far less often engaged in verbal performance in religious meetings. As discussed above, both men and women are subject to norms of *kersa* – dignified restraint or shame – although expectations of *kersa* are heightened for pious women. The rest of this chapter examines the ambiguous nature of these norms. While discourses and practices surrounding women's restrained and covered behaviour have often resulted in excluding women's voices from religious ritual contexts, women can also reconfigure and reimagine these norms to allow new modes of pious participation.

Woman's Voices in the Sacred Soundscape

After the late afternoon prayer (*'asr, tàkkusaan*) on a Friday in 2010, a research associate[8] and I sat in Sayyida Seynabou Mbathie's living room and conversed with her and her husband, a white-collar bank employee. A string of young men and women came through to greet her before heading back out to the street, where other young people had begun to spread several large woven plastic mats for the Friday *ḥaḍra* (group litany). After conversing with us for a few minutes, she stretched her hands out palms up (the motion one makes to "accept" [*nangu*] a prayer) and motioned to her husband to pray for us before we all joined the disciples outside.

Conveniently, this street in Dakar's middle-class Sicap Derklé neighbourhood was under construction, and a large pile of sand blocked cars from interrupting Sayyida Saynabou's *daayira*'s street meeting.

A larger-than-life painting of Shaykh Ibra Fall, the legendary disciple of the rival Murid Sufi order, overlooked the meeting place from a nearby wooden kiosk at an intersection popularly named "Baay Faal Corner" after Fall's followers. A couple of young men ran an extension cord from inside Sayyida Seynabou's house to an amplifier in the middle of the seating area, while several others attached two conical, grey loudspeakers to nearby electric poles. Most youth, whether men or women, wore the *daayira*'s uniform: lime-green cotton trousers and a short, white *xaftaan* (robe) with an image of a mosque and the name of the *daayira*, "Chifa Al Askham"[9] ("Healing afflictions"), stencilled in green on the back. Those without uniforms wore similarly coloured outfits, and all the women had draped their heads and shoulders in flowing white scarves.[10]

About fifteen men sat along three sides of a rectangle around the edges of a large plastic mat. The *muqaddama*'s husband sat at their head on the east side, where he would need to be when it came time to lead the dusk prayer. The men left the west edge of the rectangle open, where a roughly equal number of women sat in rows facing into the rectangle. Sayyida Seynabou sat at front and centre of the women's section, facing into the rectangle. This contrasted with most other group litanies I had attended where men formed a closed rectangle with women sitting outside. As women do not lead group litanies or ritual prayer, Sayyida Seynabou motioned to her husband to begin leading the *ḥaḍra*, and all joined in chanting the litany, counting off each short prayer formula on prayer beads (*kurus*). Many of the men projected their voices energetically as they rocked to the rhythm of the litanies, while the women mouthed the words less audibly and with a more subdued rocking motion. Once the sound men had tweaked the sound level and speakers' direction to minimize feedback, the microphones circulated between several male disciples, carrying the litanies through the neighbourhood. The chant tune distinguished this Taalibe Baay *ḥaḍra* from the same litany performed by other branches of the Tijānī order.

The *daayira* finished the Friday *ḥaḍra* just before sundown, and one of the young men who had chanted into the microphone during the litany stood to deliver a drawn-out and melodious call to prayer. The men formed lines behind Sayyida Seynabou's husband and the women behind them for the prayer. Following the sundown prayer, the participants resumed their places for the second group litany, the *waẓīfa*. As the sky quickly darkened, a nearby street lamp dimly lit the meeting. Partway through the *waẓifa,* just before disciples began chanting *Jawharat al-kamāl* ("Pearl of Perfection"), a prayer for the Prophet Muḥammad, *daayira* leaders unfolded a long, white cloth the length of the seating rectangle and weighed its corners with rocks against the wind. This cloth is to welcome the Prophet Muḥammad, Tijānīs say, who comes to sit with them at this time.

As the *daayira* members neared the end of the *waẓifa*, two young men arrived and sat in the men's circle, near where the women sat. Instead of the *daayira*'s uniform, one wore a long, shiny brown *xaftaan* (robe) and fez hat while the other wore a short white *xaftaan* and jeans. As the *waẓifa* ended, a *daayira* leader pronounced a closing prayer in Arabic – one formulated by Shaykh Ibrāhīm and typically recited after Taalibe Baay group *waẓīfa*s – and handed these two men the microphones. The young man in the brown *xaftaan* immediately opened the next phase of the meeting by chanting another long, memorized prayer in Arabic. The disciples stretched out their hands as if to catch the blessings brought by the prayer, repeating *"āmīn yā Rabbī"* ("Amen, my Lord") after each phrase. After the chanter finished, they put their hands to their faces and their hearts as if to wash the blessings over themselves. The chanter then led the congregation in reciting the *Ṣalāt al-Fātiḥ*, which is not only part of litanies but which opens, closes, and punctuates events.

Upon finishing this prayer, the man in brown immediately began slowly chanting *"Lā ilāha illā 'Llāh"* ("There is no divinity but Allāh"). His eyes closed and his face cast downward, he began with the first syllable: *"Lā."* As he drew this syllable out for several seconds, the up-close richness of his voice distorted over the loudspeaker, he and the circle of five or six young men around him began swaying slowly forward. By the end of this first word, they had swayed back again in slow unison.

He continued with the second word of the dhikr: *"ilāha."* His voice jumped up an interval of a fourth as he drew out the long second syllable. The circle of chant leaders once again swayed slowly forward, eyes cast downward, and their swaying motion soon spread to some of the young men immediately around them. The leader finished the first iteration of the *dhikr* with an insistence in his voice, joining the *"ha"* from the second word to the remaining words to yield *"hayllallāh."* Once again he drew out the final long vowel, during which he and the others swayed slowly forward then back a third time. He then repeated the whole phrase once more, this time meandering back down to the note on which he had begun. These two recitations took him more than ten seconds, after which he pointed the microphone towards several *daayira* members to broadcast their voices while dropping his own head and closing his eyes as if sleeping. The other visiting *sikkarkat* led the response into the second microphone, repeating the *dhikr* twice in the same melody as *daayira* members joined in. Many voices were audible from close range, but the speakers only broadcast the voices of these two leaders and a few male *daayira* members in the inner circle. From where I was sitting, though, I could hear that some of the women had begun chanting along, and as the *dhikr* progressed, they seemed to become more comfortable and sang with more gusto.

Near the end of the audience's second iteration, the leader inhaled and drew the microphone back to himself, joining the others in singing the final *"hayllallāh"* and then transitioning without a breath back to the initial *"Lā,"* repeating the *dhikr* twice in the same weighty melody and pace. The audience in turn joined the leaders in the second *"hayllallāh"* and then repeated the *dhikr* twice in the same fashion. As long as the *dhikr* is repeated in this interlocked fashion without pauses between, the phrase's connotation of God's indivisibility and continuity is embodied in the chant. Emphasizing this point of one divine reality, some attendees shook their right index finger in the air while using their left hand to cover an ear to hear their own pitch as they swayed and chanted.

After a little over ten minutes of repeating this *dhikr* melody with some minor melismatic variations, the lead *sikkarkat* introduced the next variation, Shaykh Ibrāhīm's original "Kossi" melody. This variation is slow but somewhat less glacial than the first. Every few minutes, the leader introduced slight variations.

As the *dhikr* progressed, more young men and women filtered into the seating area, kneeling and bowing their heads to greet Sayyida Seynabou before taking their seats. A few minutes after the *dhikr* had begun, a woman discreetly approached the group and sat next to Sayyida Seynabou at the front of the women's section and next to the male *sikkarkat*s. Like the male chant leaders, instead of the *daayira*'s colours, she wore a multicoloured Mauritanian-style *malaḥfa* (*mëlfa*) wrap. This was Aïda Faye, the current superstar of the Taalibe Baay *sikkar* circuit and, it so happens, a childhood friend of Sayyida Seynabou from Kaolack. Aïda Faye bowed her head and listened as the men led the chant for more than half an hour.

Then they handed her a microphone. She began her contribution to the night by singing a standard Arabic poem *(qaṣīda)* by Shaykh Ibrāhīm about Shaykh al-Tijānī. After every line, the other *sikkarkat*s and the audience would sing the first line of the poem as a refrain. Aïda Faye's eyes remained closed throughout her performance, her penetrating voice echoing throughout the neighbourhood yet her facial expression staying vacant, as if she were somewhere else.

She spent the next two hours alternating with – and at times engaging in virtuosic improvisational *dhikr* duels with – the male *sikkar* leaders. She punctuated her melismatic *sikkar* with more of Shaykh Ibrāhīm's *qaṣā'id* and syncopated Wolof praise songs for Baay composed by Baay's companion Ibou Diouf and more recent composers, each with its chorus sung by the audience. Almost every poetic line or improvised *dhikr* elicited calls of appreciation (*"ëskëy!," "ee waay!," "dëgg la!"* [It's true!]) from the audience. Minutes into Aïda Faye's chant, a young man entered a state of *jadhb* (ecstasy or insanity), leaping up, screaming, and thrashing about fiercely. Several other men used all their force to hold down the *majdhūb* (one experiencing *jadhb*, literally, one who is seized or dragged along) to prevent injuries, and a woman brought a cup of water for the men to give the *majdhūb*. One by one, several young men and women entered the same state. The same man who had at one moment mustered all his calm and strength to hold down one disciple at another moment suddenly became the *majdhūb*. Only occasionally have I witnessed so many people exhibiting such powerful states *(ḥāl)* in a weekly *daayira* meeting. Sayyida Seynabou had told me before the meeting that whenever she and Aïda Faye share a meeting, many people have "states" *(ḥāl)* of spiritual ecstasy. Shortly before midnight, Aïda Faye culminated her chanting with an interpretation of a rousing Mauritanian *dhikr* melody as many disciples chanted along. The intense volley of sacred chant between Aïda Faye, the other *sikkar* leaders, and the audience ended with the male *sikkarkat*s leading the standard collective recitation of the *Ṣalāt al-Fātiḥ*.

Aïda Faye then held onto the microphone and gave a short speech thanking Baay Niasse – repeating several times *"jërëjëfee Baay Ñas!"* – "Thank you, Baay Niasse!" – and apologizing to the neighbours – several of whom had been watching attentively from their windows – for the disturbance and the length of the meeting. This was one of the very few times I had heard a woman either lead the *sikkar* or directly address a Taalibe Baay meeting. Aïda Faye's gentle, friendly tone contrasted strikingly to her energetic singing, sounding less like that of the typical impassioned male orator than that of a gentle young mother.

After a short speech by the male *daayira* president, Sayyida Seynabou gave the closing speech. Instead of addressing the audience directly, she spoke almost inaudibly to a male *daayira* leader positioned at the edge of the women's section, and he relayed her words through the microphone. Nearly all the adult women I have heard address Taalibe Baay assemblies have spoken in this way through an animator (*jottalikat*). She tailored her speech to my research topic for my benefit, discussing how Islamic law *(sharīʿa)* introduced the idea of women's equality "in the visible" (*ci ẓāhir*), and how the deeper reality of Islam abolishes the very distinction between men and women "in the hidden" (*ci bāṭin*). She then had a male disciple "seal" the meeting by reciting a memorized prayer in Arabic.

Throughout the meeting, Sayyida Seynabou and Sayyida Aïda navigated in multiple ways between the shown and the hidden, assertiveness and restraint (*kersa*). Rather than merely steer a middle course, they played up the tensions between these opposites, shaping an outward image through performing inward-looking, restrained, and submissive behaviour. To any observer, these two women were the meeting's leading figures, and attendees' deference to both women was clear. Yet both women also engaged in many rituals of deference and self-effacement, which ultimately served to index piety and enhance their moral authority.

Although these women's voices were the most prominent in the meeting, both dissociated themselves – albeit in opposite ways – from the act of making their voices heard. Sayyida Seynabou did so through designating someone else as the "animator" of the words of which she was the "author" (Goffman 1981). Inversely, Aïda Faye presented her physical form as the "animator" while suggesting through her vacant expression that she was not the "author" of this act of chanting. Her shy-sounding speaking voice belied any suggestion that this potent chanting voice was all her own.

In numerous ways Sayyida Seynabou demonstrated deference to her husband as master of the house: she asked him to pray for us visitors rather than praying for us herself, as a religious figure normally does for all visitors. She also had him lead congregational prayer and litanies. On previous visits, whenever her husband was absent, she always had us greet him over her cell phone, fulfilling her religious obligation to seek a husband's consent to talk to other men. However, despite her rituals of submission, she was clearly the one delegating, and attendees surely perceived his more visible position as deriving from her more subdued position. She managed the meeting in other ways while remaining properly "enclosed" (Boddy 1989), speaking almost inaudibly through an animator and then asking a male disciple to pray for the congregation to close the meeting. By orchestrating a meeting seen and heard throughout the neighbourhood without broadcasting her voice, she demonstrated that restraint is power. Her silent message about empowering women through Islam was heard through the animator and demonstrated through the meeting itself.

In short, these felicitous performances of wrapped piety successfully differentiated humility from abasement, as Shaykh Ibrāhīm exhorted disciples to do (see chapter 3).

The Woman's Voice and *Kersa*

By the time I attended this meeting, I had attended many dozens of Taalibe Baay meetings and had only seen a handful of women address the audience. There seemed to be a rule that a pious woman of a certain social rank does not raise her voice in a religious meeting. Nearly all the women I had seen speak in religious meetings had been young students asked to demonstrate mastery of their lessons or speak on some assigned theme – usually "The Woman in Islam" – and they had spoken early in the program well before the male keynote speaker.

Several interlocutors explicitly mentioned the belief, widespread throughout the Muslim world, that not only a woman's body but also her voice is *'awra,* something protected from exposure, generally because it can arouse sexual desire (this belief is mentioned in Schielke 2008; Frishkopf 2009, 83n; Janson 2014, 176n). Whether or not they explicitly described the woman's voice as *'awra,* most *muqaddama*s acted as if there were some truth to the claim. Some refrained from addressing public assemblies altogether, while others attenuated their voices, often by relaying their speech through an animator (*jottalikat*). Nonetheless, none of the *muqaddama*s and few Taalibe Baay I spoke with in Dakar held that Islam forbade women from speaking or chanting before a gathering. When I have asked why women rarely speak in meetings, interviewees have almost always explained that most women are simply shy about drawing attention to themselves. Perhaps this is somewhat true, yet this shyness itself is not an accident or inherent quality but is something carefully cultivated from a young age. Just as women learn to "wrap" their bodily form, they learn to wrap their voices and presence.

The notion of performing piety through wrapping the voice and other aspects of one's presence owes as much to West African traditions of power and nobility as it does to teachings derived from the Qur'ān and *ḥadīth.* In contrast to liberal assumptions that prestige and freedom require visibility and audibility in a public sphere, in traditional settings in Senegal, the ideal of *kersa* – dignified restraint or shame – requires any person of high status (*daraja*) to attenuate his or her presence – for example, never speaking with high volume, speed, or pitch.

To address an assembly while maintaining restraint requires speaking through an animator of lower status, whether by age, class, or birth – often someone born into the *géwal* (praise singer or "griot") occupational group (Irvine 1989; Heath 1990; McLaughlin 1997). Even if many high-status leaders, male and female, still opt to perform maximum *kersa* by speaking through an animator, the animator's role is optional in religious oratory today. First, a microphone can stand in for an animator, carrying a subdued voice to a large audience (Irvine 1974; Heath 1990). Furthermore, the old rules of *kersa* are often suspended in today's religious meetings. Some of Shaykh Ibrāhīm's sons speak with forcefulness and wide dynamic and tonal range, attributes understood in this context to demonstrate not a lack of *kersa* but the importance of the message. Islamic orators – especially the many Senegalese leaders who encountered various oratorical styles while studying at Al-Azhar University in Cairo – can appeal to translocal Islamic traditions of fiery Islamic oratory.

While men and women must both perform *kersa*, the norms of *kersa* are more stringent for women. If performing *kersa* sometimes binds men to address a public only through human or technological mediation, it more often leads women not to address the public at all, or to do so in such an indirect way that they appear not to be addressing. Just as forms of sartorial covering serve as "portable seclusion," mediating women's presence in public spaces while maintaining their "mystery and remoteness" (Papanek 1971), various kinds of non-sartorial wrappers mediate Taalibe Baay women's addresses to their publics outside their homes. It is important to remember that in many contexts practices of women's seclusion and veiling have marked a family's social and economic distinction (Papanek 1971; Tucker 1993; Cooper 1994, 1997b). A certain degree of seclusion and veiling is widespread among women in Senegalese clerical households, although many disciples understand these practices as not applicable to them.

The uncommon degree to which Shaykh Ibrāhīm's senior daughters veil their bodies and voices confirms this relationship between wrapping and status. Shaykh Ibrāhīm's daughter Ndèye Aïda went further than the handful of women I had seen address meetings quietly or through an animator. When she organized her annual "Maam Astou

Diankha Day" conference on women in Islam in Kaolack in 2010, she remained motionless in her seat as a younger brother read a statement she had written, translating her Arabic into Wolof. Although a foreign observer might have perceived her as subordinating herself to him by allowing him to represent her, viewers surely understood him as assuming a less prestigious position as her *jottalikat*. Many *muqaddama*s directly address small groups of disciples in their home but decline to speak outside in larger gatherings, instead assigning disciples or male relatives to speak on their behalf. When I asked them why, none of them gave a moral or religious explanation; most answered that they were simply uncomfortable speaking in public.

Considering Sayyida Seynabou's confidence and eloquence when speaking inside her house before numerous non-relatives, one cannot say that she lacks the confidence to speak publicly. Nor does she believe that a woman's voice must not be heard by unrelated men – a belief implied by a legalistic reading of "*'awra.*" Rather, her confident display of silence and use of male intermediaries to represent her to the public – to "wrap" her – served as part of a public performance of a proper Muslim woman's demure piety and withdrawal from worldly affairs. Sayyida Seynabou thus amplified conventional notions of feminine interiority, submissiveness, and nobility to heighten her spiritual authority and mystique.

Of course, publicly performing submissiveness can only augment one's moral authority if one already has sufficiently high status that such acts appear as optional acts of humble piety and not as obligatory acts of subservience. Submissiveness and reclusiveness can exemplify what Bourdieu (1991) calls "condescension," a disavowal of the very hierarchies from which one benefits in a way that enhances one's status. The legendary models of feminine piety known in Senegal are those of saints' mothers who are celebrated for their absolute devotion and submission to their husbands. Murids say that the mother of Amadou Bamba Mbacké, Maam Diarra Bousso, was asked to hold a wooden beam by her husband, who then forgot to tell her to stop holding it and left her standing all night in the rain (Augis 2005, 314). Pape Amadi ("Baay") Diouf's well-known song praising Shaykh Ibrāhīm's mother, Maam Astou Diankha, instead of concrete biographical information, lists qualities that could describe any pious woman: "She never fought and never harmed him [Baay]. Astou Diankha was a noble woman … She had no use for sitting around blaming people … She never quarreled or laughed out loud … Ever pure for her leader [husband], she never left without permission ... Astou's qualities atonish me. May every lady imitate her" (A. Diouf 2004). Drawing on such models, Sayyida Seynabou consecrates acts of wifely submission as acts of piety before God, using submission to God's *ẓāhir* prescriptions to reveal a contrasting *bāṭin* truth. To count as pious humility rather than abasement, such acts must be perceived as a choice made by someone who could otherwise have set herself above everyone else.

Is the Woman's Voice *'Awra?*

In 2010, I asked Shaykh Ibrāhīm's daughter Sayyida Ruqayya Niasse (b. 1931) whether she agreed with the claim that a woman's voice is *'awra.* Sitting on her bed, where she normally receives visitors, the eighty-year-old scholar and Qur'ān teacher who has travelled the world giving speeches paused and then answered, "Some people say that." Although Sayyida Ruqayya is a scholar qualified to provide a juridical explanation either affirming or denying this view, she instead told me an ambiguous story.

Once while travelling in Sierra Leone with her husband ('Umar Ma'abdu Niang, the son of Baay's probable first *muqaddam),* she said, she was introduced to a large group of people who wanted to convert to Islam. They asked her to address them, but some local scholars *('ulamā')* entreated her to refuse because a woman's voice was *'awra.* She went ahead and spoke to the assembly. When she later asked Shaykh Ibrāhīm for his opinion, he told her that she had done well. If there was any sin in raising her voice publicly, he said, the good in introducing people to God's religion outweighed it. While to some this story might suggest that it is a sin for women to speak publicly except in rare, urgent situations, Sayyida Ruqayya's actions contradict such an interpretation. She went on to give countless public speeches in Medina Baay and around the world to religious and secular audiences. As I was writing this chapter, she was a speaker at a meeting held by the Carter Center in Atlanta.

Shaykh Ibrāhīm's writings are similarly ambiguous on the question. As far as I am aware, nowhere does he explicitly endorse the view that a woman's voice is *'awra* or forbid women from being heard in religious meetings. Yet he sometimes suggests that it is more meritorious – though not imperative – for women to worship and perform *sikkar* silently. In the same fatwa in which he writes that women can be given all the divine secrets, Shaykh Ibrāhīm says that he performs *dhikr* both quietly and aloud, as the Prophet's grandson Ḥasan did, yet he qualifies that "silence may suffice for women, for silence is God's" ([Niasse] 1969, 1:131). This preference for women's silent worship may be inspired by the Mālikī jurisprudence texts that govern ritual practice in the region; these texts prescribe that while performing prayers women should attenuate their movements and should not recite aloud as men do (see, for example, Al-Azharī n.d., 116; see also Geissinger 2013 on prescriptions for women's attenuated movements and voice during prayer).

Although Shaykh Ibrāhīm is not known to have categorically prohibited women from performing *sikkar* aloud or in public, anecdotes depict him as not encouraging them to do so. Several interviewees described one of his wives, Faat Ndiaye Touré, as a gifted *sikkarkat* who only performed for him in their bedroom. Commenting on this example, a male *daayira* president in Dakar explained that this was "because she was his wife and [her voice] was *'awra.*" The other women known to perform *sikkar* in Baay's presence were of *géwal* status, and even they did not do so in public. As one woman of *géwal* heritage who received *tarbiya* from Baay, Mengué Thiam, told us, "Only I dared to stand at the door of Baay Niasse and sing [meaning perform *sikkar*] ... He [Baay] made me know God, gave me clothing, and said: 'You are to sing; nothing bad will happen to you.'" Aïda Faye's story below tells of another *géwal* woman, her own grandmother, who also performed *sikkar* for Baay in his home.

Although Shaykh Ibrāhīm did request that girls at his Islamic Institute in Kaolack speak at their demonstrations in front of foreign dignitaries,[11] the only woman known to speak in a large religious meeting in his presence is his daughter Ruqayya, whom he assigned numerous times to give a short speech on some theme during the annual Medina Baay *gàmmu* when she was a student.[12] It is noteworthy that all the women Shaykh Ibrāhīm asked to speak in meetings seem to have been unmarried students. Pedagogical purposes and their junior status apparently justified any perceived breach of decorum. Following this precedent, almost every woman I have seen address a large Taalibe Baay *gàmmu* or conference has been a young student, most often either reciting the Qur'ān or speaking about women in Islam. In short, Shaykh Ibrāhīm's precedent and writings implicitly seem to treat women's voices as *'awra,* not as an absolute law but as a general principle of socially decorous *kersa.*

My interviews and observations reveal a similarly ambiguous approach among prominent Fayḍa women today. They widely accept that *sharī'a* teaches that the woman's voice is *'awra;* they deny the interpretation that this actually forbids or discourages women from speaking truth in public; yet they voluntarily restrict or attenuate their own vocal participation in religious gatherings as part of their performances of feminine piety. They suggest that women have the right to speak yet opt not to do so to demonstrate exemplary piety and dignity, guarding their voices and bodies from the public (especially male) gaze. They suggest that treating one's voice as *ʿawra* is less an Islamic legal obligation than an index of pious dignity.

Several *muqaddamas* endorsed the notion that a woman's voice is *ʿawra,* yet, like Shaykh Ibrāhīm, maintained an open-ended interpretation. Some interpreted the teaching as simply implying that women's voices should only be used for morally positive purposes, while others suggested that this teaching only applied to the ritual domain, and even then not absolutely. Sayyida Awa Cissé implicitly affirmed that the woman's voice was *ʿawra* yet suggested that this only applied to speech that has negative effects. As she explained,

> They say a woman's voice should not go out in the open. If you hear people saying that, it means you shouldn't stand there saying ugly things for everyone to hear. But if you are preaching about God, saying good things that will help people, then even if you have loudspeakers, put them up and say it! It's not forbidden.[13]

Explaining why women do not act as imams, the *muqaddama* Sayyida Khadi Fall told us that "even the voice of a woman can be *ʿawra* for a man,"[14] or a source of sexual temptation like the bodily form. "However," she qualified, "a woman can *sikkar,* but if she does, her voice should not be extremely loud." Still, she continued, women do perform *sikkar* today without restrictions and even sell albums, and "ultimately, that's art … There's religion, but art and religion go together in that respect." This ambivalent explanation echoes an attitude widespread among Fayḍa adherents that, in ritual contexts, it is decorous for women to defer to long-standing norms of feminine piety, but that these norms are neither moral imperatives nor equally applicable in other fields, such as "art," including religious art. Thus, while a Muslim woman university professor may increase her academic authority through addressing a lecture hall full of academics, the same woman baldly addressing a religious gathering may compromise her performance of exemplary piety and hence her authority to address the meeting in the first place.

Religious singing or chanting, of course, is an area where one cannot perform through an intermediary in the traditional sense. Women singers must find other alibis for presenting their voices in public. They do this in two principal ways: first, by representing themselves not as agents of their singing but as intermediaries of forces they do not control; and second, by using technological intermediaries that allow them to reach an audience indirectly. Much like women who participate in spirit possession rituals throughout Africa and beyond (Boddy 1989; Masquelier 2001), women Sufi singers narrate their trajectory into singing – as into the Fayḍa itself – as something they did not choose or control. They perform in a way suggestive of a trance-like state or mystical *ḥāl*, closing their eyes and seeming to be "pulled along" *(majdhūb)* by a power larger than themselves. The microphone and various technologies used to disseminate and circulate recordings also seem to serve as a veil separating performer and listener, such that they are not co-present in a questionable relationship.[15] The distortion and reverberations that some outsiders may perceive as degrading the natural quality of chanters' voices is actually highly appreciated, both concealing and embellishing their voices, much as their clothing does their body (A.K. Rasmussen 2010 makes a similar observation regarding Indonesia).

The remainder of this chapter illustrates these principles through a discussion of the two best-known Taalibe Baay women *sikkarkat*s, Sayyidas Khady Ndiaye and Aïda Faye. These two women surprised me by breaking with the apparent consensus that a pious woman must not display herself in the open, whether visually, aurally, or otherwise. Their stories suggest answers to this book's central question of how novel authoritative performances become naturalized with little controversy.

Khady Ndiaye: A Pioneer of *Sikkar*

By 1985, more than two decades before Aïda Faye became a sensation, Khady Ndiaye had become perhaps the first woman to perform regularly in Fayḍa *daayira* meetings and *gàmmu*s. Although viral media have less often carried her voice beyond these meetings, many people I spoke with in Dakar were familiar with her and had heard bootleg recordings of her. On 1 June 2014, she invited my assistant, Nazirou Thiam, and me to attend a *gàmmu* organized by her younger full brother, Cheikh Babacar Ndiaye, a *muqaddam* and *sikkarkat* (figure 6.1). He leads a growing *daayira* on the far side of the new but quickly growing north-eastern Dakar suburb of Yeumbeul, where this *gàmmu* took place. This was the first of two all-night *gàmmu*s we saw that summer featuring the sister-brother pair, both of which we filmed for their and our own archives.

Figure 6.1 Khady Ndiaye and her younger brother, Babacar Ndiaye (left), leading *sikkar* at a *gàmmu* in 2014.

Near midnight, just after dinner, Khady Ndiaye was able to find an hour to talk with us between eating dinner; preparing for the *gàmmu*; the hubbub of the arriving leader, Baay Sokhna; and her visits to relatives in the neighbourhood. This evening was the first time I met Khady Ndiaye, and I was struck by how youthful this veteran *sikkarkat* looked. When we interviewed her, she wore a bright pink dress and hair tie, the kind women wear at weddings and other major social events; but when she appeared in the tent later as the evening's head *sikkarkat*, she wore a more enclosing Mauritanian-style *malaḥfa* (body wrap). Her change in dress accompanied a dramatic change in verbal style, from gentle, jovial, and humorous to powerful, assertive, mysterious, and sombre. She joined Cheikh Babacar, another full younger brother and sister, and several other male and female *sikkarkat*s around the *sikkar* table. All took turns leading, although Khady Ndiaye and Cheikh Babacar were the primary leaders. The *gàmmu* continued from midnight until well after sunrise. A week later, we returned to the same public square in Yeumbeul to see the sister-brother duo once again lead *sikkar* at a larger *gàmmu*, this one organized by a different *daayira*, Chababoul Fayḍa ("Youth of the Fayḍa"), presided over by Shaykh Ibrāhīm's youngest son, Sëriñ Babacar "Baay Mbay Emcee" Niasse.

Khady Ndiaye was born in the town of Fatick, about forty kilometres north-west of Kaolack on the road to Dakar. Although she was unsure about numerical years, her narrative suggested that she was born around 1970. She told us she had been singing in *gàmmus* for nearly thirty years, or since around 1985, not long after her husband gave her *tarbiya* when she was a thirteen-year-old new mother. Her parents were adherents of the Tivaouane-based branch of the Tijāniyya, and her father would sing in this group's meetings, although both parents' roots were in Muridism.[16] So she grew up singing *sikkar* according to the melodies of Tivaouane, which she would sing around the house and later in *daayira* meetings of this branch of the Tijāniyya, even though she was just a child and had not officially taken the *wird*.

She was a thirteen-year-old Qur'ān student in Fatick (sometime around 1983) when her family married her off to a Qur'ān teacher and Islamic scholar who lived to the east in Kaffrine. Within a year, she had her first child and came from Kaffrine to stay with her mother in Fatick. Her husband soon joined her there, yet she soon returned to his family in Kaffrine while he remained with her parents in Fatick, having been invited to stay through the month of Ramadan to deliver the customary daily Qur'ān exegesis (*piri, tafsīr*) at the mosque. Her husband was then a follower of Shaykh Ibrāhīm's older brother, Khalīfa Niasse. Yet during that month of Ramadan while staying at her parents' house, he had a waking vision of Shaykh Ibrāhīm in his room.

Overcome with the need to know God immediately, he left the next morning after daybreak prayers, neither bidding farewell to Khady's parents nor fulfilling his commitment to finish the month-long Qur'ānic exegesis. When he arrived in Medina Baay, he asked for Baay Niasse and was told that he had passed away some years before but was represented by his oldest son, Al-Ḥājj 'Abdallāh, who was then visiting the village of Taïba Niassène. He went to the village and presented himself to Al-Ḥājj 'Abdallāh, telling him of his vision and saying, "Knowing God is what I'm after." Apparently testing his resolve, Al-Ḥājj 'Abdallāh told him that since it was Ramadan and he was a head of household and a religious leader, he should go back to Kaffrine until Ramadan was over. He replied, "I don't need Ramadan. I don't need family. I'm here to know God, and I will not leave Taïba Niassène without getting what I'm after." Al-Ḥājj 'Abdallāh then knew that this person was true in God.

Khady Ndiaye's husband gave Al-Ḥājj 'Abdallāh the robe he was carrying, as well as the gold jewellery Khady Ndiaye's family had given him to bring to her, telling him he gave him everything and no longer needed anything. Al-Ḥājj ʿAbdallāh initiated his *tarbiya* and then returned to Kaolack, entrusting him to another *muqaddam* in Taïba Niassène to finish his *tarbiya*. During his *tarbiya*, her husband did service *(khidma)* for the *shaykh*, cutting wood and clearing fields. As he worked and recited the *tarbiya* litanies in the fields, he wrote a Wolof song (which he later translated into Arabic) about Shaykh Ibrāhīm and his family. After he achieved *fatḥ*, the immediate goal of *tarbiya*, he stopped by Kaolack to visit Al-Ḥājj ʿAbdallāh Niasse on his way back to Kaffrine. Al-Ḥājj ʿAbdallāh gave him an unlimited *ijāza* on the spot.

Now that he was a *muqaddam*, Khady Ndiaye's husband immediately set about spreading knowledge of God. The first person to whom he gave *tarbiya* was his first wife, followed by his second wife, Khady Ndiaye, who had given birth just two months earlier. Although she had given up her formal Qurʾānic education when she married, her husband continued informally to teach her the Qurʾān as well as religious poetry that she would later sing in meetings. Already familiar with religious singing, soon after her *tarbiya* she began singing first in local *daayira* meetings and then in large *gàmmu*s in the area. Khady Ndiaye was the first of many to perform her husband's song publicly, and she says anyone who has sung it since then has learned it from her.

All of Khady Ndiaye's brothers and sisters who share the same mother and father followed her lead, becoming both Taalibe Baay and *sikkarkat*s. While her younger brother, Cheikh Babacar, is a committed follower of Baay Sokhna and is the *muqaddam* in charge of the Yeumbeul *daayira* affiliated with him, Khady Ndiaye describes herself as unaffiliated with any *daayira* or *muqaddam*. She explained that if she were affiliated, people would assume that she was only interested in performing *sikkar* for that *daayira*, whereas she will come to "anyone who needs [her] for Mawlānā Shaykh Ibrāhīm, wherever they may need [her]." Although she is no longer married to her first husband, she says she still maintains good relations with him and that he is the closest thing she has to a spiritual leader. She lives largely independently of her current husband in the Dakar suburb of Keur Massar while her husband lives in a small town in Saalum.

Khady Ndiaye told us that when she started performing *sikkar* publicly, "no woman in the community of Baay Niasse was *sikkar*-ing. Back then, Aïda Faye was a small child." Yet if it was shocking for some to see a woman singing intense full-throated chants in the public square, her voice broadcast throughout the town over loudspeakers, Khady does not let on that it was ever an issue. When I asked if she had ever heard people saying women should not do this sort of thing, she immediately said, "Yes! I sometimes hear it! That a woman's voice is *'awra,* that it should not show!" Yet she clarified that she had never heard such a thing from anyone "in Baay's community (*péey*)." Only once has her being a woman been an issue, when she was leading *sikkar* in a village *gàmmu* three years ago. There, the visiting authority from Medina Baay told the *sikkarkat*s – rightly, she added – "Let the men sit away from the young woman who is *sikkar*-ing – give her some space – don't sit near her, because a woman should not be next to a man."

The overwhelming response from leaders has been one not of criticism but of support. Khady Ndiaye mentioned several sons of Shaykh Ibrāhīm and other major leaders with whom she has relationships and who have expressed appreciation for her work. One wrote a poem specifically for her to sing. Another senior son of Shaykh Ibrāhīm, she told us, came to her as he was leaving a *gàmmu* and said, "Thank you. I listened to you. Never stop the way I heard you *sikkar*." He told her he knew it came from the heart.

To my surprise, she also insists that no one within the community had ever suggested upholding the purity of the division of the ritual space into men's and women's sections, much less suggested that women should not sing in public. When she performs, she sits at the same table where male *sikkarkat*s sit, within the larger men's section.

Like all other Fayḍa adherents I spoke to who defended the propriety of women's performing sacred chant, she did not openly contest the juridical notion of the woman's voice being *'awra* but rather appealed to mystical transcendence:

> In the community of Baay Niasse, when we hear a woman's voice – or a man's voice – we do not experience anything but God. So in that case we don't even see that the person speaking is a woman in order to feel something towards her. We don't look at who is speaking. It is what that person is saying that we desire. It is because we are experiencing God that what the person is saying is all that we desire, to the point that we don't see the body that speaks.

Therefore, if under some circumstances a woman's voice could make hearers "feel something towards her," the reason for her voice being called *'awra,* this is not relevant to a community that only cares about and sees God.

Like many others, when I asked her why so few women *sikkar*, her answer cited not social norms but individual ability and inclination. She said some women would like to *sikkar* but "a good voice is something God gives to a person." One woman she has been teaching for years "still can't sing." No matter how hard one tries, "*sikkar* is a gift from God ... *Sikkar* is hard! Especially *sikkar* of Baay Niasse's people – it's hard." She explained that it "requires strength" (*laaj doole*), to the point that if she were leading and I were singing the response (*awu*), I would get tired but she would continue throughout the night. She even becomes ill from expending so much energy performing *sikkar*, and sometimes she spends all the money she is given for a *gàmmu* to pay for prescriptions necessitated by her performance. She attributes her diabetes and general fatigue to her constant *sikkar* performances. Just two months before our interview, she was in the hospital, and the doctor forbade her to perform and told her to rest for at least two months. Yet she cannot stop, she told us. Only three or four days after leaving the hospital, she was performing.

For Khady Ndiaye, then, *sikkar* is not a personal preference but an inexorable mission, one in which her gender plays a purely positive role. She told us of people who had entered Islam and the Fayḍa through hearing her *sikkar*. In one case, a group of five Séeréer Christians from a village in Saalum heard her singing at a *gàmmu* in Dakar and were amazed to see a woman performing in a *gàmmu*. The morning after the *gàmmu*, they approached her and asked, "How does one become part of this?" She answered that it was easy – you just need to approach a *muqaddam* of Baay Niasse and receive *tarbiya*. They continued, "Ok, now, what if one hasn't converted, if one isn't a Muslim?" She answered that one must first be a Muslim. They asked her to give them *tarbiya*, but she answered that she did not have authorization *(ijāza)* to do so, so they would have to find someone else. When they started *tarbiya*, they called her and asked her to pray for them to reach God (*àgg ci Yàlla*) soon. They called her again after reaching God, telling her they wanted her to come to their village to perform a *gàmmu* for them. She has gone to the village every year since. Over the years she saw the place where they would gather to drink alcohol and drum and dance transformed into a Friday mosque.

This story presents Khady Ndiaye's womanhood not merely as a superficial distinction transcended in divine unity but as precisely what caught the Christians' attention. Whether or not her narrative adequately accounts for their conversion, it illustrates her own perception that her gender helps her reach people.

A pioneer of women's *sikkar*, Khady Ndiaye led the *sikkar* at dozens of *gàmmus* decades before most Taalibe Baay were aware that women could do so. Yet she has not attained the same superstar status that Aïda Faye has. She attributes this to the fact that she lacks the time, resources, and connections to produce a studio album as Aïda Faye has. The only studio production in which she has participated is a song by a Taalibe Baay rapper incorporating *sikkar* and Baay Niasse's poetry. Now, she says, she is too busy travelling from village to village to think about producing an album.

Aïda Faye: A Viral Superstar

Aïda Faye describes Khady Ndiaye as a mother figure, in terms of both influence and age difference. Yet Aïda Faye has eclipsed not only Khady Ndiaye but perhaps all other Taalibe Baay *sikkarkat*s in popular recognition through the viral power of ringtones, cell phone media collections, and YouTube videos. Beyond the bootleg recordings of her performances in night meetings found on nearly every Taalibe Baay cell phone or portable computer, she has produced a studio album of religious chants with backup singers and subdued electronic accompaniment. In 2007 she and her collaborators produced a glossy YouTube video for one of the songs from the album, "Delou Ci Yalla" ("Return to God").[17] In the same year she also contributed vocals to and featured in the video of a popular hip hop song – "Soldarou Baye" or "Soldier of Baay"[18] – by Daddy Bibson, a famous rapper who shares a *daayira* and spiritual guide with her. She is one of the most sought-after *sikkarkat*s on the *sikkar* scene, performing at dozens of *gàmmus* and *daayira* meetings throughout the year (figure 6.2).

Aïda Faye's gentle speaking voice contrasts starkly to her energetic, high-intensity singing voice. Whether performing or sitting at home, she often covers herself in the colourful *malaḥfa* typical of Mauritanian Arab women, and her self-effacing speech demonstrates exemplary feminine *kersa*. At home, she is deferential to her husband, a *muqaddam* of ʿAbdallāh Wilane of Kaffrine. Over the past few years she has had two small children, whom she often brings with her to her *sikkar* performances. In 2014, she occasionally nursed her baby as another *sikkarkat* took over leading.

Like Khady Ndiaye, Aïda Faye was born into a family of *sikkarkat*s, although she was born into a Taalibe Baay family in Medina Baay. Her grandparents were personally close to Shaykh Ibrāhīm. In an interview

Figure 6.2 Aïda Faye leading *sikkar* at a *gàmmu* in 2014.

conducted in her home in Dakar in 2014,[19] she told us that her mother's father helped carry Shaykh Ibrāhīm's books from Léona Niassène to Medina Baay, which would have been around 1932.

Her father's mother performed domestic service for Shaykh Ibrāhīm's wife Faat Ndiaye Touré, and the two women used to sing *sikkar* to Baay inside and at the doorway of his room. A son of Shaykh Ibrāhīm and Faat Ndiaye Touré told Aïda Faye of one occasion when Shaykh Ibrāhīm was in a strong spiritual state *(ḥāl)* and secluded himself in his room, where no one dared disturb him. The two women sat outside the room *sikkar*-ing for a long time, "until Baay opened the door and asked, who is that?" When they identified themselves, he came out and talked to them.

On another occasion, Aïda Faye told us, her grandmother was ironing Baay's clothes while chanting a number of *sikkar* melodies. When a *ḥāl* moved her to begin a new melody, Baay approached and asked where she learned that melody. She responded, "I was just *sikkar*-ing and then a *ḥāl* inspired me with it." Baay told her, "Set aside that one [the melody] for now. Its owner will not come for a little while." She clarified that he did not mean that it was not time for women to perform *sikkar* out loud but that this particular melody was to appear later. Years later, her grandmother cried as she heard Aïda Faye and her uncle, a *sikkarkat* who lives in Medina Baay, singing the same *sikkar* melody. She realized that these *sikkarkat*s were the ones whose mission was to introduce that *sikkar*. The *sikkar* became widely known, she says, after they taught it to *sikkarkat*s from Ndukkumaan (the area around Kaffrine, east of Kaolack).

Growing up in Medina Baay, Aïda Faye studied the Qur'ān for several years in the *daara* (Qur'ānic school) of "Yaa Nafi Kaaŋ" (lit. "Mother Nafi Master"), officially Nafīsatu Al-Ḥājj Bābakar Niasse, a daughter of Shaykh Ibrāhīm's older brother.[20] Yaa Nafi is also a *muqaddama* who gave *tarbiya* to several of Aïda Faye's relatives. Aïda Faye helped form and remains a member of a *daayira* that includes Nafi's disciples and former Qur'ān students.

Several of Aïda Faye's older relatives were prominent *sikkarkat*s in Medina Baay who had learned Ibou Diouf's songs directly from their composer. Although she became familiar with many of these songs as a child, she says, she thought they were silly at the time and only much later had the opportunity to relearn and perform them. She received *tarbiya* some time around 2000 in Medina Baay from a male *muqaddam* of Shaykh Ibrāhīm's daughter Ndèye Khady, who oversees a group of *daayira*s in Kaolack and elsewhere. Before long, she came to Dakar and joined the *daayira* of the young *muqaddam* Shaykh Mamour Insa Diop. At the time, Mamour Insa was just beginning to have wide repute as the leader of several of Senegal's most famous rappers. Since then, partly thanks to Aïda Faye and these rappers, he has become one of the best-known and most-followed Islamic leaders in Dakar.

Although she was surrounded by *sikkarkat*s growing up, Aïda Faye says no one taught her *sikkar*. She learned to *sikkar* not in Medina Baay while with her family but in Dakar while a member of Mamour Insa's *daayira* around 2002. No one in the *daayira* knew how to lead *sikkar* well, she said, which was a problem during one meeting when they had esteemed guests from Medina Baay and wanted to *sikkar* for them. Shaykh Mamour Insa, who may have previously heard her chanting along, was sitting at the front and told a *daayira* leader to go to the women's section and tell Aïda Faye to lead the *sikkar*. She answered that she did not know how. The *daayira* leader relayed her message back to Shaykh Mamour. After she had been asked and had refused twice, Shaykh Mamour sent the *daayira* leader back to tell her "It's an order" (*ndigal*).[21] So she followed the order and led *sikkar*. A man present, a doctor, was undergoing *tarbiya* at the time, and it was during her *sikkar* performance that he attained *fatḥ*.

During those early days, Shaykh Mamour told Aïda Faye that her voice would be heard everywhere in the world, even in the Western countries (*ci réew i tubaab yi*). She did not personally know any women *sikkarkat*s at that time, although she had heard some of the recordings of Khady Ndiaye that relatives would play when she was a child. When she became serious about learning *sikkar*, she once again listened to Khady Ndiaye's cassettes and got to know her personally. She received invitations to perform in more and more *daayira*s' meetings. One Taalibe Baay musician who was well connected in the recording industry in Senegal and England heard her *sikkar* and proposed producing an album and music video, which came out in 2007. Although Taalibe Baay do not customarily use musical instruments in their chants as some other Sufi groups do, this album involved electric keyboard accompaniment. While I wondered if this development might be controversial, Aïda Faye told me that sons of Shaykh Ibrāhīm encouraged her to do it, telling her that Shaykh Ibrāhīm was a great admirer of legendary Egyptian singer Umm Kulthūm, who praised the Prophet accompanied by an orchestra. Shaykh Ibrāhīm had even written a song he intended her to perform.

Aïda Faye describes the gift of being able to *sikkar* as a mission from God: "This is something that has been done to me. It's not something I invented or did to myself … God does whatever he pleases." She explained that the divine origin of her *sikkar* is why she does not "charge" (*fayeeku*) for it but accepts whatever people can scrape together to compensate for her transport and efforts. Although she lives in Dakar and performs frequently there, she spends months of each year in Kaolack to be closer to the many Taalibe Baay-dominated villages whose *daayira*s invite her to perform at their meetings. She says these communities do their best to compensate her for her hard work but that they themselves are struggling and often have little to give. Her well-appointed home and clothing suggest that she is making a respectable living but has not become unusually wealthy through her renown as a *sikkarkat*.

When I first met her in 2010, a few people close to her had learned of her recent appointment as a *muqaddama* by a son of Sayyida Ruqayya Niasse. This chain of authority seems appropriate, as Sayyida Ruqayya was for years the only woman to speak in the main Medina Baay *gàmmu* meeting. Yet in interviews, Aïda Faye herself downplayed this appointment, saying she had never consented to give *wird* or *tarbiya* and had not publicized the appointment. Her mission, for now, is "naming God" in as many places as possible.

When I asked Aïda Faye why so few women performed *sikkar* publicly, her answer resembled that of Khady Ndiaye: "Yes … you know, in *sharīʿa* they say that, *sharīʿa* forbids a woman's voice from being heard loudly … They say a woman's voice is *ʿawra.*" However, she said, when you drink from the knowledge Shaykh Ibrāhīm brought, "you can't distinguish man from woman, because Baay himself stood and said, 'My men are men and my women are men.'"[22] One must follow *sharīʿa,* she explained, but one can reach a level at which one "erases" (*effacer*) *sharīʿa*. Paraphrasing a line from Baay, she described him as teaching that his women should compete "in what the men of God compete in."[23] *Sikkar* is one of those things.

Aïda Faye recounted that Shaykh Ibrāhīm's daughter Ruqayya had told her of quietly singing *sikkar* in one room when Shaykh Ibrāhīm heard her from the next room and told her, "Hey, louder!" (*Yëkkëti ko waay!*). Like Sayyida Ruqayya and Khady Ndiaye, Aïda Faye said that many people have told her that hearing her has led them to change for the better, in many cases by converting to Islam and entering the Fayḍa. Hence, those whose voices are *ʿawra,* she said, are the many women who raise their voices about things of which God disapproves.

Conclusion

This chapter's threads can be tied together as an answer to the following question: In a context where women's voices have been overwhelmingly absent from public religious meetings, what conditions have allowed some women's speeches and chants to become part of felicitous performances? Like the other instances of feminine authority discussed throughout this book, women *sikkarkat*s and orators legitimize unusual roles through subtly reconfiguring the same religious discourses and practices that have often excluded them, bending them to fit new purposes.

Where women's voices are absent from religious ritual spaces, this is not necessarily a direct expression of the devaluation of women. Rather, there is a perceived contradiction between the norms of *kersa* and reserved feminine piety and the visibility and audibility entailed by addressing a large meeting. Norms of *kersa* and piety apply to men, too, but require far less self-wrapping and restraint. In addition to the juridical concept of *ʿawra* and more general expectations of reserved feminine piety, the routine spatial organization of religious meetings takes for granted that only men will speak in meetings.

These attitudes and practices seem not to have been subject to any open critique within the Fayḍa community. Hence my surprise at witnessing a dramatic growth in women's vocal participation in meetings, starting around 2009 and increasing even more since 2014. Women who speak or chant in religious meetings draw on multiple resources as they present themselves as authoritative figures whose participation in religious meetings respects norms of feminine piety.

These women provide new yet ambiguous reinterpretations of already ambiguous teachings. As we have seen, many of my interviewees were familiar with the notion that the woman's voice is *'awra,* and hints of this teaching can be found in Shaykh Ibrāhīm's writings and precedent. Although interviewees generally accept that the woman's voice is *'awra* according to *sharī'a,* they deny the literal interpretation that women's voices should never be heard in public or by non-relative males. Rather, they qualify this teaching as only applicable where the harm of speaking or singing outweighs its benefit. Thus, they describe as *'awra* the voices of women who speak too loudly (although the upper limit is never clear) and women who say ungodly things that encourage bad behaviour. Circumventing legalistic questions over what counts as *'awra,* they emphasize mystical discourses of transcending gender and Shaykh Ibrāhīm's ambiguous exhortation to women to "compete" in spiritual matters. How these teachings apply is highly ambiguous and context-dependent, since everyone agrees that no one unequivocally transcends gender. Previously, not everyone would have agreed that standing before an audience to perform *sikkar* out loud is entirely "spiritual" and not "material." Moreover, while these explanations suggest that these women's voices are not strictly *'awra,* these women still veil their own voices in some way, apparently recognizing that their persona as pious women still depends on wrapping their voices *as if* they were *'awra.*

For orators, this vocal wrapping or veiling can take several forms. The most obvious way to wrap one's presence is to refrain from addressing the assembly directly. This may involve speaking through an animator (*jottalikat*) as Sayyida Seynabou did, asking an intermediary to read a statement as Sayyida Ndèye Aïda Niasse did, or simply absenting oneself or delegating all the speaking to men as many women leaders do.

Since not being heard is not an option for female *sikkarkat*s, they instead dissociate their individual selves from the act of performing *sikkar*. They present their physical presence (*jëmm*) as a mere wrapper for a powerful reality that resonates through them without their choosing.

Their narratives discursively communicate this dissociation, while their bodily performance, as if they are personally vacant during a powerful *ḥāl,* communicates that this assertive – even deafening – voice is not actually a "woman's" voice. They present their bodies as animators for an invisible author and their vocation as a mission for which they are not the agents. Unsurprisingly, male *sikkarkat*s similarly dissociate themselves, as *sikkar* is an otherworldly activity that requires a far higher dynamic and tonal range than *kersa* normally allows. Electronic mediation, including amplification and dissemination, wraps the presence of both male and female chanters, not just through offering a level of indirection but through intentional distortion and other effects that conceal and embellish the naked voice.

Women's participation in public *sikkar* has also required reconfiguring ritual space. Sayyida Seynabou simply turned the men's section around so its chant leaders were next to the part of the women's section that contained female leaders and *sikkarkat*s. The space of a larger *gàmmu* is not as easy to reconfigure, and both Aïda Faye and Khady Ndiaye usually just sit around the *sikkar* table, sometimes putting some distance between themselves and unrelated male *sikkarkat*s. Their presence is exceptional, as the rest of the audience is entirely segregated. I was surprised to find that no one openly contested this arrangement, suggesting that general rules of decorum are not perceived as absolute laws.

All of these subtle changes in interpretation and practice are instances of "performativity," or the fact of constituting social reality through reiterating more or less convention-governed acts (Austin 1962). As Judith Butler shows (1990, 1993), performative acts not only reproduce norms and conventions but also subtly modify them. Through reiterating norms in somewhat different ways, all these women's performances in some sense modify norms, even without claiming to do so. The next chapter introduces a woman who perhaps more strikingly exemplifies this phenomenon of implicitly yet significantly challenging norms through a subtly different performance.

Chapter Seven

The Ascetic and the Mother of the Knowers

A Compound Shaykh

A casual look at the glossy invitation (figure 7.1) to the 2014 *gàmmu* organized by the religious association Fédération Hinlmou Imamoul Hamal[1] in Dakar suggests an unusual relationship between the federation's spiritual guides, the husband-and-wife duo Baay Mokhtar Ka and Yaay Aïcha Sow. The front cover of the invitation features a photo of Baay Mokhtar on the left and one of Yaay Aïcha on the right. The back cover features another photo of her, underneath which is printed, "Dieuredieuféééééé Yaye" (Thank youuuuuu, Yaay [Mother]). The inside left page invites the reader to attend the annual *gàmmu*, stating that the meeting will feature "Cheikh El Hadji Baye Mouhamadoul Moukhtar Ka [Baay Mokhtar Ka], under the effective presence of our beloved Mother Aicha Sow Oumoul Hanrifina [Mother of the Knowers]."[2] The final event listed in the program on the inner right page states, "1:00AM: Arrival of BAYE and YAYE / Thank you, Yaye!"[3] Next to the program listing is another photo of Baay Mokhtar. This is the only time I have seen a *gàmmu* speaker's wife mentioned in the program, much less pictured and thanked twice. The phrase "Thank you, Yaye!" is a variation on the phrase often repeated at Taalibe Baay meetings, "*Jërejëfee Baay!*" ("Thank you, Baay!"). Curiously, the program includes variations of "Thank you, Yaye!" twice yet lacks similar thanks for Baay Niasse or Baay Mokhtar.

Within the larger Fayḍa Tijāniyya community in Senegal, Baay Mokhtar is the one known as a leader. Yet as this invitation hints, within the couple's own community of disciples, Yaay Aïcha – the "Mother of the Knowers" – may be at least as important a figure. Perhaps more to the

Figure 7.1 Invitation to Baay Mokhtar Ka's *daayira*'s 2014 *gàmmu*, recto and verso.

point, one might say, the couple operates as an inseparable leadership unit. This has not always been the case. For decades, Baay Mokhtar Ka was widely reputed as a great "knower of God" (*ʿārif bi-Llāh*), a formidable healer and diviner, a teacher of Islamic texts, and an otherworldly Sufi ascetic and spiritual guide (*shaykh murabbī*) who was too lost in God to marry. With his dreadlocks, unkempt clothes, and lack of interest in eating, sleeping, or marrying, Baay Mokhtar exemplified the classic liminal Sufi figure for whom nothing exists but God. Yet the otherworldly wandering mystic is not the ideal Sufi leader among his fellow Tijānīs, who tend to adhere to the *ṭarīqa* founder's injunctions to balance the worldly and the mystical and to preserve the mystical from public view.

Baay Mokhtar finally agreed to marry around 1996, and his new wife immediately took charge. She reorganized his work and his disciple community, had him shave his dreadlocks and dress presentably, and effectively became a highly assertive handler. Although Baay Mokhtar today outwardly resembles more the model Islamic leader, he retains his otherworldly Sufi proclivities. His wife organizes his life and community in minute detail. He has also delegated to her important functions in spiritually guiding disciples. Baay Mokhtar and his disciples treat her as the ultimate decision maker and planner, while he acts as a conduit of spiritual knowledge and power largely channelled through his wife. Thus, only together do Baay Mokhtar and Yaay Aïcha act as a complete Tijānī shaykh.

This arrangement is unlike anything else I have seen in the Fayḍa Tijāniyya movement. Typically, wives of male religious leaders do not appear publicly with them at religious functions and do not directly take part in their leadership activities. Female leaders may delegate husbands and other male kin to handle ritual functions, such as leading prayer or group litanies, that women are excluded from performing, yet they typically sit in separate men's and women's sections, whereas Baay Mokhtar and Yaay Aïcha sit next to one another. Just as unusual as this couple's inseparability in their everyday work and in their public appearances is Yaay Aïcha's influence over her husband. As with the other cases discussed in this book, the examples of Baay Mokhtar and Yaay Aïcha are instructive not because they are typical but because they illustrate how far-from-typical possibilities can be derived through creatively reconfiguring established norms. This chapter approaches Islamic authority as, in part, a performance whose effectiveness depends on convincingly reiterating prevalent norms and citing authoritative models.

As Judith Butler argues, norms are naturalized as a sedimentation of reiterative performances. The need for constant repetition opens up "gaps and fissures" through which certain performances can "coopt" the power of the norm and produce it differently, potentially subverting what the norm is generally assumed to mean (J. Butler 1993, 10–15). While Butler is primarily interested in openly transgressive practices, this chapter illustrates more subtle reconfigurations of norms. Assessing the implications of hegemonic discourses and practices requires examining the range of performances that invoke them to sometimes opposing ends. It also requires looking at how such performances are evaluated differently by various parties. For example, some who witness Baay Mokhtar and Yaay Aïcha's unusual performances of religious authority contest their "felicity" (Austin 1962) – or the validity resulting from a match between performance and convention – partly because they reverse or significantly bend typical gender roles. Yet the couple and their close supporters present their joint authority as felicitous on a deeper level, even as a miraculous complementarity, and their disciple community and Baay Mokhtar's healing practice have flourished.

Baay Mokhtar and Yaay Aïcha's performances of gender and religious authority are woven of the same culturally hegemonic threads that run through the stories of nearly all the women leaders discussed in this book. These include the pervasive metaphor of women's authority as motherhood (see chapter 4); a woman's performance of pious wifely submission regardless of her actual influence (see chapter 3); the male household head's formal position as the household's public face and ultimate authority; Sufi discourses of the spiritually powerful woman as "man"; and the insistence on masculine and feminine as complementary principles. Yet Baay Mokhtar and Yaay Aïcha weave these threads in surprising ways, yielding patterns contrasting sharply to typical examples of religious authority and conjugal relations. Yaay Aïcha is the only woman leader discussed in this book who clearly exercises religious authority in conjunction with her husband. She is also the only one who sits front and centre at all religious meetings and who clearly directs the community's affairs and even her husband's actions. Like other prominent, pious women, she attenuates her visibility somewhat, making sure her husband is presented more visually prominently as the main authority. Yet she pushes this logic to its limits, ceremonially standing just behind her husband yet not concealing her influence over him, making some uncomfortable.

In many ways, then, the relationship between Baay Mokhtar and Yaay Aïcha disrupts or reverses the roles and attributes typically ascribed to men and women, husbands and wives, in this context. In chapter 3, I showed how one can draw homologies between the male/female binary and other binaries such as apparent *(ẓāhir)*/inner *(bāṭin)*, exteriority/interiority, structure/communitas, law *(sharīʿa)*/reality *(ḥaqīqa)*. Indeed, the women leaders I interviewed, far more often than their male counterparts, emphasized *bāṭin* over *ẓāhir*, mystical over legal, *ḥaqīqa* over *sharīʿa*. They often highlighted consonances between the inner and hidden knowledge sought by Sufism and the self-concealed nature of pious Muslim women, even explicitly linking the "Muḥammadan Reality" *(Ḥaqīqa Muḥammadiyya)* – the single hidden reality through which God engendered all of creation – to motherhood and femininity. Yaay Aïcha performs feminine piety in similarly interior ways – for example, by wearing concealing clothing, often presenting herself as standing behind and below her husband, and only speaking in enclosed spaces rather than in large meetings.

Yet in other ways her relationship to her husband reverses these gendered associations. Baay Mokhtar is far more associated with *bāṭin* knowledge and the lack of order resulting from being lost in *ḥaqīqa*, while Yaay Aïcha is known for having brought order and law to the community. Whereas a husband is often assumed to represent the wife publicly while the wife obeys her husband's commands, Yaay Aïcha appears publicly, visibly steering her husband's actions and mediating between him and others. Although her clothing, speech, and spatial practices suggest attenuated presence, in fact she appears as visibly as her husband, and anyone wishing to reach him must usually go through her.

In short, this case may appear to reverse overriding structural relationships and to transgress prevalent husband-wife roles. Yet this couple and their followers frame reversals of certain norms as necessary to uphold more important ones. While masculinity and femininity can sometimes be presented as structural analogues to oppositions such as *ẓāhir* and *bāṭin*, these connections are not stable but are always contextually produced. Prevalent discourses and practices can be emphasized and deemphasized to connect men and women to different attributes under different circumstances. Even if men and women have sometimes found it useful and natural to connect men to reason and social order while connecting women to emotion and primal forces (Ortner 1972), from the perspective of the home, women have been associated with maintaining order and discipline through managing household affairs, disciplining children, and taking care of their husbands' needs. Thus, when Yaay Aïcha organizes the community, initiates disciples into the Sufi order, and sits by her husband's side to manage his personal life, she can be seen as extending her conventional roles as manager, motherly educator, and caring wife from the literal household to the metaphorical household of disciples.

In addition to reconfiguring prevalent gender norms, this couple draws on Islamic historical models to legitimize alternative gender roles. For example, even if Islam in this context is understood to prescribe that husbands provide economically for their households, this couple cites the model of Islam's first couple, Muḥammad and Khadīja, to justify the opposite relationship of a more economically established wife supporting her husband and investing her wealth into his religious mission. This chapter shows how these two leaders draw on repertoires of gendered discourses, roles, and images to expand the possibilities of legitimate religious authority to accommodate their particular situation.

Before discussing Baay Mokhtar and Yaay Aïcha's life narratives as told by themselves and others we interviewed,[4] I will illustrate this couple's unusual relationship by describing their appearance together at their community's annual *gàmmu* meeting. The *gàmmu* is perhaps their most dramatic performance of unity as a single and singular leadership unit.

Reconfiguring the Classic *Gàmmu (Mawlid)*

During their community's 2013 *gàmmu*, to accommodate the presence of their "mother," the event's organizers maintained conventional gender segregation while reconfiguring it to give it unconventional implications. The video that their *daayira* uploaded to the video-sharing website YouTube[5] shows the leading couple entering together into the crowded tent area well after midnight, Yaay Aïcha first, surrounded by several *daayira* leaders and members of the *daayira*'s security corps. The audience, counting several thousand people inside the tent in addition to probably many more gathered in the area around it, stands to welcome them, many of them exuberantly swaying and chanting along with the amplified *sikkar* leaders. Baay Mokhtar and Yaay Aïcha gradually make their way up the aisle between the men's section to the right and the women's section to the left, finally emerging on the raised platform at the front. Yaay's shiny dress and matching head wrap are largely covered by a slightly translucent, white prayer shawl wrapped over her head, shoulders, and upper body. Baay Mokhtar wears the white robe with golden trimming and matching white cap typical of an imam or a man presiding at a *gàmmu*. He also carries a set of prayer beads (*kurus*) and displays an additional set around his neck, a somewhat controversial practice that distinguishes his community from most of the Fayḍa movement.

Normally, there would be no place on the platform for Yaay, as the leaders' section at the front of the *gàmmu* space is usually within the men's section. Yet here the organizers have divided the leaders' stand down the middle into men's and women's spaces. As Yaay enters, a line of young women decked out in white and pink dresses and prayer shawls stands prominently in the women's space, swaying along with the *sikkar*. Two armchairs have been placed side by side at the front of the platform at the dividing line between the men's and women's sections. Baay Mokhtar stands before the chair at the edge of the men's space while Yaay stands before the one in the women's section, swaying gently and raising her arms to the rhythm of the *sikkar*. Baay Mokhtar does the same, his index fingers extended to echo the unicity of God expressed in the *sikkar*. Yaay, still standing, then gently tugs Baay Mokhtar's raised arm, motioning him to sit. As he sits, she turns to the audience and motions downward with both arms, suggesting that they should sit, too, and she and the audience sit. A minute later, Baay Mokhtar stands and raises his palms, pointing and shaking both hands insistently towards the seated Yaay. Many in the audience stand once again and cheer, many joining more intensely in *sikkar*ing and swaying. She smiles and then stands once again, putting her arm on Baay Mokhtar's shoulder, then after a minute or so once again signals to Baay Mokhtar that they should both sit down. Seated, both continue to sway in rhythm with the *sikkar*, Baay Mokhtar still extending his index fingers.

After several minutes of *sikkar*, Yaay signals to the *sikkarkat*s to stop. They close this opening *sikkar*, as is traditional in Tijānī meetings, with the *Ṣalāt al-Fātiḥ*. As they are wrapping up this opening segment, the *daayira* president, an approximately thirty-year-old man wearing a white *xaftaan*, kneels in front of Yaay, apparently discussing with her the next steps of the *gàmmu*. The *sikkarkat*s immediately follow the *Ṣalāt al-Fātiḥ* with their own distinctive addition, a short and simple song praising Yaay: "Thank you, Yaay! Thank you, Yaay!" they sing. "Mom, may God give you long life and health! Baay Mokhtar, may God give you long life and health!" She and the audience answer "Amin!" The *daayira* president stands and welcomes everyone to the *gàmmu*, including the delegations representing various leaders and families.

After this welcoming address, before turning the time over to Baay Mokhtar to talk about the life of the Prophet, the *daayira* president announces a Qur'ānic recitation by two students from the *daara* (Qur'ānic school) in Kóofa Mbooro, the village founded by Yaay Aïcha. *Gàmmus* almost always open with a Qur'ānic recitation, either by an outstanding *daara* student or by a descendant of Shaykh Ibrāhīm or another leader. Less typical in this case, both reciters are girls, who stand to Yaay's right side in the women's section of the stage. Yet what started as a women's space soon seems to be a flexible space, as the area directly in front of Yaay is soon filled with boys and girls from the Kóofa Qur'ānic school, who remain there throughout much of the rest of the meeting. Throughout the meeting, Yaay continues to orchestrate events, even if she never formally speaks, and her husband speaks for nearly two hours. The evening proceeds much as did the dozens of other *gàmmus* I have attended, with several speeches interspersed with *sikkar* and several chanted poems about the Prophet Muḥammad.

The most visually striking departure from typical practice comes during the daybreak prayer, when Yaay and Baay present the visual appearance of co-leading the prayer. After Baay Mokhtar has spoken for around an hour, Yaay sits forward and turns to him. Suddenly stopping his speech, he announces that it is time for daybreak prayer *(fajr)*. While Baay Mokhtar leads the prayer, Yaay remains directly next to him – although still inside the women's section – standing, kneeling, and prostrating in near unison with him as the rest of the crowd follows closely after in response to the *mu'adhdhin*'s calls.[6] In such large meetings, it is typical to be less exacting than in mosque prayers about women praying in a space not visible to the men, as the space tends to be crowded and difficult to reorganize in time for the prayer. Thus, at such meetings I have often seen several men's sections interspersed with several women's sections, some of which might end up in front of or beside the prayer leader. Yet this is the only case I have seen in the Fayḍa community where a woman conspicuously prayed directly next to the prayer leader, visually suggesting that the couple is leading the prayer together despite technically being in separate sections.

Another point where the heightened participation of Yaay and female disciples comes to the fore is when, after a long interval of *sikkar* chanting by the male *sikkarkats*, the microphone is handed to a group of girls sitting in the mostly women's section of the stand near Yaay. All apparently between the ages of twelve and sixteen, they wear brightly coloured dresses and headscarves and, like other attendees, prayer beads around their necks. As they begin chanting, Yaay immediately stands up and frantically motions for them to stand and come next to her. They chant *sikkar* for a couple of minutes next to Yaay, and then the microphone returns to the male *sikkarkats*, who close the *sikkar* once again with the *Ṣalāt al-Fātiḥ* and then the same short song thanking Yaay.

Later, near the end of Baay Mokhtar's closing speech, Yaay stretches out her hands, palms facing up as if accepting a prayer, visibly signalling that it is time to wrap up his speech and pray for the congregation. He finishes his thought, then says, as if closing, "So, that is your *gàmmu*." When he adds a couple more sentences, Yaay lifts her arms higher and more insistently. When he appears ready to finish, she lowers her hands, yet then he begins to speak on another topic. She again lifts her hands signalling for him to stop but desists when she realizes that this point is the highlight of his speech, which partly has to do with her own spiritual status. He brings the audience to cheers and then sits down, effectively ending the *gàmmu*.

At the end of the *gàmmu*, well after the sun has come up, the same core group of disciples and *daayira* security officers accompanies the couple, Yaay first, down the steps and into a jeep waiting inside the tent. Disciples *sikkar* as they form lines on either side of a path cleared for the jeep. As the jeep slowly leaves, the two lines of disciples march forward on both sides of it, continuing their *sikkar* through the streets of suburban Dakar.

In most domains in Senegal today it is no surprise to see husbands and wives collaborating and appearing together. Yet it can be particularly tricky to change religious ritual performances, whose success depends on reenacting timeless, sacred models bequeathed by those divinely invested with knowledge and authority. This *gàmmu* arguably respected the gender-segregated space, the ritual sequence, and the content that Taalibe Baay *gàmmus* have had since Shaykh Ibrāhīm himself fixed the *gàmmu*'s canonical form during the 1930s in Medina Baay. Yet in important ways this one was different from the dozens of *gàmmus* I have attended. Most of these differences derived from Yaay's partnership with her husband. In reorganizing the ritual space to allow Yaay to sit in the leaders' section, the organizers chose, instead of making her a singular exception, to place her in a novel women's section within the leaders' section. The *gàmmu* followed the classic sequence, yet with variations – for example, in having girls perform Qur'ānic recitation and *sikkar*. This is unusual but no longer unheard of or controversial. It is significant that the handful of women whose voices were heard were all unmarried students, following a precedent modelled by Shaykh Ibrāhīm. Conversely, the voice of the most notable woman in the meeting, Yaay, was never heard. This illustrates the points made in chapter 6, that Taalibe Baay may speak and act as if a woman's voice were *'awra* – something not to be shown in public – yet not as a juridical prohibition affecting all women but as a sign of status and *kersa* applying especially to higher-status women known for their piety and religious authority.

However, even though Yaay never spoke, her presence at this meeting rivalled – even blurred together with – that of her husband. An onlooker might have wondered if she was the ultimate authority whose husband spoke on her behalf. In short, this couple models an apparently unique spousal relationship among Fayḍa Tijāniyya adherents, not through openly challenging but through subtly – or some might say not so subtly – reconfiguring the community's norms governing gender and religious authority.

The Liminal Sufi

Ibn al-Jawzī's twelfth-century encyclopedia of holy men and women of Islamic history identifies a number of people in various times and places under the category *majnūn,* which most often means "insane" or "possessed by *jinn*" yet can also refer to someone consumed by love or passion. As I read Al-Jawzī's accounts, I wondered how many of those dismissed in my own society as raving lunatics might have been understood in many moments in Sufi history as spiritually powerful sages, as threadbare spots in the veil between God and creation. Sufi poets throughout the Islamic world have invoked the pre-Islamic Arab romance of Majnūn Laylā, the tale of a man consumed by passion for his beloved Laylā, as a metaphor for the Sufi aspirant's consuming love for God. Many Taalibe Baay told me that Shaykh Ibrāhīm had dubbed himself "the Shaykh of the crazy people" (*Shaykh al-majānīn, sëriñ i dof yi*), because his followers, when absorbed in a knowledge of God, often spoke and acted in ways that onlookers described as collective folly. It is very common for Taalibe Baay proudly to describe themselves or others in the movement as "crazy" (*dof*). The ancient trope of the Sufi as a liminal figure absorbed in God to the point of apparent folly is thus an important part of Fayḍa discourse.

However, even if the Sufi is one part wandering ascetic or holy recluse, Shaykh Ibrāhīm taught that the true gnostic *(ʿārif bi-Llāh)* is one who inwardly passes through this dissolution *(fanāʾ)* of the self, time, and space in the sea of divine unity yet outwardly shows persistence *(baqāʾ)* in following God's prescriptions *(sharīʿa)* ([Niasse] 1969, 1:131). Shaykh Aḥmad al-Tijānī himself rejected spiritual practice centred on reclusion and asceticism, something he witnessed while participating in the Khalwatiyya Sufi order in Cairo (see ʿAlī Ḥarāzim 2002; Wright 2005). Shaykh al-Tijānī instructed his disciples to give both *ẓāhir* and *bāṭin* their rightful place, maintaining decorum and seeking what is good in this earthly life while not visibly displaying signs of one's spiritual pursuits. I have encountered many "liminal" Sufi figures in the Fayḍa movement in Senegal, many of whom, like Baay Mokhtar Ka, are known as extraordinarily powerful diviners, healers, and saintly figures. Yet these figures are seldom described as examples to emulate or as what Shaykh Ibrāhīm described as "the complete shaykh" *(al-shaykh al-kāmil)* (see Niasse 1998).

Baay Mokhtar Ka was and to a large extent remains the paradigmatic example of the liminal Sufi figure, one not so much contemptuous of the world as blissfully unaware of it, lost in God and the unseen. Several people I spoke to about him described him as a "true Sufi" (*sufiyanke dëgg*), citing his non-stop prayer and recitation of litanies at the expense of eating, sleeping, and otherwise taking care of himself. However, he long fell short of the ideal model of "the complete shaykh" among Tijānīs and more particularly the Fayḍa community. Although some of my interlocutors who knew him prior to his marriage with Yaay Aïcha Sow bemoaned the degree to which she controls and limits access to him, most still thought it good that he had finally married someone who imposed some order on his life, taming his asceticism and protecting him from his naive and unlimited generosity. To return to imagery introduced in chapter 3, Yaay Aïcha has come to play the role of the shell that encompasses, protects, and represents the potent yet fragile kernel that is Baay Mokhtar.

In an interview I conducted with Baay Mokhtar Ka and Yaay Aïcha, aided by two of my research associates,[7] Baay Mokhtar told us he was born in 1941 to a family of Fulbe semipastoralists and Islamic scholars in a village in Casamance, the southern sliver of Senegal. His father was a Tijānī *muqaddam* associated with the spiritual lineage of Cerno Aḥmadu

Diallo of Subulde. After both his parents had died, Baay Mokhtar took the Tijānī *wird* from a relative of his affiliated with the Tivaouane branch of the Tijāniyya. Before becoming a disciple of Shaykh Ibrāhīm, Baay Mokhtar studied the various Islamic sciences with many teachers throughout Casamance and then other regions of Senegal. At some point he actually lived in Tivaouane, where he was a personal assistant (*bëkk-néeg*) for Sëriñ Manṣūr Sy (d. 2012), a son of Al-Ḥājj Mālik Sy and later that family's General Khalīfa.[8]

In 1964, Baay Mokhtar told us, he entered a period of spiritual seclusion *(khalwa)* in the village of Gunjur Kombo, during which Baay (then living) appeared to him in a dream and said to him, "You're my disciple" (*Sama taalibe nga*). Yet Baay Mokhtar took no action at the time, instead continuing to visit teachers in search of Islamic knowledge. In 1973, Baay Mokhtar moved to Dakar, living alone in an old wooden shack on the corner of Rue 15 and Rue 16 in the old popular quarter of Medina. (I was told there were many of these shacks in Medina, but that they are all gone now.) He continued to seek knowledge while taking on his own students, teaching them the standard books of Islamic jurisprudence and other disciplines in his simple room. In July 1975, he travelled to the northern Senegalese city of St-Louis. While there, he entered another period of *khalwa*. On the seventeenth and last night of this *khalwa*, he told us, Baay appeared to him again in a dream, this time giving him more specific instructions. Baay said to him, "Come hold on to me. I have finished *(jéexal)* today. I will go away, so when you come to take hold, you will not find me there. But entrust this to my disciple Ibra Fall. He is your doorway to me." In that dream, Baay showed him his assigned leader, Shaykh Ibra Fall, a member of his inner circle, so that Baay Mokhtar would recognize him when he saw him. He later found that Baay had passed away in London on the same night.

Baay Mokhtar returned to Dakar for several months after this and then went to Medina Baay seeking Shaykh Ibra Fall. He continued on to Kossi Mbitéyène, the village near Kaolack where Ibra Fall lived, but found that his assigned leader had gone to Chad for an extended trip just after Shaykh Ibrāhīm's death and was not expected any time soon. In a hurry to know God, Mokhtar returned to Medina Baay and asked at least five prominent leaders there, including sons of Shaykh Ibrāhīm, to give him *tarbiya*. Each refused, saying that Baay had assigned him to a great leader and that they lacked permission to give him *tarbiya*. Finally, in 1976, a close relative of Baay, Sëriñ ʿUthmān Faati Niasse, agreed to give him *tarbiya*. Baay Mokhtar then stayed in Medina Baay for more than a year and a half, continuing his spiritual progression *(sayr)* with the leaders there. The same night he left for Dakar, Shaykh Ibra Fall returned from Chad. After hearing the good news the next day, he went to visit Shaykh Ibra Fall but found he had already left for Mauritania. At the end of 1978, after waiting for his leader for several months, Mokhtar Ka approached one of Shaykh Ibra Fall's prominent disciples and asked him to accompany him to Mauritania. They finally were able to locate the shaykh among the Bedouin camps in Mauritania. More than fourteen years after Baay had claimed him as his disciple, Baay Mokhtar Ka finally joined his assigned leader.

After meeting his "doorway to Baay" in 1978, Baay Mokhtar continued teaching and healing in his hut in Dakar but often travelled to Kossi, where Shaykh Ibra Fall lived. His shaykh wrote him an *ijāza* in 1984, appointing him as a *muqaddam* in the Tijānī order. Like many *muqaddam*s, after receiving his *ijāza* Baay Mokhtar did not immediately begin giving *wird* and *tarbiya*, as his leader had only explicitly instructed him to give spiritual instruction *(sayr)* to those who had already gone through *tarbiya*. Only several years later did his leader clearly signal that the time had come. This happened during a visit to Kossi during the late 1980s (he doesn't remember the exact year). Ibra Fall's own daughter came to her father to ask for *wird* and *tarbiya*, and he assigned Mokhtar to give it to her, which he did in his leader's own bedroom. After returning to Dakar, now that he had received the signal to start giving *tarbiya*, he initiated anyone who came. During the late 1980s and 1990s a group of committed disciples quickly gathered around him.

This made him one of the first *muqaddam*s with a large following in the Dakar area, where the Fayḍa was still little known. Yet according to long-time leaders of the Dakar Anṣār al-Dīn Federation, which in principle encompasses all the Fayḍa Tijāniyya *daayira*s in the Dakar area (see chapter 1), Baay Mokhtar has never been an active part of the federation. Not much of a public figure or organizer, Baay Mokhtar was known as a holy recluse who might spend a month in meditative prayer with almost no food, water, or sleep. He cared little for personal care or appearance, letting his hair grow into long, matted dreadlocks and seldom changing or washing his threadbare clothes. He would pronounce the *Ṣalāt al-Fạtiḥ* prayer so many thousands of times a day that he was known for wearing seven strings of prayer beads (*kurus*) to count them on. Baay Mokhtar himself explained to us that he spent twenty years (during the 1980s and 1990s) in almost constant seclusion, repeating the *Ṣalāt al-Fạtiḥ* tens of thousands of times per day, praying that the Fayḍa would take hold in Dakar. During that period, Taalibe Baay were few and nearly invisible in Dakar, and those who wanted to "know God" through *tarbiya* often travelled far from Dakar to do so. Baay Mokhtar told us he attributes the Fayḍa's current rapid growth in Dakar to these prayers.

Indeed, Baay Mokhtar's non-stop preoccupation with the recitation of such sacred litanies *(wird,* pl. *awrād)* has become legendary among the Taalibe Baay community and has contributed to his widespread reputation for uncanny spiritual power even among those who are not his followers. One of my assistants who accompanied me during my interview with Baay Mokhtar was a child in Medina Baay during the late 1980s, when he recalls seeing a solitary and unkempt man repeating *wird*s night and day in the Medina Baay mosque. He later learned that this was Baay Mokhtar Ka and that he was staying in a disciple's house near his own family's house. My assistant's parents soon took him to have Baay Mokhtar pray for him. In a place full of major and minor religious figures, including Shaykh Ibrāhīm's direct descendants, it is significant that Baay Mokhtar's prayers were perceived as unusually powerful even in Medina Baay.

Another interviewee who was part of Baay Mokhtar's inner circle for several years, Sayyida Ndèye Maguète Niang, told us that he would *wird* so much that he would bleed. His companions would set large, empty tomato paste cans in front of him, taking them away to empty them when they would fill with blood. She cites the fact that he didn't bleed to death even after losing litres of blood as evidence of "Baay's guarantee" that one will not lose by following him. Another interviewee in Dakar told me that in order to keep himself awake while pronouncing prayers through the night, Baay Mokhtar would sit on a plank suspended over a well so that staying awake would be a matter of life and death. Whatever the factual veracity of all these stories, they show the legendary mystique surrounding Baay Mokhtar as a holy hermit during the late 1980s and 1990s.

In addition to wearing dreadlocks and maintaining an unkempt appearance, another practice that characterized Baye Mokhtar and his followers was *yëngu,* the controversial practice of accompanying *sikkar (dhikr)* with frenetic drumming and dancing (Hill 2016c). *Yëngu* was introduced probably around 1980 by Ibra Fall's best-known *muqaddam,* Shaykh ʿAbdallāh Wilane,[9] who has a large following throughout Senegal and especially around his hometown of Kaffrine, east of Kaolack. As ʿAbdallāh Wilane had hoped, the practice successfully attracted youth into the Fayḍa, providing an Islamic alternative to the drinking, nightclubs, and sensual traditional dancing (*sabar*) that were commonplace in the area. While *yëngu* likely boosted Baay Mokhtar's popularity among young men and women, it also contributed to Baay Mokhtar's and his community's marginalization from the core Fayḍa organization.

Baay Mokhtar's otherworldliness also entailed a lack of concern for money and marriage. Some who knew him during the 1980s and 1990s told me that his disciples and clients would bring him large amounts of money, which he would promptly give away to anyone he thought needed it. One of my interviewees, Absa Samb,[10] knew Baay Mokhtar during the 1990s and glowingly testified to how generous and "consumed in God" (*jéex ci Yàlla*) he was. She told me, "Then, he was a Sufi who didn't want anything! He didn't even wear nice clothes … He just wore a simple cap and messy Baay Faal[11] clothes, and helped God's servants [people]." He would give any monetary offerings (*àddiya*) away without counting.[12] "He wouldn't keep anything," she told me. "He didn't need anything! Just God!" Absa Samb had recently been widowed and was trying to raise her seven children through petty commerce. From a family of Murids and Tijānīs of the Tivaouane branch, she was a new Taalibe Baay and had received *wird* and *tarbiya* after her husband's death from another *muqaddam* in Dakar. She told me that Baay Mokhtar treated her "like his own daughter," taking care of her electric bill, water bill, and other needs. Late one night, after she had not visited him for several days, one of Baay Mokhtar's *muqaddam*s knocked on her door, telling her Baay Mokhtar had not seen her for a while and hoped she was all right. When she apologized and told him she would come tomorrow, the *muqaddam* told her that he was there in the taxi. She approached the taxi and knelt to greet him. Baay Mokhtar said to her, "Don't stay away! Anything I have belongs to those who love God." He reached into his pocket and pulled out "a lot of money" and gave it to her.

Although Baay Mokhtar is best known as a charismatic liminal figure, it is important to remember that he has devoted much of his life to studying and teaching the Qur'ān and the classical corpus of Islamic texts. During the period when he lived in his shack in Medina near downtown Dakar, Baay Mokhtar opened a *daara* (Qur'ānic school) in the northern coastal suburb of Yoff, where he hired a teacher to teach. He continued to teach the core texts of Arabic and Islamic jurisprudence and to engage in frequent *khalwa* in his own small home. Any disciples who needed a temporary place to stay would stay at the larger *daara* house, which became the base of activities for the *daayira* associated with him.

I suspect that he may have based his disciple community so far from his own home because of his desire to spend most of his time praying in seclusion, a practice he continues today. Yet Absa Samb recounts that those who wanted to see him could easily see him, and that "whatever time you came, you would see him. You know? He didn't have anyone helping him – he did everything according to his spiritual state *(ḥāl)*." Yet she admitted that this lack of barriers taxed him. She continued, "And he's generous. He would be really, really tired, yet whenever you came … he would receive you, *ndeysaan*."[13] Baay Mokhtar was especially fatigued by performing all-night *gàmmus*, after which he would go right back to his prayerful meditation and receiving people, despite the fact that "he would be so tired he would shake, but he would just sit" and receive people. Others who knew Baay Mokhtar during this period similarly praised Baay Mokhtar's generosity and openness while admitting that it wore him out.

From Solitary Sufi to "Complete Shaykh"

Up until this point, then, Baay Mokhtar was a liminal figure in Turner's classic sense of the term (V. Turner 1967, 1995), a somewhat socially marginal recluse yet one perceived to have tremendous spiritual power. In the Fayḍa Tijāniyya community, such visible liminality is only generally acceptable for short periods of time – for example, during one's *tarbiya* or during the onset of an ecstatic spiritual state *(ḥāl)*. When I mentioned Baay Mokhtar and similarly liminal figures to some more core *muqaddams* in the Fayḍa community, some of them spoke dismissively, saying that once one has gone through *tarbiya* and reached *fanāʾ* (obliteration of the self), one may legitimately set aside social decorum for a day or two. Yet that is all the time it should take for a competent *muqaddam* to "bring you down" *(wàcce la)*, after which one must act with exemplary social decorum regardless of one's inner experience. It is a sign of spiritual maturity, I was told, to balance *ẓāhir* and *bāṭin*, *sharīʿa* (law) and *ḥaqīqa* (deeper reality), *baqāʾ* (persistence in law) and *fanāʾ*.

Sayyida Ndèye Maguète told me that she, too, supported this ideal – which is apparent in her tidy appearance and home – yet she insists that the dishevelled period that she and others associated with Baay Mokhtar went through did not stem from carelessness or ostentation. Rather, "all those who do this are seeking something in God, and he

[Baay Mokhtar] still hasn't found what he's seeking in God." People in Medina Baay, she told me, used to say, "Oh, he's just messing around, since he has his hair in dreadlocks," yet "they wouldn't seek to understand what might lead his head to be messed up like that." They should have known better, for Shaykh Ibrāhīm himself had gone through such a period while initiating the Fayḍa movement in Kossi, before founding Medina Baay. She told me that Ibra Fall had told her that "only in Medina did they see a dry-eyed [lit: white-eyed] Baay Niasse; in Kossi, no one ever saw a dry-eyed Baay Niasse." Shaykh Ibrāhīm and his first group of disciples, including Shaykh Ibra Fall, wore rags while in Kossi and shared one nice garment between them that any one of them who was to visit Kaolack would wear. Although this had more to do with poverty than asceticism, this poverty itself resulted from Baay's going "to Kossi to walk in God," whereas he only "smiled" after he found what he was looking for and came to Medina Baay. Like many accounts of saintly figures (see, for example, P. Werbner 1996), this account spatializes Shaykh Ibrāhīm's liminality, figuring the village of Kossi as the liminal wilderness of becoming and Medina Baay as the city of being. Like other accounts of Shaykh Ibrāhīm, Baay Mokhtar, and other Sufis, it also temporalizes liminality, acknowledging that ideally the Sufi ends up living in harmony with the world. The fact that Shaykh Ibrāhīm sent Shaykh Ibra Fall to live permanently in his liminal place narratively situates Shaykh Ibra Fall and his followers in this liminal space.

Some accounts suggest that, during the mid-1990s, Baay Mokhtar began to sense that he was about to experience some momentous changes. At that time, Absa Samb was supporting her family by importing and selling an assortment of small goods from the Gambia, and she would often stop by and give Baay Mokhtar some of whatever she had brought. Once she brought him a pair of sandals (*dàll i carax*). According to Absa Samb, he said:

> Oh, Mom! This means that what I don't want to happen is going to happen. What you just gave me, I'm telling you. I replied: What's that? He answered: I don't want to go abroad. The people in America are calling me to do a *gàmmu* there, but I don't want to go … I prefer these humble people here to those rich people there. But these shoes that you gave me … [they mean] I will move!

However much his reclusive asceticism contributed to his Sufi mystique, several of my interviewees told me that those around Baay

Mokhtar insisted for many years that he would be better off if he married so that someone would look after him. Yet he always refused, asking why he would need a wife when he had God. Absa Samb described him as saying to her, "My people[14] are saying they want to give me a wife. But I'm not ready for a wife. They just want to bring me problems – I don't need one." She replied, "Hey, just take one so we can have a mother." Sayyida Ndèye Maguète Niang told us that on a single day in 1995 he finally gave in and quietly married two women. Baay Mokhtar dissolved both marriages almost immediately, apparently without consummation. Many who knew him did not even know about these brief marriages while others avoid mentioning them.

My interlocutors placed Baay Mokhtar's marriage to Yaay Aïcha Sow in 1996 or 1997.[15] Many described it as a divinely ordained match that brought much-needed structure to Baay Mokhtar's perpetual anti-structure, a decorous wrapper to contain Baay Mokhtar's spiritual power. Yet the marriage has been controversial, not only because the arrangement challenges typical conjugal roles but also because Yaay Aïcha came to exercise nearly complete control, and many who were close to Baay Mokhtar have since been excluded or have left.

Sayyida Aïda Thiam, a *muqaddama* in the Dakar suburb of Yeumbeul (see chapter 5), knew Yaay Aïcha while she lived in Kaolack before their marriage. Sayyida Aïda is among the few I have met outside the couple's inner circle of disciples who have maintained close social relations with them. During the mid-1990s, Sayyida Aïda Thiam and Yaay Aïcha still lived in Kaolack. Their mothers were from the same village, and consequently they had known each other since childhood. Aïda describes Aïcha as a hard worker and as someone "accustomed to prayer beads," meaning that she spent much time meditating on sacred litanies *(wird)*. After finishing her secondary studies in Kaolack (at Lycée Valdiodio Ndiaye), Aïcha had married an Arabic teacher, had several children, and divorced. She then ran a market stall where Aïda would often come to visit her. When Aïda had a daughter, she invited Aïcha to the naming ceremony and named her daughter after her. Just a few days after the naming ceremony, Aïda was surprised not to find Aïcha in the market. She asked around and learned that she had suddenly married and moved to Dakar. When told that her husband was Baay Mokhtar, she said, "Ah, so she has a good husband, as God willed *(mā shā' Allāh)*."

By then, Baay Mokhtar had moved from his shack in the Medina neighbourhood of downtown Dakar to an apartment in the sprawling Parcelles Assainies suburb north of Dakar, although he would often come through Medina Baay to visit other leaders and his own disciples in the area. Sayyida Aïda did not know Baay Mokhtar personally at that point, yet she occasionally saw him during his visits to Medina Baay as he walked to *daayira* meetings surrounded by an exuberant crowd of disciples *sikkar*-ing in unison. She told me she would join in a crowd of people from the neighbourhood to watch the procession go by and would ask, "What was that all about?" People would tell her: "Baay Mokhtar came."

Not long after Baay Mokhtar and Yaay Aïcha's marriage, Sayyida Aïda herself came to Dakar, where she resumed her friendship with Yaay Aïcha. Sayyida Aïda commented that Baay Mokhtar had had many disciples before marrying Aïcha but not nearly the number one sees today. "He was just being a Sufi. So Aïcha, as God willed (Ar. *mā shā Allāh*), has done great work there. She has held the community together. She has brought everything." Before that, she said, Baay Mokhtar cared about nothing but "working for God," and his disciples, like him, "used to be dirty, wear many prayer beads, and so on, but she got rid of all that." Now "they're all proper, clean, and following God."

Yaay Aïcha herself told us how, as soon as she arrived, she set about changing the way things were done. Those who opposed her changes far outnumbered those who accepted them. The night she arrived at his house, she was presented with a beautiful ivory string of prayer beads and told to wear them around her neck. She asked why, and her husband answered that everyone there wore prayer beads. She answered that she would not wear it, explaining, "My leader disapproves," meaning Al-Ḥājj ʿAbdallāh Niasse, Shaykh Ibrāhīm's eldest son and official successor. When Baay Mokhtar cited the Qurʾān and *ḥadīth* to explain that wearing the *kurus* was not forbidden in Islam, she answered that this did not matter, because her leader was her "Qurʾān of this time," and because his disapproval was equivalent to Shaykh Ibrāhīm's disapproval. In the end, she compromised on the prayer beads after being reassured that Al-Ḥājj ʿAbdallāh did not outright forbid wearing a single string of beads. However, she insisted that Baay Mokhtar and his followers wear no more than one string of prayer beads, potentially while carrying another. Baay Mokhtar agreed, and instructed his disciples to do the same. Since her arrival in the household, the community has held to this practice. She also insisted that Baay Mokhtar shave his dreadlocks, dress cleanly and neatly, and bathe and eat regularly. Once again her rationale was that Shaykh Ibrāhīm's successor insisted on these things. Many dreadlocked disciples soon followed suit, some shaving their heads and others maintaining clean, short, and neatly coiffed dreadlocks.

One of Baay Mokhtar's disciples, a rapper and slam poet in Dakar who goes by the artist name of Bill Barham, has been a disciple of Baay Mokhtar since the age of fourteen in 1994. He had previously followed his older brother into the Baay Faal movement, growing dreadlocks and wandering and reciting Sufi poetry with his brother for spare change. He took the *wird* from Baay Mokhtar when the leader came through his family's village of Keur Madiabel (east of Kaolack), after which Baay Mokhtar had one of his *muqaddam*s give him *tarbiya*. The visual style of Baay Mokhtar's disciples then was similar to that of the Baay Faals, and Bill Barham continued to grow out his dreadlocks and wore the same tattered outfit every day, plus seven strings of prayer beads, like his leader. Six years later, in 2000, he saw that his leader now opposed this look. He told us:

> I cut my dreadlocks because when – since I have a leader, who is the one I believe in and follow – the period when he came to us … he gave us the counsel (*ndigal*) to cut the dreadlocks, reduce the prayer beads, start wearing clean clothes. That was what I did too, since a disciple relies on counsel. That was when I cut my dreadlocks, took off the clothes I was wearing, started wearing clean clothes, and also started wearing one string of prayer beads, and carrying one set of prayer beads.

When I have attended Baay Mokhtar's *daayira*'s Friday litany *(ḥaḍra)*, I have found that many disciples continue to have a certain flair. Most have shaved heads, although some maintain shorter and neatly coiffed dreadlocks; all wear one string of prayer beads around their necks while holding another in their hand to count *wirds*; and they tend to wear clean and well-maintained although often colourful and quirky clothes. Yaay's campaign to polish the community's outer appearance was by and large a success.

More contentious than Yaay's campaign for neatness was her campaign to eradicate the practice of *yëngu* in the community. As with other practices she forbade, Yaay Aïcha was not concerned with any juridical rationale behind forbidding *yëngu*. She even admitted to us that for some it was a genuine manifestation of a spiritual state. Rather, she again insisted that "my leader disapproves," a sufficient reason in itself. As *yëngu* was an important part of this disciple community's gatherings, many people fought her on the issue and believed she was forcing her will on her guileless husband. "At the beginning, it was very hard," she told us. "Because even now if you ask who Yaay is, I think more people disagree with me than agree with me." Yet she defended her intervention, saying, "Everything that the community [of Baay, as represented by his successors] doesn't approve, no one – I will not agree – and no one will do it when I am present." Despite strong opposition within the community, Baay Mokhtar forbade the practice except at marriages and child-naming festivities. Although *yëngu* is not practised in the central *daayira* directly overseen by Baay Mokhtar, some *muqaddams* and their *daayiras* who were once or are still associated with him continue to practise *yëngu*. Many dismiss its prohibition as due solely to his wife's pressure.

One of these is Sayyida Ndèye Maguète Niang. Although she did not discuss with us her own break with the community, one of Baay Mokhtar's assistants told us that she had not had any contact with Baay Mokhtar for at least seven years, which would have been around 2007, about a decade after the marriage. The assistant implied that this break had to do with Ndèye Maguète's and her disciples' persistence in practising *yëngu*. Yet when I mentioned to Sayyida Ndèye Maguète that Baay Mokhtar had long since abandoned *yëngu*, she replied with apparent surprise, "Oh, he abandonded it?!" Then she speculated: "Could it be that his wife forbade it?" I replied in the affirmative, to which she answered: "Yes, yes, exactly! As for me, I don't have anyone forbidding me!" It is inconceivable that Sayyida Ndèye Maguète had never heard of the prohibition during the ten years she remained in contact with Baay Mokhtar after his marriage. More likely, her response was intentionally ambivalent, the kind of statement abundant in Taalibe Baay discourse (Hill 2010, 2013b). Her apparent expression of *surprise* at hearing that Baay Mokhtar had forbidden the practice seemed to veil an expression of *disbelief* that Baay Mokhtar was the one doing the forbidding.

Beyond her campaigns against controversial dress and dance, Yaay has brought organization, order, and even economic capital to her husband's work, turning his life of seclusion into a well-organized business. As mentioned above, his earlier companions described visiting him without protocol. He had no fixed price for his services, and he would soon give away any money people brought. Yaay Aïcha instituted regular consultation hours, much like a physician. From Monday afternoon through Thursday afternoon, each client buys a ticket for 2,000 FCFA (around $4) and waits in line to see the shaykh. Baay Mokhtar then uses various esoteric practices to diagnose and deal with his clients' needs, whether this involves curing physical ailments, doing prayers or making amulets to help obtain work or visas, or divining which life choice is more auspicious. Like many healers, beyond the initial consultation, he may spend long stretches of time in seclusion on behalf of a client, doing divinatory prayer *(istikhāra)* or repeated litanies *(wird)* to pray for desired results.

Although this consultation system is designed for clients and not for those who wish to see him for social or religious reasons, several people I spoke to who had known him before his marriage believed that they would need to buy the 2,000 FCFA ticket and wait in line to see him. As seeing him can otherwise prove difficult, anyone who wants to visit him may see little option other than buying a ticket. One woman who had not seen him since his marriage told us she had decided she must visit him, even if she must buy a ticket. Yet she said she understood the necessity of the current arrangement, which protects Baay Mokhtar from his own generosity and allows him to focus on his work. Before, she said, he would drop whatever he was doing to help anyone who came, "but now, you know, he's married, and his wife helps him." She makes sure he eats and sleeps enough, having him rest for a whole month in solitude after performing an all-night *gàmmu*.

Beyond a core group of *daayira* leaders, Baay Mokhtar's face-to-face interactions with disciples appear to be limited. Like many leaders, he typically gives *wird* at large events and then delegates *tarbiya* and *sayr* to a number of men and women he has authorized to do these things, especially Yaay. When my collaborators and I wanted to interview him, the disciples who coordinate with visitors had us come back numerous times. We finally found the two at a *ḥaḍra,* and Yaay agreed to receive us for an interview afterwards. Although I at first wondered if *daayira* leaders were suspicious of my research, many others reported the same difficulty. Other major leaders, including Shaykh Ibrāhīm's senior sons, have hours nearly every day when they open their doors and anyone can see them, and they make their cell phone numbers easily available and answer them personally.

In our interview with Baay Mokhtar and Yaay Aïcha, my assistants and I saw at first hand how Yaay and his inner circle mediate between him and outsiders, seemingly out of concern for his well-being. Yaay and *daayira* leaders vetted my questions before the interview, and during the interview Baay Mokhtar often turned to Yaay for confirmation that he should answer a question. She sometimes instructed him to skip a question or to go only so far in answering it, while she sometimes fielded the question herself. He occasionally overrode her, reassuring her that he would not say anything potentially controversial. Those around them construe Yaay's assertiveness not as a violation of the man's ultimate authority in the household but as an extension of her role of caring for her husband. His inner circle seemed anxious to protect him from his own innocence and generosity, lest he give too freely of his time and knowledge or speak too freely of potentially misconstrued esoteric doctrines.

Perhaps even more concretely than the other women leaders discussed in this book, Yaay Aïcha not only amplifies certain aspects of feminine piety and motherhood but is also described in terms of the ancient Sufi trope of the transcendent woman who becomes an honorary "man." Absa Samb, even while lamenting the difficulty of seeing Baay Mokhtar since his marriage, says, "His wife helps him. She performs the role of a man. His wife! ... I don't even know his wife, but just from seeing how she organizes things I know she's a warrior." Beyond attaining the same spiritual level as Sufi men, Yaay Aïcha can claim to be manlike in the roles she plays in the household and religious community. Islamic jurisprudence is widely understood, including in Senegal, as prescribing that a husband economically support his wife and children while the wife takes care of maintaining the home and raising children. A good Muslim husband, I have often been told, makes the big decisions, while a good Muslim wife accepts his decisions and only offers her views when asked. Even pious women who claim the spiritual status of a man typically acknowledge these ideals regardless of complex realities.

One factor that may contribute to Yaay's ability to act "like a man" is that, like the *muqaddama*s discussed in chapter 2, she can in some way dissociate herself from ritually impure female reproductive functions. Although Yaay has children from her previous marriage, she has had none with Baay Mokhtar, and Baay Mokhtar himself has never had children or shown any carnal interest in women. Thus, their union could be perceived as an asexual one and both Baay Mokhtar and Yaay as asexual beings. This may contribute to Yaay Aïcha's ability to openly perform typically masculine roles on behalf of her husband.

The financial means and expertise Yaay Aïcha acquired through trading in bulk foodstuffs have allowed her to play roles typically played by husbands. A leader in the couple's *daayira* specifically framed her economic contributions to her husband and the religious community in terms of playing roles typically associated with men in Senegal. For example, this *daayira* leader cited the fact that she used her own income to pay for Baay Mokhtar's pilgrimage to Mecca in 2007, something he explained that Senegalese wives typically expect their husbands to finance.

Yaay Aïcha also founded a village that she populated with disciples, a common practice for centuries among male Islamic leaders in Senegal yet something I have never heard attributed to a woman. The *daayira* leader told us that once, while Baay Mokhtar was away on a trip, Yaay Aïcha went with some disciples to a spot eighty-two kilometres from Dakar and located the place for her village. She procured the land from the government and cleared the brush with the disciples. They called the village Kóofa Mbooro after the ancient city of Kūfa and the neighbouring village of Mbooro. The *daayira* leader explained that Yaay financially helped disciples who struggled to make a living in Dakar to build houses and live there. Also using her own funds, she set up a Qur'ānic school there – whose students recited the Qur'ān at the *gàmmu* discussed above – and organized farming, orchard, and vegetable gardening projects. Baay Mokhtar told me that this village is where he now obtains the ingredients for his herbal medicines. This project clearly brings Yaay away from the feminized sphere of the inner courtyard and kitchen to the masculinized space of the village square.

Yet however masculine her activities may appear, Yaay still performs them as a wife, and as such these activities must be situated within the accepted images and models of wifehood. Even if Yaay is often as prominent and influential as her husband, Baay Mokhtar and other members of the community continue to describe her primarily as a wife supporting her husband's work. When I asked Baay Mokhtar to describe their relationship, he invoked in Arabic the old saying that "behind every great man is a great woman."[16] Appealing to a higher model than routine conjugal roles, he described Yaay Aïcha as "my Khadīja," comparing her to the Prophet Muḥammad's first wife:

> She helps me as Khadīja helped the Prophet, Prayer and Peace be upon him. Also, it [this marriage] is a sacred trust, a will and testament that Maam Ibrayima Fall entrusted to me, telling me: I will put you together with my granddaughter[17] … He told me: You are my helper … But also, her – he [Ibrayima Fall] pointed her out to me and said – she will be that [helper] to you.

Aïcha Sow fits Khadīja's mould in coming into the marriage already financially established and previously married with children. Like

Khadīja, she has used her means to advance her husband's religious mission. Perhaps most importantly, just as Khadīja assertively counselled and questioned her husband, Aïcha immediately made her presence felt in the household and religious community. Carrying this parallel further, Yaay Aïcha's epithet is "Mother of the Knowers [of God]" *(Umm al-'ārifīn)*, a variation on the title "Mother of the Believers" *(Umm al-mu'minīn)*, a title designating the Prophet Muḥammad's wives in the Qur'ān and other Islamic literature.

Bending or Breaking the Norms?

Certainly everyone – including Baay Mokhtar and Yaay Aïcha, their disciples, and puzzled onlookers – recognizes that these two perform religious authority in unique ways that challenge prevalent gender roles. They are clearly an exception, not the rule. Where their supporters and detractors may disagree is over whether they actually break norms – or perhaps perform them badly – or simply bend them to accommodate exceptional circumstances. Members of this community are well aware that some perceive their leaders as flouting proper conventions, and even some of Baay Mokhtar's supporters perceive Yaay as shamelessly manipulating and monopolizing her guileless husband. Yet the couple's supporters perceive both Baay Mokhtar's unusual nature and the relationship through which this nature is channelled as miraculous signs. While the outcome is unlike anything I have seen, Baay Mokhtar and Yaay Aïcha achieve this result through the same idioms of masculine and feminine piety and Sufi transcendence we have seen to be prevalent in the larger Fayḍa community.

For example, as I have argued, Yaay Aïcha visibly performs the role of a pious Muslim woman and wife. She wears form-concealing clothing, speaks gently and quietly, does not speak in gatherings outside the home, does not sit above her husband, refers to him as the head of the household and community, and spiritually guides with his authorization. All her activities are presented as necessary to support and care for her husband, who presumably needs her assistance in order to attain his potential.

Yet the necessity of playing this supporting wifely role justifies Yaay Aïcha's incursion into leadership roles strongly associated with men and perhaps otherwise off-limits to her. It is unheard of, for example, for a woman to sit front and centre at a *gàmmu*, much less to visibly direct each step of the meeting. Her alibi for doing so is to allow her husband to manage his own presence and the meeting. Also, one would never expect to see a woman in Senegal stand and pray openly next to the imam during congregational prayer. This result stems indirectly (whether intentionally or not) from the unusual placement of a women's section, which leads her to be next to the imam (her husband) when prayer time comes. While formally following the established rules of maintaining separate sections for men and women, this arrangement of sections yields a striking depiction of this couple's unusual joint religious authority.

Yaay Aïcha visibly directs the community's activities, from the minutiae of the *gàmmu* to the foundation of a disciple village, all roles almost universally played by men. All these roles are framed as helping her husband, who is described as needing her organizational skills to do such things. In this way, she often appears to act as the ultimate authority through effectively exercising her husband's power of attorney. Formally, this authority derives from him, yet he mostly submits to her practical judgment, a fact that has dramatically transformed him and the religious community. As well as being presented in terms of conventional feminine piety and wifely support, Yaay Aïcha's unconventional roles are also explained as an example of the ancient Sufi trope of the holy woman as a "man" and as a recapitulation of Khadīja's exceptional example.

What implications does this story have for the study of gender and Islamic authority? Perhaps many, but here I want to highlight the importance of focusing not only on stated norms, intentions, and imperatives but also on how performances incorporate all of these with unpredictable outcomes. As discussed in the introduction to this book, studies of Islam and gender have often focused either on norms themselves – especially how they contrast to liberal norms of gender equality – or on how women either inhabit or resist these norms. Although there are limits to how one successful performance can deviate from previous successful performances, a given set of norms does not predetermine the range of possible outcomes.

This couple presents one example of changing gender roles despite the absence of significant discussion of gender roles. Even if an exceptional case, Yaay's exceptional role accompanies greater than usual women's participation in ritual gatherings, which suggests that she might be contributing to a broader shift. This is not a linear shift towards liberal models of gender equality but a shift towards greater women's participation in religious practice shaped by gendered cultural practices.

While this couple and their followers are certainly aware of discourses of Muslim women and equality, the driving forces behind the changes seen here are far more subtle than conversations about equality in a Habermasian public sphere (Habermas 1989). This is not to minimize the usefulness or validity of approaches that use *ijtihād* (critical interpretation of Islamic texts) to reexamine hegemonic gender relations in Islam (e.g., Wadud 1992; Barlas 2002; Safi 2003; Ali, Hammer, and Silvers 2013). Rather, this case suggests that, for many Muslims, changes in religious practice depend more on performative reconfigurations and recontextualization of existing norms than on discursive argumentation from religious texts.

Epilogue: Islam as a Numinous, Performative Tradition

The last interview of my 2014 research trip with a Taalibe Baay woman was not meant to be. Or perhaps it was. While most subjects of this book have attained some repute – even formal appointments – in the Fayḍa community, in more than one sense, this happenstance interviewee had not yet arrived at her destination. In August 2014, as my wife, Marwa, and I were returning from four months in Senegal, our cancelled flight to Canada left us trapped for nearly thirty-six hours in a Brussels airport terminal. As we waited for airline staff to set up cots for the stranded passengers, Marwa struck up a conversation with Rokhy,[1] a sharply dressed, middle-class Senegalese woman apparently in her early thirties. After two months spent visiting family in Dakar, Rokhy was returning to Montreal with her two young daughters. Marwa told Rokhy about her work for a health NGO and mentioned my research on the Fayḍa. Rokhy answered that she herself was a Taalibe Baay – or at least hoped to be one.

Marwa beckoned to me, and we shared insider talk about people and places we knew. Rokhy held up her smart phone to show its background image, a photograph of Baay. She then tapped into her music library and resumed where she had last left off listening: a *sikkar* performed by the famous *sikkarkat* Aïda Faye (see chapter 6). I told her I had just visited Aïda Faye a couple of days earlier and had filmed her leading *sikkar* at a *gàmmu*. I showed her my computer screen, revealing that at that moment I had been entering notes on that meeting.

As she told us her story – in French, for Marwa's benefit – and I realized its relevance to my research themes, I obtained her consent to jot it down to use in my book. Without prompting, Rokhy told a story strikingly similar to those of the *muqaddama*s I had interviewed.

When Rokhy told me she considered herself a Taalibe Baay but had not yet done *tarbiya,* I imagined she was like the many people with Taalibe Baay parents who identify with the community but have never taken the time to undergo *tarbiya* or participate in a *daayira*. Yet this was far from the case. In fact, she had only discovered Baay during this summer visit to Senegal.

In the Jolof area of Senegal where Rokhy's family has its roots, most people associate with the Tivaouane branch of the Tijāniyya, and many are unaware of any other Tijānī groups. Rokhy had thus always considered herself Tijānī through family association without taking the Tijānī *wird*. When I lived in Jolof, years before, I observed that the *wird* was mostly something certain mature men did, while most others identified as Tijānī by general family association.

While living in Montreal, Rokhy said, she increasingly felt a spiritual lack, yet did not know what was missing. Although she always fasted and did her daily prayers, she often felt that she was just going through the motions. While in Senegal, she mentioned her spiritual lack to her brother, who told her that clearly what she sought was Baay. Knowing little about Baay and doubting he could bring her anything new, she shrugged his suggestion off.

Then, at a time when Rokhy was not sure what Baay even looked like, he appeared to her in a series of dreams. She told us vivid details from these dreams, which seemed to her as real as waking situations. The first night, Baay appeared to her three times. During one of these dreams he gave her the Tijānī *wird*. A few nights later, he returned and gave her *tarbiya*. During that dream, Rokhy dreamed of sitting before the daybreak prayer *(fajr)* when Baay appeared and told her to get ready to pray. After she prayed, he told her he had committed to do a *dog* – a set number of *wird* divided among several people – of 25 million *Ṣalāt al-Fātiḥ* (prayers for the Prophet) and wanted her to do part of it. She gladly accepted but awoke before she could ask how many times she was to repeat it. She decided to do whatever she could, so after waking and praying *fajr*, she began counting repetitions of the *Ṣalāt al-Fātiḥ* on her prayer beads (*kurus*). After the ninetieth time, she started going into a "trance." Marwa asked what this meant, and Rokhy explained it as *fanaawu* (Wol.) – *fanā'* (Ar.), the extinction of the self that normally follows *tarbiya*. (Here she may have been using it in the loose sense referring to any ecstatic state.)

By the hundredth time, overwhelmed with a feeling she cannot describe, she began to laugh and cry simultaneously. As she continued reciting, her state intensified until she dropped her prayer beads (*kurus*) and lay down, continuing to laugh and cry. As she narrated, Rokhy emphasized repeatedly that this experience was beyond all description and that only one who had lived it could understand. The next day, Rokhy called and told her experience to her non-Taalibe Baay sister, who herself fell into a trance as Rokhy spoke. When she told her Taalibe Baay brother about her experience, he played her a recorded speech by *sikkarkat* Babacar Thiam describing *fanāʾ* as something that simultaneously brings laughter and crying. Her brother was convinced that she had actually received *wird* and *tarbiya* directly from Baay, yet to be certain, she determined to receive them through a living shaykh.

The following weekend, just two weeks before we met Rokhy on her way back to Canada, Rokhy's other sister – a Taalibe Baay – hosted her *daayira*'s weekly *sikkar* meeting. Rokhy approached the *daayira*'s *muqaddam* and received the *wird* from him. Because she would soon be leaving Senegal, some advised her not to undergo *tarbiya* before her departure, as she might enter a difficult spiritual state (*ḥāl*) with no nearby *muqaddam* to "bring her down" (*wàcce ko*). She told us she hoped to find a living *muqaddam* in Montreal to give her *tarbiya*. In an e-mail exchange in 2016, she told me she had received *tarbiya* by "long distance" (using electronic communication) in October 2014.

I found the resemblances between Rokhy's apparently little-rehearsed story of an incipient spiritual journey and those of more seasoned *muqaddamas* striking. Baay's posthumous presence is a remarkably consistent actor across new and long-standing disciples' narratives. Time and again it is Baay – not painstaking disciplinary practices or persuasive proselytizers – who gathers often unsuspecting disciples, transforming them into drops in his flood.

Unlike most of the women discussed in this book, Rokhy claims no religious authority over anyone. However, her account can still be approached in terms of Islamic authority. Like any narrative, hers does not merely retell the facts but is to some degree tailored to influence. Telling her story, she says, guided her sister towards divine knowledge, and it is easy to imagine her returning to Montreal and planting the seeds of others' experiences of Baay through retelling this story. Influencing others through conversation and example is precisely how many Muslim women exercise varying degrees of de facto authority (Augis 2014; Frede 2014; Frede and Hill 2014).

Like the *muqaddamas* encountered in this book, Rokhy is less concerned with arguing from texts to prove the most "orthodox" position than with showing the possibility of transcending questions of textual orthodoxy. What she had been missing, she says, was not knowledge or application of Islam's prescriptions – one might say the nutshell (see chapter 3) – but something beyond them – the kernel itself, which Baay himself gave her freely.

Her story and others discussed in this book highlight blind spots in current academic approaches to studying Islam. Among anthropologists and many other scholars today, the most widely accepted and perhaps fruitful way of conceptualizing Islam comes from Talal Asad, who suggests beginning by approaching Islam, "as Muslims do," as "a discursive tradition that includes and relates itself to the founding texts of the Qur'an and the Hadith" (T. Asad 1986, 14). Asad's approach elegantly clears away problems with previous approaches that assumed Islam to be either one transhistorical abstraction, a collection of discrete local "Islams," or a notion too incoherent for study. If our aim is to delineate "Islam" as a field of study allowing us to trace connections between Muslims of various times, places, and persuasions, we could scarcely improve upon this conception. As an antidote to persistent colonial assumptions of an orthodox versus a syncretistic "African Islam," Benjamin Soares has advocated this approach in the African context to highlight how African Muslims relate to "supralocal discourses of Islam" (Soares 2000, 282). Although some have critiqued Asad's conception – for example, for implying that this discursive tradition is a "coherent entity" (Schielke 2009, S37) or for privileging discourse over practice (Janson 2014, 11) – I still find it useful in analytically demarcating an academic field.

Yet no single attempt to *define* Islam does so "as Muslims do." According to Nietzsche, "it is only that which has no history which can be defined" (Nietzsche 1918, 70). Even if we can agree to identify as "Islamic" anything that refers to the Qur'ān and Sunna as authoritative texts, this does not mean that "Islam" for Muslims is coextensive with discourse surrounding these texts. All Muslims are certainly part of an Islamic discursive tradition, yet they may understand Islam as something that transcends the discourse about it and is potentially known through channels that circumvent or exceed textual references. Rokhy seems to conceive of Islamic knowledge as something beyond discourse and not necessarily rooted in text. She approaches correct Islamic knowledge and practice as established not only through texts but also through dreams and mystical states. Even if Shaykh al-Tijānī and Shaykh Ibrāhīm often insisted that all their teachings were consistent with the Qur'ān and Sunna (the example of the Prophet), they promised knowledge and experience exceeding these texts.

Understanding Rokhy's experience of Islam requires taking seriously her experience of numinous forces. Still, like any self-narrator, she shapes her narrative to contribute to her social performance of a coherent self and possessor of truth. Like many Taalibe Baay, Rokhy attributes becoming Baay's disciple entirely to Baay himself, demoting at least two Taalibe Baay siblings to secondary roles and not addressing whether worldly events like divorce or emigration contributed to her sense of crisis. Narratives that highlight the self–Baay relationship at the expense of others seem to say, "I may not be the author of my spiritual journey, but it is entirely *my* journey."

Often, religious truths are established not through debates and logical proofs but through demonstration and practical proofs. Perhaps if we are interested in *describing* and not just *locating* Islam anthropologically, we could simply approach it as a "tradition" – one that is discursive, numinous, performative, disciplined, and so on. Throughout this book I have focused on the numinous and performative aspects of Islamic experience. Islam for any given Muslim may be constituted largely by what she experiences as the uncanny and miraculous – that which is beyond articulation and *ẓāhir* explanation. Rather than through textual argumentation, she may legitimate and communicate her Islamic knowledge through demonstration – that she is the kind of moral person one might expect to bear such knowledge, that her intuitive knowledge harmonizes with that of others on some spiritual level, and that she can transmit such knowledge to others. Supporting one's position through demonstrating exemplary piety and devotion is what I have called elsewhere "performative apologetics" (Hill 2016c; 2016b).

It is likely easier to talk about "global discourses" than "global numinosities" or "global performativities." We can easily imagine "discourse" travelling easily over global networks. As anthropologists have increasingly recognized the inherence of the numinous and the occult in modernity and global neoliberalism (Comaroff and Comaroff 1999, 2000; Meyer and Pels 2003), it has remained easy to imagine the numinous as a local response to global discourses and institutions. Likewise, within Islam, it would be easy to imagine discourse – represented, for example, by scripturalist reform tendencies – as representing a universal "Great Tradition" (Redfield 1956), "orthodox" Islam (Gellner 1969), or "global" Islam, while imagining the "numinous" as representing the "Little Tradition," "heterodox," or "local" Islam. The Fayḍa is a clear example of the globalization of the numinous, with similar accounts of Baay's choosing his disciples all over West Africa and increasingly in the United States, South Africa, and Europe. My point is not that Fayḍa adherents depend less on discourse than anyone else does but that discourse is not the only thing that regulates religious practice or produces religious knowledge. Rather than constituting religious knowledge, discourse may only obliquely index its inarticulable existence, as in the statement "I am God."

This idea of establishing religious knowledge and authority more through showing than through telling suffuses the narratives of the women leaders discussed throughout this book. Changes in gendered religious roles, I have argued, have had less to do with reopening the gates of *ijtihād* – or systematically reinterpreting Islamic texts and norms – than with modelling new performances of piety and discipleship and demonstrating their compatibility with prevalent Islamic norms. Women's religious authority among Taalibe Baay is almost always connected to the numinous. Their alibi for their unusual work is that they did not choose it but discovered the unique mission Baay assigned them through dreams and ecstatic experiences.

While these points are not specific to women, a shift away from privileging discursive reasoning and towards acknowledging multiple modes of establishing religious truth and authority is one step towards the project of "en-gendering" Islamic authority (Frede and Hill 2014). Muslim women around the world increasingly act as scholars and teachers of Islamic texts (Islam 2012; Rausch 2012) and have created new spaces of women's authority through the Internet and radio (Le Renard 2012; Schulz 2012b). Yet Islamic textual study in most contexts continues to be male-dominated, and many women remain more likely to base authority on intuitive experience and performances of exemplary piety than on textual study and exegesis. This more often entails resignifying and reconfiguring prevalent norms of feminine piety than subverting them.

A result of this approach is to allow spiritual narratives and experiences to retain their ambiguity. Narratives often do not clarify where a person's responsibility ends and that of Baay and larger institutions and conditions begins. Explaining why Baay's disciples have so many different – and sometimes conflicting – ways of doing things, several Taalibe Baay told me that "Baay takes on many forms" ("*Baay ay melokaanam ñoo bari*"). As Malaw Camara explained the changes Baay had posthumously decided to implement in the organization of religious life, "times change" ("*jamano dafay dox*"). In his multitudinous and changing forms, Baay is simultaneously a numinous presence that transcends changing material and social conditions and "the solution" – the slogan of some *muqaddams* I interviewed – that takes a form appropriate to each condition. It is this simultaneity of diverse and changing conditions and timeless truths that Taalibe Baay women leaders navigate, improvising new roles while performatively situating them as manifestations of timeless Islamic principles and Baay's numinous presence.

Notes

Transliteration Note

1 Here I differ from the ALA-LC convention, which is to represent the feminine *nisba* as *-īyah*. I represent all *shadda*s as double consonants.

Introduction

1 *Sayyida* (Arabic: a noble woman): A title for a woman of high spiritual rank. I use the Arabic spelling for this and other titles of Arabic origin. Its Wolof pronunciation is not standardized, but it is most commonly pronounced *Zeydaa*, the "z" being a hypercorrection for Wolof's lack of native "z." The same women are sometimes given the title "*Ajaa*," from Arabic *Ḥajja*, if they have undertaken the pilgrimage to Mecca.
2 The general 2013 census document (the "Rapport définitif," République du Sénégal 2013, 300) mentions a population of 96 per cent Muslims in passing, although it gives no further information about religious affiliation. The religion survey (République du Sénégal 2015) breaks the population down into religions and Sufi adherences. This survey yielded slightly different results, with 93 per cent of respondents identifying as Muslim, although it is based on a much smaller sample size (65,826).
3 I had interviewed Diénaba Guèye in Kaolack in 2001 and Sayyida Moussoukoro Mbaye in Dakar in 2004 (see chapters 4 and 5).
4 See Hill 2013a for more details about her.
5 *"Muqaddam tur la rekk me jigéen ñépp muqaddam lañu paskë jigéen ñépp ay yarkat lañu."* Note that the masculine form *"muqaddam"* is used in Wolof contexts to refer to men and women because Wolof is grammatically genderless.

6 Here I am synthesizing reports from many interviews over the years. I plan to publish a far more detailed account of early women in the Fayḍa.
7 In this book I use "reformism" to designate literalist tendencies, including both Islamist/Salafī-style movements that ultimately seek an Islamic state and Islamic *da'wa* (preaching) movements such as the Tablīgh Jamā'at for whom this is not explicitly part of their program.
8 "*dafay xeex pour droits de la femme.*" Interview in Dakar, 30 August 2004, with the assistance of Cheikh Baye Thiam and El Hadj Abdoulaye Bitèye. Sayyida Moussoukoro is discussed further in chapters 2, 4, and 5.
9 "*Loolu mooy libération bu dof. Loolu mooy liberté bu dof. Moom la tubaab yi indi.*" Speech given by Ustādh Bashīr Niasse on 22 October 2005 in Dakar.
10 I have analysed this speech in greater detail in Hill 2011. See Al-Hibri (1997, 2000a) for an analogous argument that the Islamic marriage contract, if implemented correctly, benefits women more than liberal Western ideals of equality. See Ali (2003) for a critique of this view of the Islamic marriage contract.
11 Here, *sharī'a* suggests not a state-enforced legal code but regulations surrounding worship and social relationships based in the discipline of Islamic jurisprudence *(fiqh).*
12 "*Soldarou Baye*" (*soldaar u Baay*).
13 El-Hadji Baye Thioub speaking at a *daayira* meeting in Medina Baay, 14 May 2001.
14 In his magnum opus, *Kāshif al-Ilbās* (Niasse 2010), Shakyh Ibrāhīm explains what gnostics mean by "seeing" God and mentions both these meanings.
15 In defining "ethics," Mahmood (2005, 28) quotes Foucault's definition of "technologies of the self" quoted above, showing that she approaches these terms as synonyms.
16 Both Mahmood and Hirschkind sharply differentiate the Aristotelian ethical conception of "habitus" from that of Bourdieu (1977), who sees habitus as a largely unintentional by-product of class upbringing.
17 *Adab* has many potential translations, among them "good behaviour" and "etiquette," or, as Wright (2015, 14) suggests, "habitus." The transitive verb "*addaba*" can mean to discipline, punish, or chastise. In his translation of *Rūḥ al-Adab,* Shaykh Hasan Cissé sometimes translates "*adab*" as "discipline" (Niasse 1998, 19).

1 An Emerging Urban Youth Movement

1 Interview with Malaw Camara and Sayyida Awa Cissé in Dakar, 30 June 2010.

2 "*Xéjna jigéen ñi ba léegi des na ci seen comportement … seen itte moo ci tolloogut noonu.*" Interview with Sayyida Awa Cissé conducted on my behalf by Cheikh Baye Thiam in Dakar, 18 March 2010.

3 The "Women in Development" paradigm that dominated international development circles in the 1970s has more recently given way to "Gender and Development." Although the theory behind these paradigms is different (Rathgeber 1990; Razavi and Miller 1995), their effects on connecting women and a country's development at a local level worldwide have been similar.

4 Cheikh Hassan Cissé's African American Islamic Institute is a prime example (see Renders 2002).

5 Speech given at the Mame Astou Diankha Day conference, Kaolack, Saturday, 12 June 2010.

6 Speech by ʿAbd al-Bāqī Dem.

7 These include followers of the Tijānī leader Imam Kabir Barry of Velingara Walo and the followers of the Baay Faal Murid leader Shaykh Musā Cissé, nicknamed Njàmbe Daaru. The latter are popularly nicknamed "Yàlla Yàlla" (God God) for their incessant talk of God.

8 Oral accounts usually date the letter as 1960 or 1962, but it is dated 22 Shaʿbān 1383 *h.*, approximately 7 January 1964.

9 At the end of his 1964 letter to disciples, Shaykh Ibrāhīm identifies this phrase as the federation's motto.

10 This section condenses multiple interviews each with *daayira* co-founders Modou Niang, Papa Maḥmūd Niasse, Malaw Camara, Sayyida Awa Cissé, Sayyida Diarra Ndiaye, and Astou Diop conducted between 2004 and 2014.

11 Shaykha Maryam Niasse had been present in Dakar since 1952 and has held an *ijāza* for decades, yet out of respect for her husband's position, she only started discreetly giving *tarbiya* after his death in 1984 and has never headed a particular *daayira*.

12 She showed me a photocopy of the *ijāza*, which was dated the Islamic month of Dhū al-Ḥijja, 1400 *h.*, which started on 10 October 1980. If he held onto the *ijāza* for six months, as she reports, he would have given it to her around April 1981.

13 We had four interviews with Sayyida Awa Cissé and Malaw Camara together in their home in the neighbourhood of Ouakam: 22 July 2009 (conducted with Alioune Seck); 18 March 2010 (conducted by Cheikh Baye Thiam in my absence); 30 June 2010 (conducted with El Hadj Abdoulaye "Aas" Bitèye); and 25 August 2014 (with Alioune Seck).

14 Her family history and the narrative of how she became a disciple come from an interview with her and her husband, Malaw Camara, 22 July 2009, assisted by Alioune Seck.

15 Sayyidinā Cissé was less well known than his three brothers, who are grandsons of Shaykh Ibrāhīm through their mother, Sayyida Fāṭima al-Zahrā' Niasse.

2 The New *Muqaddamas*

1 Interview with Anṣār al-Dīn Dakar president Malaw Camara, 25 August 2014.
2 *"Ammā al-maqāṣidu fa-ḥaẓẓu al-'ārif … Hādhā huwa 'l-rajulu unthā aw dhakar."*
3 I adopt the spelling used on her business card, although she and community members often preserve the initial "Z" of the original Arabic when speaking. For consistency, I use the title "Sayyida" as I do for all *muqaddamas*, which is often used interchangeably with "Sokhna" (*Soxna*). "Ndèye" is often dropped for brevity, as I do here. In standard Wolof orthography, her name would be spelled Ndey Seynabu Mbaj.
4 "*And ligeeyal baye niass*." In Wolof orthography, this would be written "*Ànd liggéeyal Baay Ñas*."
5 Although many esoteric healers say they heal problems caused by *rab* (spirits), she insisted that *rab* are fictions of Lebu folklore. She insisted that the spiritual beings relevant to humans are *jinne (jinn),* which are mentioned in the Qur'ān and *ḥadīth*. Many of my interlocutors treated these two terms as synonyms, assimilating local beliefs in nature spirits (*rab*) with Arabo-Islamic beliefs in *jinn*. In both traditions, spirits can harm or help people. Other interlocutors described *rab* as beneficial and *jinne* as harmful or vice versa.
6 She showed me the *ijāza,* a professionally colour-printed sheet with a space for the signature. It is signed "Aḥmad Ibrāhīm" next to a stamp of Shaykh Aḥmad's son Sīdī Ḥabīb, who has written at the bottom that he is the one who wrote (filled in) the *ijāza* on behalf of his father. It is not dated, but she dated it to 2007.
7 These generalizations do not apply to all Baay Faal, although I have spoken to numerous Baay Faal who confirm them.
8 She calls this part of Kaolack "Njolofeen" after its recently migrated founders, although "Njolofeen" also refers to a group of families in Saalum, including Kaolack, whose ancestors migrated from Jolof during the late nineteenth century (Hill 2007).
9 Interview with Sayyida Ndèye Seynabou Mbathie conducted by Cheikh Baye Thiam in Dakar, 2010.
10 Interview 2 July 2014.
11 Interview with El-Hadji Moumine Dia, Dakar, 7 July 2014.

12 Interview 2 July 2014.

13 These details are from Cheikh Baye Thiam's interview with her on my behalf in early 2010.

14 Interview 2 July 2014.

15 "Our" here is the "royal we," often used by interviewees regardless of status.

16 She told this story in most detail during her 2010 interview with Cheikh Baye Thiam, although she referenced it and other stories of disciples' quitting smoking during several other interviews.

17 Interview 2 July 2014.

18 Sayyida Khadi Fall's actual curriculum vitae can be found at http://senegermanistik.ucad.sn/Fall-CV.pdf (accessed 6 August 2016).

19 The French title of her position is "Ministre de la décentralisation et de l'aménagement du territoire."

20 In 2016, I happened to become acquainted with Abdourahmane Guèye, who confirmed the general outline of this story and added a few details.

21 Numerous interlocutors in Medina Baay and Mauritania reported these details.

22 Interview with Sayyida Khadi Fall, 20 July 2009, assisted by Alioune Seck.

3 Wrapping

1 https://www.facebook.com/hijab4men.

2 While preparing this book for publication, I came across recent works on semiotics by Massimo Leone that use the term "wrapping" in discussing related topics but develop the term in different and more abstract ways. The first (2010) mentions the term in a discussion of the semiotics of Muslim women's headscarves in Europe. The second (2014) more explicitly develops the concept of "wrapping" in a discussion of how medieval Christian reliquaries semiotically enshroud relics, simultaneously indexing their transcendence and removing them from the direct contact of worshipers. Unfortunately, time and space do not permit fully discussing these works here.

3 *"wa-baththa minhumā rijālan kathīran wa-nisāʾan."* Note that in Arabic, adjectives follow the noun they modify, so the "many" (*kathīran*) explicitly modifies "men" (*rijālan*) but not "women" (*nisāʾan*).

4 *"Ishāratan ilā anna al-nisāʾa ḥaqquhunna al-tassatur."*

5 The exception to this is a passage that directly instructs the wives of the Prophet, telling them they are "not like any other women" (33:32). Yet despite this grammatical unwrapping, the passage instructs the Prophet's wives to wrap themselves sartorially and behaviorally.

6 When translating passages from Wolof, which has no grammatical gender, I alternate between generic third-person masculine and feminine.
7 Interview with Sayyida Seynabou Mbathie, 2010.
8 Interview with Ben Omar Kane, son of Shaykha Maryam Niasse, Mermoz, 30 June 2010.
9 The opposition between *fanāʾ* and *baqāʾ* is commonly invoked among Tijānīs and figures in an oft-cited passage by Shaykh Ibrāhīm Ñas ([Niasse] 1969, 1: 129–31).
10 Comments I saw from Taalibe Baay on public online forums mostly condemned the reported remarks, agreeing that no one outranked the Prophet Muḥammad. Yet similar statements are widespread among disciples experiencing an ecstatic *ḥāl* in Senegal.
11 *"Huwa 'l-ʾawwalu wa-'l-ʾākhiru wa-'l-ẓāhiru wa-'l-bāṭinu"* (Qurʾān 57:3). Most literally, the Arabic terms *ẓāhir* and *bāṭin* might translate respectively as "what appears" and "what is inside," although various translators give contrasting glosses, depending on how they understand the intent of the verse.
12 Different versions give different numbers. Al-Ghazālī downplays these differences, explaining that large numbers are often used to suggest multiplicity.
13 https://www.youtube.com/watch?v=YzJGH-MfSjM (22:12).
14 Shaykh Ibrāhīm references the treatise *"Tabṣirat al-anām fī jawāz ruʾyat Allāh fī yaqẓa wa-'l-manām"* ("Clarifying for creation concerning the permissibility of seeing God while awake and asleep") in the appendices to *Kāshif al-ilbās* (Niasse 2010, 241).
15 This belief derives partly from a *ḥadīth qudsī* ("sacred ḥadīth," a category of *ḥadīth* with a special status) in conjunction with Qurʾānic verses. It is mentioned in the poetic and exegetical writings of many Sufi scholars and is well known in many Sufi communities.
16 The Qurʾān never explicitly states this view, although verses 4:34 and 33:33 are often cited in support of it – for example, in a poem by Shaykh Ibrāhīm (I. Niyās [Niasse] 1993b, 87). However, jurisprudence schools *(madhhab)*, including the regionally predominant Mālikī school, explicitly exempt wives from housework obligations (al-Hibri 1997, 2000b; Ali 2003).
17 Other West African languages have near equivalents, such as *"maloo"* in Gambian Mandinko (Janson 2002, 161; McConnell 2016) and *"kumya"* in Hausa (Masquelier 2009, 217). Susan Rasmussen (2013) defines the Tuareg term *"takarakit"* similarly, although the gender association is reversed, as Tuareg men are to veil themselves more and show more reserve than Tuareg women.

18 I gloss "jottalikat" (literally "one who passes [something] on") as "animator" because it precisely fits the role of animator described by Goffman (1981) and also because Senegalese often use the French cognate *"animateur"* ("presenter") to designate someone leading or presenting to an assembly.

19 Cissé's translation of *"akhā tawāḍu*ʿ*"* – literally, "a brother of humility/lowliness."

20 The term *"sharīʿa"* comes up often in Taalibe Baay discourse and refers to the regulations by which God intends people to live, as interpreted by the discipline of *fiqh* (jurisprudence). This usage does not refer to a legal system imposed by the state.

21 This is a pseudonym, used because of the personal nature of the account.

22 Thanks to John Schaefer for pointing me to this example.

23 Today, exposing one's ankles is more associated with Salafi reformists, although photographs suggest it was common among Sufis during the early twentieth century.

24 This photograph and that of Al-Ḥājj Mālik Sy were first published in colonial scholar-administrator Paul Marty's survey of Islamic leaders in Senegal (Marty 1917).

25 This is the title of one of his works, *Al-sirr al-akbar*.

26 See chapters 1 and 5.

27 Interview in Dakar, 27 October 2009, with assistance from Cheikh Baye Thiam.

28 Interview in Medina Baay, 30 November 2004.

4 Motherhood Metamorphosis Metaphors

1 Cheikh Baye Thiam, El Hadj Abdoulaye Bitèye, and Nazirou Thiam accompanied me in succession on interviews with her between 2004 and 2014.

2 Cheikh Baye Thiam attended and recorded this meeting on my behalf on 26 March 2010, conducting an interview with Sayyida Moussoukoro afterwards.

3 Scholars in many disciplines have approached personal narrative, especially conversion narratives, as myths that help constitute a credible self (for example, Spengemann and Lundquist 1965; Griffin 1990; Stromberg 1990; Brenner 1996). Ochs and Capps (1996) review anthropological literature on self-narration and myth.

4 Simone de Beauvoir has made a similar observation from a phenomenological perspective (Beauvoir [1948] 2010).

5 *"Mukhannath"* can designate anyone perceived as essentially male yet defective in masculinity, including those designated in contemporary English as transgender, intersex, or homosexual.

6 Shaykh Ibrāhīm addressed these two cases in *Kāshif al-Ilbās* (Niasse 2010, Appendix VII).

7 I have been told that Shaykh Ibrāhīm's writings contain the same doctrine of "marriage" of opposites, although I have not yet located the precise reference.

8 Sayyida Ndèye Maguète Niang made and commented on this statement in two interviews, one on 9 July 2014, with Cheikh Baye Thiam's assistance, and the other on 7 August 2014, with Nazirou Thiam's assistance. Baay Mokhtar Ka, a *muqaddam* with whom she was long associated, made similar remarks in his 2013 gàmmu speech (https://www.youtube.com/watch?v=YzJGH-MfSjM).

9 Meeting recorded by Cheikh Baye Thiam, 26 March 2010.

10 Interview 9 July 2014.

11 *"Man maay baay ị mbindéef yépp."*

12 *"Baayi mbindéef yi Astoo ko jur."*

13 See the account of Sayyida Bousso Dramé (chapter 2) for a similar case of a *muqaddama* who learned to preach as a prominent member of an *ibaadu* community.

14 The feminine form of this term would be *"ʿārifa bi-Llāh,"* although Wolof speakers rarely borrow Arabic feminine forms because Wolof has no gender.

15 Although *fatḥ* is most often described as resulting from *tarbiya*, some narratives of the Fayḍa's beginning describe groups of people experiencing *fatḥ* spontaneously through encountering Baay. Many accounts tell of people experiencing *fatḥ* through dreams or through contact with other *muqaddams*.

16 This response may have been inspired by the verse from *Sūrat an-Nisāʾ* ("chapter of women") instructing men how to deal with rebellious wives: "And as for those women whose ill-will you have reason to fear, admonish them [first]; then leave them alone in bed; then beat them; and if thereupon they pay you heed, do not seek to harm them. Behold, God is indeed most high, great!" (Qurʾān 4:34; M. Asad 2003).

17 *"Yàlla rekk laa bëgg."* (2004)

18 *"benn tàkkusaan, diggante tàkkusaan ak timis."*

19 *"sa wayjur ci baatin."*

20 See chapter 5 for more on this event.

5 Cooking Up Spiritual Leadership

1 Buggenhagen (2012a) has similarly described a Murid family in Dakar as hiring griots to cook for a celebration marking a man's return from a pilgrimage to Mecca.
2 The notion that Islam requires a woman to take care of the home and children is upheld in Sayyida Ruqayya Niasse's books on women in Islam (Inyās [Niasse] 1964, 1975). Classical Islamic legal scholars actually insisted that a wife could rightfully demand that her husband hire servants to do these tasks (Ali 2003). Yet these tasks have almost always fallen to women, and even households that can afford servants typically hire women.
3 See the introduction on village elders' conflicting accounts of these women.
4 Both she and Diarra Ndiaye confirmed this in interviews.
5 Many other Fayḍa religious communities far from Medina Baay similarly hold their yearly *gàmmu* celebration on the same night, allowing them to attend both Medina Baay's and their own celebration.
6 Interview with Sayyida Diarra Ndiaye and Astou Diop in Dakar, 10 July 2014, with assistance from Cheikh Baye Thiam.
7 This comment was from an individual interview with Astou Diop on 5 August 2014, with Nazirou Thiam's assistance.
8 This references an oft-quoted line from Shaykh Ibrāhīm's poetry telling his daughters to compete to attain the highest stations (I. Niyās [Niasse] 1993a, 115).

6 "They Say a Woman's Voice Is *'Awra*"

1 While some Islamic chanters *(munshid)* refuse terms such as "music" and "song" that are associated with profane genres, Taalibe Baay *sikkarkat*s do not hesitate to describe themselves as "singing" (*woy*) in meetings, and they often refer to even classical Arabic poems as "songs" (*woy*). The Wolof term can also mean "praise" and has long been associated with religious genres.
2 During the same period I also saw a young woman lead a single song at a Murid meeting, although once again the chant leaders and the rest of the singers were all men.
3 Cheikh Anta Babou (2007) has mentioned a similarly sacred repertoire of Arabic-language poems *(qasāʾid)* and Wolof-language songs among Senegalese Murids.
4 A number of authors have discussed the importance of *samāʿ* to Sufi traditions and the polemics surrounding it (for example Nelson 1985, ch. 3;

Lewisohn 1997; Stokes 2002). Shaykh Ibrāhīm discussed the issue in his magnum opus, *Kāshif al-Ilbās* (Niasse 2010, Appendix VIII).

5 Muhammad Kébé interviewed in Taïba Niassène, 14 May 2014.

6 A line from one song says, "The star has fallen, gone to London in England country. God is showing that He is King, Siidi Barhaama" ("*Biddiiw ba fàq na, jëm Londar péey i Àngalteer. Yàllaa ñuy won ne mooy buur, Siidi Barhaama*").

7 "*Boo ko dégloo bu baax … benn baat u Ibbu Juuf, Mën nga cee dox sayru, bu yàgg a yàgg a yàgg.*"

8 Abdoulaye Niang accompanied me on that day, while Cheikh Baye Thiam and Nazirou Thiam participated in other interviews with Sayyida Seynabou Mbathie and Sayyida Aïda Faye.

9 A local romanization of Arabic *shifāʾ al-ʾasqām*.

10 I have noticed a growing number of similar *daayira* uniforms – typically involving Islamic green – since 2005.

11 Interview with Diénaba Guèye, Kaolack, 2009.

12 Several interviewees told me this, including Shaykh Ibrāhīm's son ʿArabī Ibrāhīm Niasse (Dakar, 21 July 2009) and Ruqayya Niasse's son Babacar Niang (Dakar, 25 August 2014).

13 Interview with Sayyida Awa Cissé conducted by Cheikh Baye Thiam on my behalf, 18 March 2010.

14 Interview with Khady Ndiaye, assisted by Alioune Seck, 30 July 2009.

15 Speaking on women radio preachers in Mali, Schulz (2012b) reports a similar logic but also a lack of consensus over whether technological mediations excuse women's audibility.

16 Her brother Cheikh Babacar told me this last detail.

17 Available at https://www.youtube.com/watch?v=aj-jZTqCgUI.

18 The music video of that song is available at: https://www.youtube.com/watch?v=KpHpzOeS-g4.

19 Mouhamed Nazirou Thiam assisted in the interview.

20 The second part of her nickname, *kaaŋ*, means someone with a thorough mastery, especially of the Qurʾān. Nafīsatu's father, Al-Ḥājj Bābakar, was an older brother of Baay who officially stayed with the Léona Niassène branch of the family. Yet three sons he sent to Baay to raise became among Medina Baay's most prominent *muqaddam*s and scholars. Less known is this daughter, along with her sister Rokhaya, a pioneer of the Fayḍa in Rufisque (see Sayyida Seynabou Mbathie's story in chapter 2).

21 "*Ndigal*" can mean authorization or permission, but in this context it means a religious leader's unequivocal command.

22 This paraphrases a line from a fatwa by Shaykh Ibrāhīm ([Niasse] 1969, 1:131).
23 This paraphrases a poem by Shaykh Ibrāhīm (I. Niyās [Niasse] 1993a, 115).

7 The Ascetic and the Mother of the Knowers

1 This is a romanization of the Arabic phrase *"Al-ʿilmu imām al-ʿamal"* ("Knowledge stands before work"), which derives from the title of one of Shaykh Ibrāhīm's books.
2 This is a local spelling of her Arabic title, *"Umm al-ʿārifīn"* ("Mother of the knowers [of God]").
3 *"01h: Arrivée de BAYE et YAYE / Dieuredieufé Yaye."*
4 This chapter draws primarily on interviews I conducted in 2014, assisted by Nazirou Thiam and Cheikh Baye Thiam.
5 https://www.youtube.com/watch?v=o3IKq92RL6A.
6 The *muʾadhdhin* is one who performs the call to prayer and, in some cases, repeats the prayer leader's (imam's) calls signalling to the congregation when to move to the next posture.
7 Nazirou Thiam and Cheikh Baye Thiam accompanied me on this interview on 4 July 2014 in Dakar.
8 This detail was provided by Sayyida Ndèye Maguète Niang.
9 In an interview on 9 August 2014, Abdu Wilane told me he could not recall the year he introduced the practice yet confirmed that it was around that time.
10 I conducted this interview on 8 July 2014, with the assistance of Cheikh Baye Thiam.
11 On Baay Faals, see page 89.
12 I have heard many stories of Shaykh Ibrāhīm himself doing this with offerings brought to him. Such generosity is often said to be the hallmark of Shaykh Ibrāhīm and his true disciples, so it is not necessarily associated with liminal figures.
13 *"Ndeysaan"*: an expression of sympathy, admiration, or grief.
14 *"Mbokk"* could refer to relatives or fellow disciples, although in this context it seems to refer to the latter.
15 During my single interview with Baay Mokhtar and Yaay Aïcha themselves, the exact year was not mentioned. Other interviewees answered indirectly, citing births and other events that happened around the same time.
16 He identified this saying as a *ḥadīth* of the Prophet Muḥammad *("Taḥta kulli rajulin ʿaẓīmin imraʾatun ʿaẓīmatun"),* although I have not been able to

confirm that the Prophet Muḥammad ever said it, and it is a well-known saying in the West.

17 They did not specify what her relationship to Shaykh Ibra Fall was, although several informants close to both families were unaware of any direct relationship between them.

Epilogue: Islam as a Numinous, Performative Tradition

1 This is a pseudonym.

References

Abou El Fadl, Khaled. 2001. *Speaking in God's Name: Islamic Law, Authority and Women*. Oxford: Oneworld.

Abu-Lughod, Lila. 1990. "The Romance of Resistance: Tracing Transformations of Power through Bedouin Women." *American Ethnologist* 17 (1): 41–55. https://doi.org/10.1525/ae.1990.17.1.02a00030.

– 1993. *Writing Women's Worlds: Bedouin Stories*. Berkeley: University of California Press.

– 1998. "Introduction: Feminist Longings and Postcolonial Conditions." In *Remaking Women: Feminism and Modernity in the Middle East*, ed. Lila Abu-Lughod, 3–31. Princeton, NJ: Princeton University Press.

– 2002. "Do Muslim Women Really Need Saving? Anthropological Reflections on Cultural Relativism and Its Others." *American Anthropologist* 104 (3): 783–90. https://doi.org/10.1525/aa.2002.104.3.783.

– 2013. *Do Muslim Women Need Saving?* Cambridge, MA: Harvard University Press.

Afsaruddin, Asma. 1999. "Introduction: The Hermeneutics of Gendered Space and Discourse." In *Hermeneutics and Honor: Negotiating Female "Public" Space in Islamic/Ate Societies*, ed. Asma Afsaruddin, 1–28. Cambridge, MA: Harvard Center for Middle Eastern Studies.

Ahmed, Leila. 2011. *A Quiet Revolution: The Veil's Resurgence, from the Middle East to America*. New Haven, CT: Yale University Press.

Al-Azharī, Ṣāliḥ ʿAbd al-Samīʿ. n.d. *Al-Thamar Al-Dānī: Sharḥ Risālat Ibn Abī Zayd Al-Qayrawānī*. Ed. ʿAbd Allāh Al-Yassār. n.p.: n.p.

Al-Fūtī [Taal], ʿUmar. 2001. *Kitāb Al-Rimāḥ*. Cairo: Dār al-Fikr.

al-Ghazālī, Abū Ḥāmid Muḥammad. 1998. *The Niche of Lights (Mishkāt al-anwār)*. Trans. David Buchman. Provo, UT: Brigham Young University Press.

al-Hibri, Azizah. 1997. "Islam, Law and Custom: Redefining Muslim Women's Rights." *American University Journal of International Law and Policy* 12:1.

– 2000a. "An Introduction to Muslim Women's Rights." In *Windows of Faith: Muslim Women Scholar-Activists in North America*, ed. Gisela Webb, 51–71. Syracuse, NY: Syracuse University Press.

– 2000b. "Muslim Women's Rights in the Global Village: Challenges and Opportunities." *Journal of Law and Religion* 15 (1/2): 37. https://doi.org/10.2307/1051514.

ʿAlī Ḥarāzim ibn al-ʿArabī Barād. 2002. *Jawāhir al-maʿānī wa-bulūgh al-amānī fī fayḍ Sayyidī Abī ʾl-ʿAbbās al-Tijānī*. Casablanca: Dār al-Rashād al-Ḥadītha.

Ali, Kecia. 2003. "Progressive Muslims and Islamic Jurisprudence: The Necessity for Critical Engagement with Marriage and Divorce Law." In *Progressive Muslims on Justice, Gender and Pluralism*, ed. Omid Safi, 163–89. Oxford: Oneworld.

Ali, Kecia, Juliane Hammer, and Laury Silvers, eds. 2013. *A Jihad for Justice: Honoring the Work and Life of Amina Wadud*. 48HrBooks. http://www.bu.edu/religion/files/2010/03/A-Jihad-for-Justice-for-Amina-Wadud-2012-1.pdf.

Alidou, Ousseina. 2005. *Engaging Modernity: Muslim Women and the Politics of Agency in Postcolonial Niger*. Madison: University of Wisconsin Press.

al-Idrīsī, Muḥammad al-Rāḍī Kanūn al-Ḥasanī. 2010. *Nisāʾ Tijāniyyāt [Tijānī Women]*. Casablanca.

Al-Sāʾiḥ, Muḥammad al-ʿArabī. 1973. *Bughyat Al-Mustafīd Li-Sharḥ Munyat Al-Murīd*. Cairo: Dār al-Fikr.

Antoun, Richard T., and Mary Elaine Heglund, eds. 1987. *Religious Resurgence: Contemporary Cases in Islam, Christianity, and Judaism*. Syracuse, NY: Syracuse University Press.

Appadurai, Arjun. 1996. *Modernity at Large*. Minneapolis: Minnesota University Press.

Asad, Muhammad. 2003. *The Message of the Qurʾān*. 2nd ed. Bitton, Glos: Book Foundation.

Asad, Talal. 1986. "The Idea of an Anthropology of Islam." Occasional Papers Series. Washington, DC: Georgetown University Center for Contemporary Arab Studies.

– 1993. *Genealogies of Religion: Discipline and Reasons of Power in Christianity and Islam*. Baltimore, MD: Johns Hopkins University Press.

Asad, Talal, and David Scott. 2006. "The Trouble of Thinking: An Interview with Talal Asad." In *Powers of the Secular Modern: Talal Asad and His Interlocutors*, 1st ed., ed. Charles Hirschkind and David Scott, 243–304. Stanford, CA: Stanford University Press.

Asma'u, Nana. 1997. *Collected Works of Nana Asma'u, Daughter of Usman Dan Fodiyo, (1793–1864)*. Ed. Jean Boyd and Beverly Blow Mack. East Lansing: Michigan State University Press.

'Aṭṭār, Farīd al-Dīn. 1966. *Muslim Saints and Mystics: Episodes from the Tadhkirat Al-Auliya'*. Trans. A.J. Arberry. Chicago: University of Chicago Press.

Augis, Erin. 2005. "Dakar's Sunnite Women: The Politics of Person." In *L'islam politique au sud du Sahara: Identités, discours et enjeux*, ed. Muriel Gomez-Perez, 309–26. Paris: Karthala.

– 2009. "Jambaar or Jumbax-out? How Sunnite Women Negotiate Power and Belief in Orthodox Islamic Femininity." In *New Perspectives on Islam in Senegal: Conversion, Migration, Wealth, Power, and Femininity*, ed. Mamadou Diouf and Mara A. Leichtman, 211–33. New York: Palgrave Macmillan.

– 2012. "'They Haven't Even Mastered the Qur'an': Young Sunnite Women's Negotiations of Social Change and Generational Hierarchies in Dakar." In *L'Afrique des générations: Entre tensions et négociations*, ed. Muriel Gomez-Perez and Marie Nathalie LeBlanc, 539–77. Paris: Karthala.

– 2014. "Aïcha's Sounith Hair Salon: Friendship, Profit, and Resistance in Dakar." *Islamic Africa* 5 (2): 199–224.

Austin, John L. 1962. *How to Do Things with Words*. Cambridge, MA: Harvard University Press.

Babou, Cheikh Anta. 2007. *Fighting the Greater Jihad: Amadu Bamba and the Founding of the Muridiyya of Senegal, 1853–1913*. Athens: Ohio University Press. https://doi.org/10.1353/book.7000.

Bakhtin, Mikhail. 1981. "Discourse in the Novel." In *The Dialogic Imagination: Four Essays*, ed. Michael Holquist, 259–422. Austin: University of Texas Press.

Banégas, Richard, and Jean-Pierre Warnier. 2001. "Nouvelles figures de la réussite et du pouvoir." *Politique Africaine* 82 (2): 5–23. https://doi.org/10.3917/polaf.082.0005.

Bano, Masooda, and Hilary Kalmbach, eds. 2012. *Women, Leadership, and Mosques: Changes in Contemporary Islamic Authority*. Leiden: Brill.

Barlas, Asma. 2002. *"Believing Women" in Islam: Unreading Patriarchal Interpretations of the Qur'ān*. Austin: University of Texas Press.

Barthes, Roland. 1972. *Mythologies*. Trans. Annette Lavers. New York: Hill and Wang.

Bava, Sophie. 2000. "Reconversions et nouveaux mondes commerciaux des mourides à Marseille." *Hommes & Migrations* 1224 (March): 46–55.

– 2003. "Les cheikhs mourides itinérants et l'espace de la *ziyâra* à Marseille." *Anthropologie et Sociétés* 27 (1): 149–66. https://doi.org/10.7202/007006ar.

Beauvoir, Simone de. 2010. *The Second Sex*. New York: Alfred A. Knopf. (Original work published 1948)

Behrman, Lucy Creevey. 1970. *Muslim Brotherhoods and Politics in Senegal*. Cambridge, MA: Harvard University Press. https://doi.org/10.4159/harvard.9780674733336.

Berger, Peter L. 1967. *The Sacred Canopy: Elements of a Sociological Theory of Religion*. New York: Anchor.

– ed. 1999. *The Desecularization of the World: Resurgent Religion and World Politics*. Grand Rapids, MI: Eerdmans.

Boddy, Janice. 1989. *Wombs and Alien Spirits: Women, Men, and the Zār Cult in Northern Sudan*. Madison: University of Wisconsin Press.

Bop, Codou. 2005. "Roles and the Position of Women in Sufi Brotherhoods in Senegal." *Journal of the American Academy of Religion* 73 (4): 1099–119. https://doi.org/10.1093/jaarel/lfi116.

Bouhdiba, Abdelwahab. 1985. *Sexuality in Islam*. Trans. Alan Sheridan. London: Routledge & Kegan Paul.

Bourdieu, Pierre. 1971. "Genèse et structure du champ religieux." *Revue Francaise de Sociologie* 12 (3): 295–334. https://doi.org/10.2307/3320234.

– 1977. *Outline of a Theory of Practice*. Cambridge: Cambridge University Press.

– 1984. *Distinction: A Social Critique of the Judgment of Taste*. Cambridge, MA: Harvard University Press.

– 1991. *Language and Symbolic Power*. Cambridge, MA: Harvard University Press.

Bourguignon, Erika. 1976. *Possession*. Novato, CA: Chandler & Sharp.

– 2004. "Suffering and Healing, Subordination and Power: Women and Possession Trance." *Ethos* 32 (4): 557–74. https://doi.org/10.1525/eth.2004.32.4.557.

Bovin, Mette. 1983. "Muslim Women in the Periphery: The West African Sahel." In *Women in Islamic Societies: Social Attitudes and Historical Perspectives*, ed. Bo Utas, 66–103. New York: Olive Branch Press.

Bowen, John R. 2004. "Muslims and Citizens: France's Headscarf Controversy." *Boston Review* 29: 31–5.

– 2006. *Why the French Don't Like Headscarves: Islam, the State, and Public Space*. Princeton, NJ: Princeton University Press.

Boyd, Jean. 1989. *The Caliph's Sister: Nana Asma'u, 1793–1865, Teacher, Poet, and Islamic Leader*. London: Frank Cass.

Boyd, Jean, and Murray Last. 1985. "The Role of Women as 'Agents religieux' in Sokoto." *Canadian Journal of African Studies / Revue Canadienne des Études Africaines* 19 (2): 283–300.

Brenner, Suzanne. 1996. "Reconstructing Self and Society: Javanese Muslim Women and 'The Veil.'" *American Ethnologist* 23 (4): 673–97. https://doi.org/10.1525/ae.1996.23.4.02a00010.

Buggenhagen, Beth. 2001. "Prophets and Profits: Gendered and Generational Visions of Wealth and Value in Senegalese Murid Households." *Journal of Religion in Africa. Religion en Afrique* 31 (4): 373–401.

– 2004. "Domestic Object(ion)s: The Senegalese Murid Trade Diaspora and the Politics of Marriage Payments, Love, and State Privatization." In *Producing African Futures: Ritual and Reproduction in a Neoliberal Age*, ed. Brad Weiss, 21–53. Leiden: Brill.

– 2009a. "Beyond Brotherhood: Gender, Religious Authority, and the Global Circuits of Senegalese Muridiyya." In *New Perspectives on Islam in Senegal: Conversion, Migration, Wealth, Power, and Femininity*, ed. Mamadou Diouf and Mara A. Leichtman, 189–210. New York: Palgrave Macmillan.

– 2009b. "Picturing Women's Worth: Muslim Visual Cultures and the Image Economy in Global Senegal." Paper presented at the American Anthropological Association Annual Meeting, 4 December, Philadelphia.

– 2012a. *Muslim Families in Global Senegal: Money Takes Care of Shame*. Bloomington: Indiana University Press.

– 2012b. "Fashioning Piety: Women's Dress, Money, and Faith among Senegalese Muslims in New York City." *City & Society* 24 (1): 84–104. https://doi.org/10.1111/j.1548-744X.2012.01069.x.

– 2013. "Islam's New Visibility and the Secular Public in Senegal." In *Tolerance, Democracy, and Sufis in Senegal*, ed. Mamadou Diouf, 51–72. New York: Columbia University Press.

– 2014. "A Snapshot of Happiness: Photo Albums, Respectability and Economic Uncertainty in Dakar." *Africa: Journal of the International Africa Institute* 84 (1): 78–100. https://doi.org/10.1017/S0001972013000612.

Burckhardt, Titus. 2008. *Introduction to Sufi Doctrine*. Library of Perennial Philosophy. Spiritual Classics Series. Bloomington, IN: World Wisdom.

Burke, Kenneth. 1962. "What Are the Signs of What?: A Theory of 'Entitlement.'" *Anthropological Linguistics* 4 (6) (June 1): 1–23.

Butler, Anthea D. 2007. *Women in the Church of God in Christ: Making a Sanctified World*. Chapel Hill: University of North Carolina Press.

Butler, Judith. 1988. "Performative Acts and Gender Constitution: An Essay in Phenomenology and Feminist Theory." *Theatre Journal* 40 (4): 519–31. https://doi.org/10.2307/3207893.

– 1990. *Gender Trouble: Feminism and the Subversion of Identity*. New York: Routledge.

– 1993. *Bodies That Matter: On the Discursive Limits of Sex*. London: Routledge.

Callaway, Barbara. 1987. *Muslim Hausa Women in Nigeria: Tradition and Change*. Syracuse, NY: Syracuse University Press.

Callaway, Barbara, and Lucy Creevey. 1994. *The Heritage of Islam: Women, Religion, and Politics in West Africa*. Boulder, CO: Lynne Rienner.

Certeau, Michel de. 1984. *The Practice of Everyday Life*. Berkeley: University of California Press.

Chakrabarty, Dipesh. 2000. *Provincializing Europe: Postcolonial Thought and Historical Difference*. Princeton, NJ: Princeton University Press.

Chumley, Lily Hope, and Nicholas Harkness. 2013. "Introduction: QUALIA." *Anthropological Theory* 13 (1–2): 3–11. https://doi.org/10.1177/1463499613483389.

Coleman, Simon. 2000. *The Globalisation of Charismatic Christianity*. Cambridge: Cambridge University Press. https://doi.org/10.1017/CBO9780511488221.

– 2004. "The Charismatic Gift." *Journal of the Royal Anthropological Institute* 10 (2): 421–42. https://doi.org/10.1111/j.1467-9655.2004.00196.x.

Comaroff, John L., and Jean Comaroff. 1999. "Occult Economies and the Violence of Abstraction: Notes from the South African Postcolony." *American Ethnologist* 26 (2): 279–303. https://doi.org/10.1525/ae.1999.26.2.279.

Comaroff, J., and J.L. Comaroff. 2000. "Millennial Capitalism: First Thoughts on a Second Coming." *Public Culture* 12 (2): 291–343. https://doi.org/10.1215/08992363-12-2-291.

Cooper, Barbara M. 1994. "Reflections on Slavery, Seclusion and Female Labor in the Maradi Region of Niger in the Nineteenth and Twentieth Centuries." *Journal of African History* 35 (1): 61–78. https://doi.org/10.1017/S0021853700025962.

– 1997a. "Gender, Movement, and History: Social and Spatial Transformations in 20th Century Maradi, Niger." *Environment and Planning. D, Society & Space* 15 (2): 195–221. https://doi.org/10.1068/d150195.

– 1997b. *Marriage in Maradi: Gender and Culture in a Hausa Society in Niger, 1900–1989*. Oxford: James Currey.

Copans, Jean. 1980. *Les marabouts de l'arachide: La confrérie mouride et les paysans du Sénégal*. Paris: Sycomore.

Corbin, Henry. 1969. *Creative Imagination in the Ṣūfism of Ibn ʿArabī*. Trans. Ralph Manheim. Princeton, NJ: Princeton University Press.

Cornell, Vincent J. 1998. *Realm of the Saint: Power and Authority in Moroccan Sufism*. Austin. University of Texas Press.

Coulon, Christian. 1981. *Le marabout et le prince: Islam et pouvoir au Sénégal*. Paris: Editions Pedone.

– 1988. "Women, Islam, and Baraka." In *Charisma and Brotherhood in African Islam*, ed. Donal B. Cruise O'Brien and Christian Coulon, 113–33. Oxford: Clarendon.

Coulon, Christian, and Odile Reveyrand. 1990. *L'Islam au féminin: Sokhna Magat Diop, cheikh de la confrérie mouride, Sénégal*. Talence: Centre d'étude d'Afrique noire, Institut d'études politiques de Bordeaux.

Creevey, Lucy. 1991. "The Impact of Islam on Women in Senegal." *Journal of Developing Areas* 25 (3): 347–68.

– 1996. "Islam, Women and the Role of the State in Senegal." *Journal of Religion in Africa. Religion en Afrique* 26 (3): 268–307. https://doi.org/10.1163/157006696X00299.

Cruise O'Brien, Donal B. 1971. *The Mourides of Senegal: The Political and Economic Organization of an Islamic Brotherhood*. Oxford: Clarendon.

Crumbley, Deidre Helen. 1992. "Impurity and Power: Women in Aladura Churches." *Africa: Journal of the International Africa Institute* 62 (4): 505–22. https://doi.org/10.2307/1161348.

Dakake, Maria M. 2007. "'Guest of the Inmost Heart': Conceptions of the Divine Beloved among Early Sufi Women." *Comparative Islamic Studies* 3 (1): 72–97. https://doi.org/10.1558/cis.v3i1.72.

Dar Al Quran Al Karim. 2011. "Fondatrice." *Dar Al Quran Al Karim*. Accessed 18 May. http://www.daralquranalkarim.org/fondatrice.htm.

Deeb, Lara. 2006. *An Enchanted Modern: Gender and Public Piety in Shi'i Lebanon*. Princeton, NJ: Princeton University Press.

– 2009. "Piety Politics and the Role of a Transnational Feminist Analysis." *Journal of the Royal Anthropological Institute* 15 (March): S112–26. https://doi.org/10.1111/j.1467-9655.2009.01545.x.

Delaney, Carol. 1991. *The Seed and the Soil: Gender and Cosmology in Turkish Village Society*. Berkeley: University of California Press.

Diaw, Aminata. 2004. "Les femmes à l'épreuve du politique: Permanences et changements." In *Gouverner le Sénégal: Entre ajustement structurel et développement durable*, ed. Momar Coumba Diop, 229–45. Paris: Karthala.

Diop, Abdoulaye-Bara. 1985. *La famille wolof: Tradition et changement*. Paris: Karthala.

Diouf, Amadi. 2004. *Mame Astou Diankha Yayou Baye*. Audio cassette. Dakar.

Diouf, Mamadou. 2000. "The Senegalese Murid Trade Diaspora and the Making of a Vernacular Cosmopolitanism." *Public Culture* 12 (3): 679–702. https://doi.org/10.1215/08992363-12-3-679.

Douglas, Mary. 1966. *Purity and Danger: An Analysis of Concepts of Pollution and Taboo*. London, New York: Routledge. https://doi.org/10.4324/9780203361832.

– 1972. "Deciphering a Meal." *Daedalus* 101 (1): 61–81.

Dozon, Jean-Pierre. 2010. "Ceci n'est pas une confrérie." *Cahiers d'Études Africaines* N° 198–199–200 (2) (1 December): 857–79.

Durkheim, Emile. 1995. *The Elementary Forms of Religious Life*. New York: Free Press.

Echard, Nicole. 1991. "Gender Relationships and Religion: Women in the Hausa Bori of Ader, Niger." In *Hausa Women in the Twentieth Century*, ed. Catherine Coles and Beverly Mack, 207–20. Madison: University of Wisconsin Press.

Edgar, Iain R. 2007. "The Inspirational Night Dream in the Motivation and Justification of Jihad." *Nova Religio* 11 (2): 59–76. https://doi.org/10.1525/nr.2007.11.2.59.

– 2011. *The Dream in Islam: From Qur'anic Tradition to Jihadist Inspiration*. New York: Berghahn.

El Guindi, Fadwa. 1999. *Veil: Modesty, Privacy and Resistance*. Oxford, New York: Berg. https://doi.org/10.2752/9781847888969.

Elias, Jamal J. 1988. "Female and Feminine in Islamic Mysticism." *Muslim World* 78 (3–4): 209–24.

Evers Rosander, Eva. 1991. *Women in a Borderland: Managing Muslim Identity Where Morocco Meets Spain*. Philadelphia: Coronet.

– 1997. "Le dahira de Mam Diarra Bousso à Mbacké: Analyse d'une association religieuse de femmes sénégalaises." In *Transformation des identités féminines: Formes d'organisations féminines en Afrique de l'Ouest*, ed. Eva Evers Rosander, 161–74. Uppsala: Nordic Africa Institute.

– 1998. "Women and Muridism in Senegal: The Case of the Mam Diarra Bousso Daira in Mbacke." In *Women and Islamization: Contemporary Dimensions of Discourse on Gender Relations*, ed. Karin Ask and Marit Tjomsland, 147–76. Oxford: Berg.

– 2003. "Mam Diarra Bousso: The Mourid-Mother of Porokhane, Senegal." *Jenda: A Journal of Culture and African Women Studies* 4: 1–12.

– 2004. "Going and Not Going to Porokhane: Mouride Women and Pilgrimage in Senegal and Spain." In *Reframing Pilrimage: Cultures in Motion*, ed. Simon Coleman and John Eade, 67–90. London: Routledge.

Ewing, Katherine P. 1990. "The Dream of Spiritual Initiation and the Organization of Self Representations among Pakistani Sufis." *American Ethnologist* 17 (1): 56–74. https://doi.org/10.1525/ae.1990.17.1.02a00040.

– 1994. "Dreams from a Saint: Anthropological Atheism and the Temptation to Believe." *American Anthropologist* 96 (3): 571–83. https://doi.org/10.1525/aa.1994.96.3.02a00080.

Fair, Laura. 2013. "Veiling, Fashion, and Social Mobility: A Century of Change in Zanzibar." In *Veiling in Africa*, ed. Elisha P. Renne, 15–33. Bloomington: Indiana University Press.

Fall, Khadi. 1989. *Mademba*. Paris: L'Harmattan.

– 1992. *Senteurs d'hivernage: Roman*. Paris: L'Harmattan.

– 1995. *Kiiraay/Masks, poèmes en prose (en wolof et anglais)*. Iowa City: University of Iowa International Writing Program.

– 1996. *Ousmane Sembènes Roman "Les bouts de bois de Dieu": Ungeschriebener Wolof-Text, französische Fassung, deutsche Übersetzung : Eine Untersuchung zu Problemen einer literarischen Kommunikation zwischen Schwarz-Afrika und dem deutschen Sprachraum*. Frankfurt: IKO/Verlag für Interkulturelle Kommunikation.

– 2008. *Éducation, culture, émergence: Sélection d'articles et de conférences (français et wolof)*. 2nd ed. Dakar: Presses Universitaires de Dakar.

Fernandez, James W. 1974. "The Mission of Metaphor in Expressive Culture." *Current Anthropology* 15 (2): 119–33. https://doi.org/10.1086/201450.

– 1980. "Edification by Puzzlement." In *Explorations in African Systems of Thought*, ed. Ivan Karp and Charles S. Bird, 44–59. Bloomington: Indiana University Press.

– ed. 1991. *Beyond Metaphor: The Theory of Tropes in Anthropology*. Stanford, CA: Stanford University Press.

Fernea, Elizabeth Warnock. 1965. *Guests of the Sheik*. 1st ed. Garden City, NY: Doubleday.

Fischler, Claude. 1988. "Food, Self and Identity." *Social Sciences Information. Information sur les Sciences Sociales* 27 (2): 275–92. https://doi.org/10.1177/053901888027002005.

Flueckiger, Joyce Burkhalter. 2006. *In Amma's Healing Room: Gender and Vernacular Islam in South India*. Bloomington: Indiana University Press.

Foucault, Michel. 1978. *The History of Sexuality, Volume 1: An Introduction*. New York: Random House.

– 1979. *Discipline and Punish*. New York: Random House.

– 1997. "Technologies of the Self." In *Ethics: Subjectivity and Truth*, ed. Paul Rabinow, 223–51. New York: New Press.

– 2000a. "Truth and Power." In *Power*, ed. James D. Faubion, 111–33. New York: New Press.

– 2000b. "Governmentality." In *Power*, ed. James D. Faubion, 201–22. New York: New Press.

Frede, Britta. 2014. "Following in the Steps of ʿĀʾisha: Ḥassāniyya-Speaking Tijānī Women as Spiritual Guides (*Muqaddamāt*) and Teaching Islamic Scholars (*Limrābuṭāt*) in Mauritania." *Islamic Africa* 5 (2): 225–73.

Frede, Britta, and Joseph Hill. 2014. "Introduction: En-Gendering Islamic Authority in West Africa." *Islamic Africa* 5 (2): 131–65.
Frishkopf, Michael. 2003. "Authorship in Sufi Poetry." *Alif: Journal of Comparative Poetics* 23: 78–108.
– 2009. "Mediated Qur'anic Recitation and the Contestation of Islam in Contemporary Egypt." In *Music and the Play of Power in the Middle East, North Africa and Central Asia*, ed. Laudan Nooshin, 75–114. Burlington, VT: Ashgate.
Geertz, Clifford. 1973. "Deep Play: Notes on the Balinese Cockfight." In *The Interpretation of Cultures*, 412–53. New York: Basic Books.
Geissinger, Aisha. 2013. "'Umm Al-Dardā' Sat in Tashahhud Like a Man': Towards the Historical Contextualization of a Portrayal of Female Religious Authority." *Muslim World* 103 (3): 305–19. https://doi.org/10.1111/muwo.12015.
Gellner, Ernest. 1969. *Saints of the Atlas*. London: Weidenfeld and Nicolson.
Gemmeke, Amber B. 2008. *Marabout Women in Dakar: Creating Trust in a Rural Urban Space*. Berlin: LIT Verlag.
– 2009. "Marabout Women in Dakar: Creating Authority in Islamic Knowledge." *Africa: Journal of the International Africa Institute* 79 (1): 128–47. https://doi.org/10.3366/E0001972008000648.
Gilmore, David D. 1996. "Above and Below: Toward a Social Geometry of Gender." *American Anthropologist* 98 (1): 54–66. https://doi.org/10.1525/aa.1996.98.1.02a00060.
Glover, John. 2007. *Sufism and Jihad in Modern Senegal: The Murid Order*. Rochester, NY: University of Rochester Press.
Goethe, Johann Wolfgang Von. 1998. *Faust: Part 2*. Trans. Martin Harry Greenberg. New Haven, CT: Yale University Press.
Goffman, Erving. 1959. *The Presentation of Self in Everyday Life*. Garden City, NY: Doubleday.
– 1969. "On Face-Work." In *Where the Action Is: Three Essays*, 1–36. London: Allen Lane.
– 1981. "Footing." In *Forms of Talk*, 124–59. Philadelphia: University of Pennsylvania Press.
Göle, Nilüfer. 1996. *The Forbidden Modern: Civilization and Veiling*. Ann Arbor: University of Michigan Press.
– 2002. "Islam in Public: New Visibilities and New Imaginaries." *Public Culture* 14 (1): 173–90. https://doi.org/10.1215/08992363-14-1-173.
Gomez-Perez, Muriel. 1998. "Associations islamiques à Dakar." In *Islam et islamismes au sud du Sahara*, ed. Ousmane Kane and Jean-Louis Triaud, 137–54. Paris: Karthala.

Gomez-Perez, Muriel, Marie-Nathalie LeBlanc, and Mathias Savadogo. 2009. "Young Men and Islam in the 1990s: Rethinking an Intergenerational Perspective." *Journal of Religion in Africa. Religion en Afrique* 39 (2): 186–218. https://doi.org/10.1163/157006609X436021.

Gomm, Roger. 1975. "Bargaining from Weakness: Spirit Possession on the South Kenya Coast." *Man* 10 (4): 530–43. https://doi.org/10.2307/2800131.

Gray, Christopher. 1998. "The Rise of the Niassene Tijaniyya, 1875 to the Present." In *Islam et islamismes au sud du Sahara*, ed. Ousmane Kane and Jean-Louis Triaud, 59–82. Paris: Karthala.

Griffin, Charles J.G. 1990. "The Rhetoric of Form in Conversion Narratives." *Quarterly Journal of Speech* 76 (2): 152–63. https://doi.org/10.1080/00335639009383911.

Habermas, Jürgen. 1989. *The Structural Transformation of the Public Sphere: An Inquiry into a Category of Bourgeois Society*. Cambridge, MA: MIT Press.

Haenni, Patrick. 2002. "Au-delà du repli identitaire … Les nouveaux prêcheurs égyptiens et la modernisation paradoxale de l'islam." *Religio-Scope* 30 (November). http://religioscope.com/pdf/precheurs.pdf.

Haenni, Patrick, and Tjitske Holtrop. 2002. "Mondaines spiritualités … 'Amr Khâlid, « Shaykh » branché de la jeunesse dorée du Caire." *Politique Africaine* 87 (3): 45–68. https://doi.org/10.3917/polaf.087.0045.

Hammer, Juliane. 2010. "Performing Gender Justice: The 2005 Woman-Led Prayer in New York." *Contemporary Islam* 4 (1): 91–116. https://doi.org/10.1007/s11562-009-0103-1.

Havard, Jean-François. 2001. "Ethos « bul faale » et nouvelles figures de la réussite au Sénégal." *Politique Africaine* 82 (2): 63–77. https://doi.org/10.3917/polaf.082.0063.

– 2016. "Le 'phénomène' Cheikh Bethio Thioune et le djihad migratoire des étudiants sénégalais 'Thiantakones.'" In *Les voyages du développement. Emigration, commerce, exil*, ed. Fariba Adelkhah and Jean-François Bayart, 309–36. Paris: Karthala.

Heath, Deborah. 1990. "Spatial Politics and Verbal Performance in Urban Senegal." *Ethnology* 29 (3): 209–23. https://doi.org/10.2307/3773567.

Hill, Joseph. 2007. "Divine Knowledge and Islamic Authority: Religious Specialization among Disciples of Baay Ñas." PhD diss., Yale University.

– 2010. "'All Women Are Guides': Sufi Leadership and Womanhood among Taalibe Baay in Senegal." *Journal of Religion in Africa. Religion en Afrique* 40 (4): 375–412. https://doi.org/10.1163/157006610X540735.

– 2011. "Languages of Islam: Hybrid Genres of Taalibe Baay Oratory in Senegal." *Islamic Africa* 2 (1): 67–103. https://doi.org/10.5192/021540993020167.

– 2012. "The Cosmopolitan Sahara: Building a Global Islamic Village in Mauritania." *City & Society* 24 (1): 62–83. https://doi.org/10.1111/j.1548-744X.2012.01068.x.
– 2013a. "Niasse, Mariama Ibrahim." Ed. John L. Esposito. *Oxford Islamic Studies Online*. Oxford: Oxford University Press. http://www.oxfordislamicstudies.com/article/opr/t343/e0087.
– 2013b. "Sovereign Islam in a Secular State: Hidden Knowledge and Sufi Governance among 'Taalibe Baay.'" In *Tolerance, Democracy, and Sufis in Senegal*, ed. Mamadou Diouf, 99–124. New York: Columbia University Press.
– 2014. "Picturing Islamic Authority: Gender Metaphors and Sufi Leadership in Senegal." *Islamic Africa* 5 (2): 275–315.
– 2016a. "Entrepreneurial Discipleship: Cooking Up Women's Sufi Leadership in Dakar." In *Cultural Entrepreneurship in Africa*, ed. Ute Röschenthaler and Dorothea E. Schulz, 58–80. London: Routledge.
– 2016b. "'Baay Is the Spiritual Leader of the Rappers': Performing Islamic Reasoning in Senegalese Sufi Hip-Hop." *Contemporary Islam: Dynamics of Muslim Life* 10 (2): 267–87. https://doi.org/10.1007/s11562-016-0359-1.
– 2016c. "God's Name Is Not a Game: Performative Apologetics in Sufi *Dhikr* Performance in Senegal." *Journal of Islamic Studies* 35: 133–62.
– 2017a. "Charismatic Discipleship: Sufi Woman and the Divine Mission of Development in Senegal." *Africa: Journal of the International African Institute* 87 (4): 832–52. https://doi.org/10.1017/S0001972017000389.
– 2017b. "A Mystical Cosmopolitanism: Sufi Hip-Hop and the Aesthetics of Islam in Dakar." *Culture and Religion* 18 (4): 388–408. https://doi.org/10.1080/14755610.2017.1376694.
Hirschkind, Charles. 2001. "The Ethics of Listening: Cassette-Sermon Audition in Contemporary Egypt." *American Ethnologist* 28 (3): 623–49. https://doi.org/10.1525/ae.2001.28.3.623.
– 2006a. *The Ethical Soundscape: Cassette Sermons and Islamic Counterpublics*. New York: Columbia University Press.
– 2006b. "Cassette Ethics: Public Piety and Popular Media in Egypt." In *Religion, Media, and the Public Sphere*, ed. Birgit Meyer and Annelies Moors, 29–51. Bloomington: Indiana University Press.
Hirschkind, Charles, and Saba Mahmood. 2002. "Feminism, the Taliban, and Politics of Counter-Insurgency." *Anthropological Quarterly* 75 (2): 339–54. https://doi.org/10.1353/anq.2002.0031.
Hirschon, Renée. 1981. "Essential Objects and the Sacred: Interior and Exterior Space in an Urban Greek Locality." In *Women and Space: Ground Rules and Social Maps*, ed. Shirley Ardener, 72–88. New York: St. Martin's Press.

Hiskett, Mervyn. 1980. "The 'Community of Grace' and Its Opponents, 'the Rejecters': A Debate about Theology and Mysticism in Muslim West Africa with Special Reference to Its Hausa Expression." *African Language Studies* 17: 99–140.

Hochschild, Arlie, and Anne Machung. 1989. *The Second Shift: Working Families and the Revolution at Home*. New York: Penguin.

Hoodfar, Homa. 1997. *Between Marriage and the Market: Intimate Politics and Survival in Cairo*. Berkeley: University of California Press.

Horvatich, Patricia. 1994. "Ways of Knowing Islam." *American Ethnologist* 21 (4): 811–26. https://doi.org/10.1525/ae.1994.21.4.02a00080.

Hubert, Henri, and Marcel Mauss. 1899. "Essai sur la nature et la fonction du sacrifice." *L'Annee Sociologique* 2: 29–138.

Hutson, Alaine S. 1997. "We Are Many: Women Sufis and Islamic Scholars in Twentieth Century Kano, Nigeria." PhD diss., Indiana University at Bloomington.

– 1999. "The Development of Women's Authority in the Kano Tijaniyya, 1894–1963." *Africa Today* 46 (3): 43–64. https://doi.org/10.1353/at.2003.0093.

– 2001. "Women, Men, and Patriarchal Bargaining in an Islamic Sufi Order: The Tijaniyya in Kano, Nigeria, 1937 to the Present." *Gender & Society* 15 (5): 734–53. https://doi.org/10.1177/089124301015005006.

– 2004. "African Sufi Women and Ritual Change." *Journal of Ritual Studies* 18 (2): 61–73.

Ibn Al-Jawzī, Abū al-Faraj ʿAbd al-Raḥmān. 1278. *Ṣifat al-ṣafwah*. Ed. Ṭāriq Muḥammad ʿAbd al-Munʿim. Alexandria: Dār Ibn Khaldūn.

Inyās [Niasse], Ibrāhīm. 2010 [1964]. *Fī riyāḍ al-tafsīr li'l-Qurʾān al-Karīm*. Ed. Muḥammad ibn al-Shakyh ʿAbd Allāh al-Tijānī. 6 vols. Tunis: Majmaʿ al-yamāma.

Inyās [Niasse], Ruqayya Ibrāhīm. 1964. *Tanbīh al-bint al-muslimah fī "l-dīn wa-'l-ḥayāh [Counsel for the Muslim Girl on Religion and Life]*. Kaolack.

– 1975. *Ḥaẓẓ al-marʾa fī 'l-Islām [The Lot of Woman in Islam]*. Kaolack.

Irvine, Judith T. 1974. "Caste and Communication in a Wolof Village." PhD diss., University of Pennsylvania.

– 1985. "Status and Style in Language." *Annual Review of Anthropology* 14 (1): 557–81. https://doi.org/10.1146/annurev.an.14.100185.003013.

– 1989. "Strategies of Status Manipulation in the Wolof Greeting." In *Explorations in the Ethnography of Speaking*, 2nd ed., ed. Richard Bauman and Joel Sherzer, 167–91. Cambridge: Cambridge University Press.

– 1995. "A Sociolinguistic Approach to Emotion Concepts in a Senegalese Community." In *Everyday Conceptions of Emotion: An Introduction to the*

Psychology, Anthropology and Linguistics of Emotion, ed. James A. Russell, José-Miguel Fernández-Dols, Antony S.R. Manstead, and J.C. Wellencamp, 251–65. Dordrecht: Kluwer.

Islam, Sarah. 2012. "The Qubaysīyyāt: The Growth of an International Muslim Women's Revivalist Movement from Syria (1960–2008)." In *Women, Leadership, and Mosques: Changes in Contemporary Islamic Authority*, ed. Masooda Bano and Hilary Kalmbach, 161–83. Leiden: Brill.

Janson, Marloes. 2002. *The Best Hand Is the Hand That Always Gives: Griottes and Their Profession in Eastern Gambia*. Leiden: Research School CNWS, Leiden University.

– 2005. "Roaming about for God's Sake: The Upsurge of the Tabligh Jama'at in the Gambia." *Journal of Religion in Africa. Religion en Afrique* 35 (December): 450–81. https://doi.org/10.1163/157006605774832199.

– 2008. "Renegotiating Gender: Changing Moral Practice in the Tablīghī Jamāʿat in the Gambia." *Journal of Islamic Studies* 28: 9–36.

– 2014. *Islam, Youth and Modernity in the Gambia: The Tablighi Jama'at*. London, New York: Cambridge University Press.

Kalmbach, Hilary. 2008. "Social and Religious Change in Damascus: One Case of Female Islamic Religious Authority." *British Journal of Middle Eastern Studies* 35 (1): 37–57. https://doi.org/10.1080/13530190801890238.

– 2012. "Introduction: Islamic Authority and the Study of Female Religious Leaders." In *Women, Leadership, and Mosques: Changes in Contemporary Islamic Authority*, ed. Masooda Bano and Hilary Kalmbach, 1–27. Leiden: Brill.

Kamarā, Al-Shaykh Mūsā. 2001. *Ashhā ʿulūm wa-aṭyab al-khabar fī sīrat al-Ḥājj ʿUmar [The Most Delightful Learning and Pleasant News, on the Life of Al-Ḥājj ʿUmar]*. Ed.Khadīm Imbākī and Aḥmad Al-Shukrī. Rabat: Maʿhad al-dirāsāt al-ifrīqiyya.

Kandiyoti, Deniz. 1988. "Bargaining with Patriarchy." *Gender & Society* 2 (3): 274–90. https://doi.org/10.1177/089124388002003004.

Kane, Ousmane. 2003. *Muslim Modernity in Postcolonial Nigeria: A Study of the Society for the Removal of Innovation and Restatement of Tradition*. Leiden: Brill.

– 2011. *The Homeland Is the Arena: Religion, Transnationalism, and the Integration of Senegalese Immigrants in America*. Oxford, New York: Oxford University Press.

Kane, Ousmane, and Leonardo A. Villalón. 1998. "Entre confrérisme, réformisme et islamisme : Les mustarshidin du Sénégal." In *Islam et Islamismes au sud du Sahara*, ed. Ousmane Kane and Jean-Louis Triaud, 263–310. Paris: Karthala.

Kanji, Saaliu Samba Malaado, and Fatou Kiné Camara. 2000. *L'union matrimoniale dans la tradition des peuples noirs*. Paris: L'Harmattan.

Katz, Cindi. 1993. "Growing Girls/Closing Circles: Limits on the Spaces of Knowing in Rural Sudan and US Cities." In *Full Circles: Geographies of Women over the Life Course*, ed. Cindi Katz and Janice J. Monk, 88–106. London, New York: Routledge.

Keane, Webb. 2003. "Semiotics and the Social Analysis of Material Things." *Language & Communication* 23 (3–4): 409–25. https://doi.org/10.1016/S0271-5309(03)00010-7.

Keddie, Nikki R. 2007. *Women in the Middle East: Past and Present*. Princeton, NJ: Princeton University Press. https://doi.org/10.1515/9781400845057.

Kenyon, Susan M. 1995. "Zar as Modernization in Contemporary Sudan." *Anthropological Quarterly* 68 (2): 107–20. https://doi.org/10.2307/3318050.

Kepel, Gilles. 1994. *The Revenge of God: The Resurgence of Islam, Christianity, and Judaism in the Modern World*. University Park, PA: University of Pennsylvania Press.

Kingsbury, Kate. 2014. "New Mouride Movements in Dakar and the Diaspora." PhD diss., University of Oxford. http://ethos.bl.uk/OrderDetails.do?uin=uk.bl.ethos.669764.

– 2016. "Modern Mouride Marabouts and Their Young Disciples in Dakar." Unpublished manuscript.

Klenk, Rebecca M. 2004. "'Who Is the Developed Woman?': Women as a Category of Development Discourse, Kumaon, India." *Development and Change* 35 (1): 57–78. https://doi.org/10.1111/j.1467-7660.2004.00342.x.

Lakoff, George, and Mark Johnson. 1980. *Metaphors We Live By*. Chicago: University of Chicago Press.

Lambek, Michael. 1981. *Human Spirits: A Cultural Account of Trance in Mayotte*. Cambridge: Cambridge University Press.

– 1993. *Knowledge and Practice in Mayotte: Local Discourses of Islam, Sorcery and Spirit Possession*. Anthropological Horizons Series. Toronto: University of Toronto Press.

Laqueur, Thomas Walter. 1990. *Making Sex: Body and Gender from the Greeks to Freud*. Cambridge, MA: Harvard University Press.

Launay, Robert. 1992. *Beyond the Stream: Islam and Society in a West African Town*. Berkeley: University of California Press.

LeBlanc, Marie Nathalie. 2000. "From Sya to Islam. Social Change and Identity among Muslim Youth in Bouaké, Côte d'Ivoire." *Paideuma* 46 (1 January): 85–109. doi:10.2307/40341784.

– 2014. "Piety, Moral Agency, and Leadership: Dynamics around the Feminization of Islamic Authority in Côte d'Ivoire." *Islamic Africa* 5 (2): 167–98.

Leone, Massimo. 2010. "Remarks for a Semiotics of the Veil." *Chinese Semiotic Studies* 4 (2): 258–78.

– 2014. "Wrapping Transcendence: The Semiotics of Reliquaries." *Signs and Society* 2 (S1) (1 March): S49–S83. https://doi.org/10.1086/67314.

Le Renard, Amélie. 2012. "From Qur'ānic Circles to the Internet: Gender Segregation and the Rise of Female Preachers in Saudi Arabia." In *Women, Leadership, and Mosques: Changes in Contemporary Islamic Authority*, ed. Masooda Bano and Hilary Kalmbach, 105–26. Leiden: Brill.

Lévi-Strauss, Claude. 1963. *Structural Anthropology*. New York: Basic Books.

– 1969. *The Raw and the Cooked*. Trans. John Weightman and Doreen Weightman. New York: Harper and Row.

– 1979. *Myth and Meaning: Cracking the Code of Culture*. New York: Shocken Books.

Lewis, I.M. 2003. *Ecstatic Religion: A Study of Shamanism and Spirit Possession*. 3rd ed. London: Routledge. (Original work published 1971)

Lewisohn, Leonard. 1997. "The Sacred Music of Islam: Samā' in the Persian Sufi Tradition." *British Journal of Ethnomusicology* 6 (1): 1–33. https://doi.org/10.1080/09681229708567259.

Loimeier, Roman. 1994. "Cheikh Touré: Du reformisme à l'islamisme, un musulman sénégalais dans le siècle." *Islam et Sociétés au Sud du Sahara* 8:55–66.

– 1996. "The Secular State and Islam in Senegal." In *Questioning the Secular State: The Worldwide Resurgence of Religion in Politics*, ed. David Westerlund, 183–97. London: Hurst.

– 1997. *Islamic Reform and Political Change in Northern Nigeria*. Evanston, IL: Northwestern University Press.

– 2000. "L'islam ne se vend plus: The Islamic Reform Movement and the State in Senegal." *Journal of Religion in Africa. Religion en Afrique* 30 (2): 168–90.

– 2003. "Patterns and Peculiarities of Islamic Reform in Africa." *Journal of Religion in Africa. Religion en Afrique* 33 (3): 237–62. https://doi.org/10.1163/157006603322663497.

Lubeck, Paul M. 2011. "Nigeria: Mapping the Shari'a Restorationist Movement." In *Shari'a Politics: Islamic Law and Society in the Modern World*, ed. Robert W. Hefner, 244–79. Bloomington: Indiana University Press; http://escholarship.org/uc/item/436307k8.

Mack, Beverly. 2004. *Muslim Women Sing: Hausa Popular Song*. Bloomington: Indiana University Press.

– 2008. "Muslim Women Scholars in the Nineteenth and Twentieth Centuries: Morocco to Nigeria." In *The Meanings of Timbuktu*, ed. Shamil Jeppie and Souleymane Bachir Diagne, 165–80. Cape Town: Human Sciences Research Council of South Africa Press and CODESRIA.

Mack, Beverly, and Jean Boyd. 2000. *One Woman's Jihad: Nana Asma'u, Scholar and Scribe*. Bloomington: Indiana University Press.

– 2013. *Educating Muslim Women: The West African Legacy of Nana Asma'u, 1793–1864*. Markham, Leics: Kube Publishing.

Mahmood, Saba. 2001a. "Feminist Theory, Embodiment, and the Docile Agent: Some Reflections on the Egyptian Islamic Revival." *Cultural Anthropology* 16 (2): 202–36. https://doi.org/10.1525/can.2001.16.2.202.

– 2001b. "Rehearsed Spontaneity and the Conventionality of Ritual: Disciplines of 'Ṣalāt.'" *American Ethnologist* 28 (4): 827–53. https://doi.org/10.1525/ae.2001.28.4.827.

– 2005. *Politics of Piety: The Islamic Revival and the Feminist Subject*. Princeton, NJ: Princeton University Press.

Malamud, Margaret. 1996. "Gender and Spiritual Self-Fashioning: The Master-Disciple Relationship in Classical Sufism." *Journal of the American Academy of Religion* 64 (1): 89–117. https://doi.org/10.1093/jaarel/LXIV.1.89.

Martin, Emily. 1991. "The Egg and the Sperm: How Science Has Constructed a Romance Based on Stereotypical Male-Female Roles." *Signs* 16 (3): 485–501. https://doi.org/10.1086/494680.

Marty, Paul. 1917. *Etudes sur l'islam au Sénégal*. 2 vols. Paris: Leroux.

Masquelier, Adeline. 1999. "Debating Muslims, Disputed Practices: Struggles for the Realization of an Alternative Moral Order in Niger." In *Civil Society and the Political Imagination in Africa: Critical Perspectives*, ed. John L. Comaroff and Jean Comaroff, 219–50. Chicago: University of Chicago Press.

– 2001. *Prayer Has Spoiled Everything: Possession, Power, and Identity in an Islamic Town of Niger*. Durham, NC: Duke University Press.

– 2009. *Women and Islamic Revival in a West African Town*. Bloomington: Indiana University Press.

– 2013. "Modest Bodies, Stylish Selves: Fashioning Virtue in Niger." In *Veiling in Africa*, ed. Elisha P. Renne, 110–36. Bloomington: Indiana University Press.

Massignon, Louis. 1994. *The Passion of Al-Hallāj: Mystic and Martyr of Islam*. Princeton, NJ: Princeton University Press.

Mauss, Marcel. 2000. *The Gift: The Form and Reason for Exchange in Archaic Societies*. New York, London: Norton.

Mbow, Penda. 1997. "Les femmes, l'islam et les associations religieuses au Sénégal." In *Transformation des identités féminines: Formes d'organisations féminines en Afrique de l'Ouest*, ed. Eva Evers Rosander, 148–59. Uppsala: Nordic Africa Institute.

– 2001. "L'islam et la femme sénégalaise." *Éthiopiques: Revue Socialiste de Culture Négro-Africaine* 66–7: 203–24.

McConnell, Bonnie B. 2016. "Women's Songs, Women's Responsibilities: Gender, Islam and Social Change in the Gambia." Paper presented at the African Studies Association Annual Meeting, 3 December, Washington, DC.

McLaughlin, Fiona. 1997. "Islam and Popular Music in Senegal: The Emergence of a 'New Tradition.'" *Africa: Journal of the International Africa Institute* 67 (4): 560–81. https://doi.org/10.2307/1161108.

Meneley, Anne. 1996. *Tournaments of Value: Sociability and Hierarchy in a Yemeni Town*. Toronto: University of Toronto Press.

Mernissi, Fatima. 1987. *Beyond the Veil: Male-Female Dynamics in Modern Muslim Society*. Bloomington: Indiana University Press.

Meyer, Birgit, and Peter Pels, eds. 2003. *Magic and Modernity: Interfaces of Revelation and Concealment*. Stanford, CA: Stanford University Press.

Mittermaier, Amira. 2011. *Dreams That Matter: Egyptian Landscapes of the Imagination*. Berkeley: University of California Press.

– 2014. "Bread, Freedom, Social Justice: The Egyptian Uprising and a Sufi Khidima." *Cultural Anthropology* 29 (1): 54–79. https://doi.org/10.14506/ca29.1.05.

Monteil, Vincent. 1980. *L'islam noir: Une religion à la conquête de l'Afrique*. Paris: Seuil.

Morris, Rosalind C. 1995. "All Made Up: Performance Theory and the New Anthropology of Sex and Gender." *Annual Review of Anthropology* 24 (1): 567–92. https://doi.org/10.1146/annurev.an.24.100195.003031.

Morsy, Soheir A. 1978. "Sex Differences and Folk Illness in an Egyptian Village." In *Women in the Muslim World*, ed. Lois Beck and Nikki R. Keddie, 599–616. Cambridge, MA: Harvard University Press. https://doi.org/10.4159/harvard.9780674733091.c34.

Mosko, Mark. 1992. "Motherless Sons: 'Divine Kings' and 'Partible Persons' in Melanesia and Polynesia." *Man* 27 (4): 697–717. https://doi.org/10.2307/2804170.

– 2010. "Partible Penitents: Dividual Personhood and Christian Practice in Melanesia and the West." *Journal of the Royal Anthropological Institute* 16 (2): 215–40. https://doi.org/10.1111/j.1467-9655.2010.01618.x.

Muhammad, Abdulsalam. 2015. "Nigeria: Why Kano Sharia Court Sentenced Woman, Eight Others to Death." *Vanguard*, 26 June. http://allafrica.com/stories/201506260619.html.

Munn, Nancy D. 1992. *The Fame of Gawa: A Symbolic Study of Value*

Transformation in a Massim (Papua New Guinea) Society. 2nd ed. Durham, NC: Duke University Press.

Munson, Henry. 1993. *Religion and Power in Morocco*. New Haven, CT: Yale University Press.

Murata, Sachiko. 1992. *The Tao of Islam: A Sourcebook on Gender Relationships in Islamic Thought*. Albany: State University of New York Press.

Mustafa, Hudita Nura. 2001. "Ruins and Spectacles: Fashion and City Life in Contemporary Senegal." *Nka: Journal of Contemporary African Art* 15: 47–53. https://doi.org/10.1215/10757163-15-1-47.

– 2006. "Eros, Beauty and Crisis: Notes from Senegal." *Feminist Africa* 6: 20–32.

Nelson, Kristina. 1985. *The Art of Reciting the Qur'an*. New ed. Cairo: American University in Cairo Press.

Neubauer, Anna. 2009. "Celle qui n'existe pas: Soufisme et autorité féminine à Istanbul." PhD diss., Université de Neuchâtel.

[Niasse], Ibrāhīm ibn ʿAbd Allāh. 1969. *Jawāhir al-rasāʾil*. Ed.Aḥmad Abū Fatḥ Al-Yarwāwī. n.p.

Niasse, Shaykh Ibrahim. 1998. *Spirit of Good Morals [Rūḥ al-ʾAdab]*. Ed. Abdul Hakim Halim. Trans. Shaykh Hassan Cisse. Kaolack: African American Islamic Institute. http://home.earthlink.net/~halimcisse/id6.html.

– 2010. *The Removal of Confusion Concerning the Flood of the Saintly Seal Aḥmad Al-Tijānī: A Translation of Kāshif Al-Ilbās ʿan Fayḍa Al-Khatm Abī Al-ʿAbbas*. Ed. Shaykh Ḥasan b. ʿAlī Cisse. Trans. Zachary Valentine Wright, Muhtar Holland, and Abdullahi El-Okene. Louisville, KY: Fons Vitae.

Nietzsche, Friedrich Wilhelm. 1918. *The Genealogy of Morals*. New York: Boni and Liveright.

Niyās [Niasse], Ibrāhīm. 1993a. "Ar-riḥla al-Kannāriyya wa-l-Kumāshiyya [Journey to Mauritania and Kumasi]." In *Majmūʿ riḥalāt al-Shaykh Ibrāhīm [Collected Travels of Shaykh Ibrahim]*, ed. Muḥammad al-Maʾmūn Ibrāhīm Niyās [Niasse], 71–101. Cairo.

– 1993b. "Nafaḥāt al-malak al-ghanī fī s-siyāḥati fī ʾarḍi Bamaku wa-Ghinī (Ar-riḥla al-Kunākriyya) [Gifts of the Wealthy King, on Travelling to the Land of Bamako and Guinea (The Journey to Conakry)]." In *Majmūʿ riḥalāt al-Shaykh ʾIbrāhīm [Collected Travels of Shaykh Ibrahim]*, ed. Muḥammad al-Maʾmūn Ibrāhīm Niyās [Niasse], 103–19. Cairo.

Nnaemeka, Obioma, ed. 1997. *The Politics of (M)Othering: Womanhood, Identity and Resistance in African Literature*. London: Routledge.

Nūrbakhsh, Javād. 1983. *Sufi Women*. New York: Khaniqahi-Nimatullahi Publications.

Ochs, Elinor. 1992. "Indexing Gender." In *Rethinking Context: Language as an Interactive Phenomenon*, ed. Alessandro Duranti and Charles Goodwin, 335–58. Cambridge, New York: Cambridge University Press.

Ochs, Elinor, and Lisa Capps. 1996. "Narrating the Self." *Annual Review of Anthropology* 25 (1): 19–43. https://doi.org/10.1146/annurev.anthro.25.1.19.

Omar, Sara. 2013. "Al-Qubaysiyyāt: Negotiating Female Religious Authority in Damascus." *Muslim World* 103 (3): 347–62. https://doi.org/10.1111/muwo.12018.

Ortner, Sherry B. 1972. "Is Female to Male as Nature Is to Culture?" *Feminist Studies* 1 (2): 5–31. https://doi.org/10.2307/3177638.

Paden, John N. 1973. *Religion and Political Culture in Kano*. Berkeley: University of California Press.

Papanek, Hanna. 1971. "Purdah in Pakistan: Seclusion and Modern Occupations for Women." *Journal of Marriage and the Family* 33 (3): 517–30. https://doi.org/10.2307/349849.

– 1973. "Purdah: Separate Worlds and Symbolic Shelter." *Comparative Studies in Society and History* 15 (3): 289–325. https://doi.org/10.1017/S001041750000712X.

Peirce, Charles Sanders. 1955. "Logic as Semiotic: The Theory of Signs." In *Philosophical Writings of Peirce*, ed. Justus Buchler, 98–119. New York: Dover.

Peirce, Leslie P. 1993. *The Imperial Harem: Women and Sovereignty in the Ottoman Empire*. Oxford: Oxford University Press.

Pemberton, Kelly. 2006. "Women Pirs, Saintly Succession, and Spiritual Guidance in South Asian Sufism." *Muslim World* 96 (1): 61–87. https://doi.org/10.1111/j.1478-1913.2006.00118.x.

Perry, Donna L. 2005. "Wolof Women, Economic Liberalization, and the Crisis of Masculinity in Rural Senegal." *Ethnology* 44 (3): 207–26. https://doi.org/10.2307/3774056.

– 2009. "Fathers, Sons, and the State: Discipline and Punishment in a Wolof Hinterland." *Cultural Anthropology* 24 (1): 33–67. https://doi.org/10.1111/j.1548-1360.2009.00026.x.

Pezeril, Charlotte. 2008a. *Islam, mysticisme et marginalité: Les Baay Faal du Sénégal*. Paris: L'Harmattan.

– 2008b. "Réflexivité et dualité sexuelle: Déconstruction d'une enquête anthropologique sur l'islam au Sénégal." *Journal des Anthropologues* (108–9) (1 June): 353–80.

Rabine, Leslie W. 2013. "Religious Modesty, Fashionable Glamour, and Cultural Text: Veiling in Senegal." In *Veiling in Africa*, ed. Elisha P. Renne, 85–109. Bloomington: Indiana University Press.

Rasmussen, Anne K. 2010. *Women, the Recited Qur'an, and Islamic Music in Indonesia*. Berkeley: University of California Press. https://doi.org/10.1525/california/9780520255487.001.0001.

Rasmussen, Susan J. 1995. *Spirit Possession and Personhood among the Kel Ewey Tuareg*. Cambridge: Cambridge University Press. https://doi.org/10.1017/CBO9780511521140.

– 2006. *Those Who Touch: Tuareg Medicine Women in Anthropological Perspective*. Dekalb, IL: Northern Illinois University Press.

– 2013. "Veiling without Veils: Modesty and Reserve in Tuareg Cultural Encounters." In *Veiling in Africa*, ed. Elisha P. Renne, 34–57. Bloomington: Indiana University Press.

Rathgeber, Eva M. 1990. "WID, WAD, GAD: Trends in Research and Practice." *Journal of Developing Areas* 24 (4): 489–502.

Rausch, Margaret J. 2012. "Women Mosque Preachers and Spiritual Guides: Publicizing and Negotiating Women's Religious Authority in Morocco." In *Women, Leadership, and Mosques: Changes in Contemporary Islamic Authority*, ed. Masooda Bano and Hilary Kalmbach, 59–83. Leiden: Brill.

Razavi, Shahrashoub, and Carol Miller. 1995. "From WID to GAD: Conceptual Shifts in the Women and Development Discourse." Occasional Paper, United Nations Research Institute for Social Development/ United Nations Development Programme 1.

Redfield, Robert. 1956. *Peasant Society and Culture: An Anthropological Approach to Civilization*. Chicago: University of Chicago Press.

Renders, Marleen. 2002. "An Ambiguous Adventure: Muslim Organisations and the Discourse of 'Development' in Senegal." *Journal of Religion in Africa. Religion en Afrique* 32 (1): 61–82. https://doi.org/10.1163/15700660260048474.

République de la France. 2004. *Article L141–5-1. Code de L'éducation*. Vol. Article L141–5-1. https://www.legifrance.gouv.fr/affichCodeArticle.do?idArticle=LEGIARTI000006524456&cidTexte=LEGITEXT000006071191.

République du Sénégal. 2013. "Recensement général de la population et de l'habitat, de l'agriculture et de l'elevage: Rapport définitif." Ministère de l'Economie, des Finances et du Plan. http://www.ansd.sn/ressources/RGPHAE-2013/ressources/doc/pdf/2.pdf.

– 2015. "Recensement général de la population et de l'habitat, de l'agriculture et de l'elevage 2013 (Dictionnaire de données: Variable B20, Religion)." *Agence Nationale de La Statistique et de La Démographie*. http://anads.ansd.sn/index.php/catalog/51/datafile/F2.

Reveyrand-Coulon, Odile. 1993. "Les énoncés féminins de l'islam." In *Religion et modernité politique en Afrique Noire: Dieu pour tous et chacun pour soi*, ed. Jean-François Bayart, 63–99. Paris: Karthala.

Riccio, Bruno. 2004. "Transnational Mouridism and the Afro-Muslim Critique of Italy." *Journal of Ethnic and Migration Studies* 30 (5): 929–44. https://doi.org/10.1080/1369183042000245624.

Rich, Adrienne Cecile. 1977. *Of Woman Born: Motherhood as Experience and Institution*. Toronto: Bantam Books.
Roberts, Allen F., and Mary Nooter Roberts. 2000. "'Paintings like Prayers': The Hidden Side of Senegalese Reverse-Glass 'Image/Texts.'" *Research in African Literatures* 31 (4): 76–96.
– 2002. "A Saint in the City: Sufi Arts of Urban Senegal (Exhibition Preview)." *African Arts* 35 (4): 52–95.
Robinson, David. 2000. *Paths of Accommodation: Muslim Societies and French Colonial Authorities in Senegal and Mauritania, 1880–1920*. Oxford: James Currey.
Röschenthaler, Ute, and Dorothea E. Schulz, eds. 2016. *Cultural Entrepreneurship in Africa*. London: Routledge.
Ross, Eric. 2006. *Sufi City: Urban Design and Archetypes in Touba*. Rochester, NY: University of Rochester Press.
Rūmī. Maulana Jalāl al-Dīn. 2004. *The Masnavi, Book One*. Trans. Jawid Mojaddedi. Oxford and New York: Oxford University Press.
Safi, Omid, ed. 2003. *Progressive Muslims: On Justice, Gender, and Pluralism*. Oxford: Oneworld.
Sahliyeh, Emile, ed. 1990. *Religious Resurgence and Politics in the Contemporary World*. Albany, NY: State University of New York Press.
Sall, Aminata. 2013. "Abdoulaye Wade et ses projets pour les femmes: Entre parité et financement des associations." In *Le Sénégal sous Abdoulaye Wade: Le sopi à l'épreuve du pouvoir*, ed. Momar-Coumba Diop, 383–408. Paris: Karthala.
Salzbrunn, Monika. 2004. "The Occupation of Public Space through Religious and Political Events: How Senegalese Migrants Became a Part of Harlem, New York." *Journal of Religion in Africa. Religion en Afrique* 34 (4): 468–92. https://doi.org/10.1163/1570066042564428.
Samson, Fabienne. 2005. *Les marabouts de l'islam politique: Le Dahiratoul Moustarchidina wal Moustarchidaty, un mouvement néo-confrérique sénégalais*. Paris: Karthala.
Samson Ndaw, Fabienne. 2009. "Nouveaux marabouts politiques au Sénégal." In *L'islam, nouvel espace public en Afrique*, ed. Gilles Holder, 149–71. Paris: Karthala.
Schielke, Samuli. 2008. "Mystic States, Motherly Virtues, Female Participation and Leadership in an Egyptian Sufi Milieu." *Journal for Islamic Studies* 28 (1): 94–126.
– 2009. "Being Good in Ramadan: Ambivalence, Fragmentation, and the Moral Self in the Lives of Young Egyptians." *Journal of the Royal Anthropological Institute* 15: S24–40. https://doi.org/10.1111/j.1467-9655.2009.01540.x.

Schimmel, Annemarie. 2003. *My Soul Is a Woman: The Feminine in Islam*. Trans. Susan H. Ray. New York: Continuum.

Schulz, Dorothea E. 2003. "'Charisma and Brotherhood' Revisited: Mass-Mediated Forms of Spirituality in Urban Mali." *Journal of Religion in Africa. Religion en Afrique* 33 (2): 146–71. https://doi.org/10.1163/15700660360703123.

– 2006. "Promises of (Im)mediate Salvation: Islam, Broadcast Media, and the Remaking of Religious Experience in Mali." *American Ethnologist* 33 (2): 210–29. https://doi.org/10.1525/ae.2006.33.2.210.

– 2007. "Competing Sartorial Assertions of Femininity and Muslim Identity in Mali." *Fashion Theory* 11 (2/3): 253–79. https://doi.org/10.2752/136270407X202808.

– 2008. "(Re)Turning to Proper Muslim Practice: Islamic Moral Renewal and Women's Conflicting Assertions of Sunni Identity in Urban Mali." *Africa Today* 54 (4): 20–43. https://doi.org/10.2979/AFT.2008.54.4.20.

– 2012a. *Muslims and New Media in West Africa: Pathways to God*. Bloomington: Indiana University Press.

– 2012b. "Dis/Embodying Authority: Female Radio 'Preachers' and the Ambivalences of Mass-Mediated Speech in Mali." *International Journal of Middle East Studies* 44 (1): 23–43. https://doi.org/10.1017/S0020743811001231.

Scott, James C. 1987. *Weapons of the Weak: Everyday Forms of Peasant Resistance*. New Haven, CT: Yale University Press.

Scott, Joan Wallach. 2007. *The Politics of the Veil*. Princeton, NJ: Princeton University Press.

Seesemann, Rüdiger. 2000. "The History of the Tijâniya and the Issue of Tarbiya in Darfur." In *La Tijâniyya: Une confrérie musulmane à la conquête de l'Afrique*, ed. Jean-Louis Triaud and David Robinson, 393–437. Paris: Karthala.

– 2004. "The Shurafa' and the 'Blacksmith': The Role of the Idaw ʿAli of Mauritania in the Career of the Senegalese Shaykh Ibrahim Niasse (1900–1975)." In *The Transmission of Learning in Islamic Africa*, ed. Scott S. Reese, 72–98. Leiden: Brill.

– 2011. *The Divine Flood: Ibrāhīm Niasse and the Roots of a Twentieth-Century Sufi Revival*. Oxford: Oxford University Press.

Silvers, Laury. 2010. "'God Loves Me': The Theological Content and Context of Early Pious and Sufi Womens' Sayings on Love." *Journal of Islamic Studies* 30: 33–59.

– 2015. "Early Pious, Mystic Sufi Women." In *The Cambridge Companion to Sufism*, ed. Lloyd V.J. Ridgeon, 24–52. Cambridge: Cambridge University Press.

Silverstein, Michael. 2003. "Indexical Order and the Dialectics of Sociolinguistic Life." *Language & Communication* 23 (3–4): 193–229. https://doi.org/10.1016/S0271-5309(03)00013-2.

Silverstein, Paul A. 2004. *Algeria in France: Transpolitics, Race, and Nation*. Bloomington: Indiana University Press.

Singer, Milton. 1955. "The Cultural Pattern of Indian Civilization: A Preliminary Report of a Methodological Field Study." *Journal of Asian Studies* 15 (1): 23–36. https://doi.org/10.2307/2942100.

Smith, Margaret. 1984. *Rābi'a the Mystic & Her Fellow-Saints in Islām: Being the Life and Teachings of Rābi'a Al-'Adawiyya Al-Qaysiyya of Baṣra Together with Some Account of the Place of the Women Saints in Islām*. Cambridge: Cambridge University Press.

Smith, William Robertson. 1894. *Religion of the Semites*. London: Adam and Charles Black.

Soares, Benjamin F. 2000. "Notes on the Anthropological Study of Islam and Muslim Societies in Africa." *Culture and Religion* 1 (2): 277–85. https://doi.org/10.1080/01438300008567155.

– 2004. "Islam and Public Piety in Mali." In *Public Islam and the Common Good*, ed. Armando Salvatore and Dale F. Eickelman, 205–26. Leiden: Brill.

– 2005. *Islam and the Prayer Economy: History and Authority in a Malian Town*. Ann Arbor: University of Michigan Press.

– 2006. "Islam in Mali in the Neoliberal Era." *African Affairs* 105 (418): 77–95.

– 2010. "'Rasta' Sufis and Muslim Youth Culture in Mali." In *Being Young and Muslim: New Cultural Politics in the Global South and North*, ed. Assef Bayat and Linda Herrera, 241–58. Oxford, New York: Oxford University Press.

Sow, Fatou. 2003. "Fundamentalisms, Globalisation and Women's Human Rights in Senegal." *Gender and Development* 11 (1): 69–76. https://doi.org/10.1080/741954255.

Spengemann, William C., and L.R. Lundquist. 1965. "Autobiography and the American Myth." *American Quarterly* 17 (3): 501–19. https://doi.org/10.2307/2710905.

Stokes, Martin. 2002. "Silver Sounds in the Inner Citadel? Reflections on Musicology and Islam." In *Interpreting Islam*, ed. Hastings Donnan, 167–89. London: Sage. https://doi.org/10.4135/9781446217467.n10.

Stoller, Paul. 1989. *Fusion of the Worlds: An Ethnography of Possession among the Songhay of Niger*. Chicago: University of Chicago Press. https://doi.org/10.7208/chicago/9780226775494.001.0001.

Strathern, Marilyn. 1988. *The Gender of the Gift: Problems with Women and Problems with Society in Melanesia*. Berkeley: University of California Press. https://doi.org/10.1525/california/9780520064232.001.0001.

Strobel, Margaret. 1979. *Muslim Women in Mombasa, 1890–1975*. New Haven, CT: Yale University Press.

Stromberg, Peter G. 1990. "Ideological Language in the Transformation of Identity." *American Anthropologist* 92 (1): 42–56. https://doi.org/10.1525/aa.1990.92.1.02a00030.

Suhrawardī, Yaḥyá ibn Ḥabash. 1999. *The Philosophy of Illumination*. Ed. John Walbridge and Hossein Ziai. Provo, UT: Brigham Young University Press.

as-Sulamī, Abū ʿAbd ar-Raḥmān. 1999. *Early Sufi Women (Dhikr an-niswa al-mutaʿabbidāt aṣ-ṣūfiyyāt)*. Trans. Rkia Elaroui Cornell. Louisville, KY: Fons Vitae.

Sule, Balaraba B.M., and Priscilla E. Starratt. 1991. "Islamic Leadership Positions for Women in Contemporary Kano Society." In *Hausa Women in the Twentieth Century*, ed. Catherine Coles and Beverly Mack, 29–49. Madison: University of Wisconsin Press.

Tarlo, Emma. 2010. *Visibly Muslim: Fashion, Politics, Faith*. Oxford: Berg. https://doi.org/10.2752/9781847888624.

Torab, Azam. 2007. *Performing Islam: Gender and Ritual in Iran*. Leiden: Brill.

Tourage, Mahdi. 2005. "The Hermeneutics of Eroticism in the Poetry of Rumi." *Comparative Studies of South Asia, Africa and the Middle East* 25 (3): 600–16. https://doi.org/10.1215/1089201X-25-3-600.

– 2007. *Rūmī and the Hermeneutics of Eroticism*. Leiden: Brill.

Treiger, Alexander. 2007. "Monism and Monotheism in Al-Ghazālī's Mishkāt Al-Anwār." *Journal of Qur'anic Studies* 9 (1): 1–27. https://doi.org/10.3366/jqs.2007.9.1.1.

Trimingham, J. Spencer. 1959. *Islam in West Africa*. Oxford: Oxford University Press.

– 1980. *The Influence of Islam upon Africa*. 2nd ed. Arab Background Series. London and New York: Longman.

– 1998. *The Sufi Orders in Islam*. New York: Oxford University Press. (Original work published 1971)

Tsing, Anna Lowenhaupt. 2005. *Friction: An Ethnography of Global Connection*. Princeton, NJ: Princeton University Press.

Tucker, Judith E. 1993. "The Arab Family in History: 'Otherness' and the Study of the Family." In *Arab Women: Old Boundaries, New Frontiers*, ed. Judith E. Tucker, 195–207. Bloomington: Indiana University Press.

Turner, Edith B. 1993. "The Reality of Spirits: A Tabooed or Permitted Field of Study?" *Anthropology of Consciousness* 4 (1): 9–12. https://doi.org/10.1525/ac.1993.4.1.9.

Turner, Terence. 1980. "The Social Skin." In *Not Work Alone: A Cross-Cultural View of Activities Superfluous to Survival*, ed. Jeremy Cherfas and Roger Lewin, 112–40. London: Temple Smith.

Turner, Victor. 1957. *Schism and Continuity in an African Society: A Study of Ndembu Village Life*. Manchester: University of Manchester Press.
– 1967. *The Forest of Symbols: Aspects of Ndembu Ritual*. Ithaca, NY: Cornell University Press.
– 1987. "Images and Reflections: Ritual, Drama, Carnival, Film, and Spectacle in Cultural Performance." In *The Anthropology of Performance*, 21–32. New York: PAJ.
– 1995. *The Ritual Process: Structure and Anti-Structure*. Chicago: Aldine.
Umar, Muhammad Sani. 2001. "Education and Islamic Trends in Northern Nigeria: 1970s–1990s." *Africa Today* 48 (2): 127–50. https://doi.org/10.1353/at.2001.0043.
van Gennep, Arnold. 1960. *Rites of Passage*. Chicago: University of Chicago Press.
Villalón, Leonardo A. 1995. *Islam and State Power in Senegal: Disciples and Citizens in Fatick*. Cambridge: Cambridge University Press. https://doi.org/10.1017/CBO9780511598647.
– 1999. "Generational Changes, Political Stagnation, and the Evolving Dynamics of Religion and Politics in Senegal." *Africa Today* 46 (3/4): 129–47.
Wadud, Amina. 1992. *Qur'an and Woman: Rereading the Sacred Text from a Woman's Perspective*. Oxford: Oxford University Press.
– 2006. *Inside the Gender Jihad: Women's Reform in Islam*. Oxford: Oneworld.
Ware, Rudolph T. 2014. *The Walking Qur'an: Islamic Education, Embodied Knowledge, and History in West Africa*. Chapel Hill: University of North Carolina Press.
Wario, Halkano Abdi. 2012. "Reforming Men, Refining Umma: Tablīghī Jamāʿat and Novel Visions of Islamic Masculinity." *Religion and Gender* 2 (2): 231–53. https://doi.org/10.18352/rg.7202.
Waugh, Earle H. 2005. *Memory, Music, and Religion: Morocco's Mystical Chanters*. Columbia: University of South Carolina Press.
Weber, Max. 1958. "Science as Vocation." In *From Max Weber: Essays in Sociology*, ed. H.H. Gerth and C. Wright Mills, 129–57. Oxford: Oxford University Press.
– 1992. *The Protestant Ethic and the Spirit of Capitalism*. London, New York: Routledge.
Wehr, Hans. 1994. *A Dictionary of Modern Written Arabic*. 4th ed. Ed. J.M. Cowan. Wiesbaden: Otto Harrassowitz.
Werbner, Pnina. 1996. "Stamping the Earth with the Name of Allah: Zikr and the Sacralizing of Space among British Muslims." *Cultural Anthropology* 11 (3): 309–38. https://doi.org/10.1525/can.1996.11.3.02a00020.

Werbner, Richard. 2011a. *Holy Hustlers, Schism, and Prophecy: Apostolic Reformation in Botswana*. Berkeley: University of California Press. https://doi.org/10.1525/california/9780520268531.001.0001.

– 2011b. "The Charismatic Dividual and the Sacred Self." *Journal of Religion in Africa. Religion en Afrique* 41 (2): 180–205. https://doi.org/10.1163/157006611X569247.

Westerlund, David, ed. 1996. *Questioning the Secular State: The Worldwide Resurgence of Religion in Politics*. London: Hurst.

Whorf, Benjamin Lee. 1941. "The Relation of Habitual Thought and Behavior to Language." In *Language, Culture, and Personality: Essays in Memory of Edward Sapir*, 197–215. Menasha, WI: Sapir Memorial Publication Fund.

Wiley, Katherine Ann. 2013. "Fashioning People, Crafting Networks: Multiple Meanings in the Mauritanian Veil (*Malaḥfa*)." In *African Dress: Fashion, Agency, Performance*, ed. Karen Tranberg Hansen and D. Soyini Madison, 77–91. London: Bloomsbury.

Wittgenstein, Ludwig. 1953. *Philosophical Investigations*. Oxford: Blackwell.

Wright, Zachary Valentine. 2005. *On the Path of the Prophet: Shaykh Ahmad Tijani and the Tariqa Muhammadiyya*. Atlanta: African American Islamic Institute.

– 2015. *Living Knowledge in West African Islam: The Sufi Community of Ibrāhīm Niasse*. Leiden: Brill.

Young, Iris Marion. 1990. *Throwing Like a Girl and Other Essays in Feminist Philosophy and Social Theory*. Bloomington: Indiana University Press.

Index

The letter *t* following a page number denotes a table, while *f* denotes a figure, and *n* denotes an endnote. Names are listed without titles, except where the title is considered an integral part of someone's name or nickname.

ANTHROPOLOGICAL HORIZONS

Editor: Michael Lambek, University of Toronto

Published to date:

The Varieties of Sensory Experience: A Sourcebook in the Anthropology of the Senses / Edited by David Howes (1991)

Arctic Homeland: Kinship, Community, and Development in Northwest Greenland / Mark Nuttall (1992)

Knowledge and Practice in Mayotte: Local Discourses of Islam, Sorcery, and Spirit Possession / Michael Lambek (1993)

Deathly Waters and Hungry Mountains: Agrarian Ritual and Class Formation in an Andean Town / Peter Gose (1994)

Paradise: Class, Commuters, and Ethnicity in Rural Ontario / Stanley R. Barrett (1994)

The Cultural World in Beowulf / John M. Hill (1995)

Making It Their Own: Severn Ojibwe Communicative Practices / Lisa Philips Valentine (1995)

Merchants and Shopkeepers: A Historical Anthropology of an Irish Market Town, 1200–1991 / Philip Gulliver and Marilyn Silverman (1995)

Tournaments of Value: Sociability and Hierarchy in a Yemeni Town / Ann Meneley (1996)

Mal'uocchiu: Ambiguity, Evil Eye, and the Language of Distress / Sam Migliore (1997)

Between History and Histories: The Production of Silences and Commemorations / Edited by Gerald Sider and Gavin Smith (1997)

Eh, Paesan! Being Italian in Toronto / Nicholas DeMaria Harney (1998)

Theorizing the Americanist Tradition / Edited by Lisa Philips Valentine and Regna Darnell (1999)

Colonial 'Reformation' in the Highlands of Central Sulawesi, Indonesia, 1892–1995 / Albert Schrauwers (2000)

The Rock Where We Stand: An Ethnography of Women's Activism in Newfoundland / Glynis George (2000)

Being Alive Well: Health and the Politics of Cree Well-Being / Naomi Adelson (2000)

Irish Travellers: Racism and the Politics of Culture / Jane Helleiner (2001)

Of Property and Propriety: The Role of Gender and Class in Imperialism and Nationalism / Edited by Himani Bannerji, Shahrzad Mojab, and Judith Whitehead (2001)

An Irish Working Class: Explorations in Political Economy and Hegemony, 1800–1950 / Marilyn Silverman (2001)
The Double Twist: From Ethnography to Morphodynamics / Edited by Pierre Maranda (2001)
The House of Difference: Cultural Politics and National Identity in Canada / Eva Mackey (2002)
Writing and Colonialism in Northern Ghana: The Encounter between the LoDagaa and the 'World on Paper,' 1892–1991 / Sean Hawkins (2002)
Guardians of the Transcendent: An Ethnography of a Jain Ascetic Community / Anne Vallely (2002)
The Hot and the Cold: Ills of Humans and Maize in Native Mexico / Jacques M. Chevalier and Andrés Sánchez Bain (2003)
Figured Worlds: Ontological Obstacles in Intercultural Relations / Edited by John Clammer, Sylvie Poirier, and Eric Schwimmer (2004)
Revenge of the Windigo: The Construction of the Mind and Mental Health of North American Aboriginal Peoples / James B. Waldram (2004)
The Cultural Politics of Markets: Economic Liberalization and Social Change in Nepal / Katherine Neilson Rankin (2004)
A World of Relationships: Itineraries, Dreams, and Events in the Australian Western Desert / Sylvie Poirier (2005)
The Politics of the Past in an Argentine Working-Class Neighbourhood / Lindsay DuBois (2005)
Youth and Identity Politics in South Africa, 1990–1994 / Sibusisiwe Nombuso Dlamini (2005)
Maps of Experience: The Anchoring of Land to Story in Secwepemc Discourse / Andie Diane Palmer (2005)
Beyond Bodies: Rain-Making and Sense-Making in Tanzania / Todd Sanders (2008)
We Are Now a Nation: Croats between 'Home' and 'Homeland' / Daphne N. Winland (2008)
Kaleidoscopic Odessa: History and Place in Post-Soviet Ukraine / Tanya Richardson (2008)
Invaders as Ancestors: On the Intercultural Making and Unmaking of Spanish Colonialism in the Andes / Peter Gose (2008)
From Equality to Inequality: Social Change among Newly Sedentary Lanoh Hunter-Gatherer Traders of Peninsular Malaysia / Csilla Dallos (2011)
Rural Nostalgias and Transnational Dreams: Identity and Modernity among Jat Sikhs / Nicola Mooney (2011)

Dimensions of Development: History, Community, and Change in Allpachico, Peru / Susan Vincent (2012)
People of Substance: An Ethnography of Morality in the Colombian Amazon / Carlos David Londoño Sulkin (2012)
'We Are Still Didene': Stories of Hunting and History from Northern British Columbia / Thomas McIlwraith (2012)
Being Māori in the City: Indigenous Everyday Life in Auckland / Natacha Gagné (2013)
The Hakkas of Sarawak: Sacrificial Gifts in Cold War Era Malaysia / Kee Howe Yong (2013)
Remembering Nayeche and the Gray Bull Engiro: African Storytellers of the Karamoja Plateau and the Plains of Turkana / Mustafa Kemal Mirzeler (2014)
In Light of Africa: Globalizing Blackness in Northeast Brazil / Allan Charles Dawson (2014)
The Land of Weddings and Rain: Nation and Modernity in Post-Socialist Lithuania / Gediminas Lankauskas (2015)
Milanese Encounters: Public Space and Vision in Contemporary Urban Italy / Cristina Moretti (2015)
Legacies of Violence: History, Society, and the State in Sardinia / Antonio Sorge (2015)
Looking Back, Moving Forward: Transformation and Ethical Practice in the Ghanaian Church of Pentecost / Girish Daswani (2015)
Why the Porcupine is Not a Bird: Explorations in the Folk Zoology of an Eastern Indonesian People / Gregory Forth (2016)
The Heart of Helambu: Ethnography and Entanglement in Nepal / Tom O'Neill (2016)
Tournaments of Value: Sociability and Hierarchy in a Yemeni Town, 20th Anniversary Edition / Ann Meneley (2016)
Europe Un-Imagined: Nation and Culture at a French-German Television Channel / Damien Stankiewicz (2017)
Transforming Indigeneity: Urbanization and Language Revitalization in the Brazilian Amazon / Sarah Shulist (2018)
Wrapping Authority: Women Islamic Leaders in a Sufi Movement in Dakar, Senegal / Joseph Hill (2018)